Naming your Baby

Julia Cresswell

A & C Black • London

www.acblack.com

First published in Great Britain in 1990
Second edition published 2000
Third edition published 2007

A & C Black Publishers Ltd
38 Soho Square, London W1D 3HB

© Julia Cresswell 1990, 2000, 2007

A CIP record for this book is available from the British Library.

ISBN: 978 0 7136 8313 4

3761 9227 05/08

This book is produced using paper that is made from wood grown in managed,
sustainable forests. It is natural, renewable and recyclable. The logging and
manufacturing processes conform to the environmental regulations of the country
of origin.

Text typeset by A & C Black
Printed in Spain by GraphyCems

Introduction

English speakers are blessed with a vast store of first names to choose from, as layer after layer of immigrants and cultures have added their names to the pool parents have to draw on. The earliest names we have are those from the indigenous Celtic peoples. Some of the Welsh names go back to Roman times, or even earlier, and many of the Irish names are nearly as old. The Irish took their language over to Scotland where subtle changes took place, adding yet more forms. Both Irish and Gaelic spelling preserve the ancient written forms of these names, while there have often been radical changes in their modern pronunciation, so I have tried to give some indication of how they should be pronounced. Many of the names already have phonetic respellings as variants, which make their pronunciation clear, although exact pronunciations can vary from region to region. In addition there have been times when English-speaking overlords tried to suppress these ancient languages, and so a system evolved of equivalent names that conformed to English traditions, and I have indicated many of these. In the Dark Ages the Anglo-Saxons settled England, bringing with them Germanic naming traditions. Speakers of this family of languages, which include German, English and the Scandinavian languages. had a tradition, at least among the aristocracy about whom we know most, of forming names by combining two elements, each of which came from a vocabulary word. Each family tended to have traditional name elements, and marriages meant they could cross from one family to another. This meant that a child might have a name newly coined for them, and although the meaning of the name might not make much sense, people could tell a lot about the family from the form the name took. The reason we have so many boy's names beginning *Ed-* is that Old English *ead* 'prosperous, fortunate' was one of the traditional elements used in the English royal family in the later Saxon period. It should be noted that the modern way of forming new names by blending together parts of established names to form names like **Jerrica** or **Jakayla** is not really that different. When the pagan Saxons converted to Christianity a whole new set of names were introduced. These were either Hebrew, from the Old Testament; or Greek, either directly from Greek or the Greek form of Hebrew names, from the New Testament. Over time many of these names have developed distinctively English forms. However, these names were rarely used until after the Norman Conquest.

When the Normans took over England (and later much of the rest of the British Isles) in 1066, they brought with them their own stock of names, which rapidly replaced most of the Anglo-Saxon names. Many of these names were actually Germanic in origin, for about the same time that the Saxons had taken over England, the related Germanic tribe of the Franks had taken over much of France. In France the names have developed along their own lines and taken new forms. In addition, the French were much more inclined to use biblical names, and also used more names inherited from the Roman past. A major source of names were those of saints. Children could either be named after a saint whose feast day was celebrated about the same time they were born, or else the name could be used to place a child under that saint's protection. The Renaissance introduced more classical names, particularly those from Greek, although these had been used on occasion throughout the Middle Ages. Names were also beginning to be taken from literature more often. However, with the Reformation in England there was a sudden change in the stock of names being used. Saint's names were rejected by reformists, and instead many more names were taken directly from the Bible, and the Puritans also chose names such as **Charity** which indicated desirable qualities in a child. This was the naming tradition taken over to America by the Founding Fathers and which still lies behind some of the major differences in the names tradition between the USA and the UK, so that names such as Reuben or Amos are far more common in the USA.

The next major change that happened was in the eighteenth century, with the beginnings of the Romantic movement. A whole new set of names came into use, often taken from the names of literary characters or from myth and legend. This trend increased with time, and the Romantic period also saw the revival of numerous Medieval names that had previously fallen out of use. With the rise of Gothic and the English High Church in the nineteenth century there was a marked trend to revive Anglo-Saxon names, particularly those of saints. In the same period the trend to use surnames as first names, which had long existed, grew stronger. In the past these names had often been mother's maiden names or the names of godparents. Now more and more upper class names were being used as first names by people who had no connections with the families. The trend to use surnames was particularly marked in the USA. In the twentieth century it became a mark of the wealthy, successful families, and associated with high status. As a result the fashion has accelerated and now a high percentage of new American names are re-used surnames. Part of the Romantic revival was a renewed interest in the Celtic ancestry of the British Isles, and this, combined with the spread of these names to Australia and North America through Irish and Scottish emigration led to an increased use of these names. This again is a trend that has continued, with more and more Celtic names entering the common stock. More recently there has been mass emigration from the Indian Subcontinent and the Middle East into English-speaking countries, which has introduced two entirely new sets of names, those from Sanskrit, used by Hindus, and those from Arabic. It would be impossible to cover the vast store of names these new groups have with any thoroughness, but I have included brief entries for some of the commoner ones. They lack the extensive background information that many of the European names have, simply because I lack the information myself and little has been published on them in a language I can read. Some of the comments on Arabic names may seem somewhat illogical, for Arabic acts in a way very different from European languages. It is based on word roots of three consonants, which can be combined with vowels and sometimes extra consonants in many different ways. Thus

Habib and **Mahbub** come from the same root; and the word *darasa* gives the name Idris. In the USA Spanish speakers now form a noticeable percentage of the population, and as a result, Spanish and South American names are making their mark, both traditional names and those that have been used in television series.

The entries in this book are arranged alphabetically by headword. Within these headwords I have grouped together a number of names that are related. I have also listed the commoner variant spellings. All these different forms have been cross-referenced, unless the cross reference would come immediately before or after the headword, or very occasionally, where the connection is clear, one cross-reference away from the headword. Therefore, to find the word you want, look at the nearest form to the one you want, and you should find it there or a cross reference to it. I have included in the entries the source and meaning of the name, when that is known, and something of the history of its use, and tried to indicate how popular it is in English-speaking countries when that information is available. I have tried to include all the basic stock of names used in recent years, and have covered the current top hundred names for boys and girls in the British Isles and the top thousand for the USA. The reason for the imbalance is in part because these are the figures that the relevant governments choose to publish, but it is justified by the enormous influence American television and film have on spreading names around the world. I hope by grouping related names together parents will find that they have a greater choice of names but are also able to refine their choice more easily. Related names are shown within an entry in **bold**, while cross references are indicated in SMALL CAPS.

The fund of names in active use has increased enormously in the last hundred years. In part this reflects the growing emphasis on individuality in Western culture over this time, but even more important has been the reduction in the use of surnames in everyday speech. In the past there were many more surnames in use than first names, and people were easily identified by these. Now that people call each other by their first names on first meeting, a greater diversity of first names is needed to avoid confusion. That does not mean that there are not trends and fashions in the names. Indeed this has got more marked as the years go on. One marked fashion is for respelling names, so that there may be a large number of possible spellings for the same name. The girl's name Mackenzie, for example, has at least 45 recorded spellings. Parents' choice of name often reflects social or regional differences, and naming trends can vary greatly even within districts in one small town. While there will be much overlap, a look at the published most popular names in England and Wales, Scotland and Northern Ireland will show major variations as well. African-Americans have marked their identity with their own set of names, and are prominent in the more general American fashion of inventing completely new names to mark their child's uniqueness. However, it is interesting to find that even these apparently random names seem to have hidden rules in their formation. When psychologists have researched a list of unique names with no discernable links to any other names, they have found that people can usually guess correctly which gender the name had been given to. And even with newly fashionable names there are still overarching trends. It is noticeable how many popular girl's names at the moment begin with an E, such as **Emily**, **Emma** and **Ella**. It has been calculated that over 40% of boys in the USA are currently being given names ending in *-an* or *-en*, particularly the sound *-aden*, such as **Aiden**, **Braden**, **Caden**, **Jaden**. These come from a variety of different sources, but something about them just feels right to the parents.

As well as made up names that contain fashionable sounds, many new names are currently coming from the general vocabulary. This is obviously nothing new, for a look through the names in this book will show that many started life in this way. Moreover, as has been said, there was a Puritan fashion for basing words on vocabulary words. This trend continued in the USA beyond its fashion in England which had largely dies out before the end of the seventeenth century. Thus while Mindwell Griswold (female) died in 1728, and Experience was born in 1709, Sedate was not born until the early nineteenth century. (I must thank Coralee Griswold and the Griswold Family Association for access to family trees from which these examples are plucked from many such, and for help with the name **Gaylord**.) As there has been a major revival of biblical Puritan names in recent years in the USA, there may have been some influence from this trend, but it is not very likely, and there is no need to look for this as a source. Place names have been a marked source of new names, giving us names such as **Asia**, **Africa**, **India**, **Paris**, **London**, **Kenya**, **Savannah**, and many more too individual to get into the general record. Sometimes these are used because a couple met there or honeymooned there, or have some special association with the place. Music has been a source of names such as **Lyric**, **Aria**, **Melody**, **Cadence**, as well as the well-established **Harmony**. The weather gives us **Misty**, **Storm** and **Stormy**, **Breeze** and **Cloudy**. Some on the more abstract names such as **Journey** or **Clemency** are closer to the old Puritan ones, and others with a distinct religious element, such as **Heaven**, **Eden**, **Messiah**, **Miracle** and **Genesis** closer still. Despite all this, most of the top names are still old ones and although they may not have been used continuously, can still be seen to have links with the past. Parents today have the freedom to choose from a vast fund of different sorts of names. I hope that this book will enable them to make this choice in a thoughtful and well-informed way.

Julia Cresswell

Bibliography

Books

Ahmet, Salahuddin *A Dictionary of Muslim Names* Hurst and Company (1999)

Beech, George T., Monique Bourin and Pascal Chareille (eds) *Personal Names Studies of Medieval Europe* Studies in Medieval Culture XLIII Medieval Institute Publications, Western Michigan University, Kalamazoo, Michigan (2002)

Cresswell, Julia *Best Baby Names* Bloomsbury (2000)

Cresswell, Julia Collins *Gem Babies Names* (2004)

Cresswell, Julia *Irish Babies Names* HarperCollins (2004)

Cresswell, Julia *Scottish First Names* HarperCollins (1999)

Davies, Norman *The Isles: A History* Macmillan (2000)

Davies, T.R. *A Book of Welsh Names* Sheppard Press (1952)

Dunkling, Leslie and William Gosling *Dictionary of First Names* Dent (1987)

Ellis, Peter Berresford *A Dictionary of Irish Mythology* Oxford University Press (1991)

Evans, Cleveland Kent *Unusual and Most Popular Baby Names* Consumer Guide (1994)

Hanks, Patrick and Flavia Hodges *A Dictionary of First Names* Oxford University Press (1990)

Hanks, Patrick and Flavia Hodges *A Dictionary of Surnames* Oxford University Press (1996)

Levitt, Steven D. and Stephen J. Dubner *Freakonomics* Allen Lane (2005)

Lewis, D. Geraint *Welsh Names* Geddes and Grosset (2001)

Mackay, George *Celtic First Names* Geddes & Grosset (1999)

Ó Corráin, Donnchadh and Fidelma Maguire *Irish Names* Lilliput Press (1990)

Patel, Vimla *Babies' Names from the Indian Subcontinent* Foulsham (1992)

Stewart, George Ripley *American Given Names: Their Origin and History in the Context of the English Language* OUP New York (1979)

Tanet, Chantal and Tristan Hordé *Dictionnaire des Prenoms* Larousse (2000)

Withycombe, E.G. *The Oxford Dictionary of English Christian Names* Oxford University Press third edition (1976)

Yonge, Charlotte M. *A History of Christian Names* revised edition (1884)

Online

National Statistics

General Register Office for Scotland - Personal Names:
http://www.gro-scotland.gov.uk/statistics/publications-and-data/popular-names/index.html
Irish first names: Central Statistics office, Ireland:
http://www.cso.ie/statistics/ top_babies_names.htm
Northern Ireland:
http://www.nisra.gov.uk/archive/demography/publications/babynames/
BabyNamesPressRelease2006.pdf
Office of National Statistics (UK): Top 100 names for baby girls in England and Wales 2002-2006:
http://www.statistics.gov.uk/specials/babiesnames_girls.asp;
for boys:
http://www.statistics.gov.uk/specials/babiesnames_boys.asp
USA:
http://www.ssa.gov/OACT/babynames/

Other sites

Baby Namer: http://www.babynamer.com/
Behind the Name: http://www.behindthename.com/
Hindustanlink.com:
http://www.hindustanlink.com/parenting/index-babynames.html
http://www.geocities.com/edgarbook/names/other/popculture.html
Indian Baby Names: http://scnc.udw.ac.za/doc/SOC-cult/names/names1.htm
Indian Child: Hindi Names: http://www.indianchild.com/hindi_names_namkaran.htm
Iranian-Persian names: http://cleo.lcs.psu.edu/girl_names.html
Wikipedia: http://en.wikipedia.org/wiki/List_of_most_popular_given_names

Contents

A

Aali, Aaliyah see Ali

Aamina see Amin

Aamir, Aamira see Amir

Aaron

In the Bible Aaron is the brother of MOSES and is the first High Priest of the Israelites who is traditionally regarded as the founder of the Jewish priesthood. There have been many attempts to explain the meaning of his name, including deriving it from Hebrew terms for 'high mountain' and 'brightness', but none of them are convincing. Most probably Aaron's name, like his brother's, was Egyptian in origin, and its meaning is lost. It has been popular in the English-speaking world for a number of years, and as a result has developed numerous variants, as well two different pronunciations. The traditional English pronunciation marks the 'aa' at the beginning by pronouncing them as in the word 'air'; but younger users tend to ignore the double a and start the name with the same sound as in 'and'. This has in turn led to the loss of the distinctive spelling, so that **Aron** and **Arron** are now quite common forms, while even **Erin** (not to be confused with the girl's name) and **Ehren**, reflecting yet another pronunciation, are found in the United States. These variant forms can overlap with other names with similar sounds so that for example in Wales, where Aron is the traditional Welsh spelling, **Aran** is a boy's name taken from a place name meaning 'high place'. There is also overlap with the names ARRAN and ARUN. Ron and Ronnie are used as pet forms of the name. The name appears in Arabic as **Haroun** or **Harun**.

Aaron was rarely used before the Reformation, but was taken up by the Puritans, which means it was well used by early settlers in America, where it entered the traditional stock of names. As a result it is more likely to be found as the name of a number of prominent Americans than elsewhere: Aaron Burr (1758–1836), vice-president and duellist; and the musician Aaron Copland (1900–90) being two examples. Elvis Presley was given the middle name Aaron, but preferred to spell it Aron, thus adding to the confusion that surrounds the name.

Abby see Abigail, Gabriel

Abdul, Abdullah

In Arabic *abd* means 'male servant' and is used in combination with names for Allah to form names. Abdul or **Abdel** 'servant of' is used as a short form of these names. Abdullah, also spelt **Abdallah**, **Abdoullah** or **Abd-Allah**, means 'servant of Allah'. This was the name of both the father of the Prophet Mohammed and of one of his sons. Other names formed in the same way are **Abdul Aziz**, 'servant of the Almighty'; **Abdul Qadir** (**Abdelkader**); 'servant of the Powerful'; **Abdul Latif** (**Abdellatif**) 'servant of the All-Gentle'. The use of prefixes that mean 'servant, devotee' is by no means restricted to Arabic names: compare, for example MALCOLM.

Abel

In the Bible Abel is the name of the second son of ADAM and EVE, who was killed in a fit of jealousy by his brother Cain. As in the case of so many early biblical names, it is difficult to work out the meaning. It has been suggested that the name comes from a word meaning 'son' or perhaps from another word meaning 'breath', the meaning of the current Hebrew form of the name **Hevel**. It was one of the rarer biblical names among the Puritans, who used Nab as a pet form, and while still not common, has probably been used more in the last 20 years than at any other time. Abel Tasman (c.1603–59) who discovered not only Tasmania, but also New Zealand, Tonga and Fiji, is a famous bearer.

Abigail

The Hebrew form of this name, **Avigayil**, is analysed as made up of *av(i)* 'father' (found in names such as ABRAHAM and ABNER) and *gayil* 'joy'. There have been various interpretations of these elements, most of which either boil down to variants 'father of joy' probably implying origin by the word father; or more convincingly 'father rejoiced' or 'a joy to her father'. In the Bible (1 Kings 25) Abigail is the wife of Nabal who is attacked by David after he refuses to help him. Abigail, who was famous for her beauty, prepares a magnificent feast with which she manages to appease David. This was a popular subject in art in the seventeenth and eighteenth centuries. After Nabal's death David marries Abigail. Abigail became a popular name in the Puritan period, and soon became a synonym for a ladies' maid. This was probably because Abigail describes herself to David in the Bible as 'your servant'. This use of 'abigail' for 'maid' led to a decline in its use. However, it was revived in the nineteenth century and became popular in the later twentieth century. It has been among the top hundred names in many countries over the last twenty years. It can be found spelt with two bs, and in forms such as **Abigayle**. **Abby** (**Abbey, Ab(b)i, Abbie**) is a short form which is also common as a given name, although occasionally this comes from GABRIEL. The alternative short form **Gail** is well established as an independent name.

Abner

This is a Biblical name that has been little used in the UK, but which was used in the USA, and which has made its mark on cultural life there. The name, **Avner** in Hebrew, appears to be made up of *av* 'father' and a second element *ner* meaning light, giving 'father of light'; but Abner's father was called Ner, and the name could simply mean 'his father is Ner'. Abner was a cousin of King Saul and commander of his army who 'displayed many good qualities'. It was regularly used in the nineteenth century, but has not been in the American top thousand names since the 1930s. It was in 1934 that the cartoon strip *Li'l Abner* by Al Capp first appeared. It ran until 1977. As its 'hero' Abner Yokum was a poor, stupid and obstinate hillbilly whose ignorance was used to satirize American society, it is no surprise the name became well nigh unusable. Abner Doubleday (1819–93) is popularly credited with inventing baseball.

Abraham

Abraham, **Avraham** in the original Hebrew, comes, according to the Bible, from *av hamon* 'father of a multitude', although some later scholars have doubted this. In the Bible, Abraham was originally called **Abram** ('high father'), but as the patriarch of the nation, his name was changed to fit his role. Abraham Lincoln's nickname 'Honest Abe' shows one short form of the name; **Aby** is also used, and **Bram** Stoker, the creator of Count Dracula, illustrates another short form. In recent years there has been an increased interest in the name in the USA. The Arabic form of the name, **Ibrahim**, is interpreted as from *abu* 'father' and *rahim* 'kind'.

Abril see April

Absolom see Axel

Achilles see Hector

Ada, Adah

These two names actually come from different roots, although in practice they are probably used interchangeably. **Ada** is a short form of the names in the ADELA group. It was introduced to the USA by German immigrants in the eighteenth century, but only came into general use among English speakers in the nineteenth. However, it is also recorded as a name used in Asia Minor in the fourth century BC, having been the name of the sister of Mausolus, who built the first mausoleum, and is recorded as the name of as abbess in seventh-century France. **Adah** is a Hebrew name, given to a number of women in the Old Testament, meaning 'an ornament', although it has also been interpreted as meaning 'brightness', in contrast to Adah's co-wife ZILLAH ('shadow'). The computer language Ada is named in honour of Byron's daughter Ada, Countess of Lovelace (1815–52), who was a gifted mathematician in her own right and a patron of Charles Babbage, encouraging him to develop his prototype computer. Ada and Babbage tried to apply their mathematical skills to predicting the outcome of horse races, and Ada died heavily in debt.

Adair

Adair is a Scottish surname, which in turn comes from the first name EDGAR. It is used for both sexes. It was introduced as a girl's name in the 1980s by the long-running American television soap opera *Search for Tomorrow*, which featured a character called Adair McCleary and her brothers Hogan, Cagney and Quinn.

Adala see Adil

Adam

The name of the first man created, Adam probably comes from the Hebrew word for *adama* 'earth' with reference to the story that he was made out of earth, although some interpret it as meaning 'red', referring either to the colour of his skin or to the earth from which he was made. It has been a very popular name for many years throughout the English-speaking world. Historically, it has particularly strong associations with the Celtic areas of Britain. In Scotland its early popularity led to the development of many variants and pet forms, such as **Adie, Edie** and **Edom**. There is also a rare Scots feminine form **Adamina**. The Welsh form of Adam is **Adda**, and the Irish form is **Ádhamh**, with a subsidiary form of the name, **Adamnan** which means 'little Adam'. This was the name of an Irish saint and bishop of the seventh to eighth centuries who was renowned for his work for peace and for his writings, and who also made the earliest recorded 'sighting' of the Loch Ness Monster. The Irish form in the past has taken some strange forms including Awnan, Odonan and Junan. Forms from other languages include the Spanish **Adamo** and the Portuguese **Adão**. **Ad** and **Adie** are used as pet forms and **Adkin** and ADDISON are surnames that come from it.

Addison

This is a surname, meaning 'son of Adam', now used as a first name. It has long been used, quietly, as a masculine name – for example the acerbic theatre critic in the 1950 film *All About Eve* is call Addison De Witt. However, in the last few years it has shot up the popularity charts as a feminine name, after it was used for the female character of Dr Addison Shephard in the popular television series *Grey's Anatomy*. It has already developed an increasingly-used variant **Addyson**, and the short for **Addie** is also registering as an independent name.

Addy see Audrey

Adel see Adil

Adela

The early Frankish nobility were very keen to stress their daughters' pedigree (and thus marriageability) and were particularly fond of giving them names compounded with *Adel-*, 'noble'. This is the source of Adela, the name of one of William the Conqueror's daughters, as well as of **Adelicia** or **Adeliza** ('noble cheer'), the name of the mother of William the Conqueror and of one of his daughters; **Adelina** ('noble manner'); **Adelaide** ('noble kind'), now also spelt **Adalaide** and **Adelaida**, and **Adelinde** ('noble snake'), a name that developed into our 'Sweet **Adeline**' and also shortened forms **Alina** and **Aline**. Alina is also an Arabic name meaning 'noble'. **Addie** and **Addy** are used as short forms for all these names (but see also ADDISON, above). These names were revived in the UK in the early nineteenth century as a result of the popularity of German-born Queen Adelaide (1792–1849), wife of William IV. **Adèle** is the French spelling of Adela, which became popular in the nineteenth century, and **Aleida** is a

German name from the same root, spelt **Alida** in Hungarian. Adela is also spelt **Adella**, and is the source of the now independent name DELLA. There are faint signs of a revival of interest in this group of names. (See also ADA, ALICE, HEIDI and ADIL)

Aden see Aidan

Ádhamh see Adam

Adil

Adil, sometimes **Adel**, means 'honest, just, upright'. The feminine equivalents are **Adila** or **Adela**, and there is also a girl's name **Adala** meaning 'justice'.

Adina

Adina is an obscure biblical name meaning 'slender, delicate'. It was the name of a soldier and chief of the tribe of Reuben in Chronicles, but because of the -a ending is now understood as a feminine name. It is rarely used by English speakers, but is saved from total obscurity by being the name of a character in Donizetti's opera *L'Elisir d'Amore* and the title of a work by Henry James. It is well used in Romania, and there is a Czech actress called Adina Mandlová.

Aditya

In Hindu mythology the Aditya (literally 'belonging to **Aditi**') are a group of solar deities who are the sons of Aditi, the mother goddess of sky and fertility, and the sage Kashyapa. The *Rigveda* give their names as **Varun(a)**; **Mitra**; **Aryaman**; **Bhaga**; **Daksa**; **Ansa**; **Savitr** or **Surya**, the Sun; and RAVI, all of whose names can also be used as first names. Aditi's name, which means 'boundless', is used as a female name.

Adlai

Adlai is another rare biblical man's perhaps related to ADAH. He appears in 1 Chronicles 27:29 as the father of Shaphat, who, when David was king, had charge over 'the herds that were in the valleys'. It was made known to the general public by the politician and wit Adlai Stevenson (1900–65), who was named after his grandfather in whose family the name was traditional, and by his son and grandson, who also went into politics.

Adolf

The old Germanic name *Adwulf* was formed from the elements *ad*, a shortening of *adel* 'noble' found in named such as ADELA, and *wulf* 'wolf', a common Germanic name element found in names such as RANDOLPH, which indicated fierceness and soldierly qualities. This was shortened with time to Adolf, and adopted into French as **Adolphe**, which was fairly popular in France in the nineteenth century, and sometimes found elsewhere as **Adolph**. It was used on occasion by English speakers from the eighteenth century, sometimes in the Latinate form **Adolphus**: for example it was given to the seventh son of George III. Often this was in honour of the Swedish king Gustavus Adolphus (see further under GUSTAV). In the USA it is moderately well used in the Spanish form **Adolfo**. The notoriety of Adolf Hitler has severely reduced its use, but the short forms **Dolph** and **Dolphus** can be found, for example in the actor Dolph Lundgrun, although Dolph can also be a shortening of RANDOLPH.

Adonis

The Semitic *Adonai* 'Lord', used as a term of address to a god, became Adonis in Greek when rites associated with a fertility god who dies and rises each spring were adopted into ancient Greek culture. There, the myth developed that Aphrodite, goddess of love (see VENETIA), had fallen in love with an unusually handsome young man called Adonis. He was killed while out boar-hunting, and the blood-red anemone flower had sprung from his spilt blood. Aphrodite was heart-broken, and Zeus, king of the gods, comforted her by allowing him to be restored to life some of the year. Historically, it has not been much used. The few parents confident that their son will grow up with sufficient beauty to match such a myth have been more likely to choose **Endymion** (see SELINA), but the name started to be given to boys in the USA in the 1990s. While the traditional British pronunciation is with a long 'o' (to rhyme with 'phone'), in the USA it often used with a short 'o', giving the same sound as in the name Donald. There is a very rare feminine **Adonia**. Adonis is the pen-name of the Arabic poet Ali Ahmed Said (1930–).

Adrian, Adrienne

The Adriatic Sea probably got its name from the Latin word *ater* meaning 'black', possibly from the black sand of its beaches. The sea in turn gave its name to the town of Adria, and it was from this town that the family name of the Roman Emperor **Hadrian** (Latin *Adrianus*) came, which gave us the name Adrian. The only English pope, Nicholas Breakspeare, took the name of Adrian or Hadrian IV, perhaps from St Adrian of Canterbury (d. 710), a man who twice refused to become Archbishop of Canterbury, preferring to remain in a local monastery. The French form of the name is **Adrien**, and from this comes the most common feminine form **Adrienne**. **Adrianne**, **Adriane** and **Adrian(n)a** are also used, and can be shortened to forms such as **Riana**. Particularly in the United States, Adrian and Adrien can also be found used as girls' names, the spread of the use perhaps influenced by the character of Adrian Balboa, the hero's wife in the *Rocky* series of films made from 1976 onwards. Names in this group are not much used in the UK at the moment, but are well used in some Continental countries and a wide range is quite popular in the USA, where **Adriel** has also started to be used in the last few years. This would appear to be a variant of Adrian.

Aedan see Aidan

Aegidia, Aegidius see Giles

Aelwyn see Alvin

Aeneas, Aengus see Angus

Aeron, Aeronwen

The meaning of the Welsh name element Aeron is disputed. The word *aeron* in Welsh means 'fruit, berry'; but it has also been suggested that the name comes from the ancient Celtic goddess of battle, *Agrona*, or, particularly when used for boys, from the river name which, despite being the least romantic option, is probably the most accurate. Aeron is used for both sexes, but there are specifically feminine variants in **Aerona** and **Aeronwy**. Another feminine, **Aeronwen**, is formed from Aeron plus the suffix *gwen*, which means both 'white' and 'blessed'. The Welsh poet Dylan Thomas chose the name Aeronwy for his daughter.

Affery, Afra see Aphra

Afric, Africa

These are forms of a woman's name used in Ireland and the Isle of Man for the Celtic name **Aifric**, meaning 'pleasant', and in Scotland for the Celtic name **Oighrig**, of disputed meaning, possibly 'new speckled one'. It is an old name, going back to at least the eleventh century, and has no connection with the name of the continent. It is also found as **Affrica**, while the form **Aphria** may sometimes lead to confusion with APHRA. It has also been confused with the short forms of the name EUPHEMIA which, particularly in the form Effie, was used in Scotland to anglicise Oighrig. Africa is also used with reference to the continent, mainly by Afro-American parents to show pride in their origins, in which case it is occasionally also spelt Afrika. There may be a growth in the use of Aifric after it was used for the eponymous heroine of an Irish Language television series, first broadcast in 2006.

Agatha

Agatha comes from the Greek word *agathos* meaning 'good'. St Agatha was a third-century martyr, about whom little is known for sure. She is the patron saint of bell-founders, owing to misinterpretation of pictures of her martyrdom. One of the tortures that she was supposed to have suffered was to have her breasts cut off, and she is often painted bearing them on a dish. The bell-like shape of these objects led to her association with campanology. **Agate** is the old form of the name, based on the French pronunciation of the name. It was a popular name in the Middle Ages, and William the Conqueror used it for one of his daughters, but it later died out until revived with other medieval names in the nineteenth century. It was well used into early twentieth century, but is now little used by English speakers to whom it still sounds old-fashioned. The French form **Agathe** is, however, currently popular in France. **Aggy** or **Aggie** are shared as short forms of Agatha with AGNES. The mystery writer Agatha Christie is a famous holder.

Agnes

The Greek name *Agathe*, from *agathos* 'pure', became in Latin Agatha. This name looked to Latin speaker as if it came from *agnus*, their word for 'lamb', and also a symbol of purity. Thus the lamb became the symbol in art of St Agnes, an early Christian martyr. In the Middle Ages St Agnes was a very popular saint and her name was often used for girls. This meant that popular forms of the name developed. The form **Annis** or **Annes**, with **Annot** as a variant, reflects the medieval pronunciation which did not sound the 'g', much as the modern French form, Agnès, pronounces it as part of the 'n'. The modern hard 'g' sound comes from the spelling pronunciation of the nineteenth-century revival of the name. Annes is one of the sources of the name NANCY, probably via **Nance**. In Wales, the name became **Nest** or **Nesta** and one eleventh-century holder of that name became a byword for her beauty. In Scotland, where the name was particularly popular in the nineteenth century, the pet forms were not only the usual Aggie or Aggy (shared with AGATHA), but also **Ness** and **Nessie**, which explains why Nessie the Loch Ness Monster is usually a 'she'. There is also the peculiar development in Scotland in which the name **Senga** is formed by spelling Agnes backwards (although it has also been suggested that this could come from the Gaelic word *seang* meaning 'slender'). In Ireland Agnes was used to anglicise OONAGH, perhaps because both were thought to come from the word for 'lamb', while INA, in Irish **Aghna** may be another Irish form of the name. **Agneta** is both a Latin and Scandinavian form of the name and gives a pet form **Netta,** while **Agnethe** is a variant. The Spanish form gives us **Inez** or **Ines**. The latter is particularly popular in France at the moment, and Agnes is popular in Sweden. The name is not much used by English speakers, but as Thom Yorke of the popular group Radiohead named his daughter Agnes in 2004, may be due for a revival.

Ahmad, Ahmed

Ahmad is an Arabic word meaning 'most praised' based on the verb *hamida* 'to praise' shared with many other Muslim names, such as MOHAMMED and HAMID. It was one of the names of the Prophet Mohammed, and is one of the most popular boy's names in the Arab world. **Ahmadullah** or **Ahmad Allah** 'most praised of Allah' is a variant. In the USA Ahmad (the more popular spelling) or Ahmed is used by Afro-Americans, particularly Black Muslims. Ahmad Jamal is a well-known American jazz musician and the Turkish-American Ahmet Ertegun was enormously influential in the development of popular music.

Aibhilin see Eileen

Aïcha, Aïchoucha see Aisha

Aidan

Aidan was originally a pet form of the Irish name **Aodh** (pronounced 'ee'), the name of the old Celtic god of the sun and fire, and so means 'little fire'. St Aidan was a seventh-century missionary from Ireland who played an important part in the conversion of the pagan north of England. As a result, his name has long been used in the North or England and in Scotland, as well as in Ireland. In the twentieth century it spread more widely, and is currently enormously popular in the USA, no doubt helped by the fact that over 40% of boys names currently chosen there end with the -en sound. Aidan is the most popular form there, closely followed by **Aiden**. **Ayden**, **Aden**, **Adan**, **Aydan**, **Aydin**, **Aedan** and **Adin** all get into the top thousand names for boys in 2005, in that order of popularity, and if all the variants were added together it would probably turn out to be the most popular name given that year. Aidan and Aiden are also popular in Australia and Scotland, while Aidan has been well used in Ireland for some years.

The original Irish spelling of the name is **Aodán** or **Aodhan**. The name has always been used occasionally for girls in Ireland, and it is starting to be a girl's name in the USA, but **Enat** (Irish spelling **Aodhnait**), ENA**, Aida, Aideen** and most often **Edana** are alternative feminines.

Aifric see Afric

Ailbe, Ailbhe see Elvis

Aileen see Eileen

Ailie see Alice, Eilidh

Ailis, Ailish see Eilis

Ailsa

Some authorities have argued that this Scottish girl's name is a form of ELSA, or of Ealasaid, the Gaelic form of ELIZABETH, or of **Ailsie**, sometimes spelt Ailsa, used in Scotland as a pet form of ALICE. These have no doubt been an influence, but most people identify the name with the island, Ailsa Craig, in the Firth of Clyde. The island's name comes from Old Norse, Ailsa originally meaning 'Alfsigr's Island' (from a masculine Norse name), but it seems to have been popularly understood as 'Ailsa's rock', and so Ailsa came to be thought of as a first name. Ailsa started being used for girls some 100 years ago. Further south, Ailsa Craig became familiar to vegetable growers as the name of popular varieties of tomato and onion. Since Craig is more familiar to southerners as a surname than as a form of the word 'crag', and as many plants are named after people, this may have helped to establish Ailsa's currency as a name.

Ailsie see Alice, Ailsa

Aily see Eileen

Aimé, Aimée see Amy, Esmé

Aine

In Irish mythology, Aine is a goddess whose name means 'brightness, splendour', and who was particularly associated with Knockainey (Aine's Hill) in County Limerick. In later legend she became a fairy woman, queen of the fairies, and the kings of Munster claimed to be descended from her. So too did the Fitzgerald family (to whom we owe the name GERALDINE), and Aine is still a traditional name in their family. Aine is one of the oldest recorded Irish names and is once again popular throughout the island. It is generally pronounced with the first vowels as in *law* or the start of *oyster*, with the rest of the word much as the Spanish name Anya.

Ainsley, Ainslie

There are two place names in England called Ainsley, and there may have been more in the past. The one in Nottinghamshire is made up of the Old English elements *an*, 'one, only' and *leah* 'clearing' and the Warwickshire one from *ansetl* 'hermitage, solitary settlement' and *leah*. The place names would have become surnames, and the surnames then used as first names. The name was particularly well used in the early to mid twentieth century. Originally it was more used for boys than girls, but is now more often feminine. Ainsley Harriott is a well-known chef.

Aisha

Aisha is an Arabic name meaning 'living, prosperous'. It was the name of the third and favourite wife of the Prophet Mohammed, and is consequently a popular Arabic name. After he died in her arms, she played an important part in the political and religious events which followed his death, and is known as 'the mother of the faithful'. In the form **Ayesha** it was used by Rider Haggard for the name of She-Who-Must-Be-Obeyed in his novel *She* (1887). It is also, by tradition, the name of the wife of the Pharaoh who was drowned in the Red Sea when the Children of Israel escaped from Egypt. **Ayeisha** is also used, while in the United States, where the name has been popular, particularly with Black parents, the form **Iesha** or **Ieasha** has developed. Some American uses of Asia may be meant for Aisha, as Asia represents one American pronunciation of the name. In France the name is spelt **Aïcha**, and can have the pet forms **Aïchoucha** and **Aouïcha**.

Aislin, Aisling see **Ashling**

Aiyana see **Ayanna**

Ajay, Ajit

This is a boy's name which means 'unconquered, invincible' in Sanskrit and is an epithet of the gods Shiva and Vishnu.

Akeem, Akim see **Hakim**

Akhil

This Sanskrit boy's name means 'whole, complete'.

Akiva see **Jacob**

Al see **Alan, Albert, Alexander**

Alan, Alana

Alan is a Celtic name of unsure meaning and confused history, as it is found early on in several Celtic countries. The most convincing explanation of its meaning is that it comes from the same root as Gaelic *ailin* 'little rock', although some French authorities think that the French form, Alain, comes from the ancient tribe of the Alans. If this is to be believed, there must be a separate Celtic name. A recently found coin from Iron Age Britain bares the inscription Ale, which may be a very early form of the name. It is recorded in early Welsh records but seems to have died out, only to be re-introduced by Breton followers of William the Conqueror, such as Alan, Duke of Brittany. The name was popular in Brittany because it was that of a local fifth-century saint. It is also found in forms such as **Allan, Allen** (both common in the USA), **Alyn, Alleyn** which probably show the influence of surname spellings. Attempts have been made to distinguish the form **Alun** from other spellings, linking it with a Welsh river name, but in practice, outside Wales only a minority of parents seem likely to be aware of this distinction.

Feminine forms of the name, which have become much more common since the 1950s, include **Alana, Alena, Alan(n)ah** and **Alanna**, and the short form **Lan(n)a**, made famous by the film star Lana Turner, although it was in use in the nineteenth century. Forms such as Alannah may be influenced by the spelling of names such as Hannah, although some authorities claim that this group of female names come not from Alan, but from the affectionate Irish interjection *alannah*, which comes from the Irish Gaelic *a lenbh* ('o child'). In recent years **Alaina** and **Alayna**, perhaps a blend of Alana and ELAINE, have begun to be used in the USA. Alanis, made famous by the Canadian singer Alanis Morissette, whose father is called Alan, is generally considered a feminine form of Alan. Alani, which has recently made inroads in the USA, could also belong in this group, but is also the name of a Hawaiian tree.

Alan is currently moderately well used in Scotland, Ireland and the USA, while a number of feminine forms are also moderately well used in the USA, with both Aannah and Alanna featuring in Ireland, although Alana is preferred in Scotland. Well-known users include the computer pioneer Alan Turing and the American poet Allen Ginsberg.

Alaric

Alaric was a traditional name for the kings of the Ostrogoths, the most famous of which, Alaric I, sacked Rome in 410. The name is formed from the elements *al* 'all' and *ric* 'power, ruler' also found in such names as HENRY and RICHARD. It was introduced to England at the time of the Norman Conquest. For some reason, perhaps as a part of the admiration of things 'Gothic', perhaps in honour of the blessed Alaric, a prince who became a monk in Switzerland in the tenth century, it was revived in the nineteenth century, and is still occasionally used.

Alastair

Alastair is the commonest English spelling of the Scottish name Alasdair. It is the Gaelic form of ALEXANDER, where the name is discussed in full. The name is also spelt **Alistair** and **Alister**. It had been adopted by the Lowland Scots by the seventeenth century, and became popular outside Scotland and Ireland in the twentieth century. There are rare Irish and Scottish feminine forms of Alasdair: **Alastrina** and **Alastriona**. Alastair is still moderately well used in Scotland, but is currently declining ·in popularity.

Alba see Dawn

Alban

St Alban, who gave his name to the town which grew up around his supposed place of death, was the first British martyr. He is said to have been a Roman soldier who swapped clothes with a Christian priest who was being hunted for his faith, and was executed in his place. Alban seems to have lived in the third century, but dates suggested for his death range between 209 at the earliest to as late as 304. The name, which comes from Latin and can be interpreted either as meaning 'white' or 'man from the town of Alba' ('white town'), was revived in the nineteenth century. It is also found in the form **Albin**. Feminine names from the same root are **Albinia** and **Albina**, the name of a third-century martyr, which can be shortened to **Bina**, while BLANCHE is an alternative name with the same meaning, 'white'. The name is rare, and most likely to be used nowadays in honour of the German composer Alban Berg (1885–1955).

Albany see Avalon

Alberic see Aubrey

Albert

The old German name *Adalberht*, made up of *adel* 'noble' and *berht* 'bright, famous', was shortened in France to Albert and brought over to England by the Normans in 1066. The Anglo-Saxons already had the same name in the form **Ethelbert**, which more or less died out after Conquest until revived as a rare name in the nineteenth century. Elbert was a Dutch form of the name, which was not uncommon in the past in the USA. Albert had gone out of use in England by the time Sir Walter Scott used it for a major character in his popular novel *Anne of Geierstein* in 1829, but what really made the name popular was the marriage in 1840 of Queen Victoria to the German Prince Albert of Saxe-Coburg and Gotha. Meanwhile the German form Albrecht had been taken to the USA by German migrants, so it is found used there from the seventeenth century onwards, when it had died out in England. It was popular in the USA in the 1930s when it was already out of fashion in the UK, and is still more likely to be used there than in other English-Speaking countries, particularly in the Spanish form **Alberto**. The short forms are **Al**, shared with other Al- names and the preferred shortening in the USA, and **Bert** or **Bertie**, the usual British pet forms. **Alberta** (short form **Berta**) was coined as a feminine form for a goddaughter of Queen Victoria, and other feminines such as the French **Albertine** – familiar as the name of a popular variety of rose – and **Albertina** are also on record.

Albin, Albina, Albinia see Alban

Alby see Elvis

Aldous

Aldous most probably comes from the Germanic element *ald* 'old' probably indicating respect, although both *adal* 'noble' and *hild* 'battle' have been suggested as sources. **Aldis** is a rare variant. The Italian form **Aldo** is more common, and lies behind the famous fifteenth-century Venetian **Aldus** Manutius (given name Aldo Manuzio), founder of the Aldine Press, which beautifully printed books brought the Classics to a new audience. **Alden**, a surname which has been quietly growing in popularity as a first name over the last decade, is a distantly related name, as it comes from the Anglo-Saxon name Aldwyn, meaning 'old friend'. Aldous, a popular name in East Anglia in the Middle Ages, is now mainly kept alive by the fame of the novelist Aldous Huxley (1894–1964).

Aldred see Eldred

Alea, Aleah see Alia

Alec, Aleck, Alessandro, Alessandra see Alexander

Aled

Aled is a Welsh name taken from the name of a river and lake in Denbighshire. It was used by the fifteenth- to sixteenth-century poet Tudor Aled (d. c. 1526). The Welsh singer Aled Jones has made the name widely known outside Wales.

Aleesha see Alice

Aleida see Adela

Alejandra, Alejandro, Alessandra see Alexander, Alondra

Alethea

A woman's name which comes from the Greek word meaning 'truth', Alethea first came into fashion in the sixteenth century, perhaps as a part of the Puritan movement for naming children after abstract virtues such as PATIENCE and CHARITY. It has a variety of spellings such as **Alithea**, **Alithia**, **Alethia** and **Aletheia**. ALTHEA comes from a different root, although the two names are often confused. Charlotte M. Younge, writing on first names in the nineteenth century, says that Alethea was then notably used in Ireland and shortened to **Letty**. There is some disagreement whether the name should be accented on the first or second syllable.

Alewyn see Alvin

Alexander, Alexandra

Alexander is a very ancient and widely used name, which has been one of the key boy's names in the UK since the final third of the twentieth century, and popular in the USA since the 1990s. The various masculine and feminine forms of this name are currently in the top ten choices in an astonishing range of countries, from Estonia to Spain. The Greeks believed it came from *alexein* 'to defend' and *andros* 'men', giving a meaning 'defender of men', and it is generally so interpreted. However, there is some evidence that it may be an even earlier name coming from ancient Hittite, which was later given a Greek form. According to Greek legend, the first holder of the name was the Trojan PARIS, abductor of HELEN; he was nicknamed Alexander by some shepherds whose flocks he defended from robbers. Much later it was adopted by the Macedonian royal family, who followed the Greek custom of alternating pairs of names between generations. Thus PHILIP II of Macedon was the son of an Alexander, and his son was Alexander III, better known as Alexander the Great (356–323 BC). His conquests of Asia as far as India spread his name in forms such as **Iskander** through much of that continent (see also OLYMPIA, ROXANA). The medieval fictional account of his life in *The Romance of Alexander*, which, like a modern bestseller, was translated into a wide range of different languages, meant that the name was found throughout Europe, and gave us at least 20 saints bearing the name. The name is found in England from at least the twelfth century, but has special associations with Scotland. St Margaret of Scotland (c. 1038–93) was the daughter of an exiled Anglo-Saxon prince and a Hungarian princess. She married King Malcolm III of Scotland and one of her sons was christened Alexander, a name that had not been used in the Scottish royal family before, but which was popular in Hungary. Alexander I of Scotland reigned for 17 years, and in the following century two more Alexanders succeeded each other. Their combined reigns, lasting from 1214 to 1286, firmly established the name in Scotland. Thus it is not surprising that Scotland provides a multitude of pet forms of the name, including **Alec** and **Aleck**, **Alick**, **Eck**, **Ecky**, **Sander**, **Sandy**, **Elshander**, **Elshender**, **Elick**, **Allie** and **Ally**. In Gaelic the name became **Alasdair** (see ALASTAIR). Other pet forms are **Al**, **Alex**, **Lex**, and in the north of England and Scottish Lowlands **Sawnie** was an old pet form. **Xander** and **Zander** are short forms which are now becoming names in their own right. (See also ALEXIS, SASHA). In the USA, the Spanish forms **Alejandro** and Alexandro and the Italian **Alessandro** are well represented and the strange form Alexzander is also found.

The feminine form **Alexandra**, made popular by the Danish princess who married King Edward VII, and back in fashion on both sides of the Atlantic, is the most widely used female form of the name, but **Alexandria, Alexandrina, Alexandrine** are also used. They can be shortened to **Alex** and **Lexie**, forms shared with ALEXIS names. **Alix** and **Alyx** look as if they should also be forms of the name, but historically they are medieval spellings of ALICE. From the Italian **Alessandra** we get the names **Sandra, Sondra** and **Zandra**, while in France they use **Xandra** and **Xandrine** as pet forms. The Spanish form is **Alejandra**.

Alexis

Alexis is an English form of the Latin **Alexius**, itself from Greek *Alexios*, which comes, like Alexander, from *alexein* 'to defend, protect'. Indeed, there is much overlap between the two names, and it is not always possible to distinguish between short forms. There were numerous saints called Alexis. The one who was most popular in the Middle Ages, Alexis of Rome, probably never existed. He is said to have left home on his wedding night to go on pilgrimage, and on his return to have lived as an unrecognised pauper outside his father's house for the seventeen years before his death. While Alexis was originally a masculine name, and is still used as such in many countries, it is now also feminine in English-speaking countries. This changeover and the currency of the name owes much to the character of Alexis Carrington in the 1980s soap opera *Dynasty*. Alexis has since become very popular in the USA, reaching 3 in 1999 and still at 13 in 2005 for girls, while for boys Alexis highest ranking has been 103 in 2004. Also in the most popular rankings for girls have been **Alexa, Alexia** and **Alexus**, despite its apparently masculine ending. Shortened forms **Lexi** and **Lexie** are also used as independent names. In 2007, after footballer Steven Gerrard named his daughter Lexie, the name rose 239 places in the English charts. Sometimes the form **Lexus** is found for girls in the USA. It has been suggested that this refers to the luxury brand of car, for naming children after luxury products is a minor but distinct trend in the USA. However, it seems more likely that it is simply a shortening of Alexus, although the status of the car may well have influenced the parents' choice. Alexis is shortened to **Alex**, and can be respelt **Alexy**, reflecting the French pronunciation. French variants for girls include **Alexiane, Alexina** and **Alexine**, but these have yet to make inroads in English-speaking countries.

Alfonso

Alfonso is a name that was taken to Spain by the invading Visigoths, one of the many Germanic peoples who spread over Europe in the Dark Ages. There are various theories as to its origin, but the most likely seems to be that it is another name from *adal* 'noble' combined with *funs* 'ready, prompt, eager'. It has been a royal name in Spain since at least the seventh century. It is not among the established names of most English speakers, but is well used in the USA among those of Spanish-speaking descent, where it can be shortened to forms such as **Fonso**. The French form is **Alphonse**, which has a feminine **Alphonsine**. **Alonso** or **Alonzo** are variant forms of Alfonso and are well used in the USA. This gives short forms **Lon** and **Lonnie**.

Alfred

Alfred is an Anglo-Saxon name formed from the elements *ælfr* 'elf', which shares a common Germanic root with ALVIN, where other elf names are discussed, and *ræd* 'counsel'. Short forms are **Alf, Alfie**, and **Fred**. The name, which had become obsolete, was revived in the nineteenth century, and its very popularity then and in the early part of the twentieth century led to a decline in its use by the middle of the twentieth century. **Alured** is coinage of the nineteenth century, formed from a misunderstanding of the Latin form of the name, the 'u' being a misreading of the 'v' used for the Old English 'f'. **Avery** is a surname, now also used as a first name, which arose because the Norman French who came to rule England in the eleventh century had great difficulty pronouncing English words with groups of consonants in them, and so mangled Alfred to Avery. **Alfreda** is a feminine version of the name which can be shortened to FREDA. In Scandinavia **Alf** is an independent name, from the Old Norse form of 'elf', *alfr*. Alfred owes its nineteenth-century revival to the fame of Alfred the Great (849–901), who was not only an inspiring leader of men and a successful general, forcing the invading Danes out of southern England, but also a great patron of learning. While the full form has not regained its popularity, the pet form Alfie has been very popular in England and well used in Scotland. Alfie has long been known to small children, and hence their parents, from Shirley Hughes' wonderful picture books, and it has been suggested that the sudden appearance of Alfie among the most popular names in England in the 2000s owes much to the popular character of Alfie Moon in the television soap *East Enders*. In the USA Avery is more likely to be found, its popularity for both sexes having climbed steadily for many years. It is more common as a female name, in which case it is occasionally **Averie**.

Alfwine see Alvin

Algernon

Algernon comes from the Norman French *gernon* 'moustached' or 'with whiskers'. It started life as a nickname. For instance, William de Percy, who took part in the Norman Conquest and founded the PERCY family, was called Algernon on account of his moustache. Recent research has shown that in the Middle Ages at least, the nickname was used through all strata of society. However, its use by the Percy family has given the name distinct aristocratic associations. This led to its increased use in the nineteenth century in the UK, but also meant that it was little used in the USA. **Algy** or **Algie** is the short form. The Victorian poet Algernon Charles Swinburne (1837–1909) was a famous bearer of the name.

Ali, Alia

Ali comes from the Arabic *aliyy* 'high, lofty, sublime'. *Al-Aliy*, the All-High, is one of the names of Allah. **Aali** is another form of the name. The feminine forms of this name take many forms, the simplest being **Alia** or **Alya**. **Aaliyah**, popularised by the singer Aaliyah Houston (1974–2001), which is the most-used form among non-Muslims in the UK and USA. Other forms used in the USA include **Aliyah**, **Aliya** and even **Aleah**. Aliya(h) can also be a Hebrew name meaning 'to ascend, go up'. These names are not only very popular among Arabic speakers, but have also made inroads among Black Americans, particularly those who are also Black Muslims. The most prominent example is the boxer Muhammed Ali, who chose the name to replace his original name of Cassius Clay.

Alice

This name comes ultimately from the old German name **Adelaide** (see under ADELA) via the French shortening Adaliz or Alis, which came over to England as **Aliz**, **Alys**, **Alyx** or **Alix** (see also under ALEXANDER). The Latin form of the name gives us **Alicia**, which has the modern developments **Alis(i)a**, **Aliss(i)a**, **Alyss(i)a**, and which in turn have developed such forms as **Aleesha** and **Alisha**. **Elysia** (also found in forms such as **Eleasha**, **Elissa**, **Elisha** and **Ellicia**) can be thought of as either a development of Alicia, a blend of Elise and Alicia or a development of Elizabeth. Pet forms of these names are **Ali**, **Allie** and **Ally**. ALISON, an old pet form of Alice, is now regarded as a name in its own right. In Scotland, Alice has pet forms **Ailie**, ELLIE, **Ailsie** (sometimes written AILSA), and this, alongside ELIZABETH, is one of the sources of **Elsie. Elke** or **Elkie** is a German pet form of the name. Alice can also be found in such spellings as **Alyse** or **Alyce**. (See also EILIS.) **Alize** could be interpreted as another form of Alice or as a modern blend, just as **Aliza** can be seen variously as a respelling of Alicia, a blend of Alice and Liza or in some cases as a Jewish name, from the Hebrew for joyful. Forms of Alice were very popular in the Middle Ages, but then declined until the name was revived in the nineteenth century, most famously in *Alice in Wonderland*. Many forms of Alice are currently popular among English speakers. Alyssa is currently the most popular form in the USA but many other forms are also well used; it is also popular in Australia. Alice and Alisha, followed by Alyssa, head the list in the UK and are also popular in Ireland along with Alicia.

Alick see Alexander

Alida see Adela

Alienor see **Eleanor**

Alina, Aline see **Adela**

Alis, Alisa, Alisha see **Alice**

Alison

Alison, is a pet form of ALICE which has become an independent name. While Alison is the standard old spelling, and the one most often found to the east of the Atlantic, in the USA **Alisson** is the commonest spelling, and **Al(l)yson** and **Alysson** are also used.

Alistair, Alister see **Alexander**

Alithea, Alithia see **Alethea**

Alivia see **Olivia**

Alix, Aliz see **Alice**

Aliya, Aliyah see **Ali**

Allan, Allen, Alleyn see **Alan**

Allegra

This name means 'lively' in Italian. The poet Byron chose it for his daughter (1817–22), and his choice has been followed by later English-speaking parents, particularly in recent years.

Allie, Ally see **Alexander, Alice**

Allyson see **Alison**

Alma

Those wanting to use this girl's name can choose from many different sources and meanings. The Latin word *alma*, as in the term Alma Mater for one's school or university, means 'loving, nurturing', and is one source of the name. Then, in the sixteenth century, Edmund Spenser created a character called Alma for book II of his *Faerie Queene*, deriving the name from the Italian for 'soul'. The name remained rare until after 1854, when the British and their allies defeated the Russians in the Crimean War at the battle of Alma, named after a Crimean river. This third source gave the name a popularity that lasted well into the twentieth century. Alma is also the Spanish for 'soul', which probably lies behind many modern American uses. In Hebrew Alma means 'maiden'. Alma Cogan (1932–66) was a much-loved British singer in the 50s and 60s, and the name recently received exposure in the character of Alma Del Mar in the 2005 film *Brokeback Mountain*.

Almeric

This Germanic man's name formed from elements meaning *amal* 'work' and *ric* 'rule', found in so many men's names. It was introduced to England at the time of the Norman Conquest. It is also found in the form **Almery**. In Italy the name became Almerigo, then Amerigo, as in Amerigo Vespucci (1451–1512), after whom the continent of AMERICA is named. Almeric was one of the names revived in the nineteenth century, but it never became as popular as many of the other revivals. It was the name of the sixth-century Visigothic king and two twelfth-century kings of Jerusalem. Almeric developed into the surname **Emery** or **Emory**, used as a first name for both sexes, but currently more used for girls in the USA, as is the surname which developed from this, **Emerson**. The use for girls may stem from an association with names such as EMILY. The actress Teri Hatcher has recently named her daughter Emerson Rose.

Aloisa, Aloys, Aloyse see **Heloise, Lewis, Lois**

Alondra

Alondra is a pet form of Alejandra, the Spanish feminine form of ALEXANDER. It is also the Spanish for 'lark', and a common place name in parts of the USA. It has become quite popular as a given name there in recent years. There is a popular Mexican singer called simply Alondra.

Alonso, Alonzo see **Alfonso**

Aloysius see Lewis

Alphonse, Alphonsine see Alfonso

Althea

Althea is a Greek name, possibly meaning 'wholesome, healing' although its exact meaning is unsure. In the form **Althæa** it occurs in Greek mythology, as the mother of the hero Meleager. She was told at his birth that he would live as long as a certain log of wood on the fire remained unburned. She kept the wood safe, thus protecting him, until the day he got into a fight and killed her two brothers. In fury she threw the wood on the fire, and her son immediately died. The form Althea was introduced by the Cavalier poet Richard Lovelace (1618–59) as one of his poetic names for Lucy Sacheverell (see also LUCASTA). Lovelace would have accented the name on the second syllable, but many modern users accent it on the first. The American tennis player Althea Gibson (1927–2003) was a prominent user of the name.

Alun see Alan

Alured see Alfred

Alvin, Aylwin

Two Old English names, **Athelwine** ('noble friend') and **Alfwine** ('elf friend'), lie behind this name, both taking on the forms **Alwin** or **Alewyn** after the Norman Conquest. The name was used quietly until given a boost by the publication of Theodore Watts-Dunton's romantic novel of Gypsy life, *Aylwin*, in 1898. **Alvin** is the form of the name most popular in the United States and may show a Dutch influence. Other forms of the name are **Alvyn** and **Aylwin** or **Alewyn**. A feminine form, **Alvina**, is found in a Flemish legend in which a king's daughter of that name was rejected by her parents for marrying unsuitably. It is said that her crying can still be heard in the howling of strong winds.

The history of the name is complicated by the existence of a group of similar Welsh names – **Aelwyn**, **Alwen**, **Alwyn**, **Eilwyn** and various other forms – which could be from the same Old English source, or else from a jumble of Welsh sources, the second element meaning 'white, fair', the first any one of 'great', 'child' or 'brow'. A related name to Alvin is **Alvar**, which can be analysed as a form of the Old English name *Alfhere*, formed from 'elf' and 'warrior'. It is also used as the English form of the Spanish **Alvaro**, another Germanic name introduced to Spain by the Visigoths, formed from elements meaning 'all' and 'war'. This is the name of a number of characters in the great Spanish epic the *Cantar de Mio Cid* ('Song of My Cid'). To any British person above a certain age Alvar is best known from the veteran broadcaster Alvar Liddell. Liddell was British born but had Swedish parents. The feminine form of Alvar is **Alva** 'elf, fairy', currently a popular choice in Sweden. Other 'elf' names are found under ALFRED and AUBREY.

Alvis see Elvis

Alya see Ali

Alyce see Alice

Alyn see Alan

Alys, Alyssa see Alice

Alysson see Alison

Alyx see Alice

Amabel see Amy, Mabel

Amadea, Amadeus see Theodore

Amalia, Amalie see Amelia

Aman, Amani

For a non-Arabic speaker, sorting out the relationships between these two names can be difficult. As both a masculine and feminine name Aman is from the Arabic word for 'trust, safety, protection'. Amani, also used for both sexes, can be from the Arabic for 'wishes, aspirations'. The singular of this is **Umniya**, which is also used for girls. As a feminine form Amani can also be a Muslim name from the Persian for 'security, trust'. Amani is established as a girl's name in the USA, particularly among Black Americans. In some of these uses Amani may represent yet another word, the Swahili for 'peace'.

Amanda

Amanda means 'worthy of love' in Latin, and it is one of a large group of names connected with love, for which see further under AMY. The name probably goes back to the seventeenth century when descriptive names based on Latin roots were popular. It was used as a name by Colly Cibber in his 1696 play *Love's Last Shift* and from there much used for literary heroines in the eighteenth century. It was particularly popular as a given name in the second half of the twentieth century. It peaked in popularity in the 1960s in the UK, but not until the 1980s and 1990s in the USA, where it is still well used. The short form **Mandy** is perhaps best known as the title of a Barry Manilow song.

Amandine see Amy

Amarantha see Amaryllis

Amari

Amari, which is used for both sexes, is the commonest of a group of names which share the same sounds, but no clear history. The other names are **Amara** and **Amaris** for girls and **Amare** and **Amarion** for boys. While some sort of meaning can be given to the names, we should probably think of them as being given primarily for their sound, perhaps under the influence of **Amani**. There is a not uncommon Italian surname, Amari, which has been linked to the Latin for 'bitter'. The girl group Amari say they are named from the Swahili for 'God is Highest'. Another source gives the not very convincing information that the name is 'African' (unspecified) meaning 'builder, strong'; while another says it is a Hebrew masculine name meaning 'eternal'. The other names should probably be seen as variants, with Amarion reflecting the current popularity of -(m)arion as a name-forming element for boys, although the possible influence of names based on the Latin *amare* (AMANDA, AMY) should not be ignored.

Amaryllis

Amaryllis is a name used by pastoral poets of the classical world, notably Virgil, for a fair country girl. The name probably derives from a Greek root with the sense 'sparkling of the eyes' or 'darting quick glances'. Amaryllis was taken up in turn for their pastoral poetry firstly by Spenser and then by Milton, who immortalised the name when he wrote of the shepherd's opportunity 'To sport with Amaryllis in the shade' (*Lycidas*, 1637). It is only in modern times that Amaryllis has come to be a plant name. The similar-sounding **Amarantha**, another of Lovelace's poetic names (see ALTHEA), is however an ancient Greek flower name, the word meaning 'unfading flower'. It has been suggested that AMARA (*see* **Amari**) (see above) may be a pet form of Amarantha.

Amata see Amy

Amaya

Amaya seems to be a name without a history, which sprang into the American name charts in 1999 after a woman called Amaya Brecher appeared in the reality television show *The Real World*. The popularity of the AMY group of names and of MAYA may have influenced its adoption. The similar-sounding **Aniya(h)** or **Anaya**, which entered the charts in the same year, seems to be a variant of **Ania**, a Polish form of Ann, but both names are likely to have been chosen for their sounds.

Amber

Amber, the name of the fossilised resin used as a jewel, was used occasionally for girls in the nineteenth century, but became fashionable in the 1960s; it has again been widely popular since the 1980s. There is a French variant **Ambrine**, and related Arabic girl's name **Ambrin** meaning 'ambergris'. The name came to public attention in the 1944 novel *Forever Amber* by Kathleen Winson, and even more markedly when the film version was released in 1947 to great outcry from the self-styled guardians of public morality. The story is set in seventeenth-century England (when the name was not is use) and tells how the orphaned Amber St Clare sleeps her way to the top. In real life Amber Valletta is a famous American model.

Ambrose

Ambrose, from the same Greek root as the food of the gods, ambrosia, means 'belonging to the immortals' and was the name of one of the great doctors of the early Christian Church, the fourth-century St Ambrose, bishop of Milan. The name is found in British history in the fifth century in the person of Ambrosius Aurelianus, traditionally the uncle of King Arthur. From this Ambrosius the Welsh name **Emrys**, now more common than Ambrose, developed. There is a very rare feminine, **Ambrosine**.

Ameer, Ameera see Amir

Amelia

Although Amelia looks as if it should be from the Latin family name of Aemilia, this in fact became EMILY. Amelia, sometimes found as **Amalia** or **Amalie**, actually comes from *amal*, a Germanic word for 'work'. However, Emily and its related forms are also found as pet forms of Amelia, and may well have influenced the name's development. **Emmeline** (French **Ameline or Émiline**) is another form of Amelia and the source of the rare name **Emblem**. **Amelina, Ameline** and **Amelita** are all developments of the name. **Millie** or **Milly** are used as short forms for these names as well as for MILLICENT. The name was introduced to England from Germany by the Hanoverian monarchy in the eighteenth century and was used by Henry Fielding as the eponymous heroine of a novel in 1751, but was out of fashion when a revival of interest began in the 1980s, and it is now among the more popular names in the English-speaking world. In France **Amélie** was the title of a very successful film released in 2001.

America

America has been in use as a girl's name in the USA since the nineteenth century, but fell out of use around 1900, and does not reappear until the late 1990s, perhaps under the influence of the resurgence of patriotism brought about by 9/11 and the Iraq wars. The actress America Ferrara, star of the television series *Ugly Betty*, has recently brought the name to public attention. For the history of the word America, see under ALMERIC.

Amethyst see Jewel

Amhalgaidh, Amhlaoibh see Oliver

Amice, Amicia, Amie see Amy

Amin, Amina

Amin is the Arabic for 'trustworthy, honest', which sometimes appears as **Amine**, particularly in France and in countries where French is the basis for transcription from Arabic. Amina is the feminine form, which can have **Aminata** as a pet form. **Aamina**, 'safe' is a related name, and was borne by the mother of the Prophet Mohammed.

Aminta see Araminta

Amir, Amira

There are several Arabic names that can be transliterated as Amir, all of them related. Amir, which can also appear as **Ameer**, is the commonest of these names and usually glossed as 'prince, commander'; but it can also represent **Aamir** 'commander, leader', and there is another name Aamir (more properly **'Aamir**) which means 'prosperous, full of life'. Similarly Amira can also be **Ameera** 'princess' or **Aamira** 'prosperous'. In the sense 'prince' Amir is from the same word that gives English Emir and ultimately admiral. Amir can also be a Hebrew name meaning 'tree top' and Amira a Hebrew name meaning 'speech, speaker'.

Amit, Amitabh

These are masculine names from Sanskrit. Amit means 'limitless, infinite', and has a feminine **Amita**. Amitabh or **Amitav** is an epithet of the Buddha and means 'limitless splendour'.

Amiya, Amiyah see **Amy**

Amos

Amos is the name of an Old Testament prophet who foretold the destruction of Judah and Israel if the people did not reform. The name probably means 'bearer of a burden', although others have interpreted it as 'borne by God'. Although popular in the sixteenth century among Puritans, and well used for the next 300 years, it is not much used today.

Amy

Amy means 'loved' (from the French name **Aimée**) and is one of a group of names given to children as an expression of their parents' love. The Latin form of Amy is **Amicia**. In the early Middle Ages the English turned this form into **Amice**, a name which is still occasionally used. As well as AMANDA ('worthy to be loved') there is a French name of the same meaning, **Amandine**. **Amata** means 'beloved' and **Amabel** (Amabilla in the Middle Ages), which became MABEL, means 'loveable'. **Amorée** is a recent addition to the list, along with Amya, Amiya and Amiyah (which blend into AMAYA). Amy can also be found in spelling such as **Amie** or **Amye**. In the past there were male equivalents of many of these names, but the only one to have survived is **Amyas** ('loved'), kept alive by its use by Charles Kingsley for the hero of his *Westward Ho!* (1885). Amy and Aimee are both currently very popular in the English-speaking world.

Amynta, Amyntas, Amyntor see **Araminta**

Ana see **Anna**

Anabel, Anabella, Anabelle see **Annabel**

Anaëlle see **Anna**

Anahi

Anahi is the name of the heroine of a South American myth who was famous for her singing. It has come into use in the USA as a result of the success of the Mexican actress and singer who simply goes by the name Anahi.

Anaïs

Anaïs is a Catalan and Provencal pet form of Anna. It is recorded in France in the nineteenth century, is found as a character in Colette's *Claudine* books, and has a certain notoriety from the French-born author Anaïs Nin, but more recently became widely known as the name of a perfume. **Nais** can be used as a short form. It has been very popular in France since the 1980s and has spread to other countries.

Anand, Ananda

These are the masculine and feminine forms of a Sanskrit name meaning 'happiness'. Ananda can also appear as **Anandi**.

Anas see **Anis**

Anastasia

Anastasia comes from the Greek word for 'The Resurrection'. St Anastasia was a Christian martyr who died about 304, and whose feast day is on Christmas Day. Although there are wild and wonderful legends, almost nothing is known about her for sure. The name was found from the early twelfth century onwards in England, often in the forms **Anstace** or **Anstice**. We now tend to think of it as a Russian name, thanks to the fame of the Russian princess who is rumoured to have survived the massacre of the last Tsar and his family. Short forms include **Nastasia**, STACEY or **Stacy** (see also EUSTACE) and **Tansy**, although this can also be thought of as a use of the name of the yellow wild flower (*Tanacetum vulgare*). The singer **Anastacia** has given prominence to an alternative form of the name, while the actress **Nastassja** Kinski shows a German pet form of the name.

Anaya see **Amaya**

Anchoret see **Angharad**

Andrew, Andrea

Andrew comes from the Greek *Andreas* meaning 'manly', and thus shares part of the same root as ALEXANDER. The Apostle Andrew became the patron saint of Scotland, so it is not surprising that there it has developed its own forms **Andra** or **Andro** and **Dand**, **Dandie** or **Dandy**. Other pet forms are **Andie**, **Andy** and **Drew**; the latter is often used as an independent name and can also be derived from a Germanic-French name Drew or **Drogo** meaning 'trusty'. The Spanish form is **Andres**; the Welsh use **Andreas**. The French form, **André**, has now spread to English-speaking countries as well, while forms such as **DeAndre** are found in America.

Andrea, the most common of the feminine versions of the name, is from the Italian (where it is a masculine name), which also gives **Andreana**. **Andrée** and **Andréa** are French forms. There are also a number of feminine versions which probably started life in Scotland, as they show typical Scots forms, but which are now by no means restricted to Scotland. Included in this group are **Andrina**, **Andrene**, **Andrewena**, **Andrine**, **Andre(e)na** and their diminutives **Dreena** and **Rena**. Most of these names can be shortened to Andie or Andy.

Anemone see Flora

Aneta see Anna

Aneurin, Aneirin

This is a very old Welsh name, that of one of the earliest known Welsh poets, who lived in the sixth century. Its meaning is obscure, complicated by the fact that **Neirin**, now used alongside **Nye** as a pet form, seems to be the oldest form. It may mean 'noble', in which case the 'a' added in front would be emphatic. It has also been described as from the Latin name Honorius (see HONORIA), which would mean it was adopted before the end of the Roman occupation of Britain, although since Honorius also means 'honorable, noble' there may be a common root going back to the time before Latin and Celtic split into separate languages. It is best known from the Labour politician Nye Bevan (1897–1960), who as minister for health was largely responsible for the introduction of the National Health Service after World War II.

Angel, Angela

Angel comes from Latin *Angelus*, taken in turn from the Greek *angelos* 'messenger, angel' which also lies behind 'evangelist' and EVANGELINE names. The masculine names are mainly confined to Mediterranean, Roman-Catholic countries and groups descended from them. Angel is used in Spain and by Spanish-speakers and has spread to more general use in the USA, where it is now used for girls as well. Another masculine form is the Italian **Angelo**, which has a pet form **Lito** (via **Angelito**), and from this comes **Deangelo** and **Dangelo**, used in the USA. The character of Angel Clare in Thomas Hardy's *Tess of the D'Urbervilles* (1891), is a rare, literary, example of the use of Angel in the Protestant North.

The feminine basic form Angela has elaborations **Angelina**, currently a popular choice in the USA, but in the UK strongly associated with the *Angelina Ballerina* children's stories of a dancing mouse; **Angelica** and the French **Angelique**, associated in many minds with a racy series of historical novels; **Angeline**, which is also French in origin, and the Spanish pet form **Angelita**. Many of these are shortened to **Angie** or **Ange**, while **Anjeli** is sometimes a shortening of forms such as Angelique, although it can also be a spelling of the Indian name ANJALI. The fame of the American actress Angelina Jolie may account for the name's popularity there, while another American actress **Anjelica** Houston shows an alternative spelling of one of these names.

Angharad

Angharad, also spelt **Anghared**, is a Welsh name meaning 'much loved', which has been in use since at least the ninth century and is famous in Welsh literature as the name of the fair lady in the medieval Welsh romance *Peredur*. It was out of favour for a while because the element 'an', which in this name is an intensifier indicating 'very, much', could be understood as a negative, giving a meaning 'unloved'; but in the twentieth century it was well used in Wales and occasionally outside the country. It is one of the few Welsh names adopted by the English in the Middle Ages, anglicised to the now rare **Anchoret** or **Ankaret**.

Angie see Angel

Angus

The Scottish form of the Gaelic name **Aonghus** or **Aongus**, Angus means 'one choice'. It is an important name in Scottish history, as it was the name of one of the first Irish settlers who founded the Scots nation. The Irish form is **Aonghus** or **Aengus**, which has given the Scots surname **Innes**, reflecting the Irish pronunciation of the name. This is occasionally found as a first name. **Aeneas** or **Eneas**, the name of the Trojan founding father of the Roman people, whose name means 'praiseworthy', was used in the past when Gaelic names were frowned on, as the equivalent of Angus, and is still used in some Scots families. (For a similar use of a Trojan hero see HECTOR; see also under JULIA.) Angus is currently well used in Scotland and Australia, but not widely used elsewhere.

Angy see Angel

Ania see Amaya

Anika, Anita, Anja see Anna

Anil

Anil is a boy's name form the Sanskrit for 'air, wind' and is one of the names of the Hindu god of wind who drives Indra's golden chariot. There is a feminine form **Anila**.

Anis, Anissa

Anis, also spelt **Anees**, is the Arabic for 'friendly', used to indicate a good companion. The feminine form **Anisa** or Anissa is rather more common than the masculine. There is a related name, **Anas**, meaning 'friendship'.

Anish

This is one of the thousand names of the god Vishnu. It means 'supreme'. There is a female form **Anisha**.

Anita see Anna

Aniya, Aniyah see Amaya

Anjali, Gitanjali

These are girl's names. Anjali means 'offering' in Sanskrit, and **Gitanjali** is an offering of melody or poetry, and is related to **Geet** or **Geeti** (melody) **Gita** 'song' and **Gitali** 'melodious'.

Anjelica see Angel

Ankaret see Angharad

Anna, Anne

Ann, Anne or Anna come from the Greek form of the Hebrew name HANNAH, meaning 'God has favoured me' (often interpreted as meaning 'grace'). Tradition, rather than the New Testament, makes Anne the name of the mother of the Virgin Mary, and this St Anne or Anna was especially honoured in the Byzantine Empire, where it was frequently used as a given name. The name spread from there to Russia, and then to France in the eleventh century, after King Henry I married a Russian princess called Anna. It was a popular name in England by the fourteenth century. The main pet form is **Annie**, but there are many others which were well used in the past, such as **Nan**, **Nan(n)a** and **Nanny**. These in turn are one source of the name **Nancy** (**Nansi** in Welsh) and its short form **Nance** (see also AGNES).

Many foreign forms of the name have been adopted by English-speaking parents. From France we get ANAÏS**, Annette** (which in Scotland became **Annot**) and the diminutives **Nanette**, **Ninette** and **Ninon**. **Anita** (shortened to **Nita**) and **Ania** and its pet form **Anita**, come from Spain, with **Anya** a Russian form (see further at AMAYA), and **Anneka**, **Anika** and **Annika** are Scandinavian pet forms. The actress **Anouk** Aimée has made another Russian form better known, and Russia also gives us **Anushka,** or **Anouchka** and **Nina**. Respellings of Anna, such as **Anja** and **Annah**, are not uncommon, and Anne and Anna are often combined in forms such as Anna Mae or **Anneli** (a shortening of the German and Scandinavian **Anneliese** formed from Anne and Liese, a pet form of ELIZABETH, which is sometimes spelt **Annalise** to reflect its pronunciation). **Ana** is a spelling found in many European languages. **Aneta** is a pet form currently popular in Poland, and **Anaëlle** a Breton form well used throughout France. These numerous forms of the name are widely popular in many different countries at the moment. The pet forms are particularly well used, with plain Ann or Anne way behind Anna in English-speaking area, although beginning to make a bit of a comeback as a choice.

Annabel

Annabel presents us with something of a problem. It was well-established in Scotland by the twelfth century, long before ANNE was in use. So although it looks like an elaboration of Anne, and looks as if it is a combination of Anna and Belle 'beautiful', this cannot be its original sense. The best explanation put forward so far is that it is a version of the name Amable (see MABEL), particularly as the form Amabel is not found in Scotland at the time. Annabel can also be found as **Anabel**, Annabelle, **Anabelle** and **Annabella**, and is shortened to **Belle** or **Bella**. Annabella was the name of the mother of King James I of Scotland. The form Annabella crops up as the incestuous main female role John Ford's play *'Tis Pity She's a Whore* (first published in 1633), but is otherwise rare in England at this date. Edgar Allen Poe wrote a poem, *Anabel Lee* in memory of his dead wife, not published until his death in 1849, but despite mild interest in the name as a result, the name did not become widespread outside Scotland until the 1940s.

Annes, Annis, Annot see Agnes

Anorah, Annorah, Annora see Eleanor, Honoria

Anouk see Anna

Anour see Nur

Ansa see Aditya

Anselm

Anselm is a Germanic name formed from *ans* 'divine' and *helm* 'helmet (hence protection)'. It was introduced to Italy by the invading Lombards, and to England when St Anselm was made Archbishop of Canterbury in 1093. The American photographer **Ansel** Adams (1902–84) shows another form of the name.

Anstace, Anstice see Anastasia

Anthea

The Greek word *antheios* 'flowery' became a personal name *Antheia* which became Anthea in Latin. Anthea was an ancient title of Hera, the Greek queen of the gods, and has been in use as a literary name since at least the fourth century AD. In England it was taken up and given currency by the poets of the seventeenth century, in particular Herrick, but has only been popular as a given name since the mid-twentieth century. It is not currently particularly popular in any country, but has been given a certain exposure by the television personality Anthea Turner.

Antony, Antonia

These names come from the Roman family name of the Antonii, best known through Julius Caesar's follower Mark Antony (in Latin, *Marcus Antonius*). The meaning of the name is not clear, but the Romans derived it from a word meaning 'inestimable' or else as signifying descent from Antius, one of the sons of the hero-god Hercules. **Anthony** with an 'h' (never found in Latin) came into use in the sixteenth century in an attempt to derive the name from the Greek *anthos* (a flower), as in ANTHEA. **Tony**, and in the past **Nanty**, are pet forms. The name became popular throughout Europe through the fame of two saints, St Antony the Hermit, a third-century saint regarded as the founder of monasticism, and St Antony of Padua, a thirteenth-century saint famous for his preaching, and still one of the best-loved saints of the Roman Catholic Church. The French form of the name **Antoine**, and **Anton**, found in both Germany and Russia, have recently become more popular, particularly in the USA, where the Spanish form **Antonio**, and its shortening **Tonio** are also well used.

Antonia is the Latin feminine of Antony and is similarly abbreviated to **Tony**, or more commonly **Toni(e)**. **Tonia** and **Tonya** are also used. The French form **Antoinette**, famous from the beheaded Marie Antoinette, is shortened to **Net, Nettie** or **Netty** (see also JANE), and in the United States phonetic respellings of both Antoinette and Antoine using a 'w' or 'u' after the 't' are to be found.

Anwaar, Anwar see Nur

Anyah see Amaya

Aodan, Aodh, Aodhan Aodhnait see Aidan

Aoife

Aoife or **Aoibhe** is an ancient Irish name meaning 'beautiful, radiant', and was originally the name of a goddess. It has been one of the most popular choices among Irish parents for girls in recent years. Because of the closeness of the pronunciation is anglicised as Eva (see EVE), which explains why Eva has always been such a popular name in Ireland. Many Irish women who appear in history as Eva were originally Aoife. One legendary Aoife was a warrior-princess who first fought, and then became the lover of, the great Ulster hero Cochulainn. The related **Aoibheann** or **Aoibhin(n)** 'beautiful sheen, fair radiance', a royal name in the early Middle Ages, is anglicised Eavan, as in the Irish poet **Eavan** Boland.

Aonghus, Aongus see Angus

Aphra

This name comes from a misunderstanding of a biblical passage when, in the book of Micah (1:10) the translators gave 'in the house of Aphrah roll thyself in the dust', where the word 'Aphrah' actually means 'dust'. It is possible that the name is also confused with **Afra**, an obscure early martyr, and with forms of the Irish AFRIC. It was a not uncommon name in the seventeenth century, but its use today is almost entirely due to the fame of Mrs Aphra Behn (1640–89), spy, playwright and author of the first anti-slavery novel in English, who is reputed to be the first Englishwoman to have earned her living by her writing. She was nicknamed by her contemporary admirers 'The Incomparable **Astrea**'. Records of her life show her name spelt Afra, Aphra and Ayfara. In *Little Dorrit* (1857) Dickens has a character called **Affery** Flintwinch, which illustrates the pet form of the name.

Aphria see Afric

Aphrodite see Adonis, Julia, Venetia

Apple see Peaches

April

April is the name of the month used as a first name. Perhaps April, May and June are all used as girls' names not only because they are short, making them more suitable than, say, October, but because the months' associations with spring and early SUMMER are so attractive. They are chosen surprisingly rarely because the child is actually born in that particular month. April was particularly popular in the USA in the 1980s. Other month names are occasionally used: there is, for example, an actress called January Jones. In Wales the equivalent name is **Ebrilla**, with **Ebrillwen** as a variant, and **Abril** is the Spanish form. The French form of the name, **Avril**, is also used, although it is not noticeably common in France. Avril probably owes something to the name **Averil**, from the Old English name **Everild** or **Everilda** ('boar-battle'), the name of a rather obscure Yorkshire saint. Everild became **Averilla** and thence **Averil**. The older forms are still found today, although rarely, Averil being much more common

Arabella

This is originally a Scottish name, which may share a history with ANNABEL. However, since it sometimes appears in early texts as Orable as well as Arbel, and **Arabel**, it has been suggested that it could come from the Latin *orabile* 'easily moved by prayer', perhaps with the idea of the merciful lady of romance, but this is probably folk etymology. Arabella Stuart (1575–1615), sometimes known as Arbell in contemporary documents, had a theoretical claim to the throne on the death of Queen Elizabeth I, but was easily outmanoeuvred by her rivals. Arabella can be shortened to **Bel(le)** or BELLA. The BELINDA who was heroine of Pope's *Rape of the Lock* was really called Arabella Fermoor. The name has been fashionable but not common in the UK in recent years, but almost unknown in the USA until very recently.

Araceli

Araceli is a comparatively recent Spanish name, formed from the Latin *ara* 'altar' and *coeli* 'sky'. It is more used in Latin America and Mexico than Spain. It can be shortened to **Cheli** and sometimes appears in the USA in the anglicised form Aracely. Araceli Valdez is a Mexican actress who uses the stage name of Ara Celi, and Araceli Gonzales is a successful Argentine-born model.

Araminta

This is an elaboration of the name **Aminta** or **Amynta**, itself derived from the Macedonian Greek masculine name **Amyntas** ('defender'), used by that country's royal family from at least the fourth century BC. The masculine name was used by Spenser in his autobiographical poem 'Colin Clout' (1595) and by the Earl of Rochester (1647–80) in 'Phyllis', and in the form **Amyntor** by Beaumont and Fletcher, but the masculine name does not seem to have caught on with parents. The feminine forms have an equally literary pedigree, being poetic names of the seventeenth century; both are used by Vanbrugh, and Sir Charles Sedley addresses poems to Aminta. Aminta had already been used in the previous century by the Italian poet Tasso. Virginia Woolf's **Minta** Doyle in *To the Lighthouse* (1927) shows one short form of the names, the other being **Minty**.

Aran see Aaron, Arran, Arun

Aranrhod see Arianrhod

Arbell see Arabella

Archibald

Archibald is a Germanic name formed from the elements *ercen* meaning 'truly' and *bald* 'bold'. It was well-established among the Normans who took the name to Scotland, from where it only slowly spread to England. It had particular associations with the Campbells who used it to anglicise the native name **Gillespie** (Gaelic **Gilleasbuig**), meaning 'servant of the bishop'. Short forms of the name are usually **Arch**, **Archie** or **Archy**. Archie has been quite well used in both England and Scotland in recent years.

Ardal

Ardal (**Ardgal** or **Ardghal** in Irish) probably comes from *ard* and *gal*, words meaning 'high valour'. However it may belong with other Celtic masculine names such as ARTHUR, that come from the element *art* meaning 'bear', as indicated by early forms such as Artgal, which appears to be 'one who is fierce as a bear'. Probably, several names have fallen together to produce Ardal. Edmund Spencer, who lived for a time in Ireland (see OONAGH) calls one of his heroes Sir Artegal. He uses it to indicate 'equal to Arthur', but it is probably based on Ardal. The Irish actor Ardal O'Hanlan is a prominent user of the name.

Arel see Ariel

Areli, Arely see Aurelia

Aretha

Made famous by the singer Aretha Franklin, this unusual name comes from *arete* the Greek word for 'virtue'. It is also spelt **Areta**. From the same root comes the rarely used

Arethusa, the nymph who, in classical mythology, was chased from Greece to Sicily by an amorous river god until she turned herself into a spring to escape his attentions.

Arfon

A Welsh place name in Gwynedd meaning 'opposite Anglesey', Arfon is used as a boy's first name. **Arfona** and **Arfonia** are the female equivalents.

Ari see Ariana, Ariel

Aria

This term for an operatic song belongs with a group of new girl's names based on musical terms such as MELODY and HARMONY. It only came into significant use, in the USA, in the twenty-first century. Its growth may have been influenced by literary use, for example as a character in Elizabeth Haydon's *Rhapsody* series (published from 1999 onwards); in the spelling **Arya** in Geroge R.R. Martin's *Song of Ice and Fire* series (1998 onwards), Christopher Paiolini's novel *Eragon* (2002) (see also ARIANA below); and as **Aryah** in Brian Jacques' *Martin the Warrior* (1994).

Ariana

In Greek mythology, **Ariadne** is a Cretan princess who falls in love with Theseus and helps him to escape from the Minotaur, only to be abandoned by him. The name means 'the very holy one' from *ari* 'most' and *adnos* 'holy' and was probably originally used as a title for a goddess. Recently interest has been shown in the French form **Ariane**, perhaps because it has become well known as the name of the European space rocket. The Modern Greek and Italian **Arianna** is also found along with Ariana, both of which are well used in the USA. **Aryanna** and **Aryana** are recorded, and there may be some influence here of the name Arya (see ARIA, above). **Ari** is found as a short form. The masculine name Aryan, which has been increasingly used in the USA despite its unfortunate Nazi associations, may have been used as a masculine equivalent of the name. Both **Aryan** and **Aryana** can be interpreted as a Persian name meaning 'noble'. Princess Ariane of the Netherlands bears one version of the name, while the Greek-born American newspaper columnist and politician Arianna Stassinopoulos Huffinton has given her version a high profile.

Arianrhod

This Welsh girl's name is a modern form of Aranrhod formed from the elements *arian* 'silver' and *rod* 'wheel'. She is a character in the medieval Welsh stories of the *Mabinogion* where she is the mother of DYLAN. She seems to have originally been a moon goddess, with her name a description of her appearance. *Caer Arianrhod*, 'Arianrhod's Fortress' is a Welsh name for the Milky Way. Arianrhod is also the name of an early Welsh saint and **Arianwyn** is a rare masculine form.

Ariel

As a girl's name, this became well used in the United States after it was given to the heroine of the Disney cartoon *The Little Mermaid* (1989). In origin it probably owes something to Shakespeare's island spirit Ariel in *The Tempest,* with its associations with 'air'. It is also found in the form **Arielle** and **Arial**. As a masculine name, it is a Hebrew name, from a biblical place name, said to mean 'lion of God', which is used as a symbol of Jerusalem. It is also found in the Bible as a man's name. It is a popular name in Israel and can be found used in the USA. It has pet forms **Arel** and **Arik**. **Ari** is used as a short form, which can also be short for **Aristide** (from Greek *aristos* 'excellent') and **Aristotle** (Greek 'the best purpose') as well as being the full form of a Hebrew name meaning 'lion' and an ancient Scandinavian one meaning 'eagle'.

Arjun

Arjun or **Arjuna** means 'bright, shining, silver' is the name of a hero in the great Indian epic the *Mahabharata*. It is a popular name in India and is borne by many, including Arjun Sarja, the South Indian actor and director.

Arlene

The name **Arline** seems to have been invented by Michael William Balfe for the main character in his opera *The Bohemian Girl* (1843). Whether Arlene, which seems to have come into use in the USA and is still primarily confined there and which is also spelt **Arleen** and **Arline**, is the same name is debatable. It seems to be a fairly modern coinage, possibly derived from Charlene (see CAROL). Similarly **Arlette**, a French name made known to English speakers through the Van der Valk detective novels of Nicholas Freeling, is thought to be formed from a pet from of CHARLOTTE, or more strictly speaking Charlette, an Old French feminine form of Charles. Arlette was the name of the mother of William the Conqueror (b. 1027). **Arleth**, is a Spanish name which is probably a form of Arlette. It is just starting to make its presence felt in the USA, no doubt because of the success of the Mexican actress Arleth Teran.

Armand, Arminel, Arminelle, Armine see Herman

Armani
This is the name of the Italian fashion firm which has been used regularly if quietly in the United States as a first name since the 1990s. It is used for both sexes, but more commonly for boys. This is part of a small but definite trend to use luxury brand names such as Lexus, Bacardi, Porsche and Timberland as first names, of which Armani is the most successful. As a surname, Armani is a form of HERMAN.

Arnav
Arnav is an Indian boy's name, from the Sanskrit for 'sea, ocean'.

Arnold
Arnold is a Germanic name, originally *Arnwald*, formed from elements meaning *arin* 'eagle' and *wald* 'rule'. Its popularity in the Middle Ages is shown by its frequency as a surname, but it later died out, only to be revived, with so many other old names, in the nineteenth century. Short forms are **Arn** and **Arnie**. The success of the Austrian-born actor Arnold Schwarzenegger does not seem to have increased the popularity of the name, perhaps because he came to fame playing rather unearthly roles.

Aron see Aaron

Arran
The name of the beautiful Scottish island of Arran has been used increasingly as a boy's name in Scotland since the beginning of the century. It is part of a growing trend to use Scottish place names as first names (see IONA, SKYE) which is probably linked to the growth of nationalism, what is sometimes called the *Braveheart* factor. The meaning of the name is not known, although there may be a connection to that of the Irish Aran Isles, which means 'arched ridge'. **Aran** is occasionally used as a first name, and can also be from a Welsh place name. In some cases these forms may represent forms of AARON or ARUN.

Arron see Aaron

Art, Artan see Arthur

Artemis see Cynthia, Diana, Orion, Phoebe

Arthur
The meaning of this name is much disputed; the two main theories being that it comes from a Celtic root meaning 'bear', or that it is a form of some Roman name, such as the clan name Artorius. The name is inextricably linked with that of King Arthur of legend and possibly history, but despite its link, over-use of the name in the nineteenth century led to a decline in its popularity in the twentieth. **Art** and **Arty** are its short forms, but Art can also be a traditional Irish name (also meaning 'bear') with pet forms **Artan** and **Artin**. The name's popularity in the nineteenth century was due in part to the general revival of medieval names, but also because it was the name of the hero of Waterloo, the Duke of Wellington. It is therefore ironic that it is currently much more likely to be found used in France and Belgium than among English speakers, although there are signs that interest may be increasing. The Spanish form **Arturo** is found in the USA. (See also ARDAL)

Arun

The popular Indian boy's name Arun is the modern form of **Aruna** (a form sometimes used for girls). It means 'reddish brown' in Sanskrit, and indicates the colour of the rising sun, for Arun is the charioteer of the sun in Hindu mythology. Arun Nayar is an Indian businessman who has recently been in the international news because of his marriage to the actress Elizabeth Hurley. The similar-looking **Arundhati**, well-known from the author **Arundhati** Roy, is the name of a star, also known as Alcor, and is identified with Arundhati the wife of the sage Vasishta, who is regarded as the ideal wife in Hindu mythology.

Arwel

Arwel is a Welsh masculine name meaning 'prominent'. Arwel Hughes is a prominent Welsh composer.

Arwen, Arwyn

These are Welsh names meaning 'fair, fine', the former masculine, the latter, along with the variant **Arwenna**, feminine. The form Arwen is also found in Tolkien's *Lord of the Rings* in the character of the elf Arwen Evenstar. There the name is said to mean 'noble lady' in Elfish. Tolkien was a scholar of ancient languages including Welsh, and would have known of the name's origin.

Arya, Aryah, Aryan see Aria

Aryaman see Aditya

Aryanna see Ariana

Asa

Asa is a Hebrew name meaning 'physician', and was the name of one of the most outstanding of the Old Testament kings. In the UK it is particularly associated with Yorkshire, and is perhaps best known today from the historian Asa Briggs. In the USA it is more widely used.

Asante see Ashanti

Asha see Asher

Ashanti

Also spelt **Asante**, this is one of the names chosen by Black parents to mark their pride in their ancestry. The Ashanti are a West African tribe, mainly based in Ghana, who, in the eighteenth and nineteenth centuries, ruled a great empire which also had a fine artistic tradition. The name is used for both sexes, but is mainly female. The name **Shante** is a short form of this. Ashanti Douglas is a popular American singer.

Asher

According to the Bible (Genesis 30:13), when one of Jacob's twelve sons, who gave their names to the tribes of Israel, was born to ZILPHA, his wife Leah said 'Happy am I, for the daughters will call me blessed; and she called his name Asher', the name traditionally meaning 'fortunate, blessed'. The name was originally restricted to Jewish use, but has recently begun to be more widely used, and has even been recorded as a female name, perhaps under the influence of ASHLEY. **Ashur** is a variant, and both can be used as pet forms of Ashley. These should not be confused with **Asha**, the Hindi for 'hope', which is used as a girl's name.

Ashkon

This is a Persian boy's name, the name of the third dynasty of Persian kings. Also found as Ashkan. It is also the name of a Californian rapper and a brand of software.

Ashley

This is a surname originally given to someone who lived in an ash wood (or a clearing in one); it is now used as a first name for both sexes. It is also spelt **Ashleigh** and **Ashly**. It has been particularly popular in Australia and the United States, but is also well used in the UK and Ireland. It probably owes its use to the name given to one of her male characters in Margaret Mitchell's *Gone with the Wind* (1936), for this book and film has influenced the popularity of several names; but see further under EARTHA. The name was at first predominantly masculine, but was being used increasingly for girls in the USA from the 1940s, becoming even more popular through the 1980s, until it became the most popular name for American girls in 1991; it was still in the top three five years later and had only dropped to number 10 in 2005. In the UK the spread between girls and boys has been more even.

Two related names have recently begun to make an impact in the USA. **Ashlyn**, used for girls, may be a development of Ashley, or else an American version of ASHLING. **Ashton**, another surname, from a place name meaning 'settlement where ash trees grow', is now used as a first name for both sexes. Its spread no doubt owes much to the success of the actor Ashton Kutcher. All these names, along with those either side, can be shortened to **Ash**.

Ashling

Ashling is the phonetic spelling of the Irish feminine name **Aislin(g)**, also found as **Isleen**. It is a modern name which comes from the Irish word meaning 'dream, vision' and has been particularly popular in the last 30 years. **Ashlyn** may be an American form of this name, or a blend of ASHLEY and Lynn.

Ashlyn, Ashton see Ashley

Ashur see Asher

Asia

Sometimes the girl's name Asia may be a form of the Arabic name Aisha, but it is also quite popular in the USA as a name taken from the continent's name. In Greek myth Asia was the daughter of Ocean. Asia Argento is a well-known actress.

Aspen

Aspen has been increasingly used as a girl's name in the USA since the 1990s. The tree is especially admired for its shaking leaves. The choice of this particular name links in not only to the trend for unusual plant names, but also carries with it the prestige of the ski resort of Aspen, Colorado.

Astrea see Aphra

Astrid

Astrid is a Scandinavian name formed from elements meaning 'god' and 'beauty'. It has been used in Scandinavian royal families since at least the tenth century, but only since the twentieth century in the UK. Its spread may owe something to the popularity of Queen Astrid of the Belgians (d. 1935). The Brazilian jazz singer **Astrud** Gilberto shows another form of the name.

Atalanta

Atalanta is an ancient Greek name that has gradually been coming into use over the last 25 years. In Greek mythology Atalanta was a maiden-huntress who was determined not to marry. To this end, knowing how fast she could run, she said she would only marry the man who could beat her in a footrace. She was finally outrun by Hippomenes, who had obtained three golden apples from Aphrodite, goddess of love. Every time Atalanta was about to overtake him, he rolled one of these apples in front of her and pulled ahead as she stopped to pick them up; in the end, he just beat her. Atalanta's name and story became widely known through Swinburne's much-anthologised poetic drama *Atalanta in Calydon*, published in 1865. **Lanty** has been used as a pet form of Atalanta. The similar sounding **Atlanta** comes either from the Atlantic Ocean or from the city in Georgia. The Atlantic got its name because it was the ocean near where Atlas stood. He, in Greek myth, was a giant who held up the sky on his shoulders. Since his picture appeared in many early books of maps, these came to be known as 'an atlas' after him.

Atara

This is a Jewish girl's name, also found as Atarah. It means 'crown' in Hebrew, and was the name of a very minor biblical character

Atheldreda, Athelthryth see Audrey

Athelstan

Also spelt **Athelstane**, this is an Old English name meaning 'noble stone'. It suffered the same obscurity after the Norman Conquest as most other Old English names, but was revived in the nineteenth century, and as a result is still occasionally found.

Athelwine see Alvin

Athena

Athene, the Greek form of the name, was the great patron-goddess of the city of Athens, a warrior goddess, but also the bringer of many skills and crafts, and goddess of wisdom. The meaning of her name is not known, but goes back at least to Mycenaean times. Both Athene and the alternative form **Athena** were moderately used in the past, giving rise to people such as Athene Seyler (1889–1990), the actress. The Roman equivalent was **Minerva**. This was used in the nineteenth century, with the pet form **Minnie**, but is best known today from the character of Minerva McGonagall, professor of transfiguration, in the *Harry Potter* books.

Athol

The earls and later dukes of Athol played a prominent role in Scottish history, and the name may have come into use from the title, in much the same way that CLIFFORD and HOWARD did in England. It is also a surname and place name in Perthshire (which gave the dukes their title). The place gets its name from the Gaelic *ath Fodla*, meaning 'new Ireland', a name given it by the Gaels who immigrated to the area from Northern Ireland. As a masculine first name it is also found as **Atholl, Athole** and **Athold**.

Atlanta see Atalanta

Atticus

Atticus 'of Attica', the ancient Greek city-state headed by Athens, was the nickname given to Titus Pomponius (b. 110 BC). He was a friend and advisor of the great Roman orator and politician Cicero. The correspondence between the two, written after Atticus had retired to Athens, has survived, and is one of the most important works to have survived from that period. Atticus was a philosopher, and this no doubt lies behind the choice of the name Atticus Finch for the fearless, open-minded small-town lawyer who is the hero of HARPER Lee's novel *To Kill a Mockingbird* (1960). It is from this book that Atticus has recently come to be used as a first name in the USA.

Aubrey

Aubrey is the Norman French form of the Germanic name **Alberic** ('elf-ruler'), which was introduced into England by the Normans. Alberic was the name of the king of the elves in Germanic legend, who plays such an important part in Wagner's *Ring Cycle*. **Auberon** seems to have been a pet form of this name, and had already been used as the name of the king of the fairies before Shakespeare used the name in the form **Oberon** in *A Midsummer Night's Dream*. Throughout most of its history Aubrey has been a boy's name, and was once common enough to become a wide-spread surname, but in recent years, perhaps influenced by AUDREY, the name has begun to be used for girls, particularly in the USA. For girls it can also appear as **Aubree, Aubri(e)** and **Aubry**.

Audrey

This is a contraction of the Old English name of St **Etheldreda**, or **Ethelthryth** ('noble strength'). The full form of the name is also spelt **Atheldreda, Etheldred**, and **Athelthryth**, and is also one of the sources of the name ETHEL. The name was felt to be rustic by the sixteenth century (hence the character of Audrey in *As You Like It*) and the longer spelling was changed to what was now the pronunciation. St Etheldreda was a seventh-century East Anglian princess who founded an abbey at Ely on the site where the cathedral now stands. The name St Audrey was itself contracted to the word 'tawdry' (the 't' being run on from the end of the word 'saint'), first used to describe the sort of cheap but glittering goods sold at the famous St Audrey's Fair. Audrey is not a frequent choice of British parents at the moment, but is more likely to be found in the USA, most often as **Audrie**, and it is currently popular with French speakers. Variants such as **Audreen** and **Audrianna** can be found. All forms can be shortened to **Audie,** and occasionally **Addy**. Audrey Hepburn is its most famous holder.

Augustus, Augusta, Austin

Augustus is a Latin word meaning 'majesty', given as a title by the Roman Senate to the first Roman Emperor, Octavian, in 27 BC and adopted by him as a name (see also OCTAVIA). Augusta is the feminine form of the same word. **Gus** and **Gussie** and sometimes **Auggie** are used as pet forms of these names and of **Augustine**, pronounced with the stress on the second syllable in Britain, but on the third in the United States. Augustine was the name of an early saint and one of the great doctors of the Christian Church, and was derived from Augustus. Augustine was also the name of the man sent in 596 to England by Pope GREGORY the Great to convert the heathen Saxons to Christianity. In medieval England this name was contracted to **Austin** or **Austen** and used both as a surname and as a first name. Austin has for some time been a popular choice for boys in the USA. **August** is a German and Polish form also found in the USA and **Agustin** the Spanish form. The month of August was named after the Emperor Augustus, and August is occasionally used as a month name for both sexes.

Auley, Auliffe see Oliver

Aure see Dawn

Aurelius, Aurelia

These are the masculine and feminine forms of a Roman family name meaning 'golden'. **Aurelian**, the name of one of the Roman emperors, is an alternative masculine form, which is currently quite well used in France. From Aurelia come **Auriel** and **Auriol**; **Oriel** and **Oriole** are spelling variants of this name. ORLA is the Irish equivalent of this name. **Arely** or **Areli** are Spanish pet forms.

Aurnia see Orla

Aurora, Aurore see Dawn

Austen, Austin see Augustus

Autumn

This vocabulary word, with its associations of glowing leaves and the richness of the harvest, is the most successful of the seasons used as a girl's name. Although it was used in the 1980s and earlier, it only made its mark in the 1990s. In the USA Autumn is currently the most popular of the season names, with SUMMER the next most popular of the seasons, followed by **Spring** (but see AVIVA), but the month names – APRIL, MAY, JUNE – also cover these seasons. Winter has too many negative associations ever to become popular. In the UK Summer is currently very much more popular than Autumn. There is a successful American model called Autumn Hyle.

Ava

The history of the name Ava is muddled. It is found in the early Middle Ages when it is the name of a ninth-century saint, where it is probably a pet form of names, such as Avaline, beginning 'av-', but then disappears from the records. Other uses may be as a form of Eva. Modern use of the name seems to start with Ava Lowle Willing (1868–1958), who was born in Philadelphia and married first John Jacob Astor IV and then Thomas Lister, Lord Ribblesdale, both prominent on the social scene. Ava was very beautiful and her first husband famously ugly, and they were nicknamed 'beauty and the beast'. Their daughter was also called Ava. In this way the name was established in High Society, but what brought it to the masses was the enormous success of the film star Ava Gardner (1922–90). By the time she died the name was hardly given to girls at all, but then in 1999 the actress Reese Witherspoon called her baby Ava, and a number of other celebrities have also used the name. Within a few years the name was among the most popular girl's names throughout the English-speaking world. As well as the English name which is usually pronounced with the first sound as in 'hay', Ava, pronounced with the first a as 'car' is a Persian name meaning 'voice, song'.

Avalon

This is an unusual, but fashionable, girl's name, from the Mystic Isle of Avalon where, according to legend, King Arthur was taken to be healed of his wounds and wait until his return to save the country. The singer Julian Cope has called his daughters Avalon and **Albany**, the old name for Britain.

Aveline see Eileen

Averie see Alfred

Averil, Averilla see April

Avery see Alfred

Avice, Avis

This is from *Aveza*, an old Germanic feminine name of unknown meaning, although the form Avis has led to its association with the Latin for 'bird'. Some French writers associate it with the German name **Hedewig** or **Hedwige**, meaning 'combat', the source of the pet forms found in Ibsen's **Hedda** Gabler and the film star **Hedy** Lamarr. **Hedwig** has enjoyed new prominence as the name of Harry Potter's pet snowy owl in the popular *Harry Potter* series of novels by J. K. Rowling.

Avigayil see Abigail

Aviva

This is a modern Jewish name from the Hebrew for 'spring' which is set to become very fashionable, although this surge may be dampened by the realisation that is also the name of one of the world's largest insurance groups. **Aviv** is the masculine equivalent.

Avner see Abner

Avraham see Abraham

Avril see April

Awena

Awena is a Welsh girl's name meaning 'muse'. **Awen** is another form used for both sexes.

Awley see Oliver

Axel

Absolom is the English form of the Hebrew name *Avshalon*, 'my father is peace'. In the Old Testament he is a son of King David who dies while leading a revolt against his father. Axel is the Scandinavian form of this name. The Guns N Roses front man, Axl Rose, has given the name some prominence, and led to an increase of use in the USA. In France both Axel and a feminine form **Axelle** are well used.

Ayala see Ayla

Ayanna

This is a girl's name used in America, particularly by African-Americans. It had a certain vogue in the 1970s, and then reappeared in the 90s. It may be a coinage, based on Anna, but is generally interpreted as from a Somali word meaning 'beautiful flower'. It is also found as **Ayana** and **Aiyana**.

Aydan, Aydin see Aidan

Ayeisha, Ayesha see Aisha

Ayla

Ayla can be a Jewish girl's name, meaning 'oak tree, terebinth' (not to be confused with **Ayala**, from the Hebrew for 'deer, gazelle'), but its use as a popular first name in the USA comes from its use as an invented name for the heroine of Jean Auel's 1980 novel *Clan of the Cave Bear.*

Aylin see Eileen

Aylmer see Elmer

Aylwin see Alvin

Aymé see **Esmé**

Aziz, Aziza

This comes from the Arabic word meaning 'mighty, strong, illustrious' but also 'highly esteemed, dearly beloved'. It is one of the titles of Allah. The names are popular with Muslims. Aziz is the masculine, Aziza the feminine.

B

Babette see **Barbara, Elizabeth**

Babs, Baibín, Báirbre see **Barbara**

Bailey

This is a surname used as a first name, originally given to someone who had the job of bailiff. It was used regularly in the nineteenth century for boys and into the early twentieth century, but was never particularly popular. It reappeared in the early eighties as a girl's name in the USA and has become increasingly popular. This reappearance has been linked to its use for a female character, Bailey Quarters, in the hit television comedy *WKRP in Cincinnati,* which originally ran 1978–82 with later repeats. Unusually, about ten years after it was already established as a popular girl's name it came back into regular use as a boy's name. Usually the traffic is from boys to girls, and traffic the other way is rare. This may have been encouraged by its use for another, male, television character, that of Bailey Salinger in the drama *Party of Five*, which ran on US television from 1994–2000, although the name was already coming back in by 1992. As a female name the second syllable can have all the variant spellings found in the name LEE, giving forms such as **Bailee** and **Baileigh**, while spellings with Bay-, such as **Baylee**, are also found. Outside the USA Bailey is increasingly popular as a boy's name, but has yet to make much of an impact for girls.

Bala

Bala means 'young' in Sanskrit, and is used for both sexes.

Baldwin, Baldric

Baldwin is a compound of *bald* 'bold' and *wine* 'friend', while Baldric combines *bald* with *ric* 'power, rule'. In the French form, Baudouin, Baldwin was a staple name in Flemish ruling families in the Middle Ages, including the leader of the first Crusade in the twelfth century, who was eventually crowned King of Jerusalem. It reappeared in the region in Baudouin I, King of the Belgians (1930–93). Baldric has never been as popular as Baldwin, but has achieved immortality in the character of the hopeless servant in the *Blackadder* television comedy series, the first series of which was first shown in 1983.

Balthazar see **Jasper**

Bambi see **Fawn**

Baptiste see **John**

Barbara

Barbara comes from the Greek word for 'foreign, strange': the same root gives us the word 'barbarian'. It may have started as a name given to a foreign slave. St Barbara, virgin and martyr, was a very popular saint from the ninth century onwards. Her symbol is the brass tower in which her father shut her before executing her for her faith. Since he was punished by being struck down by a thunderbolt, Barbara is invoked against lightning and, by an association of ideas, is also the patron saint of gunners and miners. Her story has elements found in many folk tales, and there is no evidence that she ever existed. Short forms are **Babs, Barb, Barbie** (as in the doll) and, in the US, **Bobbi**. The French pet form **Babette** (also used for ELIZABETH) is sometimes found, and **Barbra**

Streisand has popularised a variant spelling. In Irish the name became **Báirbre**, but is more likely to be found in the pet form **Baibín**, and for some reason was used as an English equivalent of **Gobnait**, a fifth-century Kerry saint. Barbara was popular in the United States through most of the twentieth century, but it is less well used now, and has been in decline in the UK since the 1950s.

Barnabas

In the Bible, Barnabas is defined as meaning 'son of consolation', although a more correct interpretation would be 'son of exhortation'. The biblical St Barnabas, 'a good man, full of the Holy Ghost and of faith' (Acts 11:24), was closely associated with St Paul in spreading Christianity through Asia Minor. **Barnaby** is an old short form of the name which has been revived as an independent name in recent years. **Barney**, a short form shared with BERNARD, is now probably best known to millions of children as the name of a lurid purple singing and dancing dinosaur on television.

Barney see Barnabas, Bernard

Barra see Barry

Barrett

Barrett is a surname used as a first name. The surname can come from a medieval term for someone who was quarrelsome, or can be a form of the name BERNARD. It never been particularly popular, but has been used steadily for boys since the 1950s.

Barry

Barry is a Celtic name with several origins. There are three main sources, which have become so confused as to be indistinguishable. There is an Irish name Barry (**Bearach** in Gaelic), which comes from the word for 'spear'. In Wales the name can be a form of the surname 'ap Harry' (son of Harry); but it can also be derived from the place name of Barry Island, in which case it comes from the Welsh word *bar* meaning 'a dune or mound'. In addition, Barry can be used in Ireland as a pet form of Finbar, 'fair head', (see FINLAY), in which case it is sometimes spelt **Barra**. Thackeray's 1844 novel *Barry Lyndon* brought what had been a mainly Irish name to general attention. Although the name was well used in many English-speaking countries in the middle of the twentieth century, it is rarely given now.

Bartholomew

Bartholomew is a Hebrew name meaning 'son of Talmai', Talmai itself meaning 'abounding in furrows'. It is thought that the apostle Bartholomew is probably the same as NATHANIEL, Bartholomew being the equivalent of a surname. **Bart** is a common short form; **Bartlemy, Bat** and **Bartly** are less common old shortenings, and **Tolomey** is also found. In Ireland, Bartholomew appears as **Parthalon** or **Partholon**.

Basil

Basil comes from *basileus* the Greek word for 'kingly', and is thus the Greek equivalent of the Latin REX. The herb name comes from the same word, because of its many excellent medicinal properties. Basil was the name of several saints in the Orthodox Church, and is very popular in Slavic countries, usually in a form beginning with a 'v', as in the Russian **Vasilie**. Short forms are **Baz** or **Bas**, and there are rare feminine forms **Basilia** and **Basilie**. Basil can also be an Arabic name meaning 'brave, valiant'.

Bastian, Bastianne, Bastienne see Sebastian

Bat see Bartholomew

Bathsheba

This Hebrew name means 'daughter of the oath'. In the Bible, King David sees Bathsheba bathing and engineers the death of her husband **Uriah** the Hittite, so that he could marry her. It was not uncommon as a given name in the Middle Ages, but is nowadays better known as a literary name from Bathsheba Everdene in Thomas Hardy's *Far from the Madding Crowd* (1874). The short form **Sheba** is occasionally found used independently, as in William Inge's 1950 play *Come Back Little Sheba* (where Sheba is a dog).

Baudoin see **Baldwin**

Baylee see **Bailey**

Baz see **Basil**

Bearach see **Barry**

Beatrice

There was a Late Latin name *Viatrix* 'voyager', indicating one voyaging through life, used often in a Christian context, but under the influence of the Latin *beatus* 'blessed', this seems to have been changed to **Beatrix**. This was in used by the fourth century, when it was the name of a saint and martyr. The name developed the form Beatrice alongside Beatrix, an alternative spelling **Beatris** and, in Wales, **Bet(t)rice** or **Bet(t)rys.** In Spanish it is **Beatriz**, currently popular in parts of South America. Short forms are **Bea, Bee, Beatty, Trix, Trixie** and **Triss**. **Beata** is from the same Latin root and means 'blessed'. The choice of Beatrice by the Duke and Duchess of York for their first child, in 1988, led to a short-lived interest in the name in the UK, but it is now not well used anywhere in the English-speaking world. Beatrice has lasting fame as the name of Dante's beloved muse and guide to Paradise in his poetry and is also the name of a popular character from Shakespeare's *Much Ado About Nothing*, while Beatrix Potter is a famous bearer of the alternative form.

Beau

Beau is the French word for 'handsome'. This boy's name has been almost entirely restricted to American use until recently, when it has started to be used in Australia as well. Although it was used as a nickname for the Regency dandy Beau Brummell (1778–1840), it was not noted as a given name until the twentieth century. Two books brought it to the general public: P.C. Wren's novel *Beau Geste* (1924), where it was again a nickname, and, more importantly, Margaret Mitchell's novel *Gone With the Wind* (1936), which featured the character Beau Wilkes and was the inspiration behind the growth in popularity of a number of names, including ASHLEY, MELANIE and SCARLETT. In his case, as with many real-life Beaus, his name was a shortening of **Beauregard** (a surname meaning 'handsome look'), a name given in honour of the US Confederate general Pierre Gustave Toutant Beauregard (1818–93), particularly in his native New Orleans. Beau is also found spelt **Bo** and **Boe**. Both Beau and Bo have been used regularly in the USA since the 1970s. The actor Beau Bridges (1941–), originally Lloyd Vernett Bridges III, got his nickname after the boy in *Gone With the Wind*.

Bebhinn, Bebhionn, Bebinn see **Bevin**

Becca, Becka, Becky see **Rebecca**

Bedelia see **Bridget**

Bedwyr

This is the Welsh form of the name more widely know as King Arthur's faithful knight **Bedivere**.

Bee see **Beatrice**

Beibhinn see **Bevin**

Bel see **Arabella, Isabel**

Belag see **Isabel**

Belén

Belén is the Spanish form of the name Bethlehem, and a term used for the model Nativity scenes made at Christmas. It is thus a companion name to the better known **Natividad**, 'nativity'. Belén has started to be used by Spanish speakers in the USA. There is a character called Belén Lopez in the successful Spanish sit-com *Aquí no hay quien viva* ('No one can live here') and another Belén in Sharon Creech's prize-winning young adult's novel *Bloomability* (1998).

Belinda

Strictly speaking Belinda is an old Germanic name, with an unknown first element and the '-linda' part meaning 'serpent', a symbol of wisdom. However, most users today probably think of it as a combination of the French 'belle' (as in the name BELLA, also used as a short form of this name) and of the Spanish 'linda'; both mean 'beautiful'. Alexander Pope seems to have had the connotations of beauty in mind when he gave this name to the heroine of *The Rape of the Lock* (1712–14). The name is one of the sources of LINDA.

Belle, Bella

Bel, Belle or Bella is usually from a shortening of names such as ANNABEL, ARABELLA, BELINDA, ISABEL. Belle and Bella were particularly used in the nineteenth century. However, some uses may have come directly from Latin or Spanish *bella* or French *belle*, 'beautiful'; and in the Southern United States may have been a use of the vocabulary word used for an attractive girl, the feminine equivalent of BEAU.

Ben see Benjamin

Benazir

Benazir is the Arabic for 'matchless, unique'. Prominent holders are the ballet dancer Benazir Hussein and Benazir Bhutto, former President of Pakistan

Benedict

Benedict comes from *benedictus*, the Latin meaning 'blessed', and owes its use as a name to St Benedict (490–c. 542), founder of the Benedictine order. **Benedick** is an old variant form of the name, found in Shakespeare's *Much Ado about Nothing*, as is the surname **Bennet(t)** slowly increasing in popularity for boys in the USA. **Benedicta** and **Benedetta** are uncommon female forms of the name, while **Benita** comes from the same root. The name **Bettina** is both an elaboration of Betty (see ELIZABETH) and an Italian pet form of Benedetta.

Benjamin

Benjamin, *Benyamin* in Hebrew, is an Old Testament name meaning 'son of the right hand', indicating qualities of strength and good fortune. In the Bible, Benjamin is the youngest of the twelve sons of JACOB, and the pet of his father and brothers, so the name has sometimes been used to signify a favourite child, or the youngest son of elderly parents. In the seventeenth and eighteenth century the name was so popular in America that 'Cousin Benjamin' could be used for shorthand for an American Puritan. Short forms are **Ben**, **Benjie**, **Bennie** or **Benny**. Both Benjamin and Ben have been particularly popular with parents throughout the English-speaking world in recent years.

Bennet, Bennett see Benedict

Bennie, Benny see Benjamin

Berenice see Veronica

Bernard

This is a Germanic name formed from *bern* 'bear' and *hard* 'brave'. **Barney**, shared with BARTHOLOMEW, is a short form used particularly in the United States. The feminine form **Bernadette** (sometimes **Bernardette**) was given popularity by St Bernadette of Lourdes. **Bernardine, Bernarda** and **Bernardetta** (shortened to **Detta**) are feminine variants, and **Bernie** is used as a short form for both sexes. In the USA, where the Spanish **Bernardo** is also used, Bernard is stressed on the second syllable, but in British English it is stressed on the first.

Bernice, Bernie see Veronica

Berry see Bertram

Bert, Bertie see Albert, Bertram, Gilbert, Herbert, Robert

Bertha

This is an old Germanic name, from *berht* originally meaning 'famous' but developing the English meaning 'bright'. It may originally have been a short form of lost longer names. It is found in various forms throughout Europe, and has been used in England since Anglo-Saxon times. Bertha Bigfoot, the mother of the emperor Charlemagne (c. 742–814), was an early holder of the name. She appears in medieval fiction as the heroine of highly romantic stories, but in her real life she was much admired as a fine ruler and a power behind her son's throne. A less attractive use of the name is Big Bertha, the name given to each of a set of four guns made by the Krupp armaments firm and used by the Germans to bombard Paris in 1918. They were named after Bertha Krupp, the heiress to the firm, and their range of 76 miles was the greatest of any gun yet made. The name died out after the Middle Ages, and was briefly revived in the nineteenth century, but is currently little used except in Iceland, where it is popular in the form **Birta**. (See further under HERBERT)

Bertram, Bertrand

Strictly speaking Bertram means 'bright raven' from Germanic elements *berht* + *hramn* and Bertrand 'bright shield' (*berht* + *rand*), but these two Germanic names early on came to be regarded as variants of the same name, with Bertrand the French form of Bertram. The commonest short forms are **Bert** and **Bertie**, but **Berry** (as in the case of the Dornford Yates character) is sometimes used, although this can also be derived from the surname, which comes from either the type of fruit or the French place name. There has been a mild fashion for 'Bertie' names in the UK as part of the revival of nineteenth century names, but some Berties may be meant for ALBERT.

Beryl

This is one of the gem names popular in the late nineteenth and early twentieth centuries. It came into use rather later in the American Middle West, where it has also been regularly recorded as a man's name.

Bess, Bessie, Bessy, Bet see Elizabeth

Beth, Bethan, Bethany

There is considerable overlap between these names, leading to some confusion about their origin. Beth is primarily a short form of ELIZABETH. It grew in popularity after the publication of Louisa M. Alcott's *Little Women* (1868) which had the attractive character of Beth March as one of the heroines. It started to be given as an independent name, and later became popular in combinations such as Beth-Ann. In some cases Bethan came about as the result of this combination, but Bethan is also a Welsh pet form of Elizabeth, now widely used as an independent name. It has also been linked with the Celtic name **Bethia**, meaning 'life', itself also a biblical place name. Bethany can be used as a pet form of Bethan, but can also be analysed as a biblical place name, the village where Jesus stayed during Holy Week and the home of St Mary of Bethany, sister of Martha and Lazarus (compare BELÉN, above). And to complete the circle, Beth is used as a short form of Bethan and Bethany. Bethany is currently popular in England and Scotland, but less so in the USA, and Beth is also well used in Scotland

Betrice, Bettrice, Betrys, Bettrys see Beatrice

Betsan, Betsy, Bettina, Betty, Bettyne see Elizabeth

Beulah see Hephzibah

Beverly, Beverley

This comes from a place and surname *beoferlic* meaning 'beaver stream'. While it can be used as a name for either sex, it is now rare as a male name, although the novelist Beverley Nichols kept alive an awareness of its masculine use. **Bev** is the short form. The name was popular in the USA from the 1920s to the 1950s, and in the 1960s in the UK, but is little chosen now. Beverly was well used as a masculine name in the nineteenth century, but the change to a girl's name was precipitated in the USA by the enormously popular novel by G.B. McCutcheon, *Beverly of Graustark* (1904). The book is set in the Southern states where the use of surnames as first names for girls was already well-established (see SCARLETT). Nevertheless Beverly was regularly used in the USA for boys into the 1950s. Beverley is the commoner form in the UK, Beverly in the USA.

Bevin

This is an Irish girl's name written **Bebhinn**, **Bebhionn**, **Bebinn** or **Beibhinn** in Irish. It means 'fair lady' and was the name of both the mother and sister of Brian Boru. There is also a mythical Bevin who appears in the Finn cycle of legends. In Macpherson's Ossian poems the name appears as **Vevina**, and in the past was anglicised as VIVIAN.

Beyoncé

This name was created for the singer and actress Beyoncé Knowles by her family. While some parents have chosen to adopt the name for their child, it is too soon to see if it has any lasting impact.

Bhaga see Aditya

Bhaskar

Bhaskara, the early form of the name, means 'shining' and is one of the many names of the sun and the god Shiva. It was the name of a famous twelfth-century Indian astronomer.

Bianca, Bibi see Blanche

Biddie, Biddy, Bidelia see Bridget

Bijou see Jewel

Bilal

Bilal or **Bilel** comes from the Arabic word meaning 'water, refreshment'. Bilal al-Habachi was a contemporary of the Prophet Muhammad who became Islam's first Muezzin.

Bill, Billie, Billy see William

Bina see Alban

Birgit, Birgita see Bridget

Birta see Bertha

Bishr see Farah

Blain

Blain is a Scottish surname that has recently found some favour with parents in the USA as a boy's first name. The surname was originally an affectionate nickname probably given to someone with blond hair, as it is a pet form of the Gaelic word *bla* ('yellow').

Blair

Like BLAIN, Blair is a Scottish surname and place name used as a first name. The place name means 'marshy plain'. It is now being used for girls as well as boys, in which case it can appear as **Blayre**. Blair has been used regularly in Scotland in recent years, and should probably be thought of as belonging to the set of names from places that have been growing in popularity alongside the growing sense of Scottish national identity.

Blaise

Blaise comes from a Latin nickname *blaseus*, meaning 'stuttering, deformed', which is probably why St Blaise, who was decapitated in 316, is invoked to cure sore throats. In Arthurian legend it is the name of Merlin's secretary, who is supposed to have written down his master's sayings. The name is more popular in France than in English-speaking countries, no doubt due in part to the fame of Blaise Pascal (1623–62). **Blaze** and **Blase** are variants, although Blaze may be the vocabulary word, used in much the same way as STORMY. It has recently started to be used as a girl's name.

Blaithin see Blathnat

Blake

Old English had two confusing words which would both be written *blac* in modern script, which differed only in whether the 'a' was pronounced as in 'cat' or 'are'. They have opposite meanings. One meant 'white, shining' and is also the ancestor of the modern 'bleak'; the other meant 'black'. They both developed into the surname Blake, now used as a first name. It is usually a masculine name, but feminine uses are also found. It is most likely to be used in the USA and Australia. The film producer and director Blake Edwards is a prominent bearer, who may have influenced its spread.

Blanche
Occasionally spelt **Blanch**, this is an old name meaning 'white', when pale skin was a sign of an aristocratic lifestyle, and white a symbol of purity and virtue. A fourteenth-century holder was Blanche, Duchess of Lancaster, the wife of John of Gaunt and heroine of Chaucer's elegy *The Book of the Duchess*. **Bianca**, which can be shortened to **Bibi**, and **Blanca**, the Italian and Spanish forms of the name, are also found, particularly in the USA. The Nicaraguan model and political activist Bianca Jagger is a famous holder of the name.

Blanid see **Blathnat**

Blase, Blaze see **Blaise**

Blathnat
Blathnat or **Blathnaid** is an Irish name for girls meaning 'little flower', and in legend is the name of a woman who loved the great hero Cuchullain. There is a phonetic spelling **Blanid** and there is an alternative form **Blaithin**.

Blayre see **Blair**

Bleu see **Blue**

Blodwen
This is a Welsh feminine name made up of elements meaning 'flower' and 'white' and therefore belongs with the flower group of names (see FLORA). Another Welsh flower name is **Blodeuwedd** ('flower-form'), the name of a woman magically created out of flowers in the medieval Welsh story of *Math son of Mathonwy*. She was unfaithful to her husband for whom she had been made, and as a punishment was turned into an owl. The legend has become familiar to modern children through its retelling in Alan Garner's *The Owl Service*. **Blodyn** or **Blodeyn**, which simply means 'flower, blossom', is another member of this group. All have an unfortunate tendency to be shortened to **Blod**.

Blossom see **Flora**

Blue
The unusual name Blue has had considerable exposure in celebrity names in recent years, particularly as a middle name. It started at least as long ago as the 1970s, when the singer Cher named her son Elijah Blue (but see also under BONNIE). Since then quite a number have followed this trend, with John Travolta giving the name a French twist when he named his daughter Ella **Bleu** in 2000. One who had gained publicity in her own right, rather than as someone's daughter, is Dakota Blue Richards, the child star of the 2007 film *The Golden Compass*. **Indigo** (the word originally indicated 'Indian dye') is another word for blue that is fashionable for both sexes. In India, where the colour can have religious associations, there are Indian girl's name **Nilima** which means 'blue, blueness', **Nila** or **Neela** 'dark blue, indigo'; while **Nilam** or **Neelam**, used for both sexes, means 'sapphire'. **Sunil** (m) and **Sunila** (f) are modern names which come from the Sanskrit for very dark blue, sometimes taken to indicate SAPPHIRE. It is possible that the acceptance of Blue as a first name in the West may be influenced by the spread of SCARLETT.

Blythe see **Bonnie**

Bo see **Beau**

Boadicea see **Victor**

Bob see **Robert**

Bobbi see **Barbara**

Bobbie, Bobby see **Robert**

Boe see **Beau**

Bonnie, Blythe

Bonnie or Bonny is the Scottish word for 'fair, fine' used as a first name. In Margaret Mitchell's novel *Gone With the Wind* (1936) the daughter of SCARLETT and RHETT Butler is officially called Eugenie Victoria, but is nicknamed Bonnie or Bonnie BLUE because her eyes were as blue as the 'bonnie blue flag' or the Confederacy. However, although the book was instrumental in promoting a number of names, including Ashley, Melanie and Scarlett, Bonnie was already well established by the 1880s, although the book may have increased its popularity for it was at its most popular in the years immediately after the book was filmed in 1939. Bonnie Parker, the notorious gangster, was born in 1910.

Blythe, an old word for 'happy' which is often linked in early verse with 'bonnie', is less common, and has been recorded for both sexes. For boys it may well be taken from the surname. The actress Blythe Danner is the mother of Gwyneth Paltrow, and is a middle name of her granddaughter, Apple (see PEACHES).

Boris

Boris is a Slavic name, probably from the earlier *Borislav* from elements meaning 'battle' and 'glory'. In early Russia it was frequently used as a royal name. Its associations are still predominantly Russian, but it is occasionally found in English-speaking countries, as in the case of the English politician Boris Johnson.

Boston

Boston is one of the surnames and place names that have recently come into use in the USA, although it was used there occasionally in the late nineteenth and early twentieth centuries. Both the surname and the American city come from the English town of Boston, which in turn means 'Botwulf's stone', from some lost Anglo-Saxon landowner.

Boudicca see Victor

Brad, Bradd see Bradley

Braden, Bradon, Braedon, Braiden see Brady

Bradley

Bradley is a boy's name that has been popular in Australia and the United States for some time, but only became noticeably popular in the UK in the late 1990s. It derives from a surname taken from a place name meaning 'broad clearing'. **Brad** is used as a short form and also as an independent name, sometimes in the form **Bradd**. A related surname, **Bradford**, from a place meaning 'broad ford', is also found. Bradley was obviously not unknown as a first name in nineteenth-century England, for the marvellously-named Bradley Headstone is a character in Charles Dickens' *Our Mutual Friend* (1865). Brad Pitt is a famous bearer of the name.

Brady, Brayden, Brody

As a surname Brady can have a number of origins, the most common of which is an Irish surname of uncertain meaning, perhaps originally a nickname given to someone with a broad chest. It has been in regular use in the USA since the nineteenth century, but has recently become much more popular. It is fashionable enough to have been chosen as the name of Miranda Hobbe's baby in the enormously cool television series *Sex in the City*. Brady is also used as a short form for the even more popular **Brayden**, which is also found, in order of popularity as **Braden**, **Braeden**, **Braydon**, **Braiden**, **Bradyn** and **Braedon**. These are forms of the Irish surname usually found as **Braden**, which comes from the Irish for 'salmon'. Brayden is also well used in Australia. Names containing the same sounds as the very popular AIDEN (*see* **Aidan**) are currently very popular for boys in the USA, which may explain its success. Similar-sounding names which are also in use for boys are **Braylon** or **Bralen** which are probably modern coinages and **Brody** or **Brodie**, a Scottish surname probably from Gaelic *brothach* 'muddy place', which is nearly as popular in the USA as Brady. Brodie is also well used in Scotland, despite the fact that Deacon Brodie (d. 1788) is one of Scotland's most notorious thieves and all-round scoundrels.

Bram see **Abraham**

Bran see **Brandon, Bronwen**

Brand see **Brenda**

Branden see **Brandon**

Brandi, Brandie see **Brandy**

Brandon, Brendon

The Irish form of Brendan, with an 'e', is **Breandán**, and is most probably a form of the Welsh word *breehin* meaning prince. This cross-cultural influence is not surprising, for the crossing from southern Ireland to Wales is not difficult, and there was much two-way traffic from earliest times. It is the name of more than one Irish saint, the most famous of which is St **Brendan** the Navigator, who sailed his coracle in the Atlantic and whose legend has been interpreted as an account of a pre-Columbian discovery of America. Brandon, a name used by Charles Kingsley in *The Water Babies* (1863), is often a variant of Brendan, although it can have other sources, including a surname, in its turn derived from either the Old English meaning '(person from the) broom-covered hill', or from the French for 'sword'. It is sometimes analysed as from Celtic *bran* 'raven', and **Bran** can be found as an independent name. Brendon has been used steadily in the UK, Ireland and the USA, but Brandon (or **Branden**) has been more popular in the USA since the late 1970s. It entered the UK most popular lists only in the late 1990s, but has been steadily popular ever since, and has also increased in popularity in Ireland. The names sometimes appear as **Brenden**. Modern popularity of the name may owe something to the child star Brandon de Wilde (1942–72) who appeared on Broadway 492 times before going on to give an Oscar-nominated performance in the 1953 film *Shane*. He went on to have his own television series and starred in many other films.

Brandy

Sometimes spelt **Brandi(e)**, this is a feminine (and rare masculine) name more likely to be found in the United States than in the UK, although it is being used increasingly in England. Although it appears to be the drink used as a first name, it may have gained popularity as it functions as a female form of Brandon. It is not a particularly new name, for the actress Jodi Foster's mother is called Brandy. There is a singer and actress called Brandy, and the name has featured in several popular songs.

Branson see **Brenda**

Branwen see **Bronwen**

Braulio

Braulio is a Spanish name meaning 'shining', sometimes found as **Bravilio** or **Bravilo**, which is beginning to make inroads in the USA. St Braulio of Zaragossa (590–651) was a scholar and advisor of kings. The increased use of his name may owe something to the success of the Puerto Rican actor Braulio Castillo who starred in numerous telenovellas in the 1960–90s throughout South American and whose teen-idol son of the same name has followed his footsteps.

Brayan see **Brian**

Brayden, Braydon, Braylon see **Brady**

Bree, Breeda see **Bridget**

Breeanna

This name, which has enjoyed considerable popularity in the United States, can be analysed as a variant of Brianna, a feminine form of BRIAN, or as a blend of Bree (see BRIDGET) and Anna, but probably owes its popularity as much as anything to the fashion for names combining 'br-', a long vowel and an 'n', as a number of these have been popular recently in the USA. These include **Brenna** (girls) and **Brennan** or **Brennen** (boys), Irish names meaning 'tear', 'sorrow', as well as other names listed here under Br-. Breanna is also found as **Breeanne**.

Brenda

Brenda is a name made popular by Sir Walter Scott, who used it in *The Pirate* (1821) for one of his heroines. It is a name from the Shetland Islands, and is probably a feminine form of the old Norse name **Brand** ('a sword'). In Ireland it is used as the feminine of BRENDAN. It was popular in the 1950s and into the 1960s, but is little used in the UK today, although it is moderately popular in the USA. Brand in turn is the origin of the surname **Branson**, which is in use for boys in the USA. In the popular American television series *Beverly Hills 90210* the fictional characters Brenda and Brandon Walsh were twins.

Brendan, Brenden see Brandon

Brenna, Brennan, Brennen see Breeanna

Brent

Originally a surname, Brent can come either from an Old English word meaning 'burnt', or from a West Country place name meaning 'hill, high place'. It has been in regular use as a boy's name, particularly in the USA, for a number of years. The similar-sounding **Brenton**, probably primarily an elaboration of Brent, is also another surname from a place, this time meaning 'Bryni's homestead', Bryni being an Old Norse name.

Bret, Brett

This name comes from the surname meaning 'Briton' or 'Breton'. Its best-known holder is probably the American poet and short story writer Bret Harte (1836–1902), whose work, now little read but at one time very popular, helped give literary form to the legends of the Far West. It has been used regularly in the USA, usually as a boy's name, but occasionally as a girl's.

Brian

A Celtic name, Brian probably comes from the word for 'a hill'. In Ireland it is famous as the name of Brian Boru, High King of Ireland (1002–14), who defeated the Viking invaders. The name was also used by Celtic-speaking Bretons who probably introduced the name into England in the Middle Ages. The common alternative **Bryan** (currently well used in France) reflects the spelling of the surname. The popularity of the name has varied from country to country. In the UK it was popular from the 1920s to the 1960s, but is now out of fashion, but in the USA it has been steadily popular since the 1960s, and the surname that derives from Brian, **Bryant**, can sometimes be found as a first name. The boy's name **Brayan** probably belongs with this group. After a time out of favour, Brian is now popular once again in Ireland. In the United States, feminine versions of the name are also popular, in the form **Brianne** (**Briann, Bryanne**), or most commonly, **Brianna** (**Briana, Bryanna**), which is also well used in Australia. **Bria** could be thought of as a form of these names or of Bree (see Bridget). (See also BRYN, BREEANNA.)

Brice see Bryce

Bridget

The Irish form of this name, meaning 'the High One', is **Brighid**, which seems to have been the title given to ancient Celtic goddesses and a name which may also be connected with the ancient British tribe of the Brigantes. The popularity of the name is due to St Bridget (c. 450–c. 523), the greatest of the Irish female saints, though little is known of her for sure, for her legend seems to have attracted stories of the original pagan goddesses. **Brigid** is an alternative form of the name, while the form **Bride** (Irish **Brid**) with its pet forms **Bridie, Biddie** or **Biddy** reflect the Gaelic pronunciation of the name. **Brigh** 'high' can be both a short form and an independent name. **Brigitte**, occasionally **Brigette**, comes from the continental form, and **Bidelia** or **Bedelia** is an Irish gentrification of the name, which has fallen out of favour as it was felt to be over-genteel. **Birgit** or **Birgita**, the Swedish form, gives us **Britt** as a short form. The name **Bree**, with its elaboration **Breeda**, can either be interpreted as an independent name from the same root, or else as a pet form of Bridget, and may be a source of BREEANNA.

Brielle see **Gabriel**

Brigh, Brighid, Brigid, Brigette, Brigitte see **Bridget**

Brion, Brioni, Briony see **Bryony**

Brisa

Brisa is the Spanish word for 'breeze' which has begun to appear as a first name for girls in the USA.

Brittany

The place name Brittany means 'country of the Bretons' who in turn were originally emigrants from Britain, hence the distinction made in the Middle Ages, when the spellings were not so distinct, between Great Britain and Little Britain or Brittany. It was one of the most popular girl's names in the USA in the late 1980s and early 1990s, and while it is dropping rapidly in popularity, it is still well used, particularly if one takes into account all the different spellings. These sometimes reduced it to two syllables, a pronunciation widely found in the States, giving forms such as **Britney** alongside **Brittney**, **Brittani** and **Brittny**. Although place names are increasingly popular as first names, and the choice of a French place is by no means unique, being found in names such as **Normandy** or **Normandie**, and to some extent **Rochelle** (see RACHEL), no one has come up with a convincing explanation of why this district of France should be used, but the sounds that make up the name can be found in other popular names, so the attraction may be the same as in the use of blends. For men BRETT has much the same meaning. The singer Britney Spears is probably the best-known bearer.

Brock

Brock or **Broc**, from a surname, has been increasingly used as a boy's name in the USA and is now gaining popularity in Australia. As a surname, it can either be a form of the surname Brook or Brooks, or may derive from an old word for 'a badger'. In Ireland, **Broc** has been used as a rare first name since the Middle Ages.

Broderick see **Roderick**

Brodie, Brody see **Brady**

Bronach, Bronagh

This is an Irish name meaning 'sorrow'. In the past Bronach was used for both sexes, but while the form **Brone** is occasionally found for boys, it is now mostly feminine.

Bronson

As a surname Bronson refers to the son of someone called Brown. Its quiet but regular use as a first name for boys must owe much to the film actor Charles Bronson and his tough, hyper-masculine film persona (compare TYSON). There is a baseball player called Bronson Arroyo.

Bronwen

This is a Welsh feminine name meaning 'fair or white breast'. The similar-sounding **Branwen**, origin of Brangwain or Brengwain, the name of ISOLDA's maid in the TRISTAN legends, means 'fair raven', indicating a dark beauty, and is the name of the heroine of one of the medieval Welsh *Mabinogion* stories. Bronwen's name may be of divine origin as the names of her father Llyr and her brother **Bran** (see BRANDON) are both those of Celtic gods.

Brooke, Brooklyn

Brook or Brooke is a surname, meaning 'brook' which has been used for both sexes, although thanks to the fame of the actress Brooke Shields it is now usually female, with the form **Brooks** used for boys in the USA. **Brooklyn**, the name of a borough of New York City, may look as if it too comes from 'brook', but is in fact a form of the Dutch *Breukelen* meaning 'broken land'. Although chosen as the name of the son of David Beckham and 'Posh Spice', and as a result primarily a boy's name in the UK, it is more likely to be found in the USA as a girl's name, sometimes in the form **Brooklynn** or **Brooklynne**, as if a blend of Brooke and Lynn. Brooke as a feminine name is not a recent phenomenon, for the famous socialite and philanthropist Brooke Astor (1902–2007) was named after her grandmother. Brooke is well used as a girl's name throughout the English-speaking world.

Bruce

The fame of the heroic King Robert the Bruce (1274–1329) is why this surname was adopted as a Scottish first name, which has since spread throughout the English-speaking world. Despite its Scottish associations, the surname comes from a Norman place name, although experts cannot agree which particular place with which particular meaning is the exact source. Around 1975 Bruce, and particularly its pet form Brucie came to be used as a synonym for 'gay' in the USA, a peculiar development given that at the same time it was considered in the UK to be the archetypal butch Australian first name.

Bruno

Bruno simply means 'brown', and is a German name which has become more common in English-speaking countries in recent years, probably via German immigrants to the United States, although the popularity of names beginning Br- may also have been influential. The rare feminine equivalents, **Brunella** and **Brunetta**, show the influence of Romance languages (see also PRUNELLA).

Bryan, Bryanna, Bryanne, Bryant see Brian

Bryce

St **Brice**, whose name goes back to ancient Gaul, was a fifth-century Frenchman, who succeeded the great St Martin as bishop of Tours. Bryce is the more popular spelling of the name in the USA, where it is well used for boys. **Bryson**, occasionally spelt **Brycen**, the surname that comes from Brice, can also well used as a first name. Bryce is also occasionally found used as a feminine name, as in the actress Bryce Dallas Howard.

Bryn

This is from the Welsh for 'a hill', and thus shares the same root as BRIAN. The elaboration **Brynmor** means 'big hill'. They are both place names that have become first names. In Wales the names are always masculine, but in the USA, Bryn particularly in the form **Brynn**, is currently more likely to be found for girls than boys. **Brynna** has also been recorded there, as has **Brynlee** or **Brynley**, for both sexes. Bryn Terfel is an internationally famous Welsh baritone.

Bryony

Bryony is a plant name introduced in the twentieth century. Unlike most of the plant names which are those of striking flowers, this is an insignificant hedge climber. It may owe its use in part to its role as a feminine form of BRIAN. It is sometimes found spelt **Briony**, or even **Brioni**, so presumably the feminine name **Brion** should be seen as a short form of this, although it had also been recorded as a masculine name, a respelling of BRIAN.

Buddic, Buddug see Victor

Buddy, Buster

These two terms for 'friend' are usually nicknames, but are occasionally used as given names for boys. It has been suggested that **Bud** or Buddy comes from baby-talk for 'brother', while Buster seems to be the vocabulary word. Buster became famous as the name of the silent film comedian Buster Keaton. **Buck** and **Bubba** are occasionally used in much the same way.

Buffy see Elizabeth

Bunnie, Bunny see Veronica

Bunty

Bunty is usually a nickname rather than a given name. Its popularity is said to date from 1911 when there was a successful comedy performed in London called *Bunty Pulls the Strings*. The name comes from the same source as the nursery song 'Bye, baby bunting',

'bunting' being a dialect word for a pet or hand-reared lamb, which came to be used as an endearment.

Burt

This is often an alternative spelling for Bert, originally short forms of ALBERT, BERTRAM, CUTHBERT, EGBERT, GILBERT, HERBERT, HUBERT, LAMBERT, OSBERT, ROBERT, WILBERT. Sometimes, as in the case of the actor Burt Reynolds, it is a shortening of the surname **Burton**, used as a first name.

Byron

Byron is the name of the Romantic poet George Gordon, Lord Byron (1788–1824), used as a first name. The first Lord Byron was John Byron (1600–52), who was created Baron Byron as a reward for his support of Charles I in the Civil War. The meaning of the place name that it comes from is far from aristocratic as it means 'at the cattle sheds', and would have been a name given to a cowman. The name is not much used in the UK, but has been used steadily in the USA since the nineteenth century.

C

Caddie, Caddy see **Candace, Carol**

Cade, Caden

These are surnames, which can come from various sources, currently popular as first names in the USA for both sexes. The names appear in multiple spellings. At the time of writing **Caden**, as a boy's name, is the most popular, followed by **Kaden**, **Kaiden**, **Cade**, **Cayden**, **Caiden**, **Kade**, **Kadin**, **Kaeden** and **Kadyn** for boys, with **Kayden** being the most popular form for girls. There are other spellings on record, but these are the most frequent. However, the distribution can be expected to change from year to year. These names share sounds that have been popular in other names in the USA in recent years.

Cadel, Cadfael, Cadwallader

The Welsh name-element *cad* means 'battle' and is used in a multitude of Welsh masculine names, some of them the names of warriors in our earliest records. Cadel or **Cadell**, combining 'battle' with an affectionate ending, is both a name in its own right and a pet form of these names. It was the name of an early king in Wales and of an early saint. **Cadfael**, a name familiar as the hero of Ellis Peters' medieval whodunnits, means 'battle-metal', a suitable name for an old and experienced soldier. It was the full name of a very popular medieval saint, better known by the pet form **Cadog**. **Cadwallader** (also spelt **Cadwalder** and **Cadwaladr**) means 'battle prince' and is a name found as early as 681. The most famous holder of this name was a Welsh ruler who led his people against the troops of Henry II and who died in 1172.

Caden see **Cade**

Cadence

This vocabulary word has grown rapidly in popularity in the USA since the start of the twenty-first century. It is usually a girl's name, but is occasionally found for boys. The forms **Kadence** and **Kaydence** have also made their mark. The use of this term links in with the trend for musical names such as HARMONY and MELODY, but, particularly as it is shortened to **Cady**, also shows the popularity of the sound, also found in names such as KADY and those listed under CADE. Cadence was the name of a character in Armistead Maupin's 1992 novel *Maybe the Moon* and was also used as a character in the 2003 film *American Wedding* (*American Pie 3*).

Cadfael, Cadog see **Cadel**

Cadi see **Katherine**

Cadwallader, Cadwaladr, Cadwaldr see **Cadel**

Cædmon see **Hilda**

Cael see **Caleb**

Caelia see **Cecilia**

Caesar see **Julia**

Cahir, Cahal see **Cathal**

Cai see **Kai**

Caiden see Cade

Caio see Kai

Caiseal see Cashel

Caitlin

Caitlin is an Irish form of KATHERINE. The Anglo-Norman conquerors of Ireland brought the name with them in the form *Cateline*, and this became Caitlin in Irish, which was later anglicised to **Kathleen**. In Ireland the first syllable of Caitlin is pronounced as in 'cat', but in the USA, where the name was among the most popular girls' names of the 1990s, it is pronounced as if a blend of 'Kate' and 'Lynn'. This is reflected in the spelling variants which can include **Katelyn(n)** and **Kaitlyn(n)**. This form has also spread throughout the English-speaking world as well, even getting in the top 50 names in Ireland. Caitlin is found in the additional forms **Caitlyn**, **Kaitlin**, **Katlyn** and **Katelin**. Both the Caitlin and Katelyn forms are very popular in the British Isles and the USA.

Caius see Kai

Calder

Calder is a Scottish surname which is beginning to be used as a first name. There are various place names that lie behind the surname, which have various origins, including Old Norse 'calf valley'.

Caleb

In the Bible, Caleb is one of only two men, among the many who leave Egypt with Moses, who lives to see the Promised Land (Numbers 26:65). The name comes from the Hebrew word for 'dog', and is usually interpreted as indicating a dog-like faithfulness and devotion to God, although it may originally have referred to a tribal totem. It was popular with the English Puritans, but thereafter became associated with rusticity, and became rare. However, the Puritans took it with them to America. It has been used there ever since, and has recently enjoyed a revival along with other Puritan names, which is beginning to be felt in the UK as well. It is already well used in Australia. **Cale** is a shortened form, and the recent name **Kalin** or **Calen** appears to be a development of this. The name is also spelt **Kaleb** and Cale can appear as **Cael** and **Kale**.

Caledonia see Callie

Caleigh, Caley see Kayleigh

Callie

Callie, more common as a girl's name in the USA than in the UK, has a number of sources. It can be a pet form of CAROLINE, but also a short form of two names based on the Greek word *kalos* ('fair, beautiful'). **Calliope** ('beautiful voice') was the name of the Muse of Heroic Epic in Greek myth. **Calista** (sometimes **Callista**) is the Latinate form of a Greek name meaning 'most beautiful'. In Greek, the name was **Callisto**, and was in legend the name of a maiden loved by Zeus and turned into a bear by Hera, Zeus's jealous wife. However, since Callisto is used in Italian as a man's name, and the -a is more obviously feminine, the Latin form is more usual. Callie has also been recorded as a short form of **Caledonia**, the ancient name for Scotland, and of **Calvina**, the feminine form of CALVIN. Some variant forms blend imperceptibly into variants of KAYLEIGH. Callie is also found as Cali and Kallie. The actress Calista Flockhart has made her name better known.

Callum, Calum

The Latin word for 'dove' is *columba,* and was a popular name in early Christian Ireland. It was the name of numerous Irish saints, the best-known of which is St Columba of Iona (see under MALCOLM). In Ireland the name became **Colm**, and St Columba is sometimes known as **Colmcille** ('Colm/Dove of the Church'). The name also appeared in Ireland as Colomb, Colom or Colum, which becomes Callum or Calum in Scotland. From there it has spread through the English-speaking world. Even in Ireland Cal(l)um is currently more popular than Colm, although this is well used. There is no significance in the spelling with one or two ls. Sometimes one is the more popular, sometimes the other, and they often appear in the charts together.

Calvin

Calvin is a surname that comes from the Old French adjective *calve* meaning 'bald'. It is used as a first name in honour of John Calvin (1509–64), the French Protestant theologian who gave his name to Calvinism and who was famous for his strict morality, his learning and his support of austerity. It was taken to America by the earliest Protestant settlers and has been regularly used ever since. It was the name of Calvin Coolidge (1872–1933), 30th President of the United States, is the name of the fashion designer Calvin Klein, and there is a popular cartoon strip showing the adventures of Calvin and Hobbes. For the feminine form see under CALLIE.

Camden

Camden is a surname of obscure meaning, which has been in use as a first name in the USA since the 1990s. It is mainly used for boys. It is part of a growing trend to use surnames as first names, its attraction probably lying in its fashionable sounds. It is occasionally spelt **Kamden**.

Cameron

A Scottish clan name used as a male first name, Cameron comes from the Gaelic *cam sron* ('crooked nose'), perhaps a nickname given to an early clansman. It started being used as a first name in the nineteenth century as part of the Romantic revival. It has been a popular first name on both sides of the Atlantic since the 1990s, and is being used increasingly for girls. In Australia, Ireland, Scotland and England it is still primarily a masculine name, spelt in the conventional way. In the USA it is still most popular as Cameron, for boys, but is also well used as a masculine name spelt **Kameron**, **Camron**, **Camren** and **Kamron** in that order of popularity. For girls there the most popular spelling is **Camryn**, closely followed by Cameron, and **Kamryn**. **Campbell** is a related surname from *cam béul* 'crooked mouth'. It is also used as a first name in the USA, although less often than Cameron, and used more for girls than boys.

Camilla

Camilla is a figure from Roman legend, whose name, it has been suggested, means 'one who assists at sacrifices to the gods'. In VIRGIL's *Aeneid*, she figures as a warrior queen who fights with Aeneas, and is described as so fast a runner that she could run over a field of wheat without bending a blade, or over the sea without getting her feet wet. It was introduced to the general public as an English first name with the publication of Fanny Burney's *Camilla* in 1796, which has a heroine of that name. The French form of the name, **Camille**, can be used for either sex. Camilla has been quite fashionable in the UK in recent years, but Camille, as a girl's name, is the more popular form in the USA. Use of Camille went up 50% in the USA in the years 1969–70 after hurricane Camille hit the Gulf Coast. Camille is also currently popular in French-speaking countries. In the US it is shortened to **Cammie** or **Kami**, sometimes given as an independent name, but because of its association with underwear it is rarely used in the UK, where the name is more likely to be shortened to **Milla** or **Milly**. Camilla has had much exposure in recent years as the name of the Duchess of Cornwall.

Campbell see Cameron

Candace, Candice

This name, which was formerly pronounced 'can-day-see' but is now usually 'can-dis', is an ancient title of the queen of Ethiopia. The name was introduced into the body of European first names through the mention of 'Candace queen of the Ethiopians' in the Acts of the Apostles (8:27), thereby making this exotic name respectable. **Candy** is a pet form of the name, shared with CANDIDA. Candice is currently popular in France. William Faulkner used the name Candace, shortened to **Caddy** in his 1929 novel *The Sound and the Fury*; otherwise the name is best known from the actress Candace Bergen.

Candida

Candida comes from the Latin for 'white', the same word that gives us 'candid' (originally 'unblemished') and 'candidate' (from the white robes worn by Roman politicians when standing for office). Although it is found as a woman's name in Roman inscriptions, it was not used thereafter, until it was 're-invented' by George Bernard Shaw for the heroine of his play *Candida* in 1897. He in his turn modelled the name on the naive hero of Voltaire's allegorical novel *Candide* (1759). The similar-sounding **Candia** is not, as it would appear, a variant of Candida or of the pet form **Candy** which it shares with CANDACE, but (according to E.G. Withycombe) a name first given to one Candia Palmer who was born while her father was travelling to Candia, the old name for Heraklion in Crete, and which then passed into use among certain families. It is currently most noted as the name of the novelist Candia McWilliam.

Candy see **Candace, Candida**

Canna, Cannelle see **Flora**

Cannon

As a surname, Cannon is either a name originally given to someone who was a canon in a cathedral, or can be from an Irish surname, O Canáin 'descendant of Canán', Canán meaning 'wolf cub'. It is probably chosen as a first name for boys by those wanting something that sounds aggressively masculine. However, it has been argued that the form **Canon** belongs with names like ARMANI, which are prestige brand names used as first names.

Caoimhe

Caoimhe is the Irish for 'beautiful, precious, beloved' and comes from the same root as Kevin. It is pronounced 'kee-va' or 'kwee'va' and can be anglicised as **Keavy** or **Keeva**. It is currently very popular throughout Ireland.

Caoimhín see **Kevin**

Caolan, Caoilfhionn

Caolan is from the Irish *caol* 'slender' and means 'little slender one, slender lad'. It is a well used name among Irish speakers, particularly in Northern Ireland. The English spellings, reflecting the pronunciation, are **Kelan, Keelan** or **Kealan**. The female equivalent is Caoilfhionn (also **Caolinn** or **Caoilainn**) from *caol + fionn* 'fair, white, pure', which was the name of an Irish saint. Her name is turned into Keelin in English, and some **Kaylyn**s (see KAYLEIGH) may be forms of her name.

Capucine

The Italian word *cappa* 'cape' developed the form *capuccio* for a little cape or hood, which gave its name to the Capucine nuns and also to the cappuccino coffee from the white cape it appears to wear. In French capucine also became the name for a nasturtium flower, from its hood-like shape. The flower name, which features in a French nursery rhyme, has been adopted as first name in France, where it is currently popular. Capucine was the name of a very glamorous French actress who lived 1931–90. She is probably best known to English speakers from her role as the wife of Inspector Clouseau in *The Pink Panther* (1963).

Cara

Cara is the Italian for 'dear' used as a girl's name, and therefore the equivalent of the French Chère (See CHERYL). The affectionate diminutives **Carina, Carita, Carissa** or **Karissa** (but see also CHARIS) are also used. These names came into use in the later nineteenth century. They have all had a certain popularity in the USA, particularly Cara, which is more likely to be spelt **Kara** there, while Carina is often **Karina**, with forms such as **Karena** shading into variants of KAREN. (See also under CATHERINE for some of these forms.) Both Cara and Kara are currently popular in Scotland and Cara in the Republic of Ireland.

Caradoc, Caradog

This comes from the Welsh word *cariad* ('love') and is therefore the masculine equivalent of the feminine names found under CERI. It is one of the oldest recorded British names, for it is the same as **Caractacos** (Latin **Caratacus**), the name of the captured British chief taken in chains to Rome in AD 51, whose noble bearing won him his liberty. Caradoc is also the name of a character in the Arthurian legends, chiefly famous for being the only man at the court who came through various magical tests to prove he had a faithful wife.

Cari see Cerys, Ceridwen

Carina, Carissa, Carita see Cara

Carl, Carlie

The Germanic word *carl* 'man' became CHARLES in French, but Karl in German. German and Scandinavian immigrants took the name to the USA, where the C spelling developed (it was already an old-fashioned spelling in Germany), and it spread to the English-speaking world from there. Meanwhile in Spain the name became **Carlos**, and **Carlo** in Italy. **Carla** or **Karla** are feminine forms, from which developed **Carly** (**Carlee, Karlee**), **Carlie** (**Karl(e)y**), **Carlyn**, **Carleen** or **Carlene**. **Carlina** has also been described as a modern coinage, but has been in use in the author's family since at least 1803. **Carlotta** or **Carlota** are the Italian and Spanish pet forms of the name, with the shortened form **Lola** being shared by Carlota and DOLORES, and with a diminutive **Carlita**. Karl has recently had some popularity in Ireland, and Carla and Carly are well used in Scotland. Carly has become more current since the singer Carly Simon came to fame in the 1970s.

Carlton

Carlton is a place and surname meaning 'settlement of the free men or peasants', based an the same word as CARL, above. **Carleton** is an alternative spelling. The name **Charlton**, as in the actor Charlton Heston, comes from a variant form of this surname.

Carly see Carl

Carmel

Carmel is the Hebrew word for 'a garden' and the name of a mountain in Israel, famous in the Bible for its fruitfulness. A monastery, dedicated to the Virgin Mary, was established there by Crusaders, and the name originally given in honour of Our Lady of Mount Carmel. **Carmella** is a diminutive form, and **Carmen**, famous from the Bizet opera (1874), is the Spanish form of the name. For boys the Italian form is **Carmine** and the Spanish **Carmelo**.

Carol, Caroline

The feminine forms of the name CHARLES are very varied, depending on whether they are based on the German form Carl, the Latin *Carolus* or on Charles itself (see under the entry for CHARLES for the history and origin of the name). Some have been dealt with under CARL and CHARLOTTE, but from the Latin form come the forms **Carol** (sometimes chosen because a child is born near Christmas) and **Caroline**, with their variants **Carole**, **Carola**, **Carolyn**, **Carolina** (one of the sources of LINA), **Karol**, **Karoline**. **Caryl** (see also CERI) is used as a variant. These names give us the pet forms **Carrie** (and nowadays **Kari**), CALLIE, **Caddy** and **Caddie**. None of these names are popular choices at the moment in the UK; but Caroline in quite popular in the USA at the moment, followed by Carolina, which perhaps reflects the trend for place names as first names; the other forms are also in use there. It was expected that the popularity of the character of Carrie in the hit television series *Sex and the City* would increase the use of the name, but it has yet to have any significant effect. For the masculine names Carol or Karol see under CHARLES.

Caron see Karen

Carrie see Carol

Carroll see Charles

Carson

Carson is a Scottish surname, possibly meaning someone who lives in a marsh, which has had a certain popularity as a boy's name in the USA, sometimes in the forms **Ka(r)son** or Cason. It does not seem to be much used as a girl's name, despite the fact that its most famous bearer, Carson McCullers (1917–67), author of *The Heart is a Lonely Hunter* and *Reflections in a Golden Eye*, was female.

Carter

This surname, from the job, is well used in the USA as a boy's name, sometimes in the form **Karter**, and has recently become increasingly popular in Northern Ireland, perhaps from President Jimmy Carter's peace-brokering activities.

Carwen, Carwyn see Cerys

Cary

Although the actor Cary Grant (Archibald Leach in real life) was not the first man to use the surname Cary as a first name, it was he who popularised it, and it has been used steadily, if quietly, ever since. The surname is usually an English West Country one, from a river whose name may mean 'pleasant stream', but it can also be from the Irish *O Ciardha* ('son of the dark one').

Caryl see Carol, Cerys

Caryn see Karen

Carys see Cerys

Casey

Although this name can be a pet form of CASIMIR, it is more commonly from the Irish surname *Cathasch*, meaning 'descendant of the vigilant one'. The most famous Casey of all, the American folk hero celebrated in song, Casey Jones (1863–1900), was in fact a railway engineer christened John Luther Jones; he was given the nickname 'Casey' because he was born near Cayce in Kentucky. As a masculine name, Casey is sometimes spelt **Casy** or with a 'K', while as a girl's name, less used than the man's, it can be found as **Kasey** and **Kaci** as well as the more usual Casey. It may also be from the initials K.C., especially in the UK. There, Hull City fans have adopted **Kaycee** as a name based on the K.C. Stadium (sponsored by Kingston Communications Co) which opened in 2002.

Cash

This is a surname, originally from *casse* the Norman French for a box, which would have been given to a box-maker. It is used quietly as a boy's name, probably as a result of the fame and image of the American singer Johnny Cash (1932–2003). It may sometimes be a short form of the next.

Cashel

This is an Irish man's name meaning 'fortified house, castle', which comes from the city's name, the ancient capital of the province of Munster. The Irish spelling is **Caiseal**, and there is a pet form **Cashlin**.

Casimir

Traditionally Casimir or **Kasimir** has been interpreted as meaning 'proclamation of peace', but recent scholars have suggested it actually means the opposite and comes from words meaning 'to spoil peace'. It is a Polish name, used in the nineteenth century among supporters of Polish independence, and introduced to the United States by Polish immigrants. CASEY (now used for both sexes, but formerly masculine) can be a pet form of Casimir.

Cason see Carson

Caspar, Casper see Jasper

Caspian

This is a name used by C.S. Lewis for the hero of his children's novel *Prince Caspian* (1951), part of the *Narnia* series, which has occasionally been used for a real boy.

Assuming he borrowed the name from the Caspian Sea in North Iran, the name comes ultimately from the Cas tribe of the area.

Cassandra, Cassidy, Cassie

Cassandra is a name from Greek legend. Its meaning is not clear, and it may be so old that it goes back to pre-Greek times, but a derivation from *kekasmai* 'shine' and *aner* 'man', giving a meaning something like 'shining upon man' has been suggested. It was one of the earliest non-Christian Greek names adopted into English and was common by the beginning of the thirteenth century. This early adoption was a result of the popularity of the *Romance of Troy*, a work that told the story of the Trojan War with sympathy firmly on the Trojan side. Given her story, it is perhaps surprising that the name has been so well used for so long. She was a Trojan princess and priestess of Apollo, who agreed to let him sleep with her in return for the gift of prophecy. However, she reneged on her side of the bargain, and as a punishment the god condemned her to prophesy the truth, but to be believed by no one. Thus she is often used as a symbol of one who foretells unpleasant events, but is ignored, and as such her name was chosen for the name of the famous column in the *Daily Mirror* whose criticisms so annoyed Churchill during World War II. After the fall of Troy Cassandra was taken as a slave-concubine back to Mycenae by Agamemnon, where she was murdered by his wife. Cassandra (sometimes **Kas(s)andra**) is shortened to **Cass** or **Cassie** (**Cassy**), which is also a short form of **Cassidy** (**Kassidy**). This is an Irish surname from the Gaelic *O Caside*, 'descendant of the curly-haired one', which can also be found used for boys. Both Cassidy and Cassandra are relatively well used in the USA at the moment; and Cassandra is currently popular in France. Cassandra Austen was the sister of the writer Jane Austen, and their delightful letters have been preserved and published.

Castor see Cosmo

Casy see Casey

Catalina, Cate see Katherine

Cathal

This is an Irish name meaning 'battle-mighty': **Cathair**, from the same root, means 'warrior'. Both versions have the anglicised forms **Cahal** and **Cahir**. For the related name **Cathan** see KEENAN. Cathal is currently popular in Ireland.

Catharine, Catherina, Catherine, Cathie, Cathy, Caterina, Cati, Catrin, Catriona, Catrina see Katherine

Caw see Kai

Cayden see Cade

Cayla see Kay

Cearbhall see Charles

Cecil

Although Cecil is sometimes thought of as a masculine form of CECILIA, it has a different origin. The Latin name **Sextus**, originally a name given to a sixth son, developed the form *Sextilius*. This was brought by the Romans to Britain, where it developed into the Old Welsh name **Seisyllt**. This in its turn became the family name Cecil, and the surname of this noble family came to be used as a first name. It was chiefly used in the nineteenth century.

Cecilia

The Roman family name *Caecilius* came, it was claimed by those who bore it, from the Latin for 'blind' in honour of a distinguished blind ancestor. In fact, like many distinguished Roman names it was probably Etruscan in origin. Its use is due to the popularity of St Cecilia, the patron saint of music, whose 'life' is now thought to be largely, if not wholly, mythical. The name was current in England from the early Middle Ages, when it generally took the form **Cecily**. The first syllable of this can be pronounced either 'ses' or, as was more usual in the past, 'sis'. This second pronunciation gave rise to the variants **Cicely** and **Sisley**, and the short forms **Sis, Cis,**

Sissy, **Sissie**, **Cissy** or **Cissie**. **Cecile** is the French form of the name. **Celia** is often used as a short form of Cecilia, but is in fact a separate name. It comes from another Roman family name, that of the *Caelii*, which was interpreted as from the word *coelum* ('heaven'), which gave rise to the old spelling **Coelia** as well as to the Latin **Caelia**. Once again this derivation is incorrect, and as the family was supposed to have been founded by an Etruscan, it seems probable that the name comes from one of the few Etruscan words we can understand: *celi* meaning 'September'. Either Cecilia or Celia was the origin of the Irish name **Sile**, anglicised to SHEILA. In the USA Cecilia is sometimes spelt **Cecelia**. These names have strong literary associations as Celia is best known as a character from Shakespeare's *As You Like It*, and Cecily from Oscar Wilde's *The Importance of Being Ernest*. Célia is currently popular in France. The actress Sissy Spacek has given her form of the name publicity.

Cedric

Cedric is a name invented by Sir Walter Scott in his novel *Ivanhoe* (1819) for the father of his hero. Cedric represents all that is good about the old Saxon landowners, in contrast with the rapacious Norman invaders. It is usually said that the name came from a misreading of Cerdic, a very early Saxon name meaning 'amiable', but others have pointed out that there is a Welsh name **Cedrych**, meaning 'pattern of bounty'. Since Scott's other 'Saxon' names are suspiciously Celtic, it may be that Scott got his cultures mixed, and is using a form of this Welsh name. Long out of fashion, there has been a mild revival of use of the name in the United States, where it is occasionally found as **Sedrick**, and can be shortened to **Rick**. The name acquired a rather effete reputation after Mary Pickford played the role of *Cedric Errol Fauntleroy*, the velvet suited, ringletted *Little Lord Fauntleroy*, in a film which was a sad perversion of the original book, in 1921.

Ceinwen

This is a Welsh name made up of elements *cain* 'lonely' and *gwen* 'holy, fair'. According to Welsh legend St Ceinwen, also known as St Keyne or Cain, was a princess living in the fifth century, who lived in Keynsham in Somerset, which is named after her. When she arrived the place was plagued by serpents. She miraculously turned these pests to stone, which explains why so many snake-like fossil ammonites are to be found in the area. Other girl's names based on *cain* are **Ceindeg**, with a second element from *teg* 'beautiful', the name of another early Welsh princess, and **Ceinlys**, which has a second element either from *melys* 'sweet' or *glwys* 'fair'.

Ceirios see **Charity**

Celeste

Celeste and its diminutive form **Celestine** come from the Latin word for 'heavenly', and therefore have links with Celia (see CECILIA). Forms such as **Celesta** and **Celestina** can also be found.

Celia see **Cecilia**

Celina, **Céline** see **Selina**

Cenydd see **Kenneth**

Ceri see **Cerys**

Cerian, **Ceril** see **Cerys**

Ceridwen

This is thought to be the name of the Celtic goddess of poetic inspiration. Her name is made up of elements meaning 'poetry' and 'white, fair, blessed'. Traditionally she is the mother of TALIESIN, one of the great early bards of the Welsh. Like all Welsh names beginning Ce- the 'c' is hard. It can be shortened to Ceri (see CERYS) or **Cari**. The name was rare in the Middle Ages, but was revived in the nineteenth century.

Cerise see **Charis, Peaches**

Cerys

This is one of a large group of Welsh girls' names that comes from the word *caru* ('love') and it is therefore the Welsh equivalent of the English AMY. After Cerys, **Ceri** (which can also be used for boys) and **Carys** are probably the most used, but other forms include **Ceril**, **Cerian**, **Cari** and **Caryl**, which is also used as a form of CAROL. Carys should not be confused with CHARIS which, although pronounced in the same way – both with a hard 'k' sound – comes from the Greek. Ceri, particularly in the form **Keri** which is sometimes found, may have contributed to the development and popularity of KERRY. From the same root comes the name **Carwen**, the second element meaning 'white, blessed', with its masculine form **Carwyn**. For other masculines see CARADOC. Cerys has been given publicity by the Welsh singer-songwriter Cerys Matthews, and is now used throughout the UK, although still most popular in Wales where it is among the top ten girl's names.

Cesar see Julia

Chad

This was the name of a seventh-century Anglo-Saxon saint and bishop whose history is told by the Venerable Bede. He was bishop of Lichfield, and the cathedral there is dedicated to him. This kept the name of this rather obscure saint current, at least locally, while in the twentieth century it was widely known thanks to the fame of the Rev. Chad Varah, who founded the Samaritans. The meaning of the name is obscure. Although he was a Saxon, it may be Celtic in origin, from the same *cad* ('battle') element that is found in names such as CADEL. Chad is also the name of a little cartoon figure shown as a bald head, two eyes and a nose peering over a brick wall associated with the phrase 'Wot, no …?' which was created in World War II by the cartoonist Chat as a comment on shortages, and which worked its way into popular culture. The name was well used in the United States in the 1970s and 80s and is still regularly used there, and has seen a mild revival in the UK. In the USA, **Chadwick** – a surname from various place names mostly meaning 'Chad's farm' – is also used as a first name.

Chae see Charles

Chaim

This comes from the Hebrew *hayyim* 'life' and is also found transliterated as Chayim, Hyam or Hiam. Chaim is the form most often used in the USA. The feminine form is usually **Chaya**. In Jewish tradition Chaim may be added to the name of someone who is seriously ill, or else used as the second name of someone who is named after a dead person. The first President of Israel was Chaim Weizmann.

Chance see Chauncey

Chandler

This is a surname used as a first name. The surname comes from the French word *chandelier* ('candle maker'). Already moderately well used as a boy's name in the USA by 1980s, the name never became quite as popular as it was expected to after the success of the television series *Friends* which had a character called Chandler, although use did increase.

Chandra

Chandra means 'moon' in Sanskrit, and is the name of a Hindu god. It is used for both sexes. A related name is **Chandrakant** (m) and **Chandrakanta** (f) 'beloved of the moon'; the term for both a gem supposedly formed from the moon's beams and a night-flowering water-lily.

Chanel

The name of the famous French perfume has been in use as a first name, particularly among Black Americans, since at least the 1980s. This particular brand name was probably chosen because the sounds fit in with other popular names, the 'cha-' sound linking to names such as CHANTAL, with the '-el' ending being a popular feminine ending. There are a number of variant spellings such as **Chan(n)el(le)** and **Shanel(le)**.

The perfume took its name from the fashion designer Coco Chanel (1883–1971). For another influential perfume name see Ciara (under KIERAN).

Chantal

This is a French surname, ultimately from the southern French word *cantal* ('a stone'). It became a first name because of St Jeanne de Chantal, a seventeenth-century French saint associated with St Francis de Sales. As well as being the grandmother of Madame de Sevigné (1626–96), she combined a romantic life-story with great worldly wisdom and true piety. She is a most attractive figure, and it is not surprising that French parents should want to name a child after her. The name was first officially accepted in France as a first name in 1913, and spread rapidly thereafter. It arrived more recently in the UK, where it has developed variants. **Chantelle**, which makes the name look as if it from the French *chanter* 'to sing', is now the most used form, particularly in Ireland and Scotland, and there are spellings with Sh- such as **Shantal**.

Chardonnay

This is the name of a variety of grape that has been very popular as the source of white wine in recent years, and which in turn gets its name from a French village. It came to public attention in 2002 as the name of one of the characters in the television series *Footballers' Wives*. Many commentators seemed to think that this was an invention of the writers for purposes of social commentary, but in fact that name had been recorded for a number of years prior to the series. The incidence of the name in the UK increased briefly while the series was showing, but it has never really become established in the general stock of names.

Charis

Charis (the 'ch' is pronounced as if a 'k') is the Greek word for 'grace'. It is tempting to link the increase of its use to the appearance of a character of that name in Georgette Heyer's novel *Frederica* (1965); but it may also be linked with the use of the Welsh name Carys (see CERYS), which is pronounced in the same way. **Charissa** is a Latinate form of the name, created by Edmund Spenser for *The Faerie Queene* (1590–96), but it could also be interpreted as a variant of Carissa (see CARA). **Charisse** is a French form of the name (pronounced with an initial 'sh' sound), which has found some popularity in the United States, often in the form **Cherise**, but variants such as **Charice, Cherice, Sharice** and **Sherise** are also found, although these can also be linked to the French name **Cerise**, 'cherry'. Use of Charisse may owe something to the film star Cyd Charisse (1921–). However, there are a number of names that seem to be developments of the sounds involved in this name, for example Cherry (see below) and Cheryl, and it is impossible to work out if they are names with traceable histories, blends or fashionable innovations. This includes **Cheryth**, or **Cherith**, and **Cherish** (the vocabulary word), as well as some of the names under CHERYL. Currently, the most-used of these names in the USA is the spelling-pronunciation **Karis**.

Charity

Formed from the same root as CHARIS, Charity is with FAITH and HOPE one of the three great Christian virtues, and all are used for girls' names. **Cherry** started life as a pet form of Charity, rather than being derived from the fruit, but it is now an independent name. The Welsh name **Ceirios** comes directly from the plant name 'cherry'. After many years out of fashion, Charity is beginning to be fashionable again. For related names, see above and at CHERYL.

Charles

The Old German word for 'a man' was *carl*, a popular name among the Frankish ruling class that dominated western Europe in the Dark Ages. The name was Latinised as *Carolus*, which in turn became Charles in French. These three forms have developed into a vast number of names for both sexes, found throughout Europe. The Germanic forms of the names are dealt with under CARL. From *Carolus* comes the eastern European form **Carol** or **Karel** found occasionally, but usually only for those of eastern European descent, although Carol can also be a masculine name in Wales. The Irish also use the surname **Carroll** (**Cearbhall**), meaning 'champion warrior', as a first name. Charles has spawned a large number of diminutives such as **Charlie** (currently more popular as a given name in the UK than the full form) or **Charley**, **Chas** or **Chaz** from the old abbreviated written form of the name, **Chae** or **Chay** in Scotland, **Chuck** mainly in the United States, while **Chilla** is said to be a form used in Australia. For the feminine forms see under CAROL and CHARLOTTE.

Charlotte

Charlotte is a feminine form of Charles. It has been enormously popular in the UK since the 1970s. It is also popular in Ireland and Australia and well used in the USA. Its short form **Charlie** or **Charli** is also well used by English speakers, although Germanic countries tend to use the alternative short form **Lotte** or **Lottie**. A variant form is **Sharlotte** (in use since the end of the nineteenth century, and not a recent form as one might expect) and the Irish forms **Charlot** or **Searlait**. **Sharley** and **Chatty** have also been used as shortenings. Variant forms from the twentieth century are **Charleen**, **Charlene** or **Sharlene**, and the actress **Charlize** Theron, whose name was coined for her by her parents, has added a new form to the stock of names. Other feminine forms of Charles can be found under CAROL.

Charlton see Carlton

Charmaine

This is a name of debated origin, particularly used in the mid-twentieth century thanks to a popular song. It now has the variant **Sharmaine**. Its origin is often linked to the much older name **Charmian**, the Greek for 'joy' and used by Shakespeare for Cleopatra's maid in *Antony and Cleopatra* (this is strictly speaking pronounced with a hard 'k' sound, but the pronunciation with a soft 'ch-' is often found), perhaps with what was felt to be a French twist; but it may simply have been invented at the time.

Chas see Charles

Chase

This surname, from the Old French word *chaceur* ('hunter'), has grown steadily in popularity as a boy's name since the 1990s in the USA.

Chastity

This Christian virtue has a long, if infrequent, history as a girl's name. In 1969 Cher and Sonny Bono chose it as the name for their daughter, and this has led to an increase in its use. It has also been suggested that the rise of the curious name **Chasity** – 252nd for girls in the USA in 1976 and still in regular use, comes from a misreading of Chastity Bono's name.

Chatty see Charlotte

Chauncey

Chauncey or **Chauncy** is a masculine name used in the United States since at least the early nineteenth century. A surname deriving from a village near the French town of Amiens, it was used as a first name in honour of Charles Chauncey (1592–1672), the second president of Harvard College (later Harvard University). The short form **Chance** is currently more popular as a given name than the full form, and well used for girls. This can also be the vocabulary word used as a first name. The popularity of Chance may owe something to the appearance of a character called Chauncey Gardiner, known as Chance, in the successful 1979 film *Being There*.

Chavon see Siobhan

Chay see Charles

Chaya see Chaim

Chayanne see Cheyenne

Chayim see Chaim

Chaz see Charles

Cheli see Araceli

Chelsea

The use of this place name as a girl's name reflects the fame of Chelsea in London and Chelsea, New York. The fame of the football club may also have been an influence. In use from at least the 1950s, the name first reached a wider public in the late 1970s when the actress Chelsea Brown was prominent in the American television comedy show *Rowan and Martin's Laugh-In*. It became popular in Australia, and was in the top two dozen most popular names in the USA by 1990, but took a few more years to become popular in the UK. It is now among the most-used names among English speakers. It is sometimes found as **Chelsey**. Chelsea Clinton, the US president's daughter, was given her name from a favourite song of her parents, Joni Mitchell's *Chelsea Morning* (1969).

Cher, Cheralyn, Chère Cherida, Cheri(e) see **Cheryl**

Cherice, Cherise, Cherish, Cherith see **Charis**

Cherokee see **Dakota**

Cherry see **Charity**

Cheryl, Cher

A modern formation, Cheryl has had currency since the 1920s. It is probably based on the name Cherry (see CHARITY) or on the French word **Cherie** ('darling'), used as a first name. Cheryl rapidly developed a number of variants, including **Cheralyn** (the most popular) and **Cheryn**. Both Cheryl and Cheralyn are found in a number of different spellings including **Sheryl, Sher(r)el(l)** and **Sher(a)lyn**. **Cher** is a short form popularised by the singer of that name (whose given name is Cherilyn), which sometimes appears as **Chère**, the French for 'dear'. Cherie is also found in the form **Sherry** or **Sherri**. **Cherida** is a rare variant, blending the Spanish and French for 'dear'.

Cheryth see **Charis**

Chester

This is the town name, derived from the Latin *castra* (a camp), used as a first name. **Chet** is used as a short form. The name has been use more in the USA than the rest of the English-speaking world. The commander of the US Pacific forces in World War II was Admiral Chester Nimitz.

Cheyenne

This is the name of a Native American nation, now an increasingly popular first name, particularly in the USA, usually for girls. The meaning of the name is disputed. It is sometimes spelt **Chayanne** or **Sheyenne**, while spellings such as **Shianne** or **Shyann(e)** reflect the pronunciation. These and the variant Cheyanne show that it sometimes being interpreted as a name incorporating ANNE. Cheyenne Brando, daughter of Marlon and born in 1970, was an early bearer of the name.

Chiara see **Clare**

Chilla see **Charles**

China

The place name China ultimately comes from the word *Qin*, the name of the dynasty that ruled China from 221 to 206 BC. It is sometimes spelt **Chyn(n)a**. The name is more usually given to girls, but the British writer China Miéville is an example of a masculine use.

Chivonne see **Siobhan**

Chloe

Chloe or Chloë comes from the Greek for 'a green shoot' and was one of the names for the fertility goddess Demeter (see DEMETRIUS) in her summer aspect (see also MELANIE). Its use is usually ascribed to the name appearing as a minor character in the New Testament, but since early uses are mainly literary it is more likely to be inspired by the Greek pastoral romance *Daphnis and Chloë*, probably from the second or third century AD. The name was not very common outside literature until about 30 years ago, when new interest was shown in it. It is currently one of the top names in many countries including England, Scotland, Ireland, Australia, France and the USA. It is occasionally spelt **Cloe**. **Chloris**, occasionally **Cloris**, is an unusual name related to Chloë since it comes from the same root, which means 'green'.

Christine
This is the most popular of the feminine names meaning 'Christian'; **Christian** itself was used originally for boys (and is currently increasingly popular), but is now used for both sexes, along with its pet form Christy. **Christy** or **Christie**, along with **Chris** and **Chrissie**, are also used as pet forms of Christine, with **Kirsty** or **Kirstie** in Scotland. **Cristyn** is the Welsh version of the name. **Christina**, with its pet form **Tina**, are popular variants, and the Scandinavian forms **Kirsten** and **Kersten** have recently come into use. **Christabel** is mainly literary, although it is found in the suffragette Christabel Pankhurst (1880–1958). Other variants include **Christiana**, **Christiane**, **Cristen**, **Kristina**, **Krystyna**, **Kiersten**, **Kirsteen** and **Kirstine**, **Kirsta**, **Krista** and **Kristin**, and spellings without the 'h' after the C. **Christelle** is a French form of the name (see also Crystal)

Christmas see Noel
Christopher
Christopher comes from the Greek for 'Christ carrier', and was the name of the giant in legend who carried the Christ Child over a river and thus became the patron saint of travellers. **Kester** is an old pet form now generally replaced by **Chris** or **Kit** and occasionally **Topher**, with **Christy** being more common in Ireland. A Scottish form of the name was Crystal or **Chrystal**, which is also used in Ireland, and found as an occasional masculine name along with the pet form **Christy**. Christopher has been a very popular name for boys since the 1990s on both sides of the Atlantic. **Cristobal** is the Spanish form of the name. The name is sometimes spelt with a K and phonetic spellings such as **Cristofer** are also found.

Chrystal see Christopher, Crystal
Chuck see Charles
Chyna, Chynna see China
Cian see Keenan
Ciara, Ciaran see Kieran
Cicely see Cecilia
Ciera, Cierra see Kieran
Cilla see Priscilla
Cillian see Killian
Cinaed see Kenneth
Cindy
Cindy started life as a short form of names such as Cynthia and Lucinda (see Lucy), but is now and independent name. It is sometimes fund as **Sindy** and **Cyndi**, as in the singer Cyndi Lauper, is a variant.

Cis, Cissie, Cissy see Cecilia
Citlali
Citlali is a Mexican name, and is the word for 'star' in the Nahuatl language of the Aztecs. It is beginning to appear in the USA. It can be used for both sexes, but is more often used for girls.

Clancey, Clancy see Clarence
Clare
Clare and its French spelling **Claire** come from the Latin word *clarus*, literally meaning 'bright, clear' but also used in the sense 'famous'. The name owes its popularity to St Clare of Assisi (c. 1194–1253), companion of St Francis and foundress of the Poor Clare order of nuns. Her Italian name would have had the form **Chiara** or **Clara**. **Clarice** is

an Italian diminutive of Clara, and featured as a literary name from the fifteenth century onwards in various romances. Other literary forms of the name are **Claribel** (masculine in Spenser), **Clarinda**, also found in Spenser, and **Clarissa**, best known as the heroine of Samuel Richardson's novel *Clarissa or The History of a Young Lady* (1747–49). **Clarisse** is a French form. **Clarry** or **Clarrie**, once almost obsolete but now familiar to listeners to *The Archers*, is used as a pet form of these names, particularly of Clarice. **Clair** was used for men in the nineteenth century, but CLARENCE is now used as a masculine form.

Clarence, Clancy

Lionel, Duke of Clarence was a son of the fourteenth-century English King. Edward III. The title of Duke of Clarence was created for him after he married an heiress with extensive land in Clare, Suffolk. The title was revived in 1890 for the elder son of Edward VII, who died in 1892. It was adopted in the nineteenth century as a first name at the same time as a number of other aristocratic names, probably as a result of its use in a novel by Maria Edgeworth. Clancy or **Clancey** is sometimes a pet form of Clarence, but this is also an Irish surname, perhaps meaning 'son of the red warrior' used as a first name, particularly in the USA. Clancy is being used for girls as well as boys now.

Claribel, Clarice, Clarinda, Clarissa, Clarisse see Clare

Clark

Clark comes from the surname, and means 'cleric'. It has become well known from the actor Clark Gable and from Clark Kent, *alter ego* of Superman. **Clarke** is also found.

Clarrie, Clarry see Clare

Claudia

Claudia comes from a Roman family name. The Claudii interpreted their name as coming from the Latin word *claudus* meaning 'lame', from the nickname of an ancestor; but this may be mere folk etymology. **Claudette** and **Claudine**, as in the novels of Colette, are further forms of the name. Claudia has a place in British folk history, for the Claudia found in the New Testament (2 Timothy 4:21) is traditionally held to be the daughter of a British prince, sister of LINUS and wife of Pudens, mentioned in the same verse. The name Pudens has been found on Roman inscriptions at Colchester, and the first-century Roman poet Martial refers to a friend Pudens who has a wife 'Claudia, the foreigner from Britain'. The Welsh name **Gladys** (**Gwladys, Gwladus**) is traditionally said to come from Claudia, but in fact probably comes from a word meaning 'ruler'. The masculine form of the name, **Claud**, once popular, is now rare; even rarer is the full Roman masculine form, **Claudius**. The French form of the name **Claude** (pronounced 'clohd') can be used for either sex, but among English speakers is usually feminine.

Claus see Nicholas

Clay, Clayton

These are surnames, originally given to someone who lived in an area of clay soil, used as first names. They have been in use since at least the nineteenth century, and are currently fashionable in the USA, particularly Clayton.

Cledwyn

This is a Welsh river name used as a first name. Various etymologies have been suggested; it may be from *caled* 'rough' combined with *gwyn* 'white'.

Clematis see Flora

Clementine

This name means 'mild, merciful' and is probably best known from the song 'My Darling Clementine'. **Clementina** is a variant. There has been something of a revival of these names in recent years, including the use of the abstract noun **Clemency**, a name used by the Puritans, along with its counterpart MERCY. Clémence is a French form currently popular in France. **Clement**, the masculine form of the name, popular with popes, has been less well used, although it too is currently popular in France. The short forms of this group of names can be illustrated from the political world, the prime minister Clement Attlee (1883–1967) being known as **Clem** and Sir Winston Churchill addressing his wife Clementine as **Clemmie**.

Cleo

Cleo is the short form of the Graeco-Egyptian name **Cleopatra**, meaning 'glory of her father', which is more frequently used than the full form. The fame of the first-century AD queen of Egypt has been too strong for the name to be more than quietly used, although there has been a certain usage among Black Americans, particularly those wanting to emphasize their African roots. **Clio**, with the 'i' usually pronounced as in 'mine', is not a variant, but the name of the Greek muse of history. The jazz singer Cleo Lane is a well-known holder of the name.

Clifford

This, with its more common short form **Cliff**, is a surname used as a first name, originally given to someone living near a cliff and ford. The name was adopted because it was the surname of a prominent aristocratic family.

Clinton

Like CLIFFORD, this is an aristocratic surname used as a first name. Henry de Clinton, founder of the family of the dukes of Newcastle in the twelfth century, held land at Glympton in Oxfordshire and the name is probably a corruption of this place name, meaning 'settlement on the River Glyme'. The actor **Clint** Eastwood has given fame to the short form of the name.

Clio see Cleo

Cliodhna, Cliodna see Clodagh

Clive

Clive is another surname used as a first name, in this case probably in honour of Robert Clive (1725–74), whose exploits in India did so much to lead to the East India Company's domination of the sub-continent, leading ultimately to the formation of the British Empire. The surname is an Old English one meaning 'dweller by the cliff'.

Clodagh

This is the name of a river in Tipperary. It was first used as a girl's name by the family of the marquises of Waterford. Its use outside Ireland may have spread through the success of the singer Clodagh Rogers, although it was also the name of the mother superior in the very successful film *Black Narcissus* (1946). The name is currently well used in Ireland, but in Northern Ireland the name is also well used in the Irish spelling **Cliodhna**, which is also found as **Cliodna**.

Cloe, Cloris see Chloe

Cloudy see Misty

Clover

This is a flower name used as a first name, particularly in the 1970s. In the *Katy* books written by Susan Coolidge (1835–1905) Clover Carr was the younger sister of Katy. Forms such as **Clova** are also recorded, which seem to be half way between this name and a feminine of Clovis (see LOUISE).

Clovis see Lewis

Clyde

This is the Scottish river and surname, used as a masculine first name. The river's name has a long history, being a pre-Roman Celtic name which probably comes from a word meaning 'to wash'. It has been suggested that it was originally the name of a pagan goddess. It seems to have developed into a first name in the USA in the nineteenth century.

Cobe, Coby see Kobe

Cody

This is an Irish surname used as a first name. It has been a popular name for boys in the USA since the 1990s, but is less frequently found for girls, when it is usually **Codi**.

Spellings such as **Codie** and **Codee** and those beginning with a 'k' can also be found. As a surname there are two possible sources. One is a Gaelic name meaning 'descendant of Cuidightheach' (originally a nickname meaning 'helpful person'), the other the Gaelic *Mac Oda* ('son of Oda'), where the meaning of Oda is not known. **Coty** as a masculine name should probably be considered a form of this name, as it is unlikely that a brand of cosmetics would be used to name a boy.

Coel see **Cole**

Coelia see **Cecilia**

Coinneach see **Kenneth**

Col see **Nicholas**

Cole

The choice of this as a first name is probably inspired by the fame of the music and sophisticated lyrics of Cole Porter (1891–1964). As a first name, Cole can have a number of origins. It is an old pet form of NICHOLAS (see also COLIN). It can be a use of the surname Cole, which can either be from Nicholas again, or from the Old English *Cola* or related Old Norse name *Koli*, both meaning '(char)coal', and probably given to someone with particularly dark colouring. Cole can also be a shortened form of other surnames used as first names: **Colby** from an English place name meaning 'Koli's settlement' (compare COLTON, below); and **Coleman**, a surname either from a charcoal burner, or from a surname based on the same name as CALLUM. **Coel**, a Welsh name with the same pronunciation, comes from a word meaning 'trust'. Coel the Adulterous, a Scottish king of the sixth century, was the original of the Old King Cole of nursery rhyme fame. Cole is being well used as a first name for boys in Scotland; otherwise the names are mainly used in the USA, where they also appear spelt with a K. They are primarily boys' names, except for Colby which is now well used for girls as well, perhaps under the influence of the character Alexis Colby from the 80s television series *Dynasty*.

Colin

Colin, now sometimes **Collin**, started life in France as a pet form of NICHOLAS, although in Scotland and Ireland it has also been associated with a Gaelic word meaning 'pup, cub' and hence 'young man'. The relationship between Colin and Nicholas can be more clearly seen in the feminine **Colette** (sometimes **Collette**) from Nicole, Nicolette. **Colinette** and **Colina** have also been recorded as feminine forms, while **Coline,** sometimes spelt **Colyne** is well used in France.

Colleen

This the Irish word for 'a girl' used as a first name. It is rarely found in Ireland itself, but has been popular in the United States and Australia where there are many families with Irish roots. Colleen Moore (1900–88) was the stage name of a silent film star whose starring role in the shocking film *Flaming Youth* (1923) helped launch the name.

Collette, Collin see **Colin**

Colm, Colmcille, Colom, Colomb see **Callum, Malcolm**

Colton

Colton or **Colten** means, like COLBY (*see* **Cole**), 'Koli's settlement' and was originally an English place name that became a surname. **Colt** can be used as a shortening. When it is used as an independent name it too can be a surname used as a first name, but is more likely to be the vocabulary word: not a young horse, but from the gun. **Kelton**, a rare boy's name, is probably best analysed as a variant of this name.

Colum, Columba see **Callum, Malcolm**

Colyn see **Colin**

Connie see **Conn, Constance**

Conor, Conn, Conan

The Irish name Conn or **Con** means 'high', and was the name of Conn of the Hundred Battles who lived about 200 AD, created the central monarchy in Ireland and gave his name to Connacht. It is used either as a name in its own right or, with **Connie**, as a short form of a number of names. These include Conor or **Connor**, the anglicised form of the Gaelic **Conchobar**, probably meaning 'lover of hounds', but often interpreted as 'high desire'. This was the name of the king of Ulster in the great Irish epic of *The Tain*. The name is currently widely popular and the spelling choice breaks down across country lines. The spelling with two ns is the norm in Australia, Canada and the USA, where **Conner**, **Konnor** and **Konner** are also used. In Scotland both forms have featured for a number of years in the top 100 names, but the two-n spelling is the more common. In Ireland the name has been very popular for the last decade, but only in the one-n form. Other related names are **Conal** ('high and mighty') and **Conan** (sometimes **Conant**), as in the *Conan the Barbarian* stories, also meaning 'high'. Conan is found as the name of the early dukes of Brittany, and it is possible that it is a Breton name that has since passed into Irish use. See also QUINN.

Conrad

This is the English form of the German name **Konrad**, meaning 'bold counsel'. There is an old pet form **Conradin**, the name of the last of the Hohenstaufen Holy Roman Emperors; it is also used by 'Saki' (H.H. Munro, 1870–1916) for a character in his short stories. The more usual short form now is **Curt** or **Kurt**.

Constance

With its masculine form **Constant**, as in the composer Constant Lambert (1905–51), Constance is a name which celebrates the Christian virtue of steadfastness. **Constancy** has also been recorded as a girl's name. There is a further Christian connection in the related **Constantine**, for it was the name of the Roman emperor who formally brought the empire into the fold of the Church. They all share the short forms **Con** and **Connie**. The Welsh form of Constantine is **Cystennin** and **Constanza** is the Spanish form of Constance. Constance was a very popular name in the nineteenth century and into the early twentieth, but then went out of fashion. However, there has been a slight revival of interest in the name in Great Britain in recent years.

Consuelo see Dolores

Cooper

Cooper is a surname that would originally have been given to a barrel-maker. It has been increasingly used as a boy's name in the USA since the 1908s, and it is also well used in Australia.

Cora see Corinna

Coral

Coral is one of the gem names introduced in the late nineteenth century. The French form is **Coralie** and dates from some 100 years earlier. Coralie became popular in France in the 1980s and is currently well used there and in Quebec. French-speakers also use **Coraline**, from the Italian form, **Coralina**.

Corbin

This surname became fashionable as a boy's name in the USA in the 1980s, no doubt helped by the success of the actor Corbin Bernsen. It comes from the French word for 'raven' and is also found as **Corben** or **Corbyn**. The related **Corbett** is also found.

Cordelia

This is one of the less frequently used Shakespearean names, but one which appears to be being used increasingly. The name may be the same as the continental **Cordula**, one of the virgins martyred with St URSULA. The name is thought to be connected with the Latin word *cor*, *cordis* ('heart'). Cordelia is shortened to **Cordy** or DELIA.

Corey

This surname, of uncertain meaning, is used as a first name for both sexes, but more commonly for boys. As a girl's name it is often **Cori**, which some users may interpret as a pet form of a name such as Cora or CORINNA. The spelling **Cory** is not uncommon and it is also found starting with a K. It started to come into general use in the USA in the 1940s and peaked in the seventies and eighties. More recently it has been popular in Scotland.

Corinna

Corinna was the name of an early Greek poetess, probably of the sixth century BC. Her name possibly comes from the Greek *kore* ('a maiden'), one of the titles of the goddess of the underworld, **Persephone**. A less respectable Corinna is the object of the poet's pursuit in Ovid's *Amores*, and it is from this source that the seventeenth- and eighteenth-century poets adopted the name for their inamoratas, as in Robert Herrick's 'Corinna's going a-Maying' (1648). **Corinne** is the French form of the name, made popular by Madame de Staël's 1807 novel of that name. **Cora** is probably an invention of James Fenimore Cooper for a woman in *The Last of the Mohicans* (1826), whence the name's popularity in the United States; but it is thought to be based on the same root. **Corisande** appears to be an elaboration of this. There is a masculine form also found in Classical poetry, where it is a typical name for a shepherd, **Corin**, which is now used for women. It is rarely found for men, but is kept in the public eye by the actor Corin Redgrave. Cora is currently well used in Northern Ireland.

Cormac

This is a Gaelic name, borne by a legendary Irish king. Its meaning is doubtful and interpretations vary widely, but include 'charioteer' and 'son of the raven'. Cormac is used steadily the Irish Republic. Cormac McCarthy is a highly-respected American novelist.

Cornelius, Cornelia

Cornelius, with its short forms **Corney** or **Corny** and **Cornel**, comes from the Roman clan name of the Cornelii, which is probably formed from *cornu belli* 'war horn'. The feminine form, **Cornelia**, is strongly associated with the famous Cornelia, mother of the Gracchi, the second-century Roman tribunes. She represented all matronly accomplishments, and devoted herself to the raising of her children. When a visitor showed off her jewels and asked to see her hostess's, Cornelia is said to have produced her sons with the words 'These are my jewels'. The Romans erected a statue in her honour. The name came into Christian use from the appearance of a Cornelius in the New Testament; it later became the name of a number of saints, particularly in the Low Countries. This led to its being associated with the Dutch, which explains its use in America by those with Dutch associations, such as Cornelius Vanderbilt.

Cortez See Curtis

Cory see Corey

Cosmo

Saints **Cosmas** and DAMIAN are said to have been twin brothers who practised medicine for free among the poor, and were martyred for their faith. Beyond the fact that they probably existed and belong to the early period of Christianity, little is known of them for sure, for their legend has become heavily adulterated by memories of the pagan heavenly twins **Castor** and **Pollux**, the sons of Zeus. Cosmas (whose name means 'order') and his brother became the patron saints of Milan, and from there the name spread throughout Italy in the form **Cosimo**. In the eighteenth century, Cosmo came to Britain via the dukes of Gordon, who had links with the dukes of Tuscany, and the name became traditional in their family. **Cosima**, the feminine form, is also used occasionally. Its use is probably inspired by the fame of the romantic Cosima, who was daughter of Franz Liszt (1811–86) and wife of Richard Wagner (1813–83).

Coty see Cody

Courtney, Courtnay

Courtney is an aristocratic surname used as a first name. The family came from a Norman village called Courtenay, which would have been named from a Gallo-Roman landlord called *Curtenus* or *Curtius*, but from early on the name was thought of and used as a nickname *court nez* ('short nose'). It was originally a masculine name, but more recently has been used for both sexes, and has become particularly popular in both the UK and USA as a girl's name.

Craig

Craig means 'cliff' and is a word still used in Scotland in that sense (see under AILSA). It has a long history as a surname given to someone who lived near a cliff, but only came into use as a first name in the twentieth century. It was particularly popular in the 1970s and 1980s in the UK, and has returned to popularity in Scotland and Ireland in recent years.

Cressida

Considering the history of the original bearer, it is surprising that this attractive-sounding name has come into use. Giovanni Boccaccio (1313–75), in his *Il Filostrato*, told the story of the love of Troilus for Cressida, showing her as a heartless and faithless woman. Chaucer (c. 1340–1400) in *Troilus and Criseyde* gives a rather more sympathetic version of her, showing her as easily led and timid rather than vicious; but by the time that Shakespeare deals with the story, she has become a downright wanton, while her uncle's name, Pandarus, became that of the common pander. However, her story must have its attractions as her name became increasingly popular through the twentieth century, while the virtuous **Troilus** is not generally used, although it has been given to Sir Laurence Olivier's grandson. Cressida has a short form, **Cressy**.

Crisiant see **Crystal**

Crispin

Crispin or **Crispian** and his brother **Crispinian** are the patron saints of shoemakers. Their name comes from the Latin meaning 'curly-haired'. The use of the name Crispin is probably helped by memories of the speech that Shakespeare gives to Henry V before the battle of Agincourt, where he tells his men: 'And gentlemen in England now a-bed/Shall think themselves accurs'd they were not here,/And hold their manhoods cheap while any speaks/That fought with us upon Saint Crispin's day'.

Cristal see **Crystal**

Cristen see **Christine**

Cristofer see **Christopher**

Cristyn see **Christine**

Cruz

This is a religious name, from the Spanish word for 'cross, crucifix'. When the Beckhams chose the name for their third son there was much comment that this was a girl's name, not a boy's. It is true that many books describe it as a feminine name, but in the United States it has been a fashionable boy's name since the early 1990s.

Crystal

As a girl's name, this belongs with the JEWEL group of names, although it is worth noting that **Kristel** is a German form of the name CHRISTINE, and **Christelle** a French one. It has been popular in the USA in the 1970s. The name also exists in a masculine guise, as a Scots pet form of the name CHRISTOPHER. The Welsh name **Crisiant** also means crystal, and has been in use since at least the twelfth century. The spellings include Krystal and Cristal, while the form Chrystal shows the influence of Chris.

Cuddie see **Cuthbert**

Curt see **Conrad**

Curtis

A surname from the French for 'courteous', Curtis is now increasingly popular as a masculine first name. It came into use in the USA in the nineteenth century and was popular by the 1880s. Thereafter it did not drop out of the top 200 names until the late 1990s, and it is still used regularly. It is currently well used in Northern Ireland. The Spanish surname **Cortez**, also used for boys in the USA, can come from the same root.

Cuthbert

St Cuthbert, whose name means 'well known and famous' in Old English, was a seventh-century bishop of Lindisfarne (Holy Island) whose simple holiness won him great love from the people he ministered to. He was buried in Lindisfarne, but frequent Viking raids led to his re-burial at Durham. His name was much used in the past in the north of England, where **Cuddie** became a pet form of the name.

Cy see Cyril, Cyrus

Cybill see Sybil

Cynan

An old Welsh masculine name meaning 'chief, pre-eminent', Cynon has the variants **Cynin**, **Cynon** and **Cymon**. **Cynyr** comes from the same root and means 'chief hero'. It was the name of St David's grandfather, who lived c. 500 AD.

Cynthia

The moon goddess Artemis or DIANA had particular associations with the Greek Mount Cynthus, and Cynthia, meaning 'of Cynthus', became one of her epithets. It was used as a name in the classical world and found in England in the seventeenth and eighteenth centuries, but did not really become popular until the nineteenth. It shares CINDY and **Sindy** as short forms with Lucinda (see LUCY).

Cynyr see Cynan

Cyprian

St Cyprian was a third-century bishop of Carthage and martyr, famous as a writer and devout Christian and for his gentle good manners and willingness to consult others. The name means 'man from Cyprus' and although rare, is occasionally used.

Cyra see Cyrus

Cyril

Cyril comes from the Greek word *kyrios* ('lord'). It was the name of one of the missionaries who brought Christianity to Russia, who gave his name to the Russian Cyrillic alphabet, devised to write down the gospels. **Syril** is a rare variant. It can be shortened to **Cy**. **Kyrie** is used as feminine versions of the name, although a male name **Kyree**, sometimes also spelt **Kyrie**, can be derived from the Arabic word *khayri* ('benevolent').

Cyrus

The name of a number of Persian kings, Cyrus may come from the Persian word for 'throne', although later commentators sometimes derived it from the same root as CYRIL. Its use, mainly in the United States, probably owes more to the mention of King Cyrus the Great in the Old Testament than to the rather obscure fourth-century martyr St Cyrus. It is shortened to **Cy**. **Cyra** and **Kyra** are feminine forms. Kyra is increasingly popular in the USA, although there is some overlap in pronunciation with the names related to KIERA (*see* **Kieran**). The actress Kyra Sedgewick has brought the name publicity.

Cystennin see Constance

D

Daffodil

One of the less common flower names, Daffodil was used in the later nineteenth and the earlier twentieth centuries when such names were at the height of their popularity, and is still occasionally found.

Dafydd see David

Dahlia

Another flower name, Dahlia comes from the name of the Swedish botanist Anders Dahl (1751–89) who brought the Mexican wild flower to Europe for cultivation. It seems to have had more popularity with authors – it is used by George Meredith in *Rhoda Fleming* (1865), and by P.G. Wodehouse for Bertie Wooster's favourite aunt – than with parents. **Dalia**, a form also found in France, is not uncommon in the USA, where it is sometimes used as a feminine form of DALE.

Dai see David

Daire

This is an Irish name meaning 'the fruitful one' which was probably originally a title of the Dagda ('the good god') who was the father god of the pagan Irish. The name is pronounced with two syllables, something like 'daw-ra'. There are feminine equivalents **Darina** and **Dareen**. Daire is well used in Ireland.

Daisy

Daisy was originally a pet form of the name MARGARET, as they both have the same meaning. When Henry James published his novel *Daisy Miller* in 1879 the name was thought of as typically American. However, it is now popular on both sides of the Atlantic.

Dakota

Like CHEYENNE, this is another Native American nation, a branch of the Sioux, whose name means 'friend'. It is used as a first name for both sexes. Although it did not start to be used regularly until the 1980s for boys and 90s for girls it was used on an occasional basis earlier than this; as in the case of the jazz and blues singer Dakota Staton (1930–2007). Other nations have been used as names, for instance **Cherokee**, but Dakota and Cheyenne are the two most popular. Dakota Fanning is a well-known child actress.

Daksa see Aditya

Dale

A surname meaning 'dweller in the dale' used as a first name, Dale was once restricted to men, but is now used for both sexes, perhaps under the influence of Dale Arden, heroine of Alex Raymond's Flash Gordon adventures. **Dayle** is an alternative spelling.

Dalida, Dalil, Dalila see Delilah

Dallas, Dallin, Dalton

These three place names and surnames, now used as boys' first names, particularly in the USA, share the same sounds but not the same histories. The most popular of them is Dalton, a common English place name meaning 'farmstead or village in the valley', and transferred to several places in the USA. Dallas, the next most popular, is famous for the Texan city, probably named after George Mifflin Dallas, vice president of the United States from 1845 to 1849, but ultimately goes back to two British place names – one Scottish, meaning 'dwelling in the valley', and one English, meaning 'house in the valley'. Dallas has been in use as a first name since the mid-nineteenth century, for in the year George Mifflin Dallas became vice president, the Texas Ranger and gunfighter Dallas Stoudenmire was born. Another Texan city, **Houston**, named after Sam Houston (1793–1863), first president of the Republic of Texas, is also used as a boy's first name. Dallin is more obscure, and probably goes back to the English place name Dalling, meaning 'settlement of the descendants of Dalla', an Anglo-Saxon name.

Damaris

Damaris is a biblical name, that of an Athenian woman converted by St Paul (Acts 17:34). As such it was adopted as a name by the Puritans. It seems to have been quite fashionable at the beginning of the twentieth century, and is still regularly, if quietly, used. It is probably a corruption of the Greek Damalis ('a heifer'). It is tempting to suggest that the new masculine name **Damari** is a version of this name, but it is more probably simply a modern invention using sounds, such as those in DeMarius (see MARIUS), **Demarion** and **Damarion** which are currently fashionable.

Damian, Damon

Damian is probably a form of the rather less common **Damon**, an old Greek name meaning 'to tame, subdue'. The story of Damon and Pythias, proverbial for loyal friendship, dates from the fourth century BC when Damon, an ardent republican, tried to assassinate Dionysius, the tyrant of Syracuse. His friend Pythias volunteered to stand surety for him while Damon went to say goodbye to his family before being executed. Dionysius was so impressed by Pythias' offer and by the fact that Damon returned rather than leave his friend to die in his place, that he pardoned them both. For the legend of St Damian see COSMO. Damon had a certain currency in the first half of the twentieth century, and is found in the authors Damon Runyon (1884–1946) and Damon Knight (1922–2002). Damian and its variants **Damien** or **Damion** have been rather more popular in the latter part of the twentieth century, although they went into steep decline for a few years after the film *The Omen* appeared in 1976, where Damian was the name given to the child born to be Antichrist.

Dana

As a masculine name, Dana is from a surname meaning 'a Dane', and **Dane** itself is sometimes found as a first name. Use of the surname as a first name is due to various prominent Americans who bore the name, most notably Richard Henry Dana (1815–82), who, in an attempt to cure his failing eyesight, signed on as a deckhand to sail round the Horn, an experience recounted in his book *Two Years Before the Mast*, and who as a result of his experiences of the privations endured by the common sailor became a reforming lawyer. As an Irish girl's name, it is said to come from the Irish word meaning 'bold'. Outside Ireland the feminine form is probably adopted from the Scandinavian pet form of Daniella (see DANIEL).

Danaë

Danaë is a character from Greek mythology. It was prophesied that her father would be killed by her son, so to try to avoid this fate he shut her in a tower of brass. However, the god Zeus fell in love with her, visited her in the form of a shower of gold, and she had a son, **Perseus**, who fulfilled the prophecy.

Dand, Dandie, Dandy see Andrew

Dane see Dana

Dangelo see Angel

Danica see Danika

Daniel

This name comes from the Hebrew and means 'God is judge'. Daniel, with his adventures in the lions' den, is one of the most attractive of the Old Testament prophets and it is not surprising that his name was popular from the beginning of the Middle Ages. **Dan** and **Danny** or **Dannie** are used as pet forms for both sexes, with **Dani** also used for girls, the feminine forms of the name being the French **Danielle**, the Italian **Daniella**, and more rarely **Danette**, **Dania** and **Danita**. In Wales, **Deiniol** or **Deinioel**, meaning 'attractive, charming' and the name of an early Welsh saint, is used as a form of Daniel. Daniel has been increasingly popular as a name for boys since the middle of the twentieth century, while Danielle has been popular since the 1980s. (See also SUSAN, DANA, DINAH)

Danika

Danika or **Danica** is a Slavic name meaning 'morning star'. Well established in eastern Europe, it is now starting to be used by English speakers. The name is usually feminine, but the 'k' spelling is also being used for boys in the USA, perhaps as an elaboration of Dan.

Dante see Donte

Daphne

Daphne is the Greek for 'laurel', and therefore the equivalent of LAURA. In mythology Daphne was a nymph with whom the god Apollo fell in love. She fled from his embraces, and when he had all but caught her, her prayers to be saved from him were answered and she was transformed into a laurel tree. Heartbroken, Apollo declared the laurel sacred to him, and wore on his head a wreath made from her leaves. This story lies behind the use of the laurel wreath as a symbol of honour or achievement in the ancient world.

Daquan see Daria

Dara

In Connemara, Ireland, the local patron saint of fishermen is known as Mac Dara, meaning 'son of the oak' ('oak' here indicating stoutheartedness), and the name Dara, a shortened form of his name, has spread from Connemara, first through Ireland, and then to other English speakers. It is usually male, but is now also used for girls, probably because most '-a' names are female. The name **Darragh** (or **Daragh**), pronounced the same way, is either a form of this or is from a related surname. The name is popular in Ireland, with the spelling Darragh the most used, followed by Dara then Daragh.

Darby see Dermot

Darcy

The original Darcy family got their name from the fact that they came from (*de*) a French place called Arcy, and the name is occasionally found in something near the original form – D'Arcy. This surname was also used in Ireland as an anglicisation of the similar-sounding surname *O Dorchaidhe* ('descendant of the dark one'). It is used as a first name for both sexes, with feminine forms including the variant spellings **Darcey**, **Darci** and **Darcie**. The name is fashionable in Australia. Darcy Bussell is a well-known ballerina.

Daria, Darius

The masculine form of this name, **Darius**, is an ancient Persian royal name meaning 'protector'. The feminine form, **Daria** (although this may owe something to **Darija**, a Russian pet form of DOROTHY), is more widely used internationally than the masculine, because it was the name of a saint martyred in 283. However, the man's name has recently become fashionable in the USA, and also appears in many altered forms. **LaDarius** has been used as a African-American name, combining the popular prefix La- with Darius, and the well-used name **Darian** could be seen as a development of Darius or Daria, although it could also be interpreted as from DORIAN. **Darian** is usually masculine, but occasionally feminine, and also occurs as **Darien**, **Darrien**, **Darrian** or

Dar(r)ion. Darius is probably the main source of the fashionable name-element Da-used to coin new names such as **Daquan**.

Darina, Dareen see Daire

Darlene
Darlene seems to be a combination of the endearment *darling* with the popular name-forming element -ene, found in names such as MARLENE. It has been used since the beginning of the twentieth century. Other forms are **Darleen**, **Darla** (popularised in the 1930s as the name of one of the characters in the *Our Gang* series of films) and **Darylyne** are related, and it has been suggested that DARYL may also belong in this group.

Darnel see Daryl

Darragh see Dara

Darrel see Daryl

Darren
This is a modern name of obscure origin. It has been described as an Irish surname, but this is not well documented. Whatever its source, this name and its variants **Darran** and **Darin** became immensely popular throughout the English-speaking world in the middle of the twentieth century. Following the fashion for De- names **DeRon** has also been used, as have forms such as Derron. Its popularity is often attributed to its use in the 1960s American TV series *Bewitched*, but while this may have helped the spread of the name, it was well used before this. The popularity of the singer Bobby Darin (1936–73) may also be influential. Darren has been well used in the Scotland and Northern Ireland in recent years.

Darrian, Darrien, Darrion see Daria

Daryl
Daryl is another surname used as a first name, although it has also been linked to the group of names found at DARLENE. The surname is French in origin, from *de Airel*, the name of someone from the Norman village of Airel. The village got its name from the Latin word for 'an open space' or 'courtyard'. **Darryl**, **Darrel** and **Darrell** are variants. The name started out as masculine, but is now used for both sexes, although the success of the actress Daryl Hannah has not led to much growth in the name as a girl's name. Darrell is currently the most popular spelling followed by Darryl, then the original Daryl. The use of the surname **Darnell** as a first name may have been influenced by the popularity of Darrell.

Dashawn see Sean

Davian see Octavia

David
The name of the killer of Goliath, and later King of Israel, is the Hebrew for 'beloved, friend'. The old short forms Daw and Dawkin have now been replaced by **Dave**, **Davie** or **Davy**. The Welsh form of the name is **Dafydd** (anglicised to **Taffy**), the form **Dewi** usually being restricted to the patron saint of Wales; short forms are **Dai**, **Deio** and **Deian**. Two surnames from the first name are used for boys. **Davis** is the less common of the two. The other is **Dawson**, which shot up in popularity in 1998 after the appearance of the character Dawson Leery in the popular television teen drama *Dawson's Creek*. **Davina** and **Davida**, with their short forms **Vina** and **Vida**, are originally Scots feminines. **Davita**, **Davinia** and **Divina** are also found. David was steadily popular throughout the twentieth century and shows no sign of falling out of favour.

Davin see Devin

Davina, Davinia, Davis, Davita see David

DaVon see Devin

Davy see David

Dawn

A modern name, Dawn was at first strongly associated with fiction and then given wider fame by several actresses. Its use may owe something to the Latin name **Aurora**, the goddess of dawn, which is increasing in popularity in the USA. The forms **Aurore** or **Aure** are well used in France. The Spanish and Italian equivalent is **Alba**. Dawn was particularly popular in both the USA and the UK in the 1960s and 1970s, while Aurora is known as the name of the Princess in the Sleeping Beauty story.

Dawson see David

Dayana see Diana

Dayanara, Deja

Dayanara is a popular Puerto Rican name, particularly associated with the Puerto Rican singer, actress and former Miss Universe Dayanara Torres. It is a form of the Spanish name **Dejanira** (also found as **Deyanira**), a form of the Greek **Deianeira**, the wife of Hercules in Greek legend. Deja can be a short form of the Spanish name, or can be a use of the French word *déjà*, as in *déjà vu*, depending on pronunciation. In addition, there was Dejah Thoris, the beautiful and capable princess of Mars in the *Barsoom* novels of Edgar Rice Burroughs (1875–1950). She first appeared in print in 1912, but Burroughs was writing about Barsoom as late as 1948, and the novels are not only still read but were very influential on, and often mentioned by, later science-fiction writers. **Diya**, which has recently appeared in the USA and Canada probably belongs with these names.

Dayle see Dale

Dayton

This is a surname from Old English, which can refer either to a place where there was dairy work going on, or to one with a ditch. It is used as a boy's name in the USA, and may have been influenced by the use of DALTON. The Dayton family were prominent politicians in the early history of the USA, and there are a number of American places named after them.

Deacon

Deacon is another surname, from the occupation, used for boys. The actress Reese Witherspoon has called her son Deacon, and there is a character called Deacon in the soap opera *The Bold and the Beautiful*.

Dean

As a surname, Dean has two sources, either an Old English name meaning 'dweller in a valley', or from the church office of Dean. Its success as a first name may owe something to the romance attached to film actor James Dean, although it was well established in the United States before he sprang to fame, as attested by the actor Dean Martin. The girl's name **Dena** may have started as a feminine form of the name, and **Deanna** or **Deanne** may also be used in the same way rather than as a respelling of DIANA. Dean is currently well used in Scotland and Ireland.

DeAndre see Andrew

DeAngelo see Angel

Deanna, Deanne see Dean, Diana

Dearbhail, Dearbhla see Dervla

Debdan see Dev

Deborah

This is the English form of the Hebrew name **Devorah** meaning 'bee'. From the account of the original Deborah in the Old Testament book of Judges, she must have been a formidable woman, for at a time when the role of women was very much that of a subordinate she was a prophetess, a Judge of the People, and even led the army. Certainly both the Puritans, who approved of biblical names but not independent women, and the Victorians who felt much the same way, did not use the name much. **Debra** is a variant, and **Debora** is also used. **Deb**, **Debbie** and **Debby** are short forms.

Declan

This is the name of an Irish saint who was a missionary associated with the southeast of Ireland from the earliest Christian times in Ireland, even before the coming of St PATRICK. The meaning is not known. **Dec** is the short form and there is a modern feminine **Decla**. Declan has been well used in the UK for a number of years.

Dee

Dee and **Dee-Dee** were originally pet forms of any name beginning with the letter 'D'. **Deeann** and **Deeanna** are forms of DIANA.

Deepak

Deepak or **Dipak** is a masculine name meaning 'to kindle' in Sanskrit. It is one of the names of KAMA, the Hindu god of love. **Deepika** is used for girls. Related names include **Deepankar** 'lamp-lighter', **Deependra** 'lord of light' and **Deepit** 'lighted' for boys, and **Deepa** 'lamp', **Deepali** 'lamps', **Deepika** 'little light' and **Deepti** 'glow, shine' for girls.

Deian see David

Deianeria see Dayanara

Deinioel, Deiniol see Daniel

Deio see David

Deirdre

This is the name of the great romantic and tragic heroine of Irish legend, whose beauty caused the death of several heroes. The meaning is debated: it has been interpreted as meaning 'the raging one', 'fear' or (most attractively) 'the broken-hearted'. The name was given wider currency by the publication of W.B. Yeats's *Deidre* (1907) and J.M. Synge's *Deidre of the Sorrows* (1910), both based on her legend. Variants include **Derdre** and **Deidre**, while the form **Deidra** is used in the USA.

Deja, Dejanira see Dayanara

DeJuan see John

Del, Dell

These are used as short forms of any name beginning Del-. A number of these are masculine and represent a fashionable use of place or surname, or of blends – a mix of elements from different names. In some cases the sense of 'del' as 'of the', found in Romance languages, can still be traced. Thus we have **Delmar**, a place and surname ('of the sea'), **Delroy**, a French surname meaning '(servant) of the king', and the blend **Delbert**, 'Del + Bert'. Del is also used as a pet form of DEREK. The singer Del Shannon (1934–90), who made the name widely known, was born Charles Westover. (See also DELYTH)

Delaney

This is a surname, which can be or either French or Irish origin, used as a first name for either sex, although it is currently used more for girls. It can be shortened to **La(i)ney**, although this can be from other sources (see under LANE).

Delbert see Del

Delia

Delia means 'girl from Delos', the Greek island sacred to Apollo and Artemis. Its use as a first name is adopted from the first-century BC Latin poet Tibullus, who celebrated Delia (a pseudonym for one Plania) in his love poems, and from its use by Virgil for one of his shepherdesses. It was popular in the seventeenth and eighteenth centuries, particularly in literature, and at one time was practically synonymous with 'sweetheart'. It can also be a short form of the name CORDELIA.

Delilah

In the Old Testament Delilah is a Philistine woman who exploits the Jewish hero SAMSON's well-known weakness for women to trim his hair and thereby leave him vulnerable to capture by his enemies. Despite these associations the name has been used for centuries. It was well used in the Middle Ages and popular with the Puritans, and is undergoing a revival in America along with other biblical names. **Dalida** is an old French form of the name, and the name of a popular French singer. The modern French form is **Dalila**. This can also be an Arabic name meaning 'guide, model, leader' which has a masculine form **Dalil**. The name Delilah is perhaps best known from a song of that name.

Della

This girl's name started life as a pet form of ADELA, but is now used as an independent name.

Delmar, Delroy see Del

Delyth

This is a Welsh girl's name meaning 'pretty'. **Del** alone is also used, as is **Delun** ('pretty one') and **Delwen** ('pretty and fair'). This has a masculine form **Delwyn**. **Dilwyn** or **Dillwyn**, also masculine, is not a variant, but comes from the name of a Herefordshire village and means either 'white honeycomb' or 'petal'.

DeMarcus see Mark

Demarion see Damaris

DeMarius see Damaris, Marius

Demelza

A Cornish feminine name, Demelza has reached a wider audience through Winston Graham's *Poldark* novels and the television series made from them. It is a place name, meaning 'the hill-fort of Maeldaf', and is said to be a twentieth-century introduction.

Demetrius, Demi

Demetrius means 'follower of **Demeter**', the Greek goddess of agriculture and mother of **Persephone** (see CORINNA, CHLOE, MELANIE). Her name means either 'earth mother' or 'corn mother'. Demetrius occurs several times in the Bible, which may in part explain its use. It is also a saint's name, found in the form **Demetrios** in the Greek Church, and as **Dimitri** in Russian. **Demitrius** is another variant. The film star **Demi** Moore has made the short form of the feminine form **Demetria** (or **Demitra**) well known. Demi has been well used in England and Scotland in recent years.

Dena see Dean

Denholm

This is a surname, made up from the place-name elements 'valley' and 'dry land in a fen'. The similar **Denham** comes from 'valley' and 'homestead'.

Denis

Denis, with its variants **Dennis** (the preferred spelling in the USA) or **Denys**, is a form of the name **Dionysius**, 'a follower of the god **Dionysos**', the Greek god of wine and poetic inspiration, whose name probably comes from the title 'son of Zeus', the king of the gods. The form Denis is the French corruption of the name of the martyr St Dionysius of Paris, who became the country's patron saint. **Den** and **Denny** are pet forms. The Greek form of the name is shortened to **Dion** or **Deon**, a name of growing popularity, which has the feminine **Dionne** as in the singer Dionne Warwick, and more rarely **Dione** and **Dionysia** (in use in England by the fourteenth century). However, **Denise** (rarely **Denisse**) is still by far the commonest feminine of the name. The new name **Denisha** is probably based on Denise.

Denzil

This is a Cornish place name of unknown meaning. Originally used as a masculine first name in the seventeenth century in a very limited way, it has now spread outside Cornwall and into more general use. The actor **Denzel** Washington is a well-known bearer of the name. The spelling of his name is closer to the original Cornish spelling of *Denzell* than the standard English spelling of the name.

Deodan see **Dev**

Deodatus see **Theodore**

Deon see **Denis**

Derby see **Dermot**

Derdre see **Deirdre**

Derek, Derrick, Deryck
This is the English form of the name **Theodoric** ('ruler of the people'), an unstable name since the German form is **Dietrich**, the Dutch **Dirk** and the French **Thierry** (one of the sources of **Terry**). Theodoric the Ostrogoth (c. 455–526) was an outstanding figure of his day, ruling northern Italy (by conquest) and parts of what are now Switzerland and Germany. After his death he became a figure in European folklore, which would explain the changes that happened to his name. The word 'derrick' for a crane is said to come from the name of a seventeenth-century hangman, whose name was first applied to the gallows and then used more generally to anything roughly that shape. DEL is occasionally used as a short form. The spellings include **Derick**.

Dermot
Dermot or **Dermod** (in Irish **Diarmuid** or **Diarmaid**) is a figure from Irish mythology, a warrior who eloped with GRAINNE. There were also 11 Irish saints of the name. The name probably means 'free from envy'. It occurs in a wide variety of forms, including **Diarmod**, and **Kermit** the Frog (from *The Muppets* TV show) owes his name to a regional variant. It was anglicised as **Darby** or **Derby**, and is the source of the popularity of this name in Ireland, although elsewhere it is from the surname which comes from the English place name, originally meaning 'farmstead where deer are kept'. Diarmuid is currently well used in the Irish Republic.

DeRon see **Darren**

Derrick see **Derek**

Derron see **Darren**

Dervla
This is the most usual anglicisation of the Irish **Dearbhail**, meaning 'true desire', which is also found in the forms **Dearbhla**, **Derval** and **Dervilia**. It is rare outside Ireland, although the travel writer Dervla Murphy has made the name much better known.

Deryck see **Derek**

Deshaun, DeShawn see **Sean**

Désirée
This is the French word for 'desired, longed for', and was used for a long-awaited child from early times, originally in its Latin form **Desiderata**. **Desiderius** ERASMUS (1466–1536), the Dutch Humanist, bore the masculine form of the name, which is also found as **Desideratus**, and which appears in French as **Didier**. **Desire** was used in the seventeenth century, mainly as a masculine name. **Desiree** (now occasionally found as **Desirae**) was introduced to the English-speaking public by the 1954 movie *Desiree* starring Marlon Brando. It was about the life of Bernardine Eugénie Désirée Clary, a woman who became engaged to Napoleon but married the future King of Sweden.

Desmond
This is an Irish surname meaning 'descendant of one from Desmond, South Munster', used as a first name. It was also the title of the influential earls of Desmond, and it is probably because of them that the name came to be used as a first name. **Des** and **Dezzi** are used as short forms.

Destiny
This vocabulary word has come to be a popular first name for girls in the USA. It is probably chosen by parents to express their hope for their child's future. It is also used

with the spellings **Destinee**, **Destini** and **Destiney** and the boy's name **Destin** may be used as a masculine equivalent, rather than as a respelling of DUSTIN. However, poor spellers need to be careful, for there is at least one child on record who is going round with the official name Density. Destiny was one of the fighter-pilot 'Angels' in the 1960s puppet series *Captain Scarlett and the Mysterons*, the others being called Symphony, MELODY, RHAPSODY, and HARMONY.

Detta see Bernard

Dev, Devi

Devi is the Sanskrit for 'goddess' and is the title of the Mother Goddess. It is used for girls, along with **Devika** 'little goddess'. The masculine equivalent is Dev 'god'. Related names are **Devdas** 'servant of the gods' and **Devdan** (also found as **Deodan** and **Debdan**) 'gift of the gods'.

Devin, Devon

There is a group of names beginning Dev- that has recently become popular, particularly in the United States. In Great Britain, Devon is the one most prominently used. It is found for both sexes, and is pronounced with the stress on the first syllable, as in the county name. In the USA these names tend to be stressed on the second syllable. Devon is primarily feminine there, but sometimes used for boys. However, boys are more likely to be **Devin**, although this too can be used for girls. Other variants of these names are **Devan**, **Deven, Davin, Draven** and **Devyn**. In addition, there are two Black American boys' names that belong in this group, **DaVon** or **DeVon(n)** and **Devonte** (**Davonte**, **Devante**), which appears to be a blend of Devon and DONTE.

Devorah see Deborah

DeWayne see Duane

Dewi see David

Dexter

This is a surname used as a first name. The surname originally came from a word meaning 'a female dyer', but the name has long since lost any feminine associations.

Deyanira see Dayanara

Dez, Dezzi see Desmond

Diamond

There has recently been a mild fashion for this jewel as a girl's first name, particularly in the USA.

Diana

Diana was the Roman goddess of the woods and wild nature, and later of the moon. She was equated with the Greek goddess **Artemis**, whose name is occasionally used as a first name. For example, the granddaughter of the famous beauty Lady Diana Cooper is called Artemis with reference to her grandmother. **Artemisia** ('follower of Artemis') is another rare name, probably used with direct reference either to the queen who fought at the battle of Salamis in 480 BC, or to the queen of Halicarnassus who built the Mausoleum, one of the Seven Wonders of the ancient world, in memory of her husband. Diana occurs in a number of variants. **Diane** is the French form which also occurs as **Dianne** or **Dian**. **Deanna** is a form introduced by the film actress Deanna Durbin; and **Deeann**, **Deanne** and **Deeanna** are now also found, along with **Dyan** and **Dyanna** or **Dayana**. Surprisingly, the enormous popularity of the Princess of Wales does not seem to have had any great influence on the popularity of the name. Other names linked with Diana as moon-goddess are PHOEBE and CYNTHIA.

Diarmaid, Diarmod, Diarmuid see Dermot

Diccon, Dick, Dickie, Dickon, Dicky see Richard

Didier see Désirée

Diego
This Spanish boy's name is traditionally analysed as a pet form of Santiago (see James), but recent authorities think it is more likely to be either from the Greek *didakhe* 'teaching' via Latin *Didacus*, or else from some lost ancient Spanish name.

Dietrich see Derek

Dieudonné see Theodore

Digby
This comes from the place name in Lincolnshire which means 'farm by the dyke'. As a surname it belonged to a notable family, the most prominent member of which was Sir KENELM Digby.

Diggory
This is a corruption of the name of a hero of medieval romance, Sir Degaré, 'the lost one'. The work, highly romantic and full of unlikely events, is not very highly thought of today, but the survival of the name must indicate a different opinion in the past.

Dilip
Dilip, also found as **Dilipa** and **Duleep**, is a boy's name that was held by several kings. It means 'protecting Delhi'.

Dillan, Dillon see Dylan

Dillwyn see Delyth

Dilwyn see Delyth

Dilys
This is a Welsh word meaning 'certain, genuine', used as a first name. It was first used by William and Jane Davis for their daughter, who was born on 11 June 1857, and they took the word from a Welsh version of the 23rd Psalm. **Dilly** is used as a short form.

Dimitri see Demetrius

Dinah
Dinah is strictly speaking a separate name from the Greek DIANA, being a Hebrew word meaning 'judgement', although it is often used as a variant of Diana. The story of Dinah's abduction and the revenge taken by her brothers is told in chapter 34 of the Book of Genesis. The name is also found in the form **Dina**. As it comes from the same root, it can also be regarded as a female equivalent of DANIEL.

Dion, Dione, Dionne, Dionysia, Dionysius, Dionysos see Denis

Dipak see Deepak

Dirk see Derek

Divina see David

Diya see Dayanara

Djamal, Djamel, Djamila, Djemila see Jamal

Djibril see Gabriel

Dodie, Dodo, Doll, Dolly see Dorothy

Dolores
A Spanish name meaning 'sorrow', Dolores is taken from the title of the Virgin Mary as Our Lady of the Sorrows, and was at first used for girls born on 15 September, the feast day of the Seven Sorrows of Mary. Despite the religious nature of the name, the pet forms have gained notoriety, one being attached to the adventuress **Lola** Montez, the other, **Lolita**, inescapably attached to Nabokov's novel (1955). Dolores was particularly popular in the USA in the 1930s. Other Spanish names associated with the Virgin Mary are **Mercedes**, 'Our Lady of Mercy', **Consuelo** from *Neustra Senora del Consuelo* 'Our Lady of Consolation', which explains the apparently masculine form, **Guadalupe** from Our Lady of Guadalupe and **Montserrat**, a Spanish place name meaning 'jagged mountain', where there is a famous monastery with a Black Madonna, which is the patron of Catalonia. **Lourdes**, where St Bernadette had a vision of Mary and which has

subsequently become a major place of healing pilgrimage, is famously the name given by Madonna to her daughter, but is recorded much earlier.

Dolph, Dolphus see **Adolf, Randolph**

Domhnall see **Donald**

Dominic
Dominic comes from the Latin meaning 'of the Lord' and therefore has the same root-sense as CYRIL. It may at first have been used for those born on a Sunday, the day of the Lord, but since the thirteenth century it has been associated with St Dominic, the founder of the Dominican Order. The old-fashioned spelling **Dominick** is sometimes used, and the name can be shortened to **Dom** and **Nic**. **Dominique**, from the French, is the usual feminine form of the name although it is also a masculine in French. The Latin **Dominica** can also be found.

Donagh see **Duncan**

Donald
Donald is the most usual form of the Celtic name **Donal** (**Domhnall**, **Domnall**), meaning 'world-mighty'; in eighth- and ninth-century Ireland it was regarded as a royal name. It was very well used in North America for the first three-quarters of the nineteenth century, where it was a particularly popular choice with those of Scottish descent. **Don** and **Donnie** or **Donny** are the short forms. There is no common feminine form, although **Donella, Donelle** and **Donalda** (particularly in Scotland) have been used (see also under DONNA).

Donna
This is the Italian word for 'lady' and is a fairly recent name, not found before the 1920s. It probably derives from **Madonna**, the Italian for 'My Lady', a title often given to the Virgin Mary. This was rarely found outside the American Middle West until given notoriety by the singer. **Ladonna**, 'the lady', also came into use in the United States in the early part of the twentieth century. Donna was very well used in the USA between the 1930s and 1970s (where it is sometimes used as a feminine of DONALD), but did not become popular in the UK until the 1960s.

Donnchadh see **Duncan**

Donovan
This is an Irish surname, originally *Donnduban*, meaning 'dark brown (person)', now used as a first name. Modern use was inspired by the Scottish-born singer Donovan Leich who, in his early career, was known only by his first name. The name is well used in the USA.

Donte, Dante
In the USA, Donte was until recently the most usual form of the Italian name better known elsewhere as **Dante**, thanks to the fame of the great Italian poet Dante Alighieri (1265–1321). Both are contractions of the name **Durante**, meaning 'enduring, steadfast' from the same Latin root as the word 'durable'. African-Americans also use the name in blends such as **Devonte** (see DEVIN) and **Dontavius**, a blend of Donte and Octavius (see OCTAVIA).

Dora see **Dorothy, Theodore**

Dorcas see **Tabitha**

Doreen, Dorinda, Dorina, Dorinne see **Dorothy**

Doris, Dorian
Doris means 'Dorian woman', the masculine name **Dorian** being 'Dorian man'. The Dorians were an early Greek tribe who gave their name to the Doric order of architecture. Doris seems to have come into use at the beginning of the nineteenth century, but became popular only at the end of that century, around the time Oscar Wilde (1854–1900) seems to have invented the masculine form for his *A Portrait of Dorian Gray* (1891). This story of a beautiful but corrupt youth with a portrait in his

attic which shows the true ravages of time and vice does not seem to have put parents off the name, which is quietly but steadily used. Doris has been little used in the UK since the 1940s, but retained its popularity for longer in the USA, perhaps thanks to the popularity of the film star Doris Day. Both Dorian and **Dorien(ne)** are now used for girls, while various elaborations and spelling variants blend names for both boys and girls into variants of DARIA and DARREN. Dorian has been little used in the UK until recently, probably because of the associations of the Wilde story, but is used regularly in the USA.

Dorothy, Dorothea

This name means 'gift of God'. It has long been a popular name, as is reflected in the use of the short forms **Doll** and **Dolly** for the toy – in use since the late seventeenth century, although earlier the word could mean 'a mistress'. Other short forms are DEE, **Dora**, **Dodie**, **Dodo**, **Dot**, **Dorrit** (unusual, but kept alive by Dickens), **Dorrie** or **Dorry** and **Thea** (shared with Theodora; see THEODORE). **Doreen** is probably an Irish elaboration of the name which was popularised by a novel with the name as its title, published in 1894, and **Dorinda** is a literary elaboration of the eighteenth century, with **Dorinne** another elaboration. An alternative form, **Dorina**, is currently popular in Hungary and France. There is no masculine form of the name, but a number of other names have the same meaning, including **Deodatus**, THEODORE and JONATHAN.

Douglas

Douglas, with its short forms **Doug**, **Dougie**, **Duggie**, is a Scottish surname derived from a river whose Gaelic name means 'blue-black'. In the Renaissance, the name was used for both sexes, but it is now exclusively masculine, with **Douglasina** a rare feminine. **Dougal** or **Dugald** comes from the same root and means 'black(-haired) stranger', a name given to the invading Danish Vikings; the name **Fingal**, 'fair stranger', being given to the blonder Norwegians (see under FINLAY). **Duff** has much the same meaning: 'dark-haired'. Outside Scotland, Douglas has not been particularly well used in the UK since the 1920s, but in the USA it was, like many other Scottish names, well used from the 1950s.

Dov

Dov is a Jewish boy's name meaning 'bear'.

Drake

As a surname Drake can either be from the word for a male duck or else from the Scandinavian word for a dragon. Use of the name as a boy's first name has been climbing steadily since the 1980s. There is a young actor called Drake Bell who has starred in a number of American TV shows.

Draven see Devin

Dreena, Drew, Drogo see Andrew

Drusilla

Drusilla is one of the names used by the Roman imperial family. According to Roman tradition, it was first used in its masculine form, **Drusus**, by a man who had killed a Gaulish chieftain called *Drausus* in battle, and who adopted the name to commemorate this deed. This name is said to mean 'firm, rigid'. Its introduction to England does not, however, come from this exalted source, but from a brief mention of a Drusilla in the Acts of the Apostles, thereby giving the name respectability in the eyes of the Puritans who first used it.

Drystan see Tristan

Duane, Dwane, Dwayne

This is an Irish surname, probably meaning 'son of the little dark one'. Its great popularity as a first name in recent decades seems to owe much to the success of the pop singer Duane Eddy in the 1950s. In recent years, the form **DeWayne**, as if combining the fashionable 'De-' prefix with WAYNE, has also appeared in the USA.

Dudley
The name of the English town of Dudley means 'Dudda's clearing or wood'; and Dudda may be an Anglo-Saxon nickname for a dumpy man. It became a surname, and in England an aristocratic title, which encouraged its use in the nineteenth century as a first name. In 1630 a man called Thomas Dudley emigrated to Massachusetts, where he married three times, had seven children and was a pillar of society until he died in 1653. His descendants used his surname as a first name, and it spread from them to the general public.

Duff see Douglas

Dugald, Duggie see Douglas

Duke see Madoc

Dulcie
This is a nineteenth-century feminine name, based on the Latin word *dulcis* ('sweet'), although forms of the name had existed in the Middle Ages, and **Dulcibella** was occasionally used in the eighteenth century. It is little used today. In the USA it has been all but extinct since the beginning of the twentieth century, probably because in slave-owning days it was a conventional name for a housemaid. However, the Spanish form **Dulce** has been increasing in use since the 1990s.

Duleep see Dilip

Duncan
This was originally a pet form of the old Gaelic name **Donagh (Donnchadh)**, which means 'brown warrior'. However, Duncan looks more as if it is derived from the Gaelic words for 'brown head', linking it with the group of names under DOUGLAS, and it is often understood in this way. The name, which is used steadily in Scotland, has strong associations with Shakespeare's *Macbeth* outside that country.

Dunstan
St Dunstan, whose name means 'dark hill', is one of the great Anglo-Saxon saints. He was archbishop of Canterbury, the adviser of the kings of his time, and responsible for the revival of monasticism in tenth-century England. He also devised a coronation service which is still the basis of the one used today.

Durante see Donte

Dustin
The spread of this surname as a first name owes much to the fame of the actor Dustin Hoffman, although there was an earlier American film actor called Dustin Farnam, after whom Hoffman is said to have been named. The origin of the surname is obscure, but it may be from the French form of the Viking name that is the origin of Thurstan (see THORA).

Dwane, Dwayne see Duane

Dwight
Modern use of this boy's name is largely inspired by the respect in which American president Dwight D. Eisenhower (1890–1969), supreme commander of the Allied forces in western Europe during World War II, is held. The original use of the name seems to have been in honour of Timothy Dwight (1752–1817), an American educator, theologian and poet who had a major influence on the thinking of his contemporaries.

Dyan, Dynna see Diana

Dylan
Dylan is a Welsh name from heroic legend, traditionally understood as 'son of the wave'. Its spread is due to the Welsh poet Dylan Thomas, and also to the singer Bob Dylan, generally referred to by his surname. Bob Dylan is said to have been inspired in his choice of stage name by the character of US Marshal Matt Dillon in the then very popular television cowboy series *Gunsmoke*, but then to have modified it to match the poet. The spellings **Dillon** or **Dillan** are also used. The Welsh pronounce the 'Y' in

Dylan with a 'u' sound, but Dylan Thomas preferred the English pronunciation, so elsewhere it is pronounced with an 'i' sound. The spelling **Dylon** has also appeared, and the name is beginning to be used for girls. The name is currently popular in many countries including Wales, Scotland, Ireland, England, Canada, the USA and France

Dymphna

Dymphna or **Dympna** is an Irish name, perhaps meaning 'befitted'. There is a St Dympna of Gheel who is the patron saint of the insane, but little is known of her, and the story of her being an early Irish princess who fled to Belgium to escape the incestuous attentions of her father owes more to folk-tale than to history.

E

Eabha see **Eve**

Eachann see **Hector**

Eadan, Eadaoin see **Etain**

Eamon, Eamonn see **Edmond**

Eanna see **Enda**

Earl

With its variant **Erle** this is the Old English word for 'a noble', now a title, used as a first name. It is rare in the United Kingdom, but not unusual in the United States, where its use may be from a family name – originally born by someone who was a servant of an earl – rather than a title.

Earnest see Ernest

Eartha

Although this name is hardly known in this country other than from the singer Eartha Kitt, it is one of a group of names well established among the African-American population of the American South. Attempts have been made to link this name with an old Germanic earth goddess, but the name has a much more recent source. According to the 1953 edition of the journal *Names*, 'if a mother has lost two children in childbirth or shortly thereafter, she can be assured of the survival of her third child, according to popular belief, only if the second dead baby lies buried face down in its grave and the new baby is named for Mother Earth'. For boys, names such as CLAY, Clayton, ASHLEY or Sandy would be chosen. For girls, the name would be taken from the word 'earth', and included Eartha, **Ertha** and **Erthel**.

Easton

Easton is a surname, from a place which was originally a 'settlement in the east', now used as a boy's first name.

Eavan see Aoife

Ebenezer

Ebenezer is a biblical name, but of a rather different kind from the majority. It is not a personal name in the Bible, but first appears as a place name (1 Samuel 4:1) and later as the name of a memorial stone erected to commemorate an Israelite victory (1 Samuel 7:12). The word means 'stone of help', and Samuel sets it up as 'hitherto hath the Lord helped us'. The name was introduced by the Puritans, and it has been suggested that it was first adopted by the early American Puritan settlers with reference to Samuel's words. It is certainly more frequently used in the United States than in Great Britain, often in its short form, **Eben**, which by the twentieth century had come to be used in American literature as a typical backwoods man.

Ebony

This is a twentieth-century girl's name, particularly popular from the 1970s-1990s among families seeking a name suggesting blackness, beauty and preciousness. **Sable** is sometimes used in the same way. Ebony is currently well used in Australia.

Ebrilla, Ebrillwen see April

Eck, Ecky see **Alexander**

Ed, Eddie see **Edgar, Edmond, Edward, Edwin**

Edana see **Aidan, Edna**

Eden

The Hebrew name for the biblical Eden means 'place of pleasure', and the choice of Eden as a first name – given to both boys and girls, but predominantly female – is part of a pattern of naming that has arisen in recent years, particularly in the USA, of using religious words, such as HEAVEN, as first names. Earlier incidents of Eden as a first name can usually be ascribed to use of the surname. The modern use of Eden seems to have started in Israel.

Edgar

Edgar comes from the common Old English name-element *ead* ('happy, fortunate') plus the common *gar* ('spear'). It remained in use after the Norman Conquest, but became obsolete in the Middle Ages, except for such uses as Shakespeare's for the virtuous brother in *King Lear*, where the names used in the play reflect the early English setting. It was revived in the later eighteenth century and use boosted in the USA, where it is currently well used, by the publication of Charles Brockden Brown's novel *Edgar Huntly* in 1800, which was one of the earliest purely American novels. It shares the short forms common to all the Ed- names: **Ed, Eddy, Ned, Neddy** and **Ted** and **Teddy**.

Edie see **Adam, Edith**

Edison

This is a surname, meaning 'son of EDWARD', which is sometimes used as a boy's first name. Thomas Edison was a prominent inventor.

Edith

Edith is the one surviving Old English feminine name that shows the common name-element *ead* ('happy, fortunate') which is found in so many masculine names. It was the name of two English kings' daughters, one in the ninth and one in the tenth century, both of whom were canonised, and the name probably owes much of its early popularity to these two saints. The original form of the name was *Eadgyth*, the second element meaning 'battle'. Edith is sometimes shortened to **Edie**, and can be found in the Latinate form **Editha**.

Edmond, Edmund

This is an Old English name formed from *ead* and *mund* giving 'happy or fortunate protection'. **Eamon** or **Eamonn** is the Irish form of the name which shares the usual short forms with other Ed- names. King Edmund the Martyr was a ninth-century king of East Anglia who, according to his Old English biographer, was taken prisoner by the Vikings because he refused to fight, wishing to follow Christ's example. He was martyred by them in a way similar to St SEBASTIAN, being used as target practice for their spears until he was covered with their missiles 'just like a hedgehog's spines'. He was buried at Bury St Edmunds, where many miracles were ascribed to him.

Edna

A name of disputed origin, Edna occurs in the Apocrypha as the name of Enoch's wife and of Tobias's mother-in-law, in which case it probably comes from the Hebrew meaning 'pleasure'. However, it has also been described as a form of the name Edwina or of Ed(a)na, a form of EITHNE. However, the use of the name in English may be as an invented name. The novelist Charlotte M. Younge used the name for a character in a novel she wrote in 1860, which is the earliest certain use of it recorded so far. But she did not include the name in her seminal two-volume book on first names, which suggests it was not in current use at the time. The name was then given wide publicity as the pen name of the very popular novelist Edna Lyell who was a commercial success from 1879.

Edom see **Adam**

Edred

An Old English name meaning 'fortunate counsel', Edred was made more widely known at the beginning of the twentieth century by its use for the hero of E. Nesbit's *The House of Arden*.

Edward

This is the most popular of the Old English names beginning with the element Ed- ('prosperous, fortunate'), this time combined with the element meaning 'guard'. Its original popularity must owe much to its being the name of two canonized English kings. The first, Edward the Martyr (c. 963–78), was a boy-king assassinated for what were probably political ends (see further under ELFRIDA). The second was King Edward the Confessor (c. 1002–66), the last legitimate Saxon king of England. He had been brought up in Normandy, favoured the Normans at his court and had no children. William the Conqueror based his claim on the English throne on his having been made, so he said, Edward's heir, which would explain why this saint's name was one of the few Old English names to survive in common use after the Conquest. It was given a further boost by Henry III, who was devoted to the cult of Edward the Confessor and who chose it in 1239 as the name of his heir, later Edward I, who was succeeded in turn by two more Edwards. It shares the short forms **Ed**, **Eddy**, **Ned**, **Neddy**, **Ted** and **Teddy** with the other names in this group. In the USA the Spanish form **Eduardo** is well used.

Edwin

Edwin is an Old English name formed from *ead* wand *win* 'friend' giving the meaning 'fortunate friend' and was the name of a seventh-century king of Northumbria who was an early convert to Christianity. **Edwina** is a feminine form of the name coined in the nineteenth century. The names have the same short forms as EDWARD.

Efa see Eve

Effie, Effy see Euphemia

Efrain, Efren see Ephraim

Egbert

This was a common Old English name, formed from *ecg* 'edge of a sword' and *beorht* 'bright'. Its users included an archbishop of York, a hermit-saint, and a tenth-century king who became overlord of the whole country. Like many other Old English names it was revived in the nineteenth century, but is now rare.

Egidia see Giles

Ehren see Aaron

Eilan see Elon

Eileen, Aileen

The Norman conquerors brought over with them the name **Aveline**, which developed into the surname **Evelyn**. This was adopted first as a man's name in the seventeenth century, but has now become predominantly feminine, although the author Evelyn Waugh (1903–66) still keeps an awareness of the masculine use very much alive. The origin of Aveline is not clear; it could be from the Old French word for 'hazel nut', or it may come from the same obscure source as AVICE. In Ireland Aveline became **Aibhilin** or **Eibhlin**. The 'bh' could either be pronounced 'v', in which case the name was anglicised as Evelyn, or be silent, in which case it was anglicised as **Aileen** or Eileen, with **Aily** or **Eily** as pet forms. The occasional use of **Aylin** should probably be seen as a variant of these. Eileen was a very popular name in Ireland and in the UK in the first half of the twentieth century, but is not notably popular now. When it is used it is more likely to be spelt Aileen. The Evelyn form is sometimes seen as an elaboration of EVE, and has various elaborations of its own: **Evelina** is the Latinate form of the name and **Evilina**, **Eveline**, **Evaline** and **Eveleen** are variants. These as pronounced with a long vowel in the UK, but with a short one in the USA. Evelyn is currently well used in the USA.

Eilian

This is a Welsh saint's name. The saint was masculine, but the name is now used for both sexes. According to legend St Eilian came to Anglesey from Rome and the king awarded Eilian as much land as his pet deer could cover before the king's hounds caught him. The deer leapt a gorge and escaped the hounds and Eilian's foundation ended up with vast lands.

Eilidh

Eilidh is the Scots Gaelic form of HELEN, so means 'bright'. It is sometimes found as **Ailie**, which reflects the pronunciation. It has been popular in Scotland for a number of years.

Eilis, Ailis

These Irish names, often spelt phonetically in forms such as **Eil(l)ish** and **Ailish**, are usually regarded as variants of the same name, although strictly speaking Eilis is an Irish form of ELIZABETH, and **Ailis** of ALICE. However, as variation between Ai- and Ei- is common in Irish names (compare EILEEN and Aileen), this distinction has been lost.

Eilon see Elon

Eiluned see Lynette

Eilwyn see Alvin

Eimear, Eimhear see Emer

Einion, Einiona see Eynon

Eira

A Welsh feminine name meaning 'snow', Eira is also found in the form **Eiry**. There are many Welsh names from this root; among the most popular are **Eirlys** ('snowdrop') **Eiriol** ('snowy') and **Eirwen** ('snow-white'), which has **Eirwyn** as a masculine form. **Gwyneira** reverses the elements, giving 'white-snow'. **Eirian**, which can be used for either sex, looks as if it should belong with the same group, but is thought by some to come from the word *arian* ('silver') although most describe it as meaning 'splendour, bright'. **Eiriana** and **Eirianedd** are specifically feminine forms of this name.

Eirene see Irene

Eithne

According to medieval legend, Eithne was the name of one of the divine inhabitants of ancient Ireland who was miraculously converted to Christianity. As a result, it became a popular name in religious circles, as well as a royal name. One of the early saints who bore her name is known as St **Ethenia**, and the name, which died out but was revived in the twentieth century, is also found as **Ethna**, **Etney** and **Ethni**. ENA and EDNA are anglicised versions of the name.

Elaine

This is an Old French form of the name HELEN. However, since it is the name of a character in the Arthurian romances – she seduces Sir Lancelot and becomes the mother of Sir Galahad – it is possible the name comes from, or has been influenced by, the Welsh name **Elain** ('a fawn'), for many of the Arthurian names have a Welsh origin. Some regard it as a short form of ELEANOR. Elaine was introduced to the general public in the nineteenth century in Alfred, Lord Tennyson's Arthurian poem sequence *Idylls of the King*, and was a popular name in the UK in the 1950s and 1960s. **Elaina** is a similar, Spanish form of Helen.

Elan see Elon

Elbert see Albert

Eldon see Elton

Eldred

Eldred, with its variant **Aldred**, is an Old English name meaning 'old (thus mature) counsel'. It was the name of the last Anglo-Saxon bishop of York who died in 1069. It was revived in the nineteenth century, but is now rarely used. The real first name of the actor Gregory Peck was Eldred.

Eleanor

Despite the popularity of this name throughout Europe, the meaning of Eleanor is obscure. It may well come from the same root as HELEN, and mean 'bright, shining', but it has also been derived from *eleos* the Greek for 'pity, mercy'; from the Arabic meaning 'god is my light'; and from a Germanic root connected with the word for 'foreign'. It first came into English from France in the form **Alienor**, and has developed spellings such as **Eleanore** and **Elinor**. Its short forms include ELLA, ELLEN, **Nell**, **Nellie**, **Nelly** and NORA, and more recently **Lainey** (but see under LANE). **Eleonora** is an Italian form of the name, which has a short form **Leonora** (sometimes **Leanora** or **Lenora**), made famous by Beethoven, while another form, **Lenore**, has been given fame by E.A. Poe (1809–49). **Annora** is said to be a northern English form of the name (see also HONORIA). ELAINE is sometimes treated as a form of the name. Eleanor has been steadily popular in the UK for a number of years.

Eleasha see Alice

Elen, Elena see Ellen, Helen

Eleri

This is the name of a fifth-century Welsh princess, as well as of a river and valley in Ceredigion. **Elerydd** is a masculine form. Its meaning is not known. Eleri is sometimes anglicised as HILARY.

Elfrida

This is an Old English name meaning 'elf strength', usually found in the history books in its old form, *Ælfthryth*. It was the name of a very forceful tenth-century queen of England, who virtually ruled the country at one time. She has been held responsible for the murder of her stepson, EDWARD the Martyr, in order to secure the throne for her own son, **Ethelred** the Unready; but despite this unsavoury reputation her name was revived in the nineteenth century and popular in the late nineteenth and early twentieth centuries, and some cases of **Freda** represent a short form. It is sometimes found in the form **Elfreda**. An allied name, revived at the same time but less popular, is **Elfgiva**, a Latinised form of *Ælfgifu* ('elf gift'), which was borne by a noblewoman whose family was persecuted by the same Ethelred. The family enmity led to her marriage to King Canute (c. 995–1035), who was fighting Ethelred for the English throne, and at one time she was his regent in Norway. She, too, had an unfortunate reputation, for she was deposed and 'Ælfgifu's days' became proverbial in Norway for bad times.

Eli

Eli was the name of the high priest in the Old Testament who was given the infant SAMUEL to bring up when he was dedicated at the temple. The name probably means 'high, elevated'. It can also be found as **Ely**, and the name is sometimes a shortening of ELIJAH and ELISHA.

Eliana

The Roman family name Aelianus (Aeliana for women) appears to have come ultimately from the Greek Helios, the sun. Aeliana became Eliana, which spread to Spanish, Italian and Portuguese via the cult of an St Eliana, an early Christian martyr. **Éliane** is the French form of the name, and there is a masculine **Elian**. The name is occasionally found spelt with two 'l's as if it is a form of ELLIE, and the name **Iliana** should probably be analysed as a form of this name, although there is a name **Ileana**, which is a Romanian form of HELEN.

Elias, El(l)iot, Elijah

Elias is the Greek form of the name, as used in the New Testament, of the Hebrew prophet **Elijah** ('Jehovah is God'). The surname **Ellis**, now used as a first name, is derived from this name, and its pet form gives us **Elliot(t)**, **Eliot** or **Eliott**. Elijah, which can be shortened to **Lige**, is a popular name in the USA. You are more likely to find Ellis or Elliot in the UK and Eliott in France, while Elias is more likely to be found in a number of Continental countries, including Finland. The actor Elijah Wood has given his name a higher profile.

Elika

Elika is a Hebrew name, said to mean 'pelican of God'. It is mentioned in passing in the Bible as one of the thirty brave men selected by David. It is now being used as a girl's name, in which case it can be a Hawaiian form of Erica (see ERIC).

Elinor see Eleanor

Elisabeth, Elise, Elisheba see Elisabeth

Elisha

Elisha means 'God saves' and was the name of an Old Testament prophet. It can be shortened to ELI. Its popularity has grown in recent years along with related Old Testament names. Elisha can now also be found as a girl's name, when it is probably best analysed as a blend of Elise and Alicia.

Elissa see Alice

Elizabeth

Elizabeth is the English spelling of the New Testament **Elisabeth**, cousin to the Virgin Mary and the mother of John the Baptist, who was the first person to recognise the significance of the child that Mary was to bear (see Luke 1: 40–45). Her role in the Bible made the name enormously popular throughout Christendom, where it took many forms, particularly in diminutives. The Hebrew form of the name is **Elisheba**, which means 'God is my oath'. English pet forms of Elizabeth include **Eliza**, **Bess**, **Bessie**, **Bessy**, **Bet**, BETH, **Betsy**, **Betty** and **Buffy**; **Libby**, **Lisa**, **Liza**, **Lisbeth**, Lizeth, **Lizbeth**, **Liz** and **Lizzie**. In Scotland, the name became **Elspeth**, with pet forms **Elspie**, **Elsie** and **Elsa**. French gives us **Babette** and **Lisette**, as well as spawning a whole set of names from the form ISABEL and its diminutives. Italy gives us **Bettina** (although this can also be a pet form of BENEDICTA (*see* **Benedict**)), which has developed **Bettyne**, while the Germanic languages give us **Elise** (now also **Elyse**), **Ilse**, **Ilsa**, **Lise** and **Liesel**. BETHAN is a Welsh pet form of **Elisabeth** (the Welsh spelling) and the popularity of BETHANY may have been influenced by this. **Betsan** is an alternative Welsh form. (See also EILIS.)

The popularity of these names has varied over the centuries. Elizabeth was rare in England the Middle Ages, but became popular when Queen Elizabeth I was on the throne, and in the seventeenth century as many as one in four girls could have the name. It became popular again in the twentieth century, first after Elizabeth Bowes-Lyon became Queen Consort and even more so after her daughter became Elizabeth II. Overuse led to a decline in the name, but in recent years it has made a comeback both in England and Scotland. In the USA Elizabeth is among the top dozen names. Lisa was enormously popular in the late twentieth century, but is now much less used in the USA, although still well used in England, Scotland, Ireland, France and several other Continental countries. Other forms of the name that get into the top 100 in England are Libby and Elise, while Elise is also well used in Scotland. Other than those names already mentioned, the names in use in the USA, in order of popularity are Lizbeth, Eliza, Elisa, Lizeth, Elyse, Elsa, Libby, and Lizette.

Elke, Elkie see Alice

Ella, Elle

A Norman French name derived from the German word for 'all', Ella is also used as a pet form of ELEANOR and **Isabella** (see ISABEL). It has been a popular choice in the UK in recent years. The similar names Elle and **Ellie** can also be pet forms of these, ALICE or ELLEN. All these names are extremely popular in many different countries. Elle was little used as an independent name before the supermodel Elle Macpherson (given name Eleanor) became so famous.

Ellen, Elen

Ellen started as a form of HELEN but has become an independent name. It is also a pet form of ELEANOR. Ellen has traditionally been associated with Scotland, and it is currently well used there and in Ireland.

Elli see Elvis

Ellicia, Ellie see Alice

Elliot, Eliott, Ellis see Elias

Elly see Elvis

Elma see William

Elmer

This is a form of the Old English name *Æthelmær* ('noble and famous'), which also gives us **Aylmer**. It is principally an American name and probably best known nowadays from the cartoon character Elmer Fudd, the implacable enemy of Bugs Bunny. Its past popularity in the United States is due to the fame of the brothers Ebenezer and Jonathan Elmer who played an important part in the American Revolution. **Elma** looks like a feminine version of the name, but is a pet form of such names as Wilhelma (see WILLIAM).

Elmo see Erasmus

Eloisa, Eloise see Heloise

Elon

Elon or Ilan is a Hebrew boy's name which is taken from a type of tree, probably the terebinth. In the Bible it is the name of one of the Judges of Israel, who was in post for ten years. The name is also found as **Eilan**, **Eilon**, **Elan** and **Ilon**. The feminine is **Ilana** (but see HELEN).

Elroy see Leroy

Elsa, Elsie see Alice, Elizabeth

Elshender see Alexander

Elspeth, Elspie see Elizabeth

Elton

Popularised through the stage name of the singer Elton John, this is a surname coming from an Old English place name meaning 'Ella's settlement'. Similarly, **Eldon** means 'Ella's mound' – 'Ella' here is a short form of an Old English name containing the same element, meaning 'elf', found in ALFRED and ELFRIDA.

Eluned see Lynette

Elvira

This is a Spanish name of debated meaning, possibly going back to the Visigoths and meaning 'noble and true'. Its associations are mainly with the arts, as it is rare in real life except for those of Spanish descent. It is familiar through the main female character in the Don Juan or Giovanni story; as the ghost in Noel Coward's *Blithe Spirit* (1941); and through the film *Elvira Madigan*.

Elvis

Elvis Presley was lucky enough to be given his father's middle name as a first name, a name so striking that there was no need for him to use a stage name. Its origin has been much debated, but Dunkling is probably right in identifying it with the Irish saint's name **Ailbe** or **Ailbhe**, usually anglicised as **Alby**, **Elli** or **Elly**. The feminine form is usually anglicised as **Elva**, and there is a place called St Elvis in Dyfed. The name is not unique to the Presley family, but received little publicity before the singer made it famous. It was used steadily since records began in 1880, and 48 other babies were named Elvis in the year Presley was born, down from 74 the year before. This rather casts in doubt the alternative interpretation of the name that, as southerners, the Presley family would have been exposed to the local traditions of creating new names for their children, and that the name is a creation, based on a name such as ALVIN or Alvis (also in use since the 1880s), a name which does seem to be a blend, of Alvin and Elvis. The similar-sounding boy's name **Elvin**, which has as long a history as Elvis in the USA, is from a surname which originally came from the name Aylwin (see ALVIN).

Ely see Eli

Elyse see Elizabeth

Elysia see Alice

Emanuel
Hebrew for 'God with us', Emanuel is the term used in the Old Testament for the Messiah. **Emmanuel** is a variant and **Manny** the short form. The name is popular with Spanish speakers in the form **Manuel**. There are feminine forms **Emanuela** or **Emmanuela** from Italian, while **Emanuelle** is the French form. The name is widely popular among Spanish-speakers and very occasionally appears in the spelling **Immanuel**.

Emblem see Amelia

Emeline see Amelia

Emer, Eimear
In Irish legend, Emer or Eimear was the wife of the great hero Cuchulainn, notable for the self-sacrificing devotion she bore him. The name is occasionally spelt **Emir**, and occurs in Scots Gaelic as Eimear or **Eimhear**. Eimear is currently the most popular form in both parts of Ireland, but Emer is well used in the Republic as well.

Emerald see Esmeralda

Emerson, Emery see Almeric

Emily
Emily comes from the Roman family name of the Aemilii, of disputed meaning. The Renaissance Italian writer Giovanni Boccaccio named one of his heroines **Emilia** in the *Teseida* (c. 1339), and when Chaucer translated this work as 'The Knight's Tale' he introduced the name as **Emily**. **Emmy**, **Emmie** and **Em** are used as short forms. (See also EMMA and AMELIA.) Emily has been one of the most popular choices for parents on both sides of the Atlantic in recent years, being the top name for ten years in the USA and the top name in 2004 in England, and in the top names in Australia and New Zealand. Variant spellings and forms include **Emely**, **Emilee**, **Emilia**, **Emilie** and **Emmalee**. For boys **Emil**, **Emile**, **Emilio** and **Emiliano** can be used, but these are much less common, although Emil is currently popular in Scandinavia.

Emir see Emer

Emlyn
Emlyn is a Welsh man's name, traditionally said to derive from the Roman name Aemilius, the same source as EMILY; in fact, it is more likely to come from a place name in Dyfed.

Emma
Emma started life as a short form of names containing the Germanic element *ermin* ('universal, entire'), such as **Ermyntrude** ('universal strength'). It was introduced in the eleventh century, has remained in use ever since, and in recent years has been one of the most popular girl's names. It shares the same short forms as EMILY, for which it is sometimes used as a pet form. The German names **Irma** and **Irm(e)gard** ('universal protection') come from the same root. Emma has topped the list of girl's names in recent years in many countries, including Scotland, Ireland, New Zealand, Belgium and Finland, and been in the top few in many more. Emma developed a pet form **Emmet** in the Middle Ages, which in turn became a surname. **Emmet** or **Emmett** is now used as a first name for both sexes, but predominantly for boys.

Emmanuel, Emmanuella see Emanuel

Emmeline see Amelia

Emmett see **Emma**

Emmie, Emmy see **Amelia, Emily, Emma**

Emory see **Almeric**

Emrys see **Ambrose**

Emyr see **Honoria**

Ena

Ena is a name with a number of different sources. It can be a pet form of names ending -ena or -ina (also giving INA), such as Eugenia or Helena, and it can be an anglicisation of EITHNE. However, its popularity in the past came from Queen Victoria's granddaughter, Princess Victoria Eugénie Julia Ena, always known as Ena, who became Queen of Spain. Her last name was to have been Eva, but at her christening the handwritten notice of her names was misread, and she became Ena.

Enat see **Aidan**

Enda

Enda (in Irish spelling **Éanna**) probably means 'bird-like' and was the name of a sixth-century saint who was influential in the development of Irish monasticism. He was a prince and soldier who was converted to religious life by his prospective bride, and is particularly associated with the Arran Isles. Enda Oates is an Irish actor.

Endymion see **Adonis, Selina**

Eneas see **Angus**

Enid

This is a Celtic name, the origin of which is debated, but it may be from the Welsh *enaid* ('soul'). In medieval literature it is the name of one of the outstanding heroines in the Arthurian stories, distinguished for her loyalty and patience, and it was brought back to the public's attention by Tennyson when he told her story in his *Geraint and Enid* (1859). In Ireland, it can be an anglicisation of Enat (see AIDAN).

Enoch

This is a rare name, made famous by the politician Enoch Powell. It was adopted by the Puritans from the Bible, where Enoch is an early descendant of Adam who has a particularly close relationship with God. According to tradition, he lived for 365 years and was then translated to Heaven without experiencing death. The meaning of the name is disputed, and it is possible that the name and stories about Enoch go back to a Babylonian sun-god.

Enola

This is a rare name that is something of a mystery, although it became famous when the United States bomber 'Enola Gay', named after the captain's mother, dropped the atom bomb on Hiroshima in 1945. It is associated with Lousiana, and was in use by the 1870s. Some claim that it is a Native American name meaning 'magnolia', but others have pointed out that it is a reversal of 'alone', and that it is also found as a place name indicating isolation.

Énora see **Honoria**

Enzo

This is an Italian boy's name currently very popular in France. There are various theories about its origin. Some say that it is an Italian form of Heinz, a German pet form of Heinrich, the German form of HENRY. Others say that it is from the old Germanic word of giant, *ent*. Others still, say it is simply a pet form from the endings of names such as Vincenzo and Lorenzo. It is possible that two or more of these have fallen together to form the name.

Eoghan, Eoin see **Ewan**

Ephraim

This name means 'fruitful'. In the Bible Ephraim is a son of JOSEPH and founder of one of the 12 tribes of Israel. It was a popular name among the early settlers in America, and for some unknown reason became a traditional name for the grizzly bear, but is now more likely to be used in the Spanish form **Efrain**, sometimes **Efren**.

Eppie see Euphemia

Erasmus

Erasmus comes from the Greek meaning 'desired, beloved' and was the name of an early Christian martyred in southern Italy. As Ermo or **Elmo**, he became the patron saint of sailors in the area, and it is after him that the strange phenomenon of St Elmo's fire is named. Gerhard Geerts (1466–1536) adopted the name Desiderius Erasmus in the mistaken belief that this was the Greek translation of his Dutch name, and the name Erasmus is now most closely associated with this great scholar. **Erastus** is a less common name from the same root and with the same meaning. **Rasmus** (popular in Estonia) and **Rastus** are the short forms of these names.

Eric

Eric is a Viking name, the second element of which is *ric* 'ruler'. The first is more of a problem, but may come either from a word meaning 'one, alone' or one meaning 'ever, always'. After the Viking age it was little used until the middle of the nineteenth century when Dean Farrar wrote the improving book *Eric, or Little by Little*, a moral tale approved of by parents but the bane of generations of children. **Erica** is a feminine form, interpreted by some as a flower name as it is the Latin for 'heather'. **Rick** and **Ricky** are used as short forms for both sexes. In recent years it has been more popular in the USA than in the UK. Eric may be found spelt **Erick** or **Erik**.

Erin

A poetic term for Ireland, Erin is used in many a sentimental poem about the country. It was turned into a first name in the USA, spread to Canada and Australia, and then to England; it has been particularly popular since the 1970s in all these countries. For a long time it was rarely used in Ireland itself, but it is currently well used both sides of the border there. Erin can also be a respelling of the boy's name **Aaron**.

Erle see Earl

Ermin, Ermine, Erminia see Herman

Ermo see Erasmus

Ermyntrude see Emma

Ernest

This German name was introduced into England by the followers of George I when he came over from Hanover to become king. It means 'seriousness, steadfastness' and has the same ultimate root as the English adjective 'earnest' and the name is sometimes spelt **Earnest** under its influence. However, the original German meaning of the name came from a word which could also be used to mean 'a battle to the death'. **Ern** or **Ernie** are short forms and the Spanish forms is **Ernesto**. **Ernestine** is a feminine form which was fairly fashionable around the end of the nineteenth century, but which is little used now.

Errol

This name, made famous by the film star Errol Flynn and in steady use ever since, has been given a variety of origins. Some have linked it with a Scottish earldom and surname; some have claimed that it is a variant of HAROLD or EARL, while others have linked it with the Welsh name **Eryl**, used for both sexes, meaning 'a look-out post'. As many men's names come from aristocratic surnames, this would seem to be the most probable source of the name, but the main source of the name may be literary. In Frances Hodgson Burnett's *Little Lord Fauntleroy* (1886) the hero, who stands up for fairness and democracy, is called Cedric Errol, and this has probably popularised the name.

Ertha, Erthel see Eartha

Erwin see Irving

Esmé

This name comes from the French word meaning 'esteemed', but was early on confused with the verb *aimer* ('to love'), whence the variants **Aimé** or **Aymé** (see also AMY). These were introduced as masculine names in the sixteenth century in Scotland, where they were used in the family of the dukes of Lennox, and spread from there. The name is now mainly feminine and has variants **Esme, Esmée, Esmee** and **Esma**. The name received publicity from the publication in 1950 of a collection of short stories by J.D.Salinger called *For Esmé with Love and Squalor*.

Esmeralda

Esmeralda is the Spanish for **Emerald**, which is also occasionally found as a first name. Use of this name owes much to the heroine of Victor Hugo's *The Hunchback of Notre Dame* (1831). Esmeralda is currently quite fashionable in the USA.

Esperanza see Hope

Ess, Essie see Esther

Estavan, Estafania, Esteban, Estefani see Stephen

Estella, Estelle, Estrella see Stella

Esther

Sometimes spelt **Ester**, Esther is said in the Old Testament to be from *hadassah*, a Hebrew name meaning 'myrtle', although it may actually be from a very similar Persian name meaning 'star'. The biblical Esther was a Jewish orphan of outstanding grace and beauty who replaced VASHTI as the queen of King Ahasuerus (Xerxes to the Greeks). When the jealous Haman plotted the death of all Jews, Esther was able to use her influence to save her people. **Hester** is an alternative form of the name which has been in use since the Middle Ages, and the names are shortened to **Ess**, **Essie** and **Hetty**.

Esyllt see Isolda

Etain

An Irish name, this is the name of the most beautiful woman in ancient Ireland, whose troubled love life was told in the 1914 opera *The Immortal Hour* by Rutland Broughton. The success of the opera led to a brief fashion for the name. It is also found as **Eadan** and **Eadaoin**.

Ethan

This is the name, meaning 'firmness', of several minor figures in the Old Testament, the most important of whom is revered for his wisdom. It has a longer history of use in the United States than in Britain, probably after Ethan Allen (1738–89), who fought the British in the American Revolution, and it has recently come back into fashion on both sides of the Atlantic. Ethan Hawke is a well-known actor.

Ethel

This was originally a short form for a number of Old English names starting with the common name-element *æthel* ('noble'). It came into use as a name in its own right in the middle of the nineteenth century as a part of the revival of Old English names (see AUDREY and ALBERT).

Ethelbert see Albert

Etheldred see Audrey, Elfrida

Etheldreda, Ethelthryth see Audrey

Ethenia, Ethna, Ethni, Etney see Eithne

Etta see Harriet

Euan, Euen see Ewan

Eugene

Deriving from the Greek *eugenes* meaning 'well born', Eugene was the name of a number of saints, the most prominent of whom was Eugenius, bishop of Carthage, who died an exile because of his faith in AD 505. The name is frequently shortened to **Gene**.

The feminine form of the name, **Eugenia**, belongs to an early saint of whom little is known, but who has acquired a highly melodramatic legend in which she figures as a reformed fallen woman, who, disguised as a man, becomes abbot of a monastery; when accused of breaking vows of chastity, she proves her innocence by revealing her true gender. The French form of the name, **Eugénie** (often spelt without the accent), became popular in the UK in the nineteenth century out of admiration and sympathy for the French Empress Eugénie (1826–1920), who spent the last 50 years of her life in retirement in England. Eugénie was the name chosen by the Duke and Duchess of York for one of their daughters, which has led to a slight increase in its use. The pet form of Eugenia is one of the sources of the name ENA.

Eulalia

This is a Greek name from *eulalos* meaning 'sweetly speaking', but the saint who spread the use of the name was Spanish. It is difficult to separate fact from fiction in her legend, but she seems to have been a 12-year-old girl who was martyred c. AD 304 after trying to stop the local magistrate persecuting Christians. It is said that after her death a dove appeared to fly from her mouth and a fall of snow covered her body. Her cult spread to Anglo-Saxon England, where several writers refer to her. Although it is a rare name, both Eulalia and the French form **Eulalie** can be found used by English speakers, and a pet form **Laia** is currently very popular in Catalonia.

Eunice

Eunice is from Greek *eunike* meaning 'good victory'. The Puritans borrowed it from the New Testament where it is the name of the mother of TIMOTHY, a Jew married to a Gentile, who had introduced him to Christianity and given him a careful religious training (2 Timothy 1:5 and Acts 16:1). The name was originally pronounced with three syllables, 'you-nice-see', but this is now very rare, and the phonetic spelling **Unice** reflects the modern pronunciation.

Euphemia

Euphemia, whose name means much the same as EULALIA, was a saint martyred just a few years later, c. AD 307. Her legend, also highly fictionalised, tells of her survival through various attempts to put her to death, until she was thrown to the wild beasts. It was particularly popular as a name in Scotland, and was much used by the Victorians and at the beginning of the twentieth century, but is rarely found in its full form. **Effie** is by far the most common short form, but **Eppie**, **Phemia** and **Phemie** are also used, and Euphemia is also one of the sources of the name PHOEBE. **Effy** and Effie were also used in Scotland to anglicise the Celtic name **Oighrig**, which developed into AFRIC.

Eurfron

A Welsh feminine name meaning 'gold breast', Eurfron is one of a large number of Welsh names beginning with the element *eu* meaning 'gold', such as **Eurwen** ('gold' + 'fair, white') and **Euryl** ('gold').

Eustace

Eustace comes from the Greek word meaning 'good harvest' and was the name of a saint who was popular in the Middle Ages but who is probably fictional. His legend has many connections with that of St HUBERT; it involves the loss of possessions, wife and children and their miraculous recovery, in a form found elsewhere in medieval romance. The name is not common now, but its pet form is one of the sources of **Stacy**. **Eustacia** is a feminine form.

Evadne

Evadne is a Greek name of unknown meaning – it is possibly pre-Greek – borne by two women in Greek legend. The best known of these features in the tale of *The Seven against Thebes* as so devoted a wife that, when her husband is killed in battle, she throws herself on to his funeral pyre in order not to be parted from him.

Evaline see **Eileen**

Evan see **Ewan**

Evangeline

This name means 'good news' and is from the same root as the word 'evangelist'. The Italian form of the name is **Evangelista**, and Henry Wadsworth Longfellow seems to have created Evangeline by giving this a French form for his poem of this name in 1847. Charlotte M. Yonge, writing in 1863, describes it as an American name, but it soon spread to the UK, in both the basic form and as **Evangelina**.

Eve

Eve is the English, **Eva** the Latin form of the name given by ADAM to the 'Mother of Mankind', probably from the Hebrew for 'life'. This meaning led early Greek writers to translate the name as ZOE. In Ireland, Eve has been used to translate the Celtic name AOIFE. It takes the form **Efa** in Welsh. **Evie** was originally used as a pet form but is now widely used as an independent name; and **Evelina**, **Eveleen** and **Evaline** are used as elaborations of both Eve and Evelyn (see EILEEN). Evie is currently very popular in England, Ireland and Scotland, and Eve and Eva are nearly as popular. In Ireland Eva appears in the list of popular names both is the English spelling as in the Irish **Eabha**.

Eveleen, Eveline, Evelyn see Eve, Eileen

Everard

Everard comes from a Germanic root via Norman French and means 'brave as a wild boar'. The surname **Everett**, occasionally used as a first name, is a variant and **Ewart** is the Scottish form of the name. For female names from the same root, see APRIL.

Everild, Everilda see April

Evie see Eve

Evonne see Yvonne

Ewan

The history of this name is rather complex. In the original Scots Gaelic it is **Eoghan**, which was anglicised as Ewan (currently the most popular spelling), **Euan**, Ewen, **Euen**, or **Evan**. In Irish, it is **Owen** and in Wales, **Owain** or Owen. These have long been thought of as the Celtic forms of EUGENE, and this may be the case, but some commentators think that this is a later rationalisation of an earlier name, perhaps meaning 'son of the yew', which may indicate a memory of ancient tree worship, or perhaps from *eoghan* ('youth'). However, these names all overlap with very similar or identical names from different sources. Evan as a Welsh surname comes from **Ieuan** (also **Iefan** and **Ifan**), an early Welsh form of JOHN. Irish **Eoin** (Scots Gaelic **Eòin**) also early forms of John, is pronounced identically with Owen, and almost identically with Eoghan. Ewan names are widely popular on both sides of the Atlantic. The actor Ewan McGregor and the Irish writer Eoin Colfer are well-known bearers of these names.

Ewart see Everard

Eynon

This is a Welsh masculine name meaning 'anvil', said to symbolise stability and endurance. **Einion** is a variant and a feminine form **Einiona** has been recorded.

Ezekiel

Ezekiel was an Old Testament prophet whose name means 'God strengthens'. The name was used regularly in the USA in the nineteenth century, and has been used increasingly since the 1970s. It is rarer in the UK. It can be shortened to **Zeke**.

Ezra

Ezra was an Old Testament prophet, whose name means 'help'. The name is chiefly associated with the poet Ezra Pound (1885–1972).

F

Faaiz Faaiza see Faiz

Fabian

The Roman patrician house of the Fabii, whose name comes from the Latin for 'bean' (presumably because some ancestor grew or sold them), gave Rome a number of eminent fighters and generals. Indeed, according to legend, at one point the family was all but wiped out fighting for their native city. The most famous of these was Quintus **Fabius** Maximus, nicknamed *Cunctator* ('the delayer'), who successfully wore down HANNIBAL and his invading forces by harrying them but refusing a direct engagement which he knew he would lose. It is after him that the Fabian Society (founded 1884) is named. A descendant of the family called Fabian was a martyred pope in the second century, thus giving the name Christian respectability. His name became **Fabio** in Spanish. There are several feminine forms: a French direct feminisation, **Fabienne**; the Latin **Fabia** and **Fabiana**, and **Fabiola**. This last was the name of an energetic and enterprising member of the Roman family, active on behalf of the Church in the fourth century and later canonized; but it is better known today as the name of Dona Fabiola de Mora y Aragon, the popular Spanish-born queen of the Belgians.

Faisal see Faysal

Faith

As one of the three great Christian virtues along with HOPE and CHARITY, Faith was popular with the Puritans. **Fay** or **Faye** was used in the past as a short form, although now used as independent names derived from the old word for 'fairy'. Although the French have a masculine name **Foy**, meaning 'faith', in most other languages the adjective rather than the noun is used, as it is with John Bunyan's character **Faithful**, which has been recorded as a real name. Thus we find Beethoven's *Fidelio* (1805), while **Fidel** Castro illustrates the Spanish form. The mainly Irish feminine name **Fidelma** seems to be an elaboration of Fidel, possibly combined with MARY. (See also VERA.) Fay(e) is little used now, having been most popular at the turn of the nineteenth to twentieth century, but Faith is well used both sides of the Atlantic. Faith and Hope are a popular choice of names for girl twins.

Faiz, Faiza

These Arabic names, sometimes spelt **Faaiz, Faaiza** or **Fayza** are the masculine and feminine forms of a name meaning 'victorious, triumphant'. Fayiz is a related name meaning VICTOR (see also FATIH).

Fallon

Fallon is an Irish surname, originally *O Fallamhain* ('descendant of the leader'), used as a first name. It came to prominence in the 1980s as the name of one of the more sympathetic female leads in the television series *Dynasty*, and has been used quietly ever since. In the UK it is currently receiving publicity as the name of a character in the popular radio soap *The Archers*.

Fanny see Francis

Farah

This is Arabic first name meaning 'joy, delight'. Related names are **Farhat** 'joys', **Farih** 'happy, delighted', **Farhan** 'glad delighted', all used for boys, and **Farha** 'gladness, delight', **Farhana** 'gladness, delight', **Farhi** 'glad, happy', used for girls. **Bishr** is a boy's name which also means 'joy'. Farah is used for both sexes in the Arab world, but in the West is strongly associated with girls, first from the 1970s when the beautiful wife, Farah Dibah, of the Shah of Iran was much photographed, and secondly from American actress **Farrah** Fawcett.

Farall see Fergus

Fareed see Farid

Fares see Faris

Farha, Farhan, Farhana, Farhat, Farhi see Farah

Farid, Farida

Farid or **Fareed** is an Arabic name meaning 'unique, matchless', which has Farida as a feminine form. Farida can also be used to indicate a precious, unique jewel. Farid was the name of a great 13th-century Persian poet, Farid al-Din (1150–1220).

Farih see Farah

Faris, Fares

This is an Arabic word literally meaning 'horseman', but with many of the implications of the English 'knight'.

Farouk

Farouk, also found as **Faruq** or **Farooq**, is an Arabic name describing someone who is able to discriminate right from wrong, and therefore related to the sense of FAYSAL.

Farrah see Farah

Farral see Fergus

Faruq see Farouk

Fatih

This is an Arabic name meaning 'victor, originator'. Related names are **Fath** 'victory, triumph', **Fathi** or **Fathy**, 'one who wins many victories', **Fattah** 'victor' with its pet form **Fattuh**. **Fawz** also means victory, and has related names **Fawiy**, **Fawzi** or **Fawzy** 'victorious' and **Fawwaz** 'repeatedly victorious'. All these are used for boys. The feminine of Fathi is **Fathiya**, Fawz can also be used for girls, and the feminine of Fawzi is **Fawziya** or **Fawziyya**.

Fatima

Fatima is primarily a Muslim name, popular because it was the name of the Prophet's daughter, who was the only one of his children to have descendants. Its meaning is unknown. It is also used by Christians in honour of Our Lady of Fatima, after a Portuguese village where visions of the Virgin Mary occurred.

Fattah, Fattuh see Fatih

Fausta, Faustina, Faustine, Faustus see Felicity

Fawiy, Fawwaz, Fawz, Fawzi, Fawziya, Fawzy, Fawziyya see Fatih

Fawn

The word for the young of the deer is occasionally used as a girl's first name, presumably on account of its connotations of large-eyed innocence. **Bambi**, the name of a fawn in a book by Felix Salten, published in 1921 and turned into a highly successful cartoon film in 1942, is also used, but usually as a nickname.

Fay, Faye see Faith

Fayiz, Fayza see Faiz

Faysal

This is the Arabic for 'judge, arbitrator' and is also found as **Faisal**. It is well used in a number of Arab ruling families.

Feargal, Fearghas, Fearghus see **Fergus**

Fedor, Fedora see **Theodore**

Felicity, Felix

The Romans worshipped *Felicitas*, the embodiment of happiness or good fortune, as a goddess. The name Felicity comes from this and was also the name of several saints, an appropriate name as they were deemed to be happy in having found their martyr's crown. **Felice**, still to be found, was the medieval form of the name, and was used for the faithful and pious wife in the Guy of Warwick legends. **Felicia** is a form of the name used in Spanish and a number of other languages, while **Felicitas**, the Latin word for 'happiness', is a rare alternative.

The masculine form of the name is Felix. This was first adopted as a name by the Roman dictator Sulla (138–78 BC), who believed that he was especially blessed with luck by the gods: not only did he fight his way to wealth and power, but he was one of the few dictators fortunate enough to be able to divest himself of power in old age and die a private citizen. Sulla had twin children whom he named **Faustus** and **Fausta**, from an adjective with the same meaning as Felix, thus introducing another new name. **Faustina** was later also used by the Romans. The French form **Faustine** was given fame by the poet Algernon Swinburne (who also wrote a poem to **Félice**), although the notoriously 'decadent' and sensual poem of that name was only written to settle a bet as to who could find the most rhymes for the word. In Ireland Felix has been used as an English form for the name **Felim** (**Felimid**, **Felimy**, **Phelim**), which means 'ever good'. The traditional use of Felix as a name for a cat is based on the similarity of the name and the Latin word for 'a cat' (*felis*).

Felipe see **Philip**

Fenella

This is the anglicised form of the Celtic name **Fionnuala**, also found as **Finnguala**, **Fionnghuala** and **Fionola** meaning 'fair, white shoulder'. This is shortened to **Finola**, and the two Celtic forms of the name produced further shortenings to **Nuala** and **Nola**, which are used as names in their own right. The form Fenella became well known in Britain as a result of Sir Walter Scott's use of it in *Peveril of the Peak*.

Feodor see **Theodore**

Ferdinand

When the Visigoths invaded Spain in the sixth century, they took with them a name based on the words *farth* ('a journey') and *nand* ('brave'); this developed into the Spanish name **Fernando** or **Hernando**, which in turn became Ferdinand in English. Short forms are **Ferd**, **Ferdie** and, rarely nowadays, **Nandy**. **Fernanda** is the Spanish feminine form.

Ferelith

This Scottish name is strangely neglected by books on names for, although by no means common, it is no rarer than many that appear regularly in the books, and is quite well represented in the public eye – dog-lovers may be familiar with it from the work of Ferelith Hamilton, there is a book illustrator called Ferelith Eccles Williams, Ferelyth Wills (1916–2005) was a distinguished sculptor and Ferelith Lean is prominent in the world of the performing arts. It is a traditional name in the Hamilton and Ramsey families, who regard it as meaning 'perfect princess', derived from the Old Irish words *fir* ('true, real, very') and *flaith* ('lady princess'). It appears to be the same name recorded in Scotland in the thirteenth century as *Forveleth*, and in eighth-century Ireland as *Forbflaith*, which one modern book on medieval Irish names glosses as meaning 'overlordship, sovereignty'. However, the form Ferelith makes it highly unlikely that it has been in continuous use since then, for the way Irish is pronounced has changed radically since the Middle Ages. The related Irish name **Gormlaith** (also found in early texts as *Gormflath*), which means 'illustrious lady' and is in current use in Ireland, has an alternative form **Gormla** (**Gormelia** in Scotland), which reflects its pronunciation, and the modern Irish pronunciation of *Forbflaith* would be something like 'furla'. Ferelith is thus probably a scholarly revival, perhaps of the nineteenth century, of an otherwise obsolete name.

Fergus

Spelt **Fearghus** in Irish and **Fearghas** in Scots Gaelic, this is a Celtic name meaning 'man of vigour'. According to tradition, it was brought from Ireland to Scotland in the fifth century by Fergus mac Erca, who led his people to settle in Scotland. Whatever the truth of that, it was certainly in use by the fifth century, for it is recorded as the name of St Columba's grandfather (see MALCOLM). From the same root comes the name **Fergal** (**Feargal** in Irish) ('man of strength'), also an early Irish name, for it was the true name of the man known as St VIRGIL of Salzburg (d. 784), in his day a highly controversial academic as well as a missionary. Fergal was sometimes anglicised as **Farrell** or **Farall**, which became a surname, now occasionally found as a first name.

Fern

Fern is a plant name which was introduced in the nineteenth century. The variant **Ferne** is also found.

Ffion

This Welsh feminine name is an old word for the foxglove. In medieval Welsh love-poetry it is a typical word used to describe the colour of a lovely girl's cheek. It has also been spelt **Fionn**, while forms such as **Ffiona** blend into the unrelated name Fiona. Ffion features regularly in the top ten names for girls in Wales.

Ffleur, Fflur see **Flora**

Fidel, Fidelma see **Faith**

Fifi see **Joseph**

Finbar, Finbarr, Findlay see **Finlay**

Fingal see **Douglas, Finlay**

Finlay, Finn

Finlay comes from a Scottish surname meaning 'fair hero' (traditionally given as the name of Macbeth's father), used as a first name. The variants **Findlay** and **Finley** are also found. It is one of a collection of masculine names based on the Celtic element *fionn* ('fair, white'). The simplest is **Finn** (sometimes **Fynn**), the name of one of the great heroes of Celtic legend. In folklore he is the giant Finn Mac Cool who builds the Giant's Causeway, but in mythology he is a hero fighting in Scotland, where he was known as *Finn na Gael* ('Finn the Foreigner'), which became **Fingal**, a form of the name well established by the fourteenth century, but made famous by the poems of James Macpherson (1736–96), purportedly by Finn's son OSSIAN (see further under DOUGLAS). **Fintan** is a diminutive of Finn. Two Irish saints bear names from the same root: the fifth- to sixth-century St **Finbar** or **Finbarr** ('fair head' i.e hair) whose name is one source of BARRY, and the sixth-century St **Finian** or **Finnian** ('the fair'). The surname **Finnegan**, sometimes used as a first name, means 'descendant of Finn'. For feminine names from the same root, see under FENELLA. Finlay, Finley and Findley are increasingly popular in Scotland, and are well used in England, with both Finn and Fionn increasingly used in the Irish Republic.

Finola see **Fenella**

Fiona

Fiona comes from the same root as the FENELLA and the FINN group of names, being the Celtic for 'white, fair' with a Latin ending. The name was invented by the Scottish poet James Macpherson, and made well known by William Sharp (1855–1905), a Scottish poet who used it for his pen name of Fiona Macleod. After many years out of favour as a result of over use, Fiona has made something of a comeback in Scotland.

Fionola, Fionnghuala, Fionnuala see **Fenella**

Flann

Flann is an ancient Irish name meaning 'blood red'. It is probably best known from Flann O'Brien, one of the pen names of Brian O'Nolan (1911–66). **Flannan** is a pet form. The surname **Flannery**, occasionally found as a first name, comes from the same root, having originally been a nickname meaning 'red eyebrows'. **Flynn**, meaning 'descendant of Flann' is an Irish surname that has become a popular first name in Australia, no doubt influenced by the fame of the rambunctious Australian dare-devil actor Errol Flynn.

Flavia, Fulvia

Flavia comes from an old Roman name, at one time the family name of the Roman emperors. The name would have started as a nickname, for it means 'golden yellow' or 'flaxen' and would have been used to describe someone of that colouring. Someone with tawny or dark yellow hair must have been the founder of the family which gave us the name **Fulvia**, the best known Roman holder of which was the wife of Mark Antony, who fought actively on his behalf in the civil war, even though at the time he was neglecting his own interests in order to dally with Cleopatra. The masculine forms of these names, Flavian or Flavius and Fulvius, do not seem to be used. The French form **Flavie** is currently in fashion in France.

Flip see Philip

Flora

The name of a Roman goddess of fertility and flowers, Flora was later seen as symbolic of spring. **Florrie** is used as a diminutive or this name and FLORENCE. In the past Flora was particularly associated with Scotland, no doubt in memory of Flora Macdonald (1722–90), who helped Bonny Prince Charlie escape. **Fleur**, the French word for 'flower', seems to have spread from its use by John Galsworthy in *The Forsyte Saga* series of novels, and it is said to have been more widely used after the successful TV version of the books, first shown in 1967. However, the similar Welsh form of the name, **Ffleur** or **Fflur**, has been in use since the mid-twelfth century. **Flor** is the Spanish form of the name. **Flower** and **Blossom**, the English translations of these names, are also found. The masculine equivalent of the name is **Florian**, which is a Roman family name based on the same root. It is the name of the third-century saint and martyr who is the patron saint of Poland and Upper Austria. Not surprisingly, the name is well used in Austria and is currently popular in France, although rare among English speakers.

One of the major trends in new names in recent years is the wider choice of plant names that have been chosen by parents. Almost any plant can now be used as a first name. Among choices recorded are **Anémone**, the French for Anemone; **Azalea**; **Canna**; **Cannelle**, the French for Cinnamon; **Clematis**; **Fuchsia**; **Genista**, the Latin name for Broom; **Japonica**; **Lavender** and **Shasta**, a type of daisy, but also used as a name in C.S. Lewis' *Narnia* books.

Florence

Florence Nightingale (1820–1910), who made Florence such a popular girl's name, was so-named because she was born in the city of Florence. This city in its turn got its name from the Latin for 'to flower, flourish', so that the name really belongs with the FLORA group. In the Middle Ages Florence or **Florent** was quite a common name, but mainly a masculine one, which has long been obsolete except in Ireland, where it is said to be used to 'translate' FLANN. When Miss Nightingale got her name it was a most unusual one. Florence is shortened to **Flo**, **Florrie**, **Flossie** and **Floy**.

Florian, Florrie, Flower see Flora

Floyd see Lloyd

Flynn see Flann

Fonso see Alfonso

Forrest
This surname and vocabulary word has been used as a first name in the USA since records began. It had a sudden blip in popularity in 1994, the year the film *Forrest Gump* was released, but has now dropped back to its lowest recorded level.

Foy see **Faith**

Francis, Frances
In the fifth century a group of Germanic tribes who called themselves the Franks invaded and took over Romanised Gaul. From these rulers the country took its new name of France via the Latin *Francia*; and since only these people were fully free, the word soon came to mean 'free'. Similarly, in England **Franklin** was firstly a title given to a free landowner, then a surname which can also be used as a first name. In the twelfth century, when France already held an important cultural position, a young Italian called Giovanni Bernardone (c. 1181–1226) was considered by his contemporaries to be so Frenchified that he was given the nickname **Francesco** ('the little Frenchman'), which became **Francisco** in Spanish. It was in honour of this man, better known as St Francis of Assisi, that the name Francis became used in various forms throughout Europe. **Frank** is used as a short form of Francis as well as a name in its own right, as are **Fran, Francie** and **Frankie**. **Frances** is the feminine, which has **Fanny** as a pet form in addition to those used for Francis. The French **Francine** can also be found, while the Italian form **Francesca** has now become popular.

Fraser, Frazer
These, along with **Frasier** and **Frazier**, are variants of a Scottish surname of unknown meaning, which are used as first names. The family name is associated with the strawberry because the strawberry plant – *fraisier* in French – was adopted as a punning heraldic symbol. Fraser has been well used in Scotland for a number of years.

Fred, Freddy see **Alfred, Frederick, Wilfred**

Freda
Freda is a short form of names such as Alfreda, ELFRIDA, Frederica and WINIFRED. It has been suggested that the Germanic spelling **Frieda** represents a feminine coinage from the popular German name Friedrich (see FREDERICK). The spelling **Frida**, although originally a Swedish and Hungarian form, is regarded as Spanish as it has spread through the popularity of the Mexican painter Frida Kahlo.

Frederick
Frederick is a Germanic name formed from *frith* and *ric* meaning 'peaceful ruler'. Although it was used by the Normans, its modern use in the UK is due to its reintroduction by the Hanoverian rulers of Britain. It is sometimes spelt **Frederic** in the French fashion and is shortened to **Fred, Freddie** or **Freddy**, and more rarely to **Rick** and **Ricky** (also used for RICHARD and ERIC). **Frederica** is the usual feminine form of the name which shares the masculine short forms. See also FREDA.

Freya
Freya was the name of the Norse goddess of fertility, so lovely that the Scandinavian myths are full of stories of the plots made to win possession of her. She also had some of the attributes of the Valkyries, and fallen heroes were feasted in her palace in Asgard. It has been quite a popular name in recent years in the UK, and is well used in Denmark in its original spelling **Freja**.

Frida, Frieda see **Freda**

Fuad
Fuad comes from the Arabic for 'heart', particularly in the spiritual sense of the word. It was the name of the first king of Egypt who died in 1936. The feminine form is **Fuada**.

Fuchsia see **Flora**

Fulvia see **Flavia**

Fynn see **Finlay**

G

Gabriel, Gabriella

The source of this biblical name, found as **Gavreil** in the original Hebrew, is probably *gheber* meaning 'man' plus the standard angel name-ending *-el* meaning 'god'. There is, however, an alternative interpretation, based on Hebrew *gabar* 'strong person'. This means that the name is open to a number of interpretations. The name is usually said to be 'man of God', but it has also been interpreted as 'God has given me strength', 'mighty God' or 'God is strong'. In the Bible the archangel Gabriel has the role of messenger, conveying God's messages to mortals. He appears to Daniel in the Old Testament (Daniel 8) and to Zacharias in the New (Luke 1), but most famously Gabriel is the messenger who tells the Virgin Mary that she has been chosen to be the mother of Christ. His appearance in innumerable paintings of the Annunciation has made him a familiar figure. It is this role as messenger which has led the Catholic Church to appointed him as the patron saint of telecommunications. Gabriel is one of only two angels named in the Bible, the other being MICHAEL, although RAPHAEL is named in the Apocrypha.

The feminine forms of Gabriel are most commonly **Gabrielle** (originally a French form), the Italian **Gabriella**, or **Gabriela**, the Spanish form. **Gabriele** is a form used by German speakers These are shortened to **Gabe**, **Gaby**, **Gabby** and **Gabey**, forms used for both sexes, while forms such as **Abby** (more usually a shortening of ABIGAIL) are used for girls. **Brielle** is used as an independent name for girls in the USA, and while it is not yet common, it has been increasing steadily in use since the late nineties. **Gay** is used as a masculine short form in Ireland. **Gabor** is the Hungarian masculine form. However the French masculine name **Gabin** and its various feminine derivatives, a name which is increasingly popular in France and which looks like a pet form of Gabriel, is actually a form of the Italian name **Gavino**, the name of an early saint. In Islam the angel appears as **Djibril**, **Jibril** or **Jabri(e)l**, depending on how it is transliterated, but it is not much used as a given name.

At one time Gabriel was a rare name in English-speaking countries, and something of a marker of Catholicism, which is why it was most likely to be found in Ireland. However it is currently enjoying worldwide popularity. While it is only just getting into the top hundred boy's names in England and Wales, it is in the top thirty in the USA and in the top five choices in countries as diverse as Brazil and Lithuania. The feminine forms have been moderately well used by English speakers for longer and are also showing world-wide popularity, although it is not as great as that for the masculine forms. Apart from the archangel, prominent bearers of the masculine name are the Colombian Nobel Prize winning author Gabriel Garcia Márquez; Gay Byrne the Irish actor and the French composer Gabriel Fauré; while the many bearers of the feminine forms include the Argentinean tennis player Gabriela Sabatini and the British singer Gabrielle.

Gael

Gaël is a commune in Brittany, and has been well-used by Bretons as a first name since at least the 1960s, and has since spread to the rest of France, losing its Breton associations in the process. The district name may be derived from the second half of the name of St Judicaël, who died at monastery there. **Judicaël**, which means 'generous leader', is also found as a first name in France. Gael is also the name of an ethno-linguistic group found in Scotland and Ireland, and sometimes used as a synonym for Celt, and some users may use the name with this meaning. The French have a feminine form **Gaëlle**. The name has been brought to the attention of a much wider audience through the success of the Mexican actor Gael Garcia Bernal

Gaenor see Jennifer

Gage

This surname which can have two origins, either referring to someone who worked as an assayer gauging weights and measures or else as a money-lender who took pledges (French *gage)*, suddenly began to be used as a boy's name in the USA after it appeared as the name of the boy who died and returned a monster in the 1989 horror film *Pet Sematary* [sic] which was based in turn on Steven King's 1982 book of the same title. It has been increasing in popularity ever since, and is found rarely in the alternative spellings **Gaige** and **Gauge**.

Gaia see George

Gail

Gail is a short form of the name ABIGAIL, now used as an independent name. **Gale** and **Gayle** are variants.

Gaius see Kai

Galfrid see Geoffrey

Galilea

Galilea is the form that the biblical place name Galilee takes in Spanish and other languages. It has been around as a name for some time – for example an asteroid was named Galilea in 1946. It entered the American name charts in 2002, and it is unlikely to be a coincidence that this was the year that the popular Mexican actress Galilea Montijo won the Mexican version of the TV competition *Big Brother*.

Gamal see Jamal

Gareth, Gary, Garth

The name Gareth was used by Sir Thomas Malory in the fifteenth century in his cycle of Arthurian stories known as *Le Morte D'Arthur*. Where Malory got the name is not clear, but he may have based it on an earlier Welsh name, and it is often linked with the Welsh word *gwared* 'gentle'. Certainly the Welsh have adopted the name as their own, and Wales is where you are most likely to find it used. **Gary** or **Garry** is often used as a short form of the name, but can also be an independent name. Gary was introduced as an independent name by the film star Gary Cooper (born Frank Cooper), who took his stage name from his home town of Gary, Indiana. This town was founded in 1906 by the United States Steel Corporation and named after the company chairman Elbert H. Gary. Gary or Garry is also used as a short form of GARFIELD and can be shortened in turn to **Gaz**. **Garth** is sometimes thought of as a pet form of Gareth, but is also an independent name, based on a surname from a northern English word for an enclosure or small cultivated area. Although it had been used beforehand, it was disseminated as a first name by the strip cartoon super-hero *Garth* which ran in the Daily Mirror from 1943 to 1997 and was syndicated throughout the English-speaking world. **Garret** (see GERALD) is not related to these names.

Use of Gareth peaked in the 1960s, and it was also mildly popular in the 1990s. Gary was popular in the USA from the 1940s to 1960s, but only became popular in the UK in the 1960s, its popularity lasting through to the 1980s. Gary is currently most likely to be found used for babies in Scotland. Apart from Gary Cooper, famous holders of these names include the American country singer Garth Brooks and the Australian children's novelist Garth Nix, while Gareth Williams is one of the most respected scrum halves ever to have played rugby for Wales.

Garfield

Garfield was originally a place name, probably referring to a triangular piece on land, the *gar-* element sharing the same origin as the term 'gore' for a triangular piece of cloth. The place-name then became a surname. Its use as a first name probably started in honour of James Garfield, the twentieth president of the United States who was assassinated in 1881. **Gary** or **Garry** (see also GARETH) are used as short forms, as in the case of the famous Barbadian cricketer, more formally known as Sir Garfield Sobers (b. 1936). The name is currently best known as that of a cartoon cat.

Garmon see Germaine

Garret, Garrett see Gerald

Garry, Garth, Gary see Gareth

Gaspar, Gaspard see Jasper

Gauge see Gage

Gavin

The history of this name presents us with some problems. Early Welsh stories of King Arthur and his knights feature the adventures of Arthur's nephew **Gwalchmai**, which is still occasionally used in Wales. Experts in Welsh seem to agree that the *gwalch* element means 'hawk', the fierceness of a hawk being suitable for a hero, but the second half has been variously interpreted to mean 'May', 'of the plains' or 'fierce'. The way is which the name changed is obscure. It may have passed through the Breton language and possibly been changed to something made up of *gwalch* and *(g)wyn* 'white', but however it happened Gwalichmai appears in early Medieval French romances with the name Gauvain, which was used as a first name in France. In English the name became **Gawain**, but the Scots kept closer to the French, and there name the became Gavin. Until the twentieth century the name was largely confined to Scotland, or to areas settled by Scots, such as Canada. It was widely used in 1980s, although it was not as well used in the USA as in other English-speaking areas. However, it has been used increasingly there ever since and is now in the top 50 boys' names, with the rare variants **Gaven** and **Gavyn**. It is still given regularly in Scotland and also currently moderately popular in Ireland. All forms can be shortened to **Gav**. Gavin or Gawin Douglas (1475–1522) managed to combine being a nobleman and bishop with being one of the foremost early Scots poets. Gavin Maxwell (1914–69) was another prominent Scots writer, best known for his influential book on otters, *Ring of Bright Water*.

Gavino, Gavreil see Gabriel

Gawain see Gavin

Gay(e), Gaylord, Happy

Gay or Gaye comes from the vocabulary word and has been used as a first name since the nineteenth century. Use has plummeted since the since the general introduction of the word 'gay' as a synonym for 'homosexual' in the 1970s. As a masculine name it is a short form of GABRIEL most often used in Ireland. Gaye Search is a prominent television gardening expert. **Gaylord** has been used as a first name in the USA since at least 1769, which saw the birth of Gaylord Griswold who later became a member of the House of Representatives. The Griswolds and the Gaylords were both prominent families in New England, among the earliest settlers, and their family trees cross a number of times. Gaylord Griswold was named after his paternal grandmother, Esther Gaylord. It was never that common a name, but was most used in the 1930s, when the baseball player Gaylord Perry was born. The surname is a corruption of the French *gaillard* 'high spirited'. **Happy** has also been used as a first name for both sexes, but is often a nickname. In the past men with the Arabic name HABIB who emigrated to the USA sometimes found that it has been turned into Happy by immigration officers. There is a Happy Acee III, a highly respected American expert in nano-technology, who is of Lebanese descent. Happy is probably best known as one of the Seven Dwarves in Snow White, although it is found elsewhere in fiction as a nickname of character in Arthur Miller's 1949 play *Death of a Salesman*. Other names with the similar meanings are MERRY, HILARY and FELIX/FELICITY.

Gayle see Abigail

Gaynor see **Jennifer**

Gaz see **Gary**

Gearalt, Gearoid, Gearoidin, Ged see **Gerald**

Geena see **Gina**

Geet, Geeti see **Anjali**

Gemma

Gemma is an old Italian name, meaning 'gem'. It is also found spelt **Jemma**. In the 1980s it was one of the most popular names in the British Isles, but is now little used in England, although still used steadily in Scotland and Northern Ireland. Gemma Donati married the poet Dante, in 1295. The most famous bearer of the name was St Gemma Galgani (1875–1903), a poor orphan who went into domestic service and suffered from ill-health all her short life, but who nevertheless experienced remarkable visions and showed on her body the marks of Christ's crucifixion. Her canonisation in 1940 probably led to the steady rise in popularity of the name. Other gem names are discussed under JEWEL.

Gena see **Gina**

Gene see **Eugene**

Generys see **Nerys**

Genesis

Genesis comes from the Greek for 'beginning, creation', and is of course the first book of the Bible. Its popularity as a first name has been growing steadily in the United States since the 1980s. It is also particularly popular in Chile. While religious motivation is no doubt important, the choice of this particular book of the Bible is probably helped by its similarity to names such as JENNIFER, a perennial favourite in the USA. Genesis is also familiar as a vocabulary word and is widely used as a name in fantasy fiction and in music. A rare masculine example of the name is that of the performer and artist Genesis P-Orridge.

Genevieve

This name first appears in France in the fifth century in the form *Genovefa*. There is some debate as to where it came from. It is generally accepted that the first half is a Celtic element meaning 'people, tribe, origin'; it has been suggested that the second half is a Germanic element with the same root and meaning as English 'wife' in the original sense 'woman', but this would be an unusual combination of elements from two different languages. **Ginette** and **Ginetta** short forms. The occasional use of **Geneva** as a first name is more likely to be a pet form of Genevieve, perhaps influenced by the Italian form **Ginevra**, rather than from the city name. St Geneviève (c. 422–512), who made the name famous, is the patron saint of Paris. As a girl living in Paris with her grandmother she was renowned for her piety, but nevertheless played a prominent part in city affairs. When it was threatened with attack by Attila the Hun, she persuaded the citizens to stand fast, and when the expected attack failed to materialise this was put down to her prayers. When the city was later besieged by the Franks, it was Geneviève who led the convoy that broke the blockade and brought food to the starving citizens. The legend of another holder of the name, Genevieve of Brabant, has been told since at least the tenth century. She is said to have been falsely accused of adultery and to have fled to the forests to raise her child, before eventually being reconciled with her husband. This story was a popular literary subject in nineteenth-century France, and this led to a revival of the name in France. For many years in Britain the name was strongly associated with the 1953 film *Genevieve*, a comedy about a vintage car of this name and the London to Brighton vintage car race. The actress Geneviève Bujold is a prominent bearer of the name.

Genista see **Flora**

Geoffrey, Jeffrey

Geoffrey is a Germanic name which was very popular with the Norman nobility, who introduced it to England. While the second half of the name is clearly from the word *frith* ('peace'), the meaning of the first half is not clear. Some people see the name as a form of GODFREY, others that it comes from *gawia* 'territory'; *walah* 'stranger' or *gisil* 'pledge, hostage'. Since all these elements could be used to form names, it seems likely that Geofffrey represents the falling together of a number of different names. A medieval Latin form of the name was *Galfridus*, sometimes found in English as **Galfrid**. Jeffrey was an early variant, and is the usual spelling in the USA (occasionally as **Jeffery**), with the G spelling more usual in the UK. They are shortened to **Geoff** or **Jeff**. The surname **Jefferson** means 'son of Jeffery' and has been used regularly as a first name in the USA. It was introduced because of the high regard in which Thomas Jefferson, principal author of the Declaration of Independence, was held.

Famous early holders of the name were Geoffrey of Monmouth, whose writings in the eleventh century started a craze for Arthurian stories, and the author Geoffrey Chaucer (c 1340–1400).

George, Georgia, Georgina

George comes from the Greek word for a farmer, itself made up of the elements *ge* 'earth', from the same root as the name of the earth goddess **Gaia** as well as words such as 'geography', and *ergein* 'to work'. Despite the fact that St George became the patron saint of England in the fourteenth century, the name was not in common use until the eighteenth century, when England had four successive kings of German extraction, of that name. St George was, according to legend, a Roman soldier martyred in Nicomedia (Asia Minor) in 303. In the eleventh century crusaders besieged in Antioch, believed he helped them, and brought his cult back to Europe. Edward III of England dedicated the order of the Garter to him in 1349, which is how he became patron saint of England. **Georgie** or **Georgy** is one pet form; in the north of England we find **Geordie**. There are a number of feminine forms: **Georgia** (with the spelling **Jorja** used in Australia), **Georgianna**, **Georgette** and **Georgina**, all of which use **Georgie** as a short form; Georgina is one source of GINA. Both masculine and feminine forms are popular at the moment in a wide range of countries. In the USA the Spanish form **Jorge** (usually pronounced with an 'h' sound for both the 'j' and 'g') is also common. **Jordi** is a Catalan form that is occasionally found elsewhere. The middle name of the football coach Sven **Goran** Ericson illustrates the Swedish form of the name.

Geraint

Geraint is a Welsh name which may be linked to the Latin (ultimately Greek) name **Gerontius**, from the word for 'old'. There was a king of Cornwall called Geraint who died in battle in AD 530. He may have been the original of the fictional Sir Geraint of King Arthur's Round Table. His story was re-told by Tennyson in *Idylls of the King* in 1859, which re-introduced the name. It was very popular in Wales in the middle of the twentieth century, but is not much used outside the country. The baritone Sir Geraint Evans is an outstanding bearer of the name.

Gerald, Geraldine

Gerald comes from the Germanic elements *ger-* 'spear' and *wald* 'rule'. This was brought to England by the Normans, but its history is confused with that of **Gerard** (originally Gerhard from *ger* + *hard*, 'brave, hardy'), which was then the more popular, and the two names were often interchanged. When the Normans invaded Ireland, their leader was a Gerald who was the founder of the Fitzgerald ('sons of Gerald') family, also known as the Geraldins. This lead to the name Gerald being adopted into Irish, where it became **Gearóid** or **Gearalt**, which was in turn re-anglicised into **Garret(t)**, which is sometimes shortened to GARY (but see also JARED). In the sixteenth century one of the Fitzgeralds, Lady Elizabeth Fitzgerald, was addressed in poetry by the earl of

Surrey as 'The Fair Geraldine', and thus a feminine form of the name was coined. **Geraldine** is found as **Gearoidin** in Irish.

Gerald is also found as **Gerold**, **Gerrold** and **Geralt** and both it and Gerard are shortened to **Ged**, **Ger** and **Gerry** or **Jerry** (also used as an independent name and as a shortening of Geraldine). Internationally, the masculine forms of the name are currently more popular than the feminine. Famous holders include the nineteenth-century poet Gerard Manly Hopkins; the Irish politician Garrett Fitzgerald and the actress Geraldine Chaplin.

Gerda

In pagan Norse mythology **Gerd** was the beautiful wife of the fertility god Freyr (the brother of FREYA). The meaning of the name is not clear, but it may be from *garthr*, an enclosure, thus making it related to Garth (see under GARETH). The form Gerda is used to make the name more like other feminine names. The name is best known outside Scandinavian stories from Hans Christian Anderson's story *The Snow Queen* where Gerda heroically rescues her friend KAI.

Gerhard see Gerald, Kai

Germain, Germaine

While this name can be analysed as related to the word 'German', and may be used by some in this sense, the Latin name *Germanus*, 'brother' which early on took on the sense of Christian brotherhood, is the true source. The masculine form, **German** or **Germain**, is rare in Great Britain, even though St Germanus of Auxerre (c. 378–448) is one of the few early saints associated with Britain. St Germanus was twice sent to Britain to counter the spread of the Pelagian heresy (see MORGAN), and is said to have won a notable victory on behalf of the British against the invading Picts and Scots. He arranged the troops in a strong and well-hidden position, and on a given signal they all cried 'Alleluia!'. The invaders are supposed to have been so taken by surprise that they fled without a blow being exchanged. 'The Alleluia victory', as it became known, was accounted a miracle. Both forms of the name are used more in the USA, usually in the form **Jermaine**. The name is found in Welsh in the form **Garmon**. Visitors to Paris will know the name from the district of Saint-Germain-des-Pres, which gets its name from a church dedicated to a French saint who became bishop of Paris in 556. The feminine form is found in yet another saint, the sixteenth-century St Germaine of Pibrac, a deformed child and a victim of what would now be called child abuse, who was nonetheless outstanding for her piety and about whom miracles were manifested both before and after her early death. Her canonisation in 1867 gave a boost to the name. The best-known holder of her name is the Australian writer and academic Germaine Greer.

Gerold see Gerald

Geronimo see Jerome

Gerontius see Geraint

Gerrold, Gerry see Gerald

Gertrude

Gertrude is a Germanic name made up of the elements *gar* 'spear' and *thruth* 'strength'. It came into general use through the cult of St Gertrude of Nivelles. She was a seventh-century Flemish noble woman who at 20 became abbess of a monastery built for her by her mother. She took a special interest in the souls of those in Purgatory, and offerings of gold and silver mice, used to represent such souls, were being made at her shrine right through into the nineteenth century. She is patron saint of cats and invoked to get rid of mice, and is often shown in art with mice at her feet or running up her staff of office. Short forms of the name include **Gert**, **Gertie** and **Trudy**, or **Trudi(e)**. The name had a certain popularity in the Romantic revival of the nineteenth century, but is now felt to be rather old-fashioned. It has been suggested that the unkind nickname 'Dirty Gertie' led to its decline. Gertrude is known in fiction as Hamlet's incestuous mother, and in real life from the American patron of the arts Gertrude Stein, while the short form is found in the actress and environmentalist Trudi Styler.

Gervais, Gervas, Gervase see **Jarvis**

Gethin

Gethin comes from a Welsh word meaning 'dark, swarthy' which would have been used originally as a nickname. It can also be found as **Gethen**. It is quite well used for boys in Wales. Rhys Gethin was a follower of Owain Glyndwr, the last Welsh Prince of Wales in the fifteenth century and Gethin Jones is a presenter of BBC television's children's program *Blue Peter*.

Geunor see **Jennifer**

Ghazal, Ghazala see **Tabitha**

Ghislaine see **Giselle**

Gia

The female name Gia, which has been being used increasingly in recent years in the USA, can be interpreted two ways. It can either be seen as a variant of **Gaia** (see GEORGE) or as a short form of the Italian name Giovanna as in the case of the Italian actress Gia Scala (real name Giovanna Scoglio). Giovanna is further discussed at GINA.

Giacomo see **James**

Giana see **Gina**

Giancarlo see **John**

Gianna, Gianni see **Gina**

Gideon

Gideon is a Hebrew name which probably means 'hewer, smiter' a suitable name for the biblical warrior whose adventures are told in the book of *Judges*. In modern Hebrew the name takes the form **Gidon**. Gideon was one of the great Old Testament leaders who liberated his people from the domination of their enemies. To help him, the Lord manifested a number of signs, including a miracle when dew fell only on a fleece laid on the ground, and not on the earth, and vice versa. The fleece became the symbol of Gideon, which led in the Middle Ages to a curious association of Gideon and the classical hero JASON, an association no doubt helped by the names sharing similar sounds. Gideon was a frequent choice for boys born to Puritans, and there has been a mild revival in the use of the name in the USA along with other Puritan names. The well-known Gideon Bible distributing organisation gets its name from its aspiration to be like the description of Gideon as 'a man who was willing to do exactly what God wanted him to do'. A very different Gideon is found as a super-villain in the Marvel comic universe.

Gilbert, Gigi

Gilbert is formed from the Germanic elements *gisil* 'pledge, hostage' and *berht* 'right, famous'. Gib, at one time proverbial as the name for a cat, is probably now obsolete as a short form, but **Gil**, **Gillie** or **Gilly** (with a hard 'g') and **Bert** are still used. It was a popular name in the Middle Ages, influenced by the fame of St Gilbert of Sempringham, the founder of the only specifically English religious order. He died, aged over 100, in 1189. His order took a special interest in caring for orphans and lepers. There is no English feminine form, but the French have a form, **Gilberte**. The heroine of Colette's 1944 novel *Gigi*, on which the musical is based, had Gilberte, shortened to **Gigi**, as a given name. While neither is particularly popular at the moment, the Spanish form **Gilberto** is slightly more common than Gilbert in the USA.

Gilda

Gilda appears to be a pet form of such names as **Hermengild**, involving the Germanic element *gild* 'sacrifice'. The name acquired an association with the *femme fatale* after the 1946 film *Gilda* with Rita Hayworth in the title role.

Giles

According to tradition St Giles was a Greek hermit called **Aegidios** (**Aegidius** in Latin) who got his name from the simple goat skin (*aigidion* is a young goat in Greek) he used to wear. His legend says he fled to the south of France seeking solitude. There the name was shortened to Gides, and then to Gilles (the consonant change is common, 'd' and 'l' being formed in the same part of the mouth), which became Giles or **Gyles** in English. He was the patron saint of Edinburgh, and for a time **Aegidia** or **Egidia** was used as a feminine form in Scotland; often these were only the official, written forms of the name, and girls, too, were called Giles when spoken to. The French still have a rare feminine form **Gilette**. For some reason the name has never really caught on in the USA, where it is thought of as typically English.

Gilleasbuig, Gillespie see Archibald
Gillian
Gillian or **Jillian** is a feminine form of the name JULIAN, discussed in full there. It is shortened to **Gill**, **Gilly**, **Jill** and **Jilly**.

Gilly see Gilbert, Gillian
Gina
Gina, now widely used as an independent name, was originally a short form of names with that sound in it, such as Georgina, Eugena and Regina. The Italian actress and photographer Gina Lollobrigida, who helped spread the name among English speakers, gets her name as a shortening of **Luigina**, a feminine form of **Luigi**, the Italian form of LEWIS. The actress **Geena** Davis, who has made an alternative spelling well known, has VIRGINIA as her given name. **Gena** is another spelling. Forms such as **Jean(n)a**, which makes the name seem a derivative of JEAN, show how difficult it is to make firm divisions between some names. These variant forms in turn merge imperceptibly into forms such as **Giana** or **Gianna**, strictly the Italian equivalent of JANE, being feminines for **Gianni**, itself a pet form of **Giovanni**, the Italian form of JOHN. Gianna is currently well used for girls in the USA, while Giovanni sometimes appears as **Jovan(n)y or Jovan(n)i**.

Ginette, Ginetta, Ginevra see Genevieve
Ginger, Ginny see Virginia
Giovanna see Gina, Jane
Giovanni see Gina, John
Giselle
This French form of a Germanic name derived from the word for 'a hostage or pledge', it can also be spelt **Gisele** or **Gisèle**. The name **Ghislaine** (the 'g' is hard and the 's' silent), far more common in France than in England, seems to come from an Old French pet form of the name. The name may have started out as a nickname, as the giving of peace pledges in the form of a wife was once common. For example Giselle, the daughter of Charles the Simple of France, was married to the Viking raider Rollo, who became First Duke of Normany by conquest, after her father made a truce with Rollo in 911. Although it was part of the stock of early noble names, Giselle only became widely used in the nineteenth century after Adolphe Adam's ballet *Giselle* was performed in 1841. Giselle has been growing in popularity in the USA in recent years. A prominent holder is the Brazilian supermodel Gisele Bundchen.

Gita, Gitali, Gitanjali see Anjali
Gladys, Gwladys, Gwladus see Claudia
Glenda
Glenda can be analysed as from Welsh, made up of words meaning 'holy, fair' and 'good', although the name may have been coined in the USA. **Glenys** comes from the same source, being *glan* ('holy, fair') plus a feminine ending. It is also spelt **Glenis** and **Glennis**. However, there is a rather grey area where the names listed under GLENN overlap with those coming from *glan*, and forms such as **Glinda** show how variable the names can be. Glenda Jackson, actress and politician, is a famous bearer of the name, while Glinda is well known as the name of the good witch in *The Wizard of Oz*.

Glenn, Glyn, Glynis

Glen(n) and Glyn come respectively from the Scottish and Welsh words for 'valley'. The place name would have become a surname, and then have been used as a first name. Glenn is predominantly a masculine name, but is also used for women along with the more obviously feminine **Glenna** and **Glenne**. Glyn is sometimes a shortened form of Welsh names such as **Glyndwr**. This is another place name, formed from *glyn* and a word for water, used in honour of the fifteenth-century Owain Glyndwr, the last Welsh prince of Wales. The feminine of Glynn is **Glynis** or **Glinys**, or occasionally **Glinis**, although some would analyse the girl's name as another formed on *glan* (see GLENDA). Glenn has always been more popular in the USA than in the UK, and became particularly popular there in the 60s, after John H. Glenn Jr became the first American to orbit the earth in 1962, although its earlier popularity is attested by bearers such as the band-leader Glenn Miller (1904–44) and the Canadian pianist Glenn Gould (1932–82). The actress Glenn Close illustrates a use of the name for women.

Glenys, Glinda see Glenda

Gloria

Names based on *gloria*, the Latin for glory, such as Glorinde, were used in Medieval romances, and **Gloriana** is well known as a poetic term of address used to Queen Elizabeth I, but the name Gloria does not seem to have been used before the late nineteenth century. It seems to have first been used in 1891, the USA, where it is still most common, as the name of the heroine of a novel, *Gloria*, by E.D.E. Southworth. Southworth was at the time a very popular novelist. It was then introduced in the UK by George Bernard Shaw, this time in his play *You Never Can Tell* (1898). The name Gloriana is occasionally found in forms such as **Glorianna** or **Gloranna** that suggest that it has been analysed as a combination of Gloria and Anna, while **Glory** is a rare alternative form. The American actress Gloria Swanson (1899–1983) did much to popularise the name and it still has associations with the media through bearers such as Gloria Estefan and Gloria Gaynor.

Glyn, Glyndwr, Glynn, Glynis see Glenn

Gobind see Gopal

Gobnait see Barbara

Godfrey

This is a Germanic name made up from the elements *god* 'God' and *frith* 'peace'. *Frith* is also the second element in the name GEOFFREY, and the two names are often confused in the surviving records. The Anglo-Saxons had a name **Godfrith**, formed from these elements, but with the Norman Conquest this was more or less superseded by the Norman form of the same name, Godfrey. Nevertheless, some of the Old English names with God- did survive, such as **Godric** ('God' and 'rule'), the name of an Anglo-Saxon saint which is still used in his native East Anglia, and **Godwin** ('God' and 'friend'), the name of the father of the last Saxon king of England, HAROLD.

Gonzalo

This name came into the repertoire of Spanish names through the Germanic speaking Visigoths who invaded Spain in the Dark Ages. An earlier stage of the name can be detected in the medieval Latin form, *Gundisalvus*. This shows that the first part is from *gund* 'war' (also found in the French name **Gontran**, which combines *gund* with *hramm* 'raven'). The source of the second half is not clear, although it has been suggested it may be from the Latin *salvus* 'safe, whole'. Like many Spanish names, it is beginning to make inroads into the stock of first names used in the USA.

Gopal, Govind

Gopal or **Gopala** is a boy's name, which literally means 'cow-protector', but is a title of Krishna and is sometimes combined with the gods name to form the name **Gopalkrishna**. Govind is a related name, meaning 'cow finder' and is also attached to Krishna. The name is sometimes **Govinda** or **Gobind**, and there is a female form **Govindi**.

Goran see **George**

Gordon

This is a Scottish place name, the first element meaning 'big, spacious' and the second 'hill, fort', which became first a surname and then a first name. Although its use as a first name is recorded before then, use really took off after the publicity over the death of Charles George Gordon (1833–85) who died defending Khartoum in the Sudan. **Gordie** and **Gordy** are pet forms. The name is currently in the news as that of the Scottish politician Gordon Brown.

Gormelia, Gormla, Gormlaith see Ferelith

Goronwy

This ancient Welsh name also occurs in such forms as **Gronwy**, **Gronw**, and **Grono**. The first part of the name means 'hero', but the second element is not understood. The name died out after the Middle Ages, but in the eighteenth century with the reassertion of Welsh nationalism, it was revived, the bard Goronwy Owen modelling his name on the medieval bard Goronwy Ddu. In medieval Welsh legend Gronw Pebr is the adulterous lover of Blodeuwedd (see BLODEUWEN).

Gottlieb see Theodore

Govind, Govinda, Govindi see Gopal

Grace

Grace is one of the vocabulary words which were popular names with Puritans, along with words such as HOPE and FAITH. As it has the same meaning as HANNAH and ANNA, it may sometimes have been used as a translation of this. Modern parents may often use it for its physical rather than religious associations. It is occasionally spelt **Grayce** (see also under GRAYSON), and has **Gracie** as a pet form. The Spanish form is **Gracia** with **Graciela** as a pet form, and the Italian equivalents are **Grazia** and **Graziella**. Germanic languages use **Gratia**. The Spanish pet form may account for the appearance of **Gracelyn** in the USA. The various forms are very popular in many countries at the moment. In the past in Ireland Grace was used to anglicise GRAINNE. There is no masculine equivalent, but **Gratian**, an ancient Roman name, comes from the same root. Famous holders include the Lancashire singer Gracie Fields (1898–1970) and the actress Grace Kelly (1928–82).

Grady

Grady is a surname which had a certain popularity in the USA as a masculine first name in the first half of the twentieth century, and is enjoying a revival again. Grady, like O'Grady, is an Irish surname which means 'descendant of *Gráda*', *Gráda* meaning 'noble'.

Graham

This is a Scottish clan name used as a first name. It comes from the town of Grantham in Lincolnshire, a place name which is spelt *Graham* in the Domesday Book and probably means 'homestead on a gravel outcrop'. William de Grantham was given lands in Scotland by King David I in the twelfth century, and thus the family name was transferred north of the border. The name is also spelt **Grahame** and **Graeme**. The novelist Graham Greene (1904–91) and Graeme Garden of *The Goodies* are famous holders.

Grainne

Grainne is an Irish name of disputed meaning. Some link it to *grán* 'grain', some to *gráin* 'revulsion' and still others to *gráidh* 'love', which despite her romantic story, is the least likely. In Irish legend Grainne was the daughter of a king of Ulster who was betrothed to the now elderly hero FINN Mac Cool. Not wanting to marry an older man, she persuades DERMOT, one of Finn's followers, to run off with her. Their legend tells of Finn's pursuit of the lovers and Dermot's early death. Although the legend shows Grainne to be shallow and selfish, the name was popular in Ireland from the Middle Ages. It was usually anglicised as GRACE (the pirate raider Grace O'Mally (c. 1530–

1600), who gave the Elizabethan authorities in Ireland so much trouble, was actually a Grainne), but could also be found turned into GERTRUDE or GRISELDA. The Latin form of the name was **Granina** and the phonetic form **Grania** is also used.

Grant
Grant comes from a surname, in origin a French nickname, *le grant*, which would have been given to a tall person. Although it is a widely found surname it is particularly associated with Scotland, where it was taken by a Norman noble family in the thirteenth century. It has been quite well used as a boy's name in Scotland in recent years, although it is declining in popularity. Its has a steady popularity in the USA, probably originally inspired by the career of General Ulysses S. Grant (1822–85), 18th president of the country.

Granville, Greville
With its variants **Grenville** and Greville, Granville was originally a surname for someone coming from Granville ('large town') in Normandy. Granville is one of the less current names derived from noble families, the Earls of Granville; and Greville is the family name of another distinguished family. Granville Hicks (1901–82) the American Marxist critic and writer, was author of the influential *The Great Tradition* (1933).

Gratia, Gratian, Grayce see Grace

Grayson
Grayson, and the less common **Greyson**, are surnames used as first names. They come from *greyve*, a Middle English term for a steward, + *-son*. It is primarily used in the USA and for boys, but is now also being used for girls, sometimes in femininised forms such as **Graycen**. In the UK the controversial potter Grayson Perry has given the name fame.

Grazia, Graziella see Grace

Gregory
Gregory comes from the Greek *Gregorios* which means 'someone vigilant'; but since the Latin form of the name, *Gregorius*, was more familiar in the Middle Ages, it was often misinterpreted as if from this language. Thus Caxton's translation (1483) of *The Golden Legend* tells us, in the life of Pope Gregory – the man responsible for the conversion of the Anglo-Saxons to Christianity and who made the name famous – 'Gregory is of the Latin Grex, which is to say a flock; and of gore, which is to say a preacher. Then Gregory is to say as a preacher to an assembly or flock of people'. Its short form is **Greg**. The Scottish form is **Gregor**, which has been quite popular there in recent years. In the 1960s the short from **Greg** was thought of as a typically Australian name, but for many years both Gregory and Greg have been commonest in the USA. Gregory the Great was only one of 16 Popes who chose the name, while the name was famous in the twentieth century as that of the Hollywood star Gregory Peck.

Grenville see Granville

Greta, Gretchen, Gretel, Grethel see Margaret

Greville see Granville

Greyson see Grayson

Griffith, Gruffydd
Griffith is the anglicised form of the name spelt more correctly in Welsh **Gruffydd** and **Gruffudd** (dd is pronounced 'th' in Welsh). The meaning of the name is unclear, although the second part probably means 'lord, prince'. **Griff** or **Gruff** are the short forms. **Griffin**, which is an alternative form of the name, is the one currently most used in the USA, but in some cases is used as with reference to the mythological animal. Gruffudd ap Llyweyn who died in 1063 was the only Welsh prince to unite most of the country under his rule. Griff Rhys Jones is a well-known comedian, author and actor.

Griselda
Griselda is a Germanic name. The second half is generally agreed to be from *hilde* 'battle' while the first part is probably *gris* 'grey'. This is a strangely aggressive

meaning for a name which has become so inextricably associated with the word 'patient', with reference to Chaucer's account of the long-suffering wife in 'The Clerk's Tale' in *Canterbury Tales*, a story he took from the Italian of Boccaccio. In Scotland, where the name has traditionally been popular, the name can take the form **Grizel** (or **Grizzel, Grissel, Grisell**). The name is occasionally spelt **Grizelda**, and is also the source of the name **Zelda**. Once mainly known as the name of the wife of the American writer F. Scott Fitzgerald, Zelda has gained international fame from the computer game *The Legend of Zelda*.

Grono, Gronw, Gronwy see **Goronwy**

Gruff, Gruffudd, Gruffydd see **Griffith**

Gruffydd, Gruffudd see **Griffith**

Guadalupe see **Dolores**

Gudrun

Gudrun is a Germanic name formed from the elements *guth* 'god' and *run* 'rune, wisdom'. It is a very common name in Norse saga and German epic. One character of that name is important in the stories that Wagner later turned into the *Ring Cycle*, and another Gudrun is central to the thirteenth-century *Laxdale Saga*, one of the best of the Icelandic sagas. It is still very popular in Iceland. In England the name is probably best known from Gudrun Brangwen, one of the main characters in D.H. Lawrence's *Women in Love* (1920).

Guendolen see **Gwen**

Guenevere, Guinevere see **Jennifer**

Guillaume see **Guy, William**

Gunnar

Gunnar is a form of the Germanic name **Gunther**, formed from the elements *gund* 'conflict' and *heri* 'army'. It is a common name in Scandinavian sagas. Although still not particularly common, it has been used increasingly for boys in the USA since the beginning of the 1990s. However, since the form **Gunner** is also showing a similar pattern of use, it is difficult to know to what extent the vocabulary word is influencing use. **Gunnhilda**, with its Latinate form **Gunilla**, from *gund* and *hildr* 'battle' (see HILDA), is the nearest feminine equivalent.

Gus, Gussie see **Augustus**

Gustav

The origin of Gustav or **Gustave** is obscure. Some claim that it is a Slavonic name, but most think it Germanic. The second element is probably *stafr* 'support, staff', but the meaning of the first element is not so clear. The most likely origin is *Gautr* 'Goth'. The name became a Swedish royal name after Gustav Vasa led the rebellion for Swedish independence against Denmark and became ruler of the country as Gustav I in 1521. This was reinforced by Gustav II Adolf, also known as Gustavus Adolphus the Great, and as the Lion of the North, who ruled Sweden from 1611 to 1632. However, currently the name is most likely to be encountered in the English-speaking world in the Spanish form, **Gustavo**, for it is currently one of the more popular names among Spanish-speakers in the USA.

Guy

The old Germanic form of Guy is *Wido*, a name of uncertain origin, possibly either from the element *widu* 'wood' or *wid* 'wide'. The name was taken up by the French where the 'w' became 'gu', a regular sound change that is also found in the French form **Guillaume** compared with the English William. The name was brought to England by the Norman invasion. There was a tenth-century Belgian saint of this name about whom very little is known, but who appears to have taken to the life of a wandering pilgrim after becoming a bankrupt; and it was known throughout the Middle Ages and later as the name of the hero of a romance, *Guy of Warwick*. However, the name became all but impossible to use in Britain after 1605 when Guy Fawkes became an object of hatred for trying to blow up the King and Parliament. In the nineteenth century writers such as Sir Walter Scott and E.A. Poe used it in their fiction which helped reintroduce it, and it was mildly popular from the end of the nineteenth century until the 1920s.

Gwalchmai see Gavin

Gwen, Gwendolen, Gwyn, Gwyneth
Gwen is an important Welsh feminine name-element, a feminine form of the word *gwyn* meaning 'white, fair, blessed'. It has been used as a name in its own right since the fifth century, and is either the first element or the final one in many Welsh names, as well as being used as a short form of many such names. Confusingly, in France there are many masculine Gwen- names, as in the Breton version of Celtic *gwen* is a masculine word, with the same meanings as Welsh *gwen*. Examples of such French names are **Gwendal** (*gwen* + *tal* 'face'), **Gwenaël** (*gwen* + *hael* 'generous') and Gwenn itself. The most common of the feminine compound names outside Wales is **Gwendolen** (also spelt **Gwendolyn, Gwendolyne, Gwendoline, Guendolen**). *Dolen* means 'bow, ring', and the name may have been that of an ancient moon-goddess. The name occurs frequently in medieval legend. One Gwendolen is discussed under SABRINA, and it is also traditionally the name of Merlin's wife, while his sister was **Gwenddydd**, 'blessed day'. **Gwenda** is a combination of *gwen* and the word for 'good', although it is also used as a short form of Gwendolen. **Gwen(n)ant**, which has a masculine equivalent of **Gwynant**, is formed from *gwen* plus *nant* 'stream', while **Gwenffrwd** uses an alternative word for stream. **Gweneira** (also found as **Gwyneira**) is *gwen* with EIRA 'snow', so makes Snow White. **Gwenfair** combines *gwen* with the Welsh form of MARY. **Gwenfrewi** (*gwen* combined with the word for 'reconciliation') was the name of the seventh-century saint known in English as WINIFRED, via the form **Gwinifrid**. **Gwenfron** ('white breast') is the reversed form of the name BRONWEN; **Gwenhwyfar** is the Welsh source for JENNIFER; while **Gwenllian** (rarely, **Gwenlian**) means 'fair and flaxen' and was in use in twelfth-century princely houses. **Gwen(n)o** and **Gwennie** are used as a pet forms of all these names, but the modern name **Gwenith** is actually the word for 'wheat'. **Gwyn** is the masculine form of the name, which is anglicised to **Wyn** or **Wynn**. It too has many compounds, the best known of which is **Gwynfor** (*gwyn* combined with *mor*, meaning 'great'), anglicised as **Wynford**. **Gwyneth** is often associated with the names in the Gwen group, but is either a feminine form of **Gwynnedd**, the Welsh place name, which is used as a man's name, or possibly from *gwynaeth* the Welsh for 'bliss, happiness'. **Gweneth** seems to be a variant of this or Gwenith. Feminine names in this group currently have a high profile with performers such as Gwyneth Paltrow and Gwen Stefani, while in the literary world Oscar Wilde's popular play *The Importance of Being Ernest* (1886) keeps Gwendoline in the public eye.

Gwil, Gwillym, Gwilym see William

Gwinifrid see Winifred

Gwyn, Gwynant, Gwynfor see Gwen

Gwyneira see Eira, Gwen

Gwyneth, Gwynneth see Gwen

Gwythyr see Victor

Gyles see Giles

H

Haakim see Hakim

Habib

Habib, with its feminine **Habiba**, come from the Arabic meaning 'beloved, friend'. **Mahbub** and **Mabuba** 'dear, beloved, sweetheart' come from the same root.

Haden see Hayden

Hadley

This is a surname, meaning 'heather field' that has recently become fashionable in the USA for girls. This is probably due to the influence of Elizabeth Hadley Richardson, known as Hadley, who was the novelist Ernest Hemingway's first wife. Their life together in Paris is told in Hemingway's *A Movable Feast* (1964).

Hadrian see Adrian

Haidee see Heidi

Hailey see Hayley

Hakim

Hakim or **Hakeem** is from the Arabic for 'wise, reasonable'. Al-Hakim 'the Wise' is one of titles of Muhammed. Hakeem is the spelling preferred in the USA, where it is also found as **Haakim**. The American name **Akim** (**Akeem**) is probably a development of it. There is a feminine **Hakima**.

Hal see Harold, Henry

Haley see Hayley

Halle

Halle Berry, the actress, was named after Halle Brother's Department store in her home town of Cleveland. Use of the name has spread because of her fame. Although the name has only been in general circulation since the early nineties, it is already mutating to forms such as **Hallie** which are half way between HAYLEY and Halle. In the past **Hally** or Hallie could be a pet form of HENRY, or more frequently HARRIET.

Hamid

Hamid or **Hameed**, with its feminine form **Hamida**, means 'praised, commendable'. Al-Hameed 'the All-laudable' is one of the names of Allah. The related **Haamid**, **Haamed** or **Hamed**, with its feminines **Haamida**, **Haameda** or **Hameda** means 'praiser of Allah'. It is one of a group of names, which includes MOHAMMED and AHMAD, based on the Arabic word *hamida* 'to praise'.

Hamish see James

Hamza

This is a masculine name from the Arabic for 'lion'. The uncle of Muhammad, who was an early convert to Islam, was known as 'The Lion of Allah' because of his bravery in battle.

Hana see Hannah

Hank see Henry

Hannah

This is a Hebrew name meaning 'God has favoured me' and is the source of the name ANNA and its variants. In the Old Testament it is the name of the mother of the prophet Samuel. It is found spelt **Hanna** and **Hana**. Hannah is currently a popular name throughout the English-speaking world.

Hannibal

This is a Phoenician man's name, meaning 'mercy of Baal'. It is said to have been particularly used in Cornwall, which has traditional, but unproved, links with Phoenician traders. The historical Hannibal was a third-century BC Carthaginian whose father brought him up from childhood to hate Rome. As an adult, Hannibal invaded Italy via the Alps, and for many years ravaged the country and almost brought about the destruction of Rome, but was finally defeated, more by force of circumstances than by superior skill. (See FABIAN.) Hannibal was in regular if uncommon use in the past, particularly in Italy in the form Annibal, but is now best known from the character Hannibal Lecter from *The Silence of the Lambs*.

Happy see Gay (*see* Gabriel)

Harlan, Harley

Harlan is a surname, from a place name meaning 'hare-land', used as a first name mainly for boys, particularly in the USA. Modern use may be influenced by respect for Supreme Court judge John Marshall Harlan (1833–1911). The name can appear as **Harlen** or **Harland** and there is feminine form **Harleen**, which has been well used in Canada. Harley, another surname used for both sexes, but commonly a girl's name, has a similar meaning ('hare-clearing'). For girls it can also be spelt **Harlee, Harleigh** and **Harli**. There is a female villain in the *Batman* stories called Harley Quinn, and the name probably gains prestige from the Harley-Davidson brand of motorcycles.

Harmony

Harmony is the vocabulary word which has been used as a first name since the 1970s. It is nearly always feminine, although the male film director Harmony Korine is a rare exception. In his case the name seems to have been used in the more abstract sense of 'peace, accord', but in most other uses it is probably used in the musical sense, part of the trend for musical names which includes ARIA, MELODY and **Rhapsody**. **Symphony**, which originally had much the same meaning as Harmony, is much rarer as a name. It is tempting to see an influence of the 1960s television puppet series *Captain Scarlet and the Mysterons*, which featured female fighter pilots, code-named angels, called DESTINY, SYMPHONY, MELODY, RHAPSODY, and Harmony.

Harold

This is the name of the last king of England before the Norman invasion; he was part Danish and bore a Scandinavian-influenced name. Harold is a typical Germanic compound made up of elements meaning 'army' and 'power'. It died out after the Norman Conquest, but was revived along with other Old English names in the nineteenth century. **Hal** is sometimes used as a short form, which is shared with HENRY. Harold was popular on both sides of the Atlantic in the first three decades of the twentieth century, and has a mild revival in the USA in the 1990s.

Haroun see Aaron

Harper

This is a surname, from the occupation, used as a first name, mainly for girls. This is because of the fame of the American novelist Harper Lee, whose 1960 novel *To Kill A Mockingbird* has become a classic of Southern life.

Harriet

Harriet is the feminine form of HENRY. It became established in England in the seventeenth century in the French form Henriette or Henrietta after Charles I married the French princess Henrietta Maria. It changed to Harriette for the same reasons as HENRY became Harry, and then the French final -te was dropped. The name was very popular in the nineteenth century, when the pet form **Hattie** was sometimes used as an independent name, and became popular again in the later twentieth century. **Hally** or **Hallie** (see also HALLE) can be pet forms of Harriet, and Henrietta can have the short form **Etta**.

Harris

Harris is on the surface a surname, derived from the name Harry (see HENRY) used as a first name. However, the name is currently popular for boys in Scotland, which suggests it may be used there after, or at least influenced by, the island of Harris, the home of Harris tweed, in the Western Isles. This would link it with names such as SKYE and IONA. The island gets its name from the Gaelic *h-earaidh* 'that which is highest'.

Harrison, Harry see Henry

Harun see Aaron

Harvey

This is a form of the French name Hervé, a Breton saint whose name meant 'battle-worthy'. Little is known about the saint's life, although according to the somewhat fantastical legends about him, he was a wandering monk and minstrel. Until the French Revolution a Breton church kept his supposed cradle as an object of veneration. The Normans brought the name over to England, and from there the name spread to the rest of the English-speaking world. Harvey was very popular in the USA in the later nineteenth century, probably because it went with other aristocratic surnames that were then popular first names, but use has declined slowly but steadily ever since. It is currently popular in the UK

Hassan

Hassan or Hasan comes from the Arabic word meaning 'good, excellent, handsome', which is also the origin of the name **Hussain** (also **Husayn**). Hassan and Hussain were the two eldest sons of FATIMA and Muhammad's cousin ALI. They were killed and are regarded as martyrs by Shiite Muslims. Hassan and Hussain are often chosen as names for twins. There are feminines **Hassana** or **Hasana** and **Hussana**.

Hattie see Harriet

Havelock see Oliver

Haven see Heaven

Hayden

There are many views about the provenance of this name. Some say that the core form is Haydn, and that it is so well used in Wales because it is a musical country and that it is used after the composer Josef Haydn (1732–1809). Other claim it is a form of AIDEN (*see* **Aidan**). However, as the most popular form is Hayden it is more likely to be from the surname, from an Old English place name meaning 'hay valley'. It is also found as **Haydon** or **Haden**. It is currently used more for girls than boys in the USA, but is predominantly male in England and Australia.

Hayley, Haley

This is a surname meaning 'hay field', now used as a first name. It owes its currency to the film actress Hayley Mills, who was named after her mother Mary Hayley Bell. The name caught the public's attention and has been very popular throughout the English-speaking world. Hayley is the usual spelling in the UK, followed by **Hailey**, but in the USA it is most usually **Haley**, with a wide range of other variants, some of which shade into versions of HALLE. The name is currently well used in Scotland and Australia and very popular in the USA.

Hazel

The name of this small nut-bearing tree does not seem to have been used as a first name before the later nineteenth century, when plant names in general were very popular. It is currently most likely to be used in the Republic of Ireland, although it is climbing in use in the USA, after a number of years of being ignored.

Heather

Like HAZEL, Heather seems to have come into fashion in the late nineteenth century along with a number of other plant names for girls. It has been most popular in the USA in recent years, and is also well used in Scotland. **Heath**, also a surname, is a synonym for the same plant and is sometimes found as a boy's name, which has been given publicity by the actor Heath Ledger. (See also HEDLEY.) Heather is currently regularly used in Scotland and Ireland.

Heaven

This vocabulary word has been climbing steadily in the American popularity charts since it first entered them in 1990. In some cases this was as a result of a novel by A.V. Andrews (published in 1990) featuring a heroine with the punning name of Heaven Leigh Casteel. A number of Heavens have Lee or Leigh as a second name (but these names are also used by a porn actress). In 2000 Sonny Sandoval, the singer in a Christian rock band, announced on television that he was intending to call his daughter Nevaeh – heaven spelt backwards. The name shot up the charts and has even developed a re-spelling **Neveah** to make pronunciation easier, even though it spoils the point. **Haven** may be used as a variant of Heaven, or be the vocabulary name used in its own right.

Hebe

In classical Greek mythology, Hebe was the goddess of youth (which is the meaning of her name) and cupbearer to the gods. Fairly popular in the nineteenth century, the name is rarely used now. As it is also the name of a group of plants, it may be thought of as one of the flower names.

Hector

Hector was the great warrior of Troy who, until he was killed in battle by the Greek hero **Achilles**, was the chief defender of the city in the Trojan War. It is therefore appropriate that his name means 'holding fast', which should probably be understood as 'defender, support'. The name can be shortened to **Heck**. It was particularly popular in Scotland, where it was used as an anglicisation of the Gaelic name **Eachann**, which means 'lord of horses'. Since the Trojan Hector is depicted by HOMER as fighting from a horse-drawn chariot, this, as much as similarity of sounds, may lie behind the association of the two names. Hector is quite well used in the USA at the present.

Hedda see Avice

Heddwen, Heddwyn

These are Welsh names, the first feminine, the second masculine, coined at the beginning of the twentieth century from elements meaning 'peace' and 'blessed, fair, holy'.

Hedewig, Hedwige see Avice

Hedley

This is a man's name which comes from a place and surname meaning 'a clearing where HEATHER grows'. It was popular at the beginning of the twentieth century, but is now little used.

Hedy see Avice

Heidi, Haidee

These are two distinct girls' names, although they may sometimes be used as variants. The first is Austrian, the second Greek: both owe their use to literary sources. Heidi, the more common of the two names, owes its introduction to the popularity of Johanna Spyri's book *Heidi*. It is a pet form of the name **Adelheid**, the German form of Adelaide (see ADELA). In the USA Heidi became established as a name in the USA after the child star Shirley Temple appeared in a film version of the book in 1937. **Haidee** is probably a form of the Greek name Haido ('to caress') and came into fashion after its introduction by Lord Byron in *Don Juan* (1819). In this poem, the adolescent Juan and Haidee fall deeply in love, and the depiction of combined innocence and passion forms some of Byron's most memorable writing.

Heinz, Heinrich see Enzo

Helen

Like HECTOR, Helen is a name from HOMER's *Iliad*. Helen, the wife of the Greek Menelaus, was the most beautiful woman alive, and her abduction, or seduction, by the Trojan prince PARIS, led to the long siege of Troy described in Homer's epic. The name means 'the light, the bright'. However, the popularity of the name throughout Europe probably owes more to St Helen or **Helena**, empress and supposed finder of the True Cross. Tradition makes her a British princess, but in fact she was born in Asia Minor of humble parents, traditionally described as innkeepers. There are many variants and short forms of the name. ELLEN, sometimes ELAINE, and **Elena** are early forms of the name, the last giving **Lena**. These are now used independently. **Nell, Nellie, Nelly** are pet forms. **Ilona,** currently well used in France, is a Hungarian form of the name, as is **Ilana**, while **Elen** is Welsh and **Elena** the Spanish form. See further under ELEANOR, EILIDH.

Helga see Olga

Heloise

Abelard and Heloise were two twelfth-century lovers whose real-life story, preserved in the letters they wrote to each other after they were parted, rivals anything to be met with in fiction. Despite the fact that Abelard had secretly married Heloise, he was castrated by her guardian for having seduced her, and they each ended their lives as the heads of learned religious institutions, only to be reunited in death, when Heloise's body was buried next to Abelard's grave. Heloise is also spelt in the French manner **Héloise** or **Héloïse**, and is frequently found in the form **Eloise** or **Eloïse**, or more rarely **Eloisa**. The origin of the name is disputed. Some derive it from an old German name Helewise, used in England until at least the thirteenth century; others argue that it is a form of the name Louise (see LEWIS), via the Provencal form **Aloys, Aloyse**, which may also have been an influence on LOIS.

Henrietta, Henriette see Harriet

Henry, Harry

Henry comes from an old Germanic name *Haimric* formed from *haim* (from the same root as 'home') and *ric* 'rule'. It was brought to England by the Normans in the French form *Henri*, and the nasalised French pronunciation is reflected in the form **Harry** which comes from it, and which was the normal English form of the name until the seventeenth century. Harry is currently the more popular given form in the UK: possible influences include Prince Harry, and the leading pupil at Hogwarts School of Witchcraft and Wizardry, Harry Potter, in the popular *Harry Potter* series of novels by J. K. Rowling. Use of 'Harry', and the pet form **Hal**, is well illustrated in Shakespeare's *Henry IV*. Henry is the more common in the USA. **Hank** is a pet form more often met with in North America. **Harrison**, the surname meaning 'son of Harry', has shown a recent increase in popularity as a first name, no doubt influenced by the actor Harrison Ford, although Harrison Ainsworth was a popular late-nineteenth-century novelist.

Hephzibah

This is a Hebrew name meaning 'my delight is in her'. In the Bible it is mentioned as the name of the mother of one of the kings of Judah, but more importantly is used by the prophet Isaiah as a symbol of Jerusalem. The name is more often found in the United States than in Britain, as is the name **Beulah** ('married'), which occurs in the same verse of Isaiah. The name is usually pronounced, and sometimes spelt, **Hepzibah**, and has a short form **Hepsie**. It is probably best known through the pianist Hephzibah Menuhin.

Herbert

Herbert is a Germanic name meaning 'army-bright' formed from *hari* and *berht* and found in early records as *Hariberht*. It is found very early in the form of Charibert, king of the Franks from 561 to 567, whose daughter BERTHA married the pagan king of Kent.

It was she who welcomed St Augustine of Canterbury to convert the English (see AUGUSTUS). The name more or less died out in the Middle Ages, but was revived again in the nineteenth century, possibly in connection with the aristocratic surname of Herbert. It shares **Bert** and **Bertie** as short forms with other names ending -bert, and **Herb** and **Herbie** are also used. *Hariberht* also lies behind the popular Spanish name **Rigoberto**.

Hereward see Howard

Herman
This is a Germanic name meaning 'army man'. It is sometimes spelt in the German manner, **Hermann**. It is an ancient name, found in Latin as Arminius, the German general who ambushed and defeated the Roman army in the Teutoburger Forest in 9 AD. The French form of the name is **Armand**, and from this come the unusual feminine names **Armine** and **Arminel(le)**, the latter regarded as a local name in Devon and Cornwall. **Hermine**, another unusual feminine name, also found as **Ermin**, **Ermine** or **Erminia**, comes from the same Indo-European root, but via the Latin family name of *Herminius*, although it has no doubt been influenced by the Germanic forms. See also ARMANI.

Hermione
This is a Greek name, meaning 'dedicated to the god Hermes'. The best-known Hermione in Greek legend was the daughter of HELEN; she was first unhappily married to Achilles' son Neoptolemus, and then to her cousin Orestes. The Athenian tragedian Euripides wrote a play on the subject, and the name probably became more widely known in the seventeenth century through the French playwright Racine's *Andromache* (1667), which adapted Euripides' work. In the twentieth century, the name was given publicity by two comic actresses, Hermione Baddeley and Hermione Gingold. Shakespeare used Hermione in *A Winter's Tale* and he introduced another form of the name, **Hermia**, in *A Midsummer Night's Dream*, but this name has not been much used by parents. Hermione has recently had new publicity in the popular *Harry Potter* series of novels by J. K. Rowling, as the name of Harry Potter's friend at Hogwarts School of Witchcraft and Wizardry, but this does not yet seem to have increased its popularity much.

Hernando see Ferdinand

Hervé see Harvey

Hester see Esther

Hetty see Esther, Harriet

Heulwen
This is a Welsh girl's name, well used at the moment. It means 'sunshine'.

Hevel see Abel

Hew see Hugh

Hiam see Chaim

Hieronymus see Jerome

Hilary, Hillary
Hilary comes from the Latin *hilarius* and means 'cheerful'. It was the name of St Hilary of Poitiers, a theologian and writer of the fourth century. Since his feast day falls in mid-January, his name was given to the 'Hilary Term' of the Law Courts and some universities, which begins at about that time. The name is used for both sexes, although there is also an uncommon feminine form, **Hilaria**. The author **Hilaire** Belloc (1870–1953) shows the French masculine form of the name. In the United States the spelling **Hillary** is usual, but in Great Britain the original spelling is the norm. The masculine use, now rare, it kept in the public eye by the politician Hilary Benn while Hillary Clinton keeps the American form of the name in the public eye. See also ELERI.

Hilda

An Old English name meaning 'battle', Hilda was the name of a Northumbrian princess who founded the monastery at Whitby where the seventh-century cowherd **Cædmon** is supposed to have written the first religious poetry in English. Hilda was a much respected woman who acted as an adviser to both kings and bishops. The name died out after the Conquest along with other Anglo-Saxon names, but was revived in the nineteenth century, and was particularly popular with campaigners trying to improve the role of women. It is occasionally spelt **Hylda**. From the same root comes the German saint's name **Hildegard**. There has recently been a revival of interest in the work of St Hildegard of Bingen (1098–1179), who was a visionary, theologian, writer on science, poet and very fine composer, and took an active part in the controversies of her day. This name has always been more common in the United States, particularly among those of German descent, than in Great Britain.

Hillary see Hilary

Hiram

Hiram is a Hebrew name meaning 'brother of the exalted one'. It was the name of a king of Tyre who was an ally of King DAVID and his son SOLOMON, and who sent building materials for the Temple at Jerusalem. It was one of the biblical names that became popular in the seventeenth century, was taken over by early settlers to America, and also had a certain popularity in the nineteenth century.

Hodge see Roger

Hoel see Hywel

Holden

This is a surname meaning 'deep valley' which has some currency as a boy's name in the USA. It undoubtedly owes its used to the character of Holden Caulfield, the narrator in J.D. Salinger's influential novel *Catcher in the Rye*. It is said that Salinger chose this name after seeing the names of the actors William Holden and Joan Caulfield juxtaposed on a film poster.

Holly

Holly is a plant name which only came into use at the beginning of the twentieth century. It is sometimes chosen because a child was born around Christmas. It has been popular among English-speakers for many years, both in the standard spelling and in the form **Hollie**.

Homer

This is the name of the great Greek poet used as a first name. It is rarely found in the UK, but is well used in the United States, where there is a long tradition of naming after heroes of the past. The British have not been reluctant to name their children after classical writers such as HORACE and TERENCE, but for some reason Homer has never caught on. The name is now heavily associated with the cartoon character Homer Simpson.

Honoria

Honoria means 'honour, honourable'. *Honorius* was a title given to Emperor Theodosius the Great, and his niece was named Honoria. The name is also found in the forms **Honor** and **Honora**. In England a form **Anora**, **Annora(h)** or **Anorah** developed, while in Ireland, where the name was particularly popular, it became NORAH (*see* **Nora**). In Welsh the masculine form of the name developed into **Emyr** and **Ynyr**. The Breton form of the name **Énora** is currently popular in France.

Hope

One of the abstract nouns that were introduced as names by the Puritans, Hope was originally used for both sexes but is now confined to women. NADIA has the same meaning, and the Spanish equivalent is **Esperanza**.

Horace

Horace is the name of the great first-century BC Latin poet, used as a first name. It was introduced during the Renaissance revival of interest in all things classical. It first seems to have appeared Italy in the form **Horatio,** the form later used as the name of Admiral Nelson. **Horatia**, the name given to his daughter by Lady Hamilton, and also used for his goddaughters, did have a certain vogue at that time, although it is rarely met with today.

Hortensia

This is the feminine form of another Latin family name, meaning 'gardener'. **Hortense** is widely used in France, and the name has sometimes been used elsewhere in this form.

Houston see Dallas

Howard

The aristocratic surname Howard was one of many adopted by parents as a first name in the nineteenth century. The origin of the surname is confused. In some cases it may be a form of the occupational term 'hayward', a man whose job it was to make sure that the hedges were kept cattle-proof; in others it may be an old Germanic name meaning 'heart-protector'. In the past it was also derived from the Old English name **Hereward**, famous as the name of one of the few to mount a guerrilla campaign against the invading Normans in 1066, but this is not now accepted. **Howie** is the most usual short form.

Howel, Howell see Hywel

Hubert

Hubert comes from a Germanic root and means 'bright-mind'. It is the name of an eighth-century saint who is the patron of hunters, having, according to his legend, been converted to the devout life as a young man by a vision of a stag with a crucifix between its antlers. The stag is his emblem in art. (See also EUSTACE)

Hudson

Hudson is a surname meaning 'son of Hudd', Hudd being a pet form of both HUGH and RICHARD in the Middle Ages. Hudson is being used as a boy's name in the USA.

Hugh

Hugh comes from the Germanic word for 'mind' or 'thought', also found in the name HUBERT, and was introduced by the Normans. The city of Lincoln can boast two St Hughs. One (c. 1135–1200) was a remarkable bishop of Lincoln, famous as much for his bold fights for justice for the common man as for his pet swan, which was reputed to be so fierce that no one else could come near him, but which was so affectionate towards Hugh that it would nestle with its head up his sleeve. The other, 'Little St Hugh', is probably apocryphal, and the sensational story of his 'martyrdom' at the hands of the local Jews was used as an excuse for much anti-Semitism. **Hew** and **Huw** are Welsh forms of the name, and the Latin and Spanish form **Hugo** is not uncommon. Pet forms are **Hughie, Huey** and **Hughy**. The Irish name **Ulick** may well come from the same ultimate source – from the Viking name *Hugleik* ('mind' + 'reward'), although it has also been explained as a pet form of Uilliam, the Irish form of WILLIAM. In Ireland Ulick is sometimes anglicised as ULYSSES.

Humbert

Humbert is a Germanic name formed from the elements *hun* 'warrior' and *beorht* 'bright'. It has gained notoriety in the form of Humbert Humbert, the narrator of Nabakov's scandalous novel *Lolita*. **Humberto** is the Spanish form and **Umberto** the Italian.

Humphrey

Humphrey is another Germanic name popularised by the Normans. The meaning of the first element of the name is uncertain, but the second element means 'peace'. **Humph** and **Hump** are used as short forms. **Humbert** is thought to come from the same unknown root as Humphrey, the second element meaning 'bright'

Hunter

An occupational surname used as a first name, Hunter seems to have come into use first in Scotland, and is currently quite fashionable in the United States and Australia.

Hussain, Hussana, Husayn see **Hassan**

Huw see **Hugh**

Hyacinth see **Iris**

Hyam see **Chaim**

Hylda see **Hilda**

Hywel

This is a Welsh name meaning 'conspicuous, eminent'. It is also spelt **Howel** or **Howell**, which reflect its pronunciation. Its pet form is **Hywyn** and there is a feminine **Hywela**. It is found as early as the ninth century, and King **Hoel** of Brittany, King Arthur's relative and ally in the legends, is probably the same name. It has become well known to the general public through the actor Hywel Bennett.

I

Iago see **James**

Ian

Ian is the Scottish form of John. **Iain** is the Gaelic spelling. Like SEAN, it is now generally used as an independent name, with no reference to John.

Ianthe see **Violet**

Ianto see **James**

Ib, Ibby see **Isabel**

Ibrahim see **Abraham**

Ida

Ida is a Germanic name, but its meaning is obscure. It probably has some connection with a word meaning 'work', and was most likely a pet form of a number of longer names containing this element. It is one of the medieval girl's name which were very popular in the nineteenth century and the first part of the twentieth. Tennyson used it in the middle of the nineteenth century as the name of the heroine of his poem mocking female pretensions to education, 'The Princess' (1847), and the name was given further currency by the adaptation of this work by Gilbert and Sullivan as *Princess Ida* (1870). In Ireland, in the forms Ida, **Ita** or **Ide**, it comes from the Irish word for 'thirst', and was the name of a sixth-century Irish saint renowned for her austerity. Ida is not much used by Anglophones at the moment, but is popular in Scandinavia.

Idonea

This unusual name is associated with the north of England. It has been suggested that it comes from a Latin adjective meaning 'fit, suitable', but, since the name is not used in countries where the language is descended from Latin, this seems unlikely. A much more attractive idea is that it is a form of the name of the Norse goddess Iduna, the guardian of the Apples of Youth, the eating of which kept the gods young. When she was abducted by the giants, the gods experienced the effects of age for the first time, although their youth was restored when they won her and the apples back. It also appears in the form **Idony**, and the rare name **Idina** may come from it or be a form of IDA.

Idris

There are two entirely different masculine names here. The first is an Arabic name, the second Welsh.

The Arabic Idris or **Idriss** comes from the verb *darasa* 'to study, learn', and is the Muslim name for the prophet who has the biblical name ENOCH. **Idrak** 'intellect, perception' would be a feminine near equivalent.

The Welsh name also has a long history. Meaning 'ardent or impulsive lord', it was held by Idris the Giant, who was killed in 632. He has entered Welsh legend as an astronomer and magician, and one of the highest mountains in Wales, Cader Idris ('Idris's Chair'), was supposed to have been his observatory. From the same root comes **Idwal** (a combination of words meaning 'lord' and 'rampart'), probably signifying 'defender', another ancient name held by two tenth-century kings of Gwynedd.

Ieasha, Iesha see **Aisha**

Iefan see **Ewan**

Iestin, Iestyn see **Justin**

Ieuan, Ifan see **Ewan**

Ifor see **Ivor**

Ignatius

This old Latin name has been interpreted as meaning 'fiery', but its use is almost entirely in association with the Spanish saint Ignatius Loyola, who founded the Jesuit order in the sixteenth century. The Spanish have two forms of the name. The first is the more obvious **Ignacio**; the other is **Inigo**. Inigo was the form given to the Catholic architect Inigo Jones (1573–1652). It had also been given to his father, and since he had been born in the reign of Mary I whose marriage to Philip of Spain led to a fashion for Spanish things, this may explain unusual choice of name. The association of 'Jones' with Wales has led to Inigo being claimed and used as a Welsh name. Inigo, long out of use among English speakers, has begun to reappear as a given name outside Wales.

Ike see **Isaac**

Ilan see **Elon**

Ilana see **Elon, Helen, Iyana**

Ileana, Iliana see **Eliana**

Illtyd, Illtud

St Illtyd was an outstanding Welsh saint of the fifth to sixth centuries, famous as a scholar and teacher, the founder of a school where numerous other Welsh saints studied. Legend credits him with introducing the plough to the Welsh, who hitherto had only used spades to turn the soil. His name is made up of elements meaning 'multitude' and 'land, people'.

Ilon see **Elon**

Ilona see **Helen**

Ilsa, Ilse see **Elizabeth**

Iman, Imani

Iman is the Arabic word for 'faith', used for both sexes. Imani is the Swahili form. It is well used in the USA, particularly by African-Americans as it has strong associations for that community. In the Kwanzaa celebrations that were created in the 1960s to provide an opportunity for Black Americans to celebrate their heritage Imani is the seventh principle of Kwanzaa, celebrated on the final day (New Year's Day).

Imelda

The name of a medieval saint, Imelda is the Italian form of the Germanic name **Irmhild**, meaning 'universal battle'. It has never been a particularly common name, although not unpopular in Ireland.

Immanuel see Emanuel

Imogen

The heroine of Shakespeare's *Cymbeline* owes her name to a misprint. The name first seems to appear in the eleventh-century *History of the Kings of Britain* by Geoffrey of Monmouth as *Ignoge*, wife of Brutus, the mythical first king of Britain. She reappears in Spenser's *Faerie Queene* as 'fayre Inogene of Italy'. Shakespeare seems to have used the 'n' spelling, for in a contemporary description of the play the name is spelt Innogen, but the form Imogen is found in the First Folio, the earliest printed text of the play. The form **Imogene** is occasionally found. The original form of the name may have come from the same root as Gaelic *inghean* 'maiden', although an alternative theory, links it to the occurrence of the name Ynoguen in c.1000 in Brittany, which appears to have a second half which is the equivalent of the Welsh *gwen* 'fair, white'.

Ina

This was originally a pet form of various names ending -ina, such as Georgina, Edwina, and so on, which has since come to be used as a name in its own right. In Ireland, Ina (Aghna) is the name of two saints, and probably represents a local form of the name AGNES. It was particularly popular in the nineteenth century.

Inderjit see **Indra**

India

This is simply the name of the country used as a girl's name. It may owe its use to the appearance of a character of that name in Margaret Mitchell's *Gone With the Wind* (1936), and it was the name given to the model India Hicks, granddaughter of Lord Mountbatten, the last Viceroy of India. Its spread may also be connected with the interest in India and its culture of the Hippy generation of the 1970s. The name India comes from the Sanskrit word for river, and is connected with the name of the sacred river of India, the Indus. For the related name **Indigo** see under BLUE. **Indiana**, famous as a masculine name from the Indiana Jones films, was used as a feminine name in Fanny Burney's 1796 novel *Camilla,* and used regularly as a girl's name in nineteenth-century America. Reciprocally, there is a town called Burney in the state of Indiana.

Indigo see **Blue, India**

Indira

This is a girl's name meaning 'beauty' in Sanskrit. Indira is one of the names of LAKSHMI, the wife of Vishnu. It was the name of Indira Gandhi, India's first female Prime Minister.

Indra, Indrajit

Indra is the name of the Hindu god who presides over battle and rain. His name means 'possessing raindrops'. Indrajit or **Inderjit** means 'conqueror of Indra' and in Indian legend is the title given by Brahma to Meghanada, king of Sri Lanka. **Jitendra** (**Jitender** and **Jeetendra, Jitinder**) has the same meaning.

Ines, Inez see **Agnes**

Ingrid

This is a Scandinavian name with connections with the pagan past. Ing was a Scandinavian god of peace and plenty, known also to the Anglo-Saxons. Ingrid has been explained in two ways: either it means 'Ing's ride, steed', probably a reference to the sacred golden boar associated with the god; or else it means 'beautiful under the protection of Ing'. The fame of the actress Ingrid Bergman undoubtedly played a large part in turning this into an international name. **Ingeborg** and its diminutives **Inge** and **Inga** (also used for Ingrid) come for the same root and mean 'Ing's protection'.

Inigo see **Ignatius**

Innes see **Angus**

Iolanthe see **Violet**

Iolo

This is the more widely used pet form of the Welsh name **Iorwerth**, formed from elements meaning 'lord' and 'value, worth'. For some unknown reason it has been used in the past as the Welsh equivalent of EDWARD, although there is no known connection between the names. There is a less common feminine form, **Iola**.

Iona

The Hebridean island of Iona was already an ancient religious site when St Columba (see MALCOLM) settled there in 563 and founded its famous monastery, which formed a base for the spread of Christianity through Scotland and the north of England. The island is still an important religious centre as well as a popular place to visit for its beauty and ancient ruins, so it is not surprising that a place name with so many associations, and with a form that fits in so well with other female names, should have come into use, at least by the beginning of the twentieth century. Its name seems to have come from a misreading of the original Celtic name which meant 'yew island', although the current form of the name in Gaelic just means 'island'. The name has been well used for the last decade in Scotland, and is part of the current trend there to use local place names for children.

Ione see Violet

Iorwerth see Iolo

Ira

A Hebrew name meaning 'watchful', Ira is found in the Bible as the name of one of King David's priests. It is little used in the UK, possibly because it is so easily mistaken for a feminine name, but is a part of the Puritan heritage of biblical names in the USA. The best-known modern holder is probably Ira Gershwin (1896–1983), lyricist to so many of his brother George's best tunes.

Irene

The old three-syllable pronunciation of this name comes from the original Greek, where the word means 'peace'; the shorter, two-syllable form is a modern pronunciation based on the spelling. Irene was the name of an early fourth-century martyr whose legend, probably embroidered, tells of her being confined, but unmolested, in a brothel before being burnt. It was also the name of a number of Byzantine empresses, one of whom, in the eighth century, managed to reign in her own right, even though holding on to the throne meant putting out the eyes of her son. The name is also spelt **Eirene**, while **Irena** reflects the Slavic form. **Renie** is a pet form.

Iris

In Greek mythology Iris is a goddess who acts as messenger for the gods. She uses the rainbow as her bridge between the heavens and earth. It is from the colours of this rainbow that the flower gets its name. The Romans used the name **Hyacinth** for what we would call an iris. In myth Hyacinth was the name of a particularly beautiful boy, accidentally killed by the god Apollo, and then transformed into a flower. It has been used as a boy's name in the past, but is rarely found now. It is, however, sometimes used as one of the flower names for girls. In France and Spain Hyacinth became **Jacinthe** and **Jacintha** (with **Jacinth** and **Jacinta** as variants), which again were originally boys' names, but are now mainly feminine. These are rare names, but are sometimes found in Ireland. The Australian model and actress **Jacinda** Barrett shows another form of the name. Iris is currently popular in the Netherlands.

Irma, Irm(e)gard see Emma

Irmhild see Imelda

Irving

This Scottish surname comes from the place and river name meaning 'west river'. It is also found in the forms **Irvin** and **Irvine**. The very similar-sounding **Irwin** or **Erwin** technically come from a different root, an Anglo-Saxon name meaning 'boar-friend' (and hence possibly linked to the sacred role of the boar mentioned under INGRID), but in practice the two names are often treated as variants of each other.

Isa see Isabel

Isaac

We are told in the Old Testament that when Abraham was 100 years old, and his wife Sarah was 90, God told him that they would have a son. Abraham's reaction to the idea of having a child at their age was to laugh, and when a son was born he was named Isaac, which is Hebrew for 'he laughed'. It has been suggested that this is merely a story designed to cover for the fact that it is a pre-Hebrew name. **Ishaq** is the Arabic spelling of the name (see ISMAEL). In the past in Britain the name tended to be associated with the Jewish community, but in the United States it was always more widely used and its modern popularity may come from the USA. It has a pet form, **Zac** (but see also ZACHARY). **Ike** is another pet form, but the use of Ike as a nickname for President Dwight D. Eisenhower is unconnected with the name Isaac. The seventeenth-century fishing enthusiast **Izaak** Walton, author of *The Compleat Angler* (1653), illustrates another spelling of the name, and the spelling **Isaak** is also on record. The name is currently well used in a variety of countries including the USA, England, Malta, Sweden and Australia.

Isabel, Isobel

These names properly belong with ELIZABETH, with which Isabel was interchangeable from the twelfth until at least the sixteenth century. The change came about when *Elisabet* was understood by the Spanish to be made up of El (that is 'the') and Isabet, and then the -et ending was replaced by the more common feminine -el. Short forms are **Bel**, **Bell**, **Belle**, ELLA and **Izzy**. In France the name, often in the forms **Isabelle** or **Isabeau**, all but replaced Elizabeth, while **Isabella** was the form adopted later in Spain. The Old Alliance between France and Scotland against the English may have helped Isabel become particularly popular in Scotland, where it developed a wide variety of pet forms including **Ib**, **Ibby**, **Isa** (currently popular in the Netherlands), **Belag**, **Tib**, **Tibbie** and **Tibby**. In Gaelic the name became **Iseabel**, from which comes the form **Ishbel** (reflecting the pronunciation), and which led to such wild variations as Easabell, Easybell and Eysie. Forms such as **Ysabel** are sometimes found.

The names are widely popular at the moment. In Scotland Isabella is the most used. In England Isabella is also the most popular, but is closely followed by Isabelle, Isabel and Isobel. In the USA Isabella is again the most popular, followed by Isabel and many other variants, but curiously the spelling Isobel is almost unknown. The names are all used regularly in Ireland but are less popular than in the previously mentioned countries, and they are also well used in Canada and Australia.

Isadora, Isadore see Isidore

Isaiah

This is a Hebrew name meaning 'salvation of the Lord', and the name of one of the great prophets of the Old Testament. It has recently become fashionable in the USA, sometimes in the forms **Isaias** which is the Late Latin form, **Izaiah, Isiah** and **Isai**.

Iseabel see Isabel

Iseult see Isolda

Ishaq see Isaac

Ishbel see Isabel

Isiah see Isaiah

Isidore, Isidora

This ancient Greek name has been interpreted as meaning 'gift of ISIS', an Egyptian goddess who was widely worshipped in the Mediterranean region in late classical times. It is a name particularly associated with Spain, thanks to St Isidore of Seville (c. 560–636), who wrote one of the first ever encyclopaedias – a fascinating combination of knowledge from the classical world, some of which would otherwise have been lost, and arrant nonsense – which formed the basis of much medieval learning. **Isodor** and **Isadore** are variants of the masculine form of the name, and it is shortened to **Izzy**. **Isadora** Duncan made the alternative spelling of the female form widely known through her innovative dancing and scandalous personal life.

Isis

Isis is the Greek form of the name of the Egyptian goddess *Esi* 'she who sits upon the throne'. Her worship spread from Egypt throughout the Roman empire. It is a fairly recent introduction and an early use was as a name given to one of Sir Laurence Olivier's grandchildren, which gave the name some publicity. It has been a mildly fashionable name in England since then, and is sometimes used with reference to the River Isis, the name given to the Thames as it runs through Oxford. It is more likely to be met with in the USA where it has been increasingly popular since the mid 1990s, and it is sometimes, but by no means invariably, used by those who want to emphasise their African roots.

Iskander see **Alexander**

Isla

This is a Scottish river name that means 'swiftly flowing'. However, the Hebridean island of **Islay** is also used as a first name (for both sexes, although Isla is only used for girls), and since Isla represents the normal local pronunciation of Islay (the 's' is silent in both cases), it may be that in origin Isla is, like IONA, an island name. Isla is popular in Scotland, but more quietly used in the rest of the UK

Isleen see **Ashling**

Ismael, Ismail

These are respectively the biblical and Arabic spelling of the name which appears in Hebrew as *Yishma'el* 'God has heard'. In biblical tradition Ismael is the son of Abraham by his concubine Hagar. The jealousy of Abraham's wife Sarah means they are turned out and nearly die in the desert. Ismael goes on to be the father of the Arab tribes. In Muslim tradition it is Ismail, not Isaac, who is offered as a sacrifice to God by Ibrahim, until his hand is stayed by God, and there are stories of the miraculous care taken of Ismail and Hagar in the desert. Ismael is regularly used in the USA, possibly encouraged by the famous opening of Herman Melville's 1851 novel *Moby Dick*, 'Call me Ishmael'.

Isobel see **Isabel**

Isodor see **Isidore**

Isolda

This name occurs in numerous different spellings and forms including **Iseult**, **Isold**, **Isolde**, **Isolt**, **Ysold**, **Ysolda**, **Ysolde**, **Yseult**, **Yseut** with **Esyllt** as the Welsh form; the variety reflecting the fame of the name through Europe. Its exact meaning has been much debated, without any convincing result. In the medieval love-tragedy of *Tristan and Isolda*, she is the heroine torn between her duties as a wife and queen and her unquenchable love for TRISTAN brought about by the accidental drinking of a love potion. Thus she becomes a symbol of undying and unhappy love. The name was popular until the sixteenth century, then went into a decline until a mild revival from the end of the nineteenth century, due in part to Celtic nationalism and in part to the success of Wagner's opera. (See also BRONWEN)

Israel

Israel is a biblical name, traditionally interpreted as meaning 'he who fights with God', with reference to the fact that in Genesis 32:28 Jacob is given this as a by-name after fighting with an angel. The name was used among Puritans in the seventeenth century, and was used steadily from the nineteenth century in the USA where it is currently undergoing something of a revival.

Ita see **Ida**

Itzel

Itzel or **Ixchel** is the name of the Mayan goddess of the earth, moon and childbirth and medicine. Her name means 'rainbow lady'. In Mayan an 'x' is pronounced 'sh'. Itzel is a popular name in Mexico, and has made inroads in the USA.

Ivan see **John**

Ivor, Ivo, Ifor

This is a confused and confusing group of names. Strictly speaking Ivor is interpreted as a Teutonic name probably connected with the god Ing (see under INGRID), Ivo is the Latinate form of Yves (see under YVONNE) and Ifor is the Welsh for 'lord'. However, these three names have become inextricably tangled, each influencing the other from an early date, and it is not really possible to draw any hard lines between the three.

Ivy

One of the plant names introduced in the nineteenth century, and popular through to the 1920s in the UK, Ivy is not much used today in the UK, but is not uncommon in the USA. Its introduction may have been helped by a feeling that there was a gap left by there being no female equivalent of the IVOR group of names, although there is a rarely found name **Iva**, which may be a feminine of IVOR or of Ivan (see JOHN).

Ixchel see Itzel

Iyana
Iyana or **Iyanna** is a rare girl's name, which has only been recorded since 2000. Its origin is a mystery at the moment, as the suggestions that it is either a form of the Hebrew name **Ilana** (see ELON) or that it is a feminine of IAN singularly fail to convince. It seems more likely that it is a combination of fashionable sounds, which will not last long.

Izaac see Isaac

Izaiah see Isaiah

Izzy see Isabel, Isidore

J

Jabari
This name, used by African-Americans, is said to be the Swahili meaning 'valiant, fearless'. Jabari has received exposure as the name of a character in the US sitcom *Girlfriends*.

Jabbar
Jabbar is the Arabic for 'powerful, mighty' and is one of the names of Allah. Abdur Jabbar means 'servant of the mighty'. Kareem Abdul Jabbar was a much admired American baseball player.

Jabez
According to the Old Testament Jabez was so-called by his mother 'because I bare him with sorrow'. He is a minor character in the Bible, with a reputation for being an honourable man.

Jabri(e)l see Gabriel

Jacalyn see Jacqueline

Jace see Jason

Jacey see Jay

Jacinda, Jacinta, Jacinth, Jacintha, Jacinthe see Iris

Jack
Jack, now used as an independent name, was originally a pet form of JOHN. The evolution is quite complex. John developed the pet form Johnkin, which in turn became Jankin (think of a West Country accent) which was then shortened to Jack. The similarity in sound to French Jacques, the French form of JAMES, is pure coincidence. **Jackie** or **Jacky** can be used as a pet form. From Jack evolved a surname **Jackson**, now well used as a first name in the USA, sometimes in the form **Jaxson**. For female forms see JACQUELINE

Jackeline, Jackelyn, Jackie, Jacky see Jacqueline

Jacob, Jake
The biblical Hebrew name *Yaakov* bercame *Iakobos* in New Testament Greek, and then *Iacobus*, later spelt *Jacobus*, in Latin. A variant spelling *Jacomus* developed, and this became JAMES, but *Jacobus* is the origin of Jacob. The name may be pre-Hebrew and go back to ancient Babylonian name meaning 'God rewards', but it is understood in the Bible to mean 'he who spurs with his heels' taken to mean 'supplanter', from the story that Jacob and his elder twin brother **Esau** fought even when in the womb and that Jacob got Esau to sell him his birthright for 'a mess of pottage'. The name is **Yakov** or **Yaakov** in Hebrew and **Akiva**, the name of a first-century Jewish sage, is the Aramaic form, also used in the USA. The Arabic form is **Yaqub**. **Jake** is a pet form, which is found as **Jaikie** in Scotland. **Jacoby**, the surname from the first name, is occasionally reused as a first name. There is a rare feminine **Jacoba**; and the form **Jacobina** was in the past a popular name for the daughters of Scottish Jacobites (i.e. followers of King James). In France Jacob became in popular speech Jacques. Both Jacob and Jake have been very popular in the UK and Jake is also popular in Ireland. Jacob has been the most popular

name in the USA for boys for the last few years, and it is also very popular in a number of other countries including New Zealand, Canada and Malta. The actor Jake Gyllenhaal is a prominent holder of the name. Akiva Goldsman is the screenwriter of a number of successful Hollywood films.

Jacqueline

Jacqueline is the usual feminine for the JACOB/JAMES names, derived from the French Jacques (see above). It also functions, particularly in its short form **Jackie** (**Jacky**, **Jacqui**), as a feminine equivalent of the unrelated JACK. It is found in a very wide variety of spellings including **Jackeline**, **Jackelyn**, **Jacalyn**, **Jaquelin**. **Jacquetta** is another form of the name, known in this country since at least the fifteenth century when Jacquetta of Luxembourg was bigamously married to Humphrey, Duke of Gloucester, then *de facto* ruler of England, as part of her long, brave, but ultimately unsuccessful attempt to inherit her duchy in her own right rather than have it pass to a distant male relative. By yet another marriage she was grandmother to the Princes in the Tower. Shakespeare uses a further form of the name, **Jacquenetta**, in *Love's Labour's Lost*, but this has never really caught on. The unusual girl's name Jakayla appears to be a blend of Jackie and KAYLA.

Jacques see Jacob

Jacy see Jay

Jade, Jaden

Although there is a long tradition of using jewels as girls' names, Jade seems to have been in use by the general public only since the 1970s. It was brought to the public's attention by its choice by the singer Mick Jagger for his first child (b. 1971) and had begun to be used by the general public by the mid 70s. The word 'jade' comes from the Spanish word *jada* meaning 'colic', because it was anciently believed to help cure that condition. **Jayde** is an occasional variant and see also Jadira at YADIRA. Since the 1970s the jade sound has become part of the stock sounds used for creating new names, particularly in the USA where they have been expanded to make new masculine names. Thus while Jade is among the top names in England, Wales, Ireland, Australia and Canada, in the USA **Jada** is the most popular form for girls, followed by Jade, then **Jayden**, **Jaden**, **Jayda**, **Jaiden**, **Jaida**, **Jaiden** and **Jaidyn**; while for boys we find **Jayden**, **Jaden**, **Jadon**, **Jaydon**, **Jadyn**, **Jaeden** and **Jaidyn**. Of these Jayden is the most used in the UK. Jadene is another form that has been recorded for girls. Jada Pinkett Smith, born the same year as Jade Jagger, is a well-known American singer and actress. Britney Spears recently chose Jayden for her second son.

Jaelyn, Jaelynn see Jay

Jago see James

Jaheim see Javon

Jai see Jay

Jaida Jaiden, Jaidyn see Jade

Jaikie see Jacob

Jaime see James

Jairo

Jairo is the Spanish form of the name **Jair**, YAIR in the original Hebrew. The name means 'he shines' in Hebrew, often interpreted as 'God enlightens'. In the Old Testament Jair is one of the judges of the Israelites. In the New Testament Jairus is the name of ruler of the synagogue whose daughter Jesus raises from the dead (Mark 5:22; Luke 8:41). Jairo is a very popular name in Latin America, and is consequently well used in the USA.

Jakayla see Jacqueline

Jake see Jacob, Jesse

Jaleesa see Whitney

Jalen, Jaliyah, Jalon, Jalyn, Jalynn see Jay

Jamal, Jamila

The is the Arabic for 'beautiful'. It sometimes appears spelt **Gamal**, **Jamaal** or **Jemal**, depending on how the Arabic has been transliterated. The feminines are **Jamila** or **Jemila**. In France, among the North African immigrant population they also appear as **Djamel**, **Djamal**, **Djamilia** and **Djemila**. They have been well used in recent years in the USA, particularly among Black Muslims, which they can also appear as **Jamel**, **Jamil** and **Jamilla**. **Jamar** is thought to be a variant, and from this Jam- has come to be used as an element in a variety of names such as **Jamarion**, **Jamari**, and **Jamir**.

James

In Latin the name JACOB occurs in two forms: *Jacobus*, from which we get Jacob, and *Jacomus*, from which we get James. The two forms have proved useful for distinguishing the Old Testament patriarch Jacob from the New Testament saints James the Less, the brother of Jesus, and James the Great, the son of ZEBEDEE. The shrine of St James the Great at Santiago de Compostella in Spain was one of the most popular places of pilgrimage throughout the Middle Ages, and this has resulted in James, in its various forms, being one of the most widely spread names in western Europe. In the British Isles alone it occurs as **Hamish** in Scotland; as SEAMUS in Ireland; as **Iago**, with its pet form **Ianto**, in Wales; and **Jago** in Cornwall. **Jim** (**Jimmie, Jimmy**) and **Jamie** are the commonest pet forms of James, while **Jem** and **Jemmie** were common in the past. **Jaime** is the Spanish form and **Giacomo** the Italian. Iago is also an old Spanish form of James, used to form **Santiago**. This is also used as a first name by Spanish-speakers and can be shortened to **Tiago**. The surnames **Jameson** or **Jamison** is also found as a first name.

JACQUELINE is the commonest feminine form, but **Jamesina** is an old Scottish name used by the Jacobites. **Jamie** is well used for girls as well as boys, sometimes in the Spanish form Jaime, although sometimes this is used with reference to the French *j'aime*. **Jamya** may also be a feminine form of James. Jamesha (**Jamisha, Jameisha**, etc) seems to be a blend of James and Aisha.

James is currently very popular throughout the English-speaking world, and Hamish used regularly in Scotland and New Zealand.

Jamila, Jamilla, Jamir see Jamal

Jamisha, Jamya see James

Jan see John, Jane

Jane, Jean, Joan

All the names in this large group are feminine forms of the name JOHN, the first two coming from the early French form *Jehane*, the third from the Latin *Johanna*. All three have developed a large number of variants and pet forms. **Joan** seems to have been the earliest form of the name. It gives us the forms nearer to its Latin root such as **Johanna** and **Joanna**; is sometimes spelt **Joanne** and has the pet form **Joanie**. **Jane** seems to have come into use in the fifteenth century and developed into **Janet, Janette, Janetta**, with pet forms **Netta** and **Nettie**. In the twentieth century all sorts of variants have become popular, such as **Janine** and **Janina**, **Janice** and **Janis**, **Jana** (particularly in Ireland), **Jan** and **Jancis**, which was made better known through its use for a character in Mary Webb's highly successful novel *Precious Bane* (1924). Pet forms include **Janie, Janey, Jen** and **Jenny** (see also JENNIFER), and the name is also spelt **Jayne**. **Jean** started life as the Scottish form of Jane or Joan, and has given rise under French influence to **Jeanette** or **Jeanet** and **Janetta**. **Jeannie** is the usual pet form, but in Scotland **Jess, Jessie, Jessy** (see also JESSICA) are used, as well as **Jinty, Janny, Jancey** and **Jinsie** (see also under GINA). The Spanish forms of the name **Juana** and its pet forms **Juanita** and **Nita** and are also found, mostly in the USA, along with the Italian **Giovanna**. More recently still, elaborations such as **Janelle, Jonelle, Janiya(h), Janae** and **Janessa** have made their mark. For the Celtic forms see under SIAN, SHEENA and SIOBHAN.

Japonica see **Flora**

Jaquan see **Javon**

Jaquelin see **Jacqueline**

Jared

In the book of Genesis Jared is the father of ENOCH, but the only information we are given about him is that he lived for 962 years. The name is of disputed origin, and may not be Hebrew. It was used by the Puritans, but then went into decline and was used only occasionally until a revival in the 1960s. In recent years it has become very popular in the United States and Australia. **Jarrad**, **Jareth**, **Jarrath**, **Jered** are variants, with the forms **Jarett** and **Jarrod** also being used, although technically these come from surnames derived from Garret (see GERALD). **Jaron** and **Jaren** are modern developments of the name. The scientist Jared Diamond is a well-known bearer of the name.

Jarvis

Jarvis is a respelling, but now the most used form, of **Gervase** or **Gervais**. The meaning of the name is obscure, but may come from the same root, meaning 'spear', found in other Gar- and Ger- names. It was the name of a martyr of unknown date and history, whose remains were exhumed in Milan in AD 386 after a 'presentiment' by St Ambrose that they would be found. Despite his obscurity, Gervase was widely revered and his cult spread through western Europe. **Gervas** and **Jervis** are variants and there is a feminine form **Gervaise**. The singer Javis Cocker is a well-known holder of the name.

Jasmine

The name of the sweet-scented jasmine flower can be traced back to ancient Persia, where scented oil was made from the plant. The Arabic forms of the name, **Yasmin** and **Yasmine**, are also sometimes used. **Jessamy** is an old form of the word, which was once synonymous with a fop; and **Jessamine**, with a pet form **Jess**, was also found. Jasmine is well used in England and Scoltand, and Yasmine makes its mark in England. In the USA Jasmine is also popular, but its popularity is perhaps masked by the vast number of variant spellings that are used, at least 10 being in regular use, and many more found occasionally.

Jason

Jason is the Greek form given to the Hebrew JOSHUA. There are at least four Jasons in the Bible, and it is also the name of the reputed author of the Old Testament book of *Ecclesiasticus*, so that when it was adopted in the seventeenth century it was thought of as a biblical name. However, it is highly unlikely that, when the name came back into fashion in the 1960s, parents associated it with anyone from the past other than the hero of Greek myth, leader of the Argonauts and winner of the Golden Fleece. The name means 'healer'. **Jace** is a pet form sometimes used as an independent name, and it is sometimes spelt **Jayce**, **Jayson** or **Jazon**.

Jasper

Jasper is the English form of the traditional name of one of the three Magi (the others being **Balthazar**, which is very occasionally found, and **Melchior**) and as such comes appropriately from the Persian meaning 'master of the treasure'. **Caspar**, **Casper** or **Kasper** are the German forms of the name, and **Gaspar** and **Gaspard** the French.

Javier, Javiera see **Xavier**

Javon

In recent years in the USA there has been a particular fashion for forming names out of fashionable sounds. At the moment it is possible to form a name from almost any combination of J+vowel+v+vowel+n, and even more names if you substitute an r, l or d for the v. Javon is currently the most popular of these, followed by **Javion** and **Jovan**. The footballer **Jevon** Kearse shows another variant, and forms such as **Javan** and **Jevin** are only examples of the many others. There have been attempts to find sources for these – Jovan is a Serbian form of JOHN; Javan is said in Genesis to be the ancestor of the

Ionian Greeks and so on, but this is largely coincidental, although is likely that Jovan is influenced if not directly derived from **Jovanny**, a respelling of Giovanni, the Italian form of JOHN. Another influence may have been the occasional spelling of the name Yvonne as **Javonne**. Other well used Ja- names boys which are modern coinages include Jaheim, publicised by **Jaheim** Hoagland, an American R&B singer who came to public attention in 2000, and whose name got into the top 500 boy's names in the USA the next year, but use has rapidly declined since; and **Jaquan**, which combines two popular name elements.

Jaxson see **Jack**

Jay, Jaye
Now established as an independent name, in the past this was often just a pet form of any name beginning with J. It can also be derived from the surname, which in its turn was originally a nickname, implying that the person so-called was a chatterer, from the noise made by the bird. It is used for both sexes, but is most frequently male, with **Jai** a respelling and **Jaya** an occasional feminine variant. The recent girl's name **Jacy** looks and sounds as if it is from a similar source, the initials J.C., but may be a development of Jace, the short form of JASON, for which there is otherwise no feminine form.

The trend for creating names from fashionable sounds has particularly focused on Jay. Some are listed under JADE and JAVON. Other names that are fashionable involving the jay or ja- sound are, in order of popularity, for boys: **Jaylen**; **Jalen**; **Jaylin**; **Jalon**; **Jaylan**; and for girls **Jayla**; **Jaelyn**; **Jaylin**; **Jaylynn**; **Jacey**; **Jaycee**; **Jaylene**; **Jaylee**; **Jaelynn**; **Jalynn**; **Jayleen**; **Jaliyah**; **Jalyn**.

Jay has recently been quite popular in England and Scotland, although currently declining in use.

There is a separate name Jay from the Sanskrit for 'victory' which overlaps with many of the forms above. It is sometimes spelt **Jai**, and appears as **Jaya** in the feminine. **Jayant** means 'victory' and is used for boys. **Jayanti** is the female equivalent, and is a title of the Hindu goddess Durga.

Jayce see **Jason**

Jaycee see **Jay**

Jayda, Jayde, Jayden, Jaydon see **Jade**

Jayla, Jaylan, Jaylee, Jayleen, Jaylene, Jaylin, Jaylynn see **Jay**

Jayne see **Jane**

Jayson see **Jason**

Jazon see **Jason**

Jeana, Jeanna see **Gina**

Jean Jeanet, Jeanette, Jeannie see **Jane**

Jeb, Jed
Jeb is a name with several sources. It can be a pet form of JACOB or Jeremiah (see JEREMY). In the southern USA it can be used in honour of the dashing Confederate cavalry officer James Ewell Brown Stuart, known to his friends as Jeb from his initials. In the case of the best-known current Jeb, Jeb Bush, Governor of Florida, it is used in a similar way, as his real name is John Ellis Bush, so his initials spell Jeb. Some have claimed that Jeb is short for Jebidiah. This is a corruption of **Jedidiah**, which is an Old Testament masculine name adopted by the Puritans and more commonly used in the United States. It means 'beloved of the Lord' and was a title given to King Solomon. **Jedediah** is an alternative spelling, while the short form Jed seems to have become a stock name for minor characters in Westerns.

Jeetendra see **Indra**

Jeff, Jefferson, Jeffery, Jeffrey see **Geoffrey**

Jem see **James**

Jemal, Jemil, Jemila see **Jamal**

Jemima
The biblical Jemima was the eldest daughter of JOB. She was born after her father's return to prosperity, so escaped the calamities which befell him. We are told that 'in all the land were no women found so fair as the daughters of Job', which would support those who want to interpret the name as meaning 'fair as the day' rather than the more usual 'dove'. **Mima** is an occasional short form. (See further under KEZIAH)

Jemma see **Gemma**

Jemmie see **James**

Jen, Jenae, Jennie see **Jane, Jennifer**

Jennifer
This is the Cornish form of **Guenevere** or **Guinevere**. The Welsh form of the name is **Gwenhwyfar**, meaning 'fair' or 'white' and 'smooth, yielding'. This was shortened in Wales to forms such as **Gaenor**, **Gaynor** and **Geunor**, recorded from the sixteenth century, and which then spread to England. In Scotland it became **Vanora**, and in Cornwall Jennifer or **Jenifer**. Although it is possible to find examples of the name being used, for example, at the end of the nineteenth century, it was for a long time a rare name, regarded as strictly local, until it became fashionable in the 1930s, possibly as a result of its use for characters in plays by George Bernard Shaw and Noel Coward. It has remained popular ever since. Short forms are **Jen**, **Jennie** and **Jenny**, which were earlier used as a pet form of JANE and Janet. The popularity since the 1980s of **Jenna**, another Cornish form of the name, can no doubt be attributed to the exposure given to it on the TV 'soap' *Dallas*, while **Jenae** is a new name which has the appearance of a blend between Jenny and a name like Renée but which may just be a respelling of Jenny. Jennifer spent fifteen consecutive years as the most popular name for girls in the USA from 1970, and is still in the top 50. Jennifer is well used in England, Scotland and Ireland, and Jenna also well-used in Scotland.

Jered see **Jared**

Jeremy
Jeremy is the English form of **Jeremiah**, the Old Testament prophet whose dire warnings and reproofs to the people of his times gave rise to the term 'jeremiad'. The name comes from the Hebrew *Yirmyahu* and means 'appointed by God'. **Jeremias**, the Greek form of the name, is occasionally found, as is the spelling **Jeramiah**. The pet form **Jerry** is shared with a number of other names. **Jerrica**, used for girls in the USA, looks like a blend of Jerry and Erica (see ERIC), while the new masculine name **Jerrell** or **Jerryl** looks like a blend of Jerry and **Daryl**. Use of Jeremy increased enormously in the UK after the popular novelist Hugh Walpole (1884–1941) wrote a series of school stories about someone of that name, the first of which *Jeremy* was published in 1919. Jeremy was almost unknown in the United Sates until the 1940s. It became a popular name there in the 1970s and is still quite well used, although the full Jeremiah is currently the more popular. Jeremy is well used a present in Canada, Australia and France.

Jermaine see **Germain**

Jerome
This comes from a pre-Christian Greek name meaning 'sacred name', which was adopted by Christians in honour of St Jerome (c. 342–420), the hermit and great Bible scholar whose translation of the Bible into Latin was used by the Catholic Church until recently. The Latin form of St Jerome's name was **Hieronymus**, as in the painter Hieronymus Bosch, while the Native American chief **Geronimo** (real name Goyathlay) was given the Italian form of the name by the Mexicans. **Jerry** is used as a short form of Jerome.

Jerrell, Jerrica see **Jeremy**

Jerry see **Gerald, Jeremy, Jerome**

Jervis see **Jarvis**

Jess see Jane, Jasmine, Jessica

Jessamine, Jessamy see Jasmine

Jesse

In the Bible Jesse, whose name means 'God is', is the father of DAVID. He is regarded as the founder of the family which culminated in Jesus Christ, and 'Jesse windows' can sometimes be found in medieval churches showing this descent. **Jess** (and occasionally **Jake**, although this is more usual for JACOB) are used as pet forms. Because of the ambiguity of the spelling, nowadays Jesse can be found spelt Jessie, particularly in the USA, where jessie does not seem to have the derogatory meaning it has in the UK. Jesse is currently well used in the Netherlands and Australia. After the Biblical character the best known bearer of the name is probably the outlaw Jesse James (1847–82).

Jessica

Jessica is a difficult name. There have been at least half a dozen different attempts to derive it from different Hebrew words, of which the most convincing is that it means 'God is looking'. However, there is no record of the name before it appears in Shakespeare's *The Merchant of Venice*, and it appears to have been made up by him, probably based on a name JESSE. The significance of the name would then be that while the first part of her name is Jewish, the ending is Venetian, a transition which reflects her role in the play. **Jess** and **Jessie** (also a Scottish pet form of Jean, see JANE) are used as pet forms. Whatever its origin, the name has been very popular on both sides of the Atlantic since the 1980s. In 2005 it was the top name in both the USA and England.

Jessie, Jessy see Jane, Jesse, Jessica

Jesus see Joshua

Jet, Jett see Jewel

Jethro

This is another biblical name, that of the father-in-law of Moses, meaning 'pre-eminence, excellence'. It was introduced in the sixteenth century with other biblical names. Its most famous bearer was Jethro Tull, the eighteenth-century agricultural reformer.

Jevin, Jevon see Javon

Jewel

Also spelt **Jewell** and **Jewelle**, this name came into use in the 1920s when exotic precious stones for women's names came into fashion; some women, such as **Emerald** Cunard (see ESMERALDA), even went so far as to change their names to suit the fashion. Jewel was used regularly from the later nineteenth century up to the 1970s, but then disappeared, only to come back into use in the later 1990s. The revival of the name has coincided with the popularity of the American singer Jewel Kilcher. The singer and actress **Bijou** Phillips shows the French equivalent of 'jewel'. Many other jewel names that were popular in the late nineteenth century and early twentieth have followed a similar pattern to Jewel – see for example RUBY. Others, like AMBER and JADE have been new introductions. A number of stone names will be found under their own entries, but unusual ones that have been recorded include **Opal**, **Amethyst**, **Jet**, **Onyx** and **Topaz**. GEMMA is another jewel name. **Jet**, often **Jett**, is also used for boys.

Jibril see Gabriel

Jill, Jillian, Jilly see Julia, Gillian

Jim see James

Jimena see Ximena

Jimmie, Jimmy see James

Jinny see Virginia

Jinsie, Jinty see Jane

Jitender, Jitendra, Jitinder see Indra

Jo, Joe

As a masculine name, usually spelt Joe, this is a pet form of JOSEPH; for women, usually Jo, it is a form of names such as Joanna (see JANE) and Josephine (see JOSEPH). It is also well used in blends and compounds such as **Billy-Joe** (for both sexes) and **Jolette, Jolene** or **Joleen**.

Joachim, Joaquin

Joaquin is the Spanish form of the biblical Joachim. In Hebrew *Yoyaqim* means 'he who God has established'. In Christian tradition Joachim was the name of the husband of St Anne, the mother of the Virgin Mary. The name Joaquin (pronounced wha-keen) was adopted as a pseudonym by the nineteenth-century American poet Joaquin Miller, but is now better known as that of the actor Joaquin Phoenix.

Joan, Joanie, Joanna, Joanne see Jane

Job

Job is interpreted as the Hebrew for 'persecuted', reflecting the afflictions, ranging from the deaths of his family to a plague of boils, sent by God in the Old Testament *Book of Job* to test this 'perfect and upright' man. He is eventually restored to greater prosperity than ever. It has pet forms **Joby**, **Jobie**, **Joabee**, **Jobey**. Job's daughters are described under JEMIMA and KEZIAH.

Jocelyn, Joscelin

Experts try to distinguish between the two forms of this name, deriving Jocelyn from the Latin for 'sportive' and Joscelin from the Latin for 'just', the same root as for JUSTIN. The name has also been derived from the word for 'a Goth'. In practice the two forms are so confused that it is pointless to try to distinguish them. Jocelyn or **Jocelin** was a common name for men in the Middle Ages, as in the chronicler Jocelin de Brakelond, but the name is now uncommon for men. The form **Joycelin** is also found, possibly through combination with the name JOYCE. Jocelyn is currently in the top hundred girl's names in the USA, sometimes as Joselyn or **Joslyn** and occasionally as what appears to be a variant **Yoselin**.

Jock, Jockie see John

Jodi, Jodie, Jody see Judith

Joel

The name of one of the Old Testament prophets, Joel means 'Jehovah is God'. It was introduced into England by the Puritans and taken by them to North America, where it has been more used than in Great Britain. A recent increase of interest in the name may owe something to the success of the actor Joel Grey. In France a feminine form **Joelle** is also used. There are other feminines such as Joely (as in the actress **Joely** Richardson) and **Joley** which also function as female forms of Joel. The name Jolie is the French for 'pretty', but is often pronounced jo-lee, when it also belongs in this group.

Joey see Joseph

Johanna see Jane

John

Derived from the Hebrew *Johanan* meaning 'the Lord is gracious', John has been one of the most popular names for boys since the early Middle Ages. It is the name of numerous saints, notably John the Baptist and John the Divine. As in the case of the feminine form JANE, the name has developed a wide variety of forms in the British Isles, the number being multiplied by duplicate forms derived from both the Latin form of the name *Iohannes* or *Johannes* found in the Bible, and the Norman-French form *Jehan* (modern French *Jean*) adopted from the Norman conquerors.

In Wales the Latin forms developed into the names under EWAN, but the French form became Siôn (see further under SEAN), a form of John that comes from the fact that Welsh, like other Celtic languages, has no j. The Scots form of the name is IAN, as well as the archetypal **Jock** and **Jockie**. Irish gives us the names under SEAN and **Eoin** (under EWAN) directly from the Latin.

From further afield the Russian **Ivan** is sometimes used (although this can also represent a spelling of the Welsh IFAN) which is shortenable to **Van**; **Jan** is a Germanic form of the name as well as being the traditional West Country pronunciation; and **Juan**, the Spanish form, is well used in the United States, and has also been elaborated into **DeJuan**. **Giovanni** (sometimes **Giovanny** in the US or **Jovanny**) is the Italian form, and also the source of **Giancarlo** ('John-Charles'). In Breton and other languages *Johannes* became **Yan(n)**, with a pet form **Yannick**. John the Baptist gives rise to names such as **Baptiste**, currently popular in France.

Jack (derived via the old pet form **Jankin** which was then shortened to Jack) is a common pet form, and at the time of writing in its twelfth year as the most popular name for boys in the UK. **Johnnie** and **Jackie** are further pet forms. The spelling **Jon** is also used, although this properly belongs to the related JONATHAN. Sometimes a child is named directly after one of the saints and called **St John**, in which case the name is pronounced 'sin-jn'.

Joi, Joie see **Joy**

Jojo see **Joseph**

Joleen, Jolene, Jolette see **Jo**

Joley, Jolie see **Joel**

Jolly, Jolyon see **Julia**

Jon see **John, Jonathan**

Jonah, Jonas

The Hebrew form of this name is **Yonah**, meaning 'dove, pigeon'. The name became famous from the Old Testament story, which tells how Jonah tried to escape the task God has set him, was thrown overboard by the crew of the ship he was running away in, and swallowed by a whale. The name became such a byword for bad luck that only the most dismal of Puritans would saddle their child with such a burden. Consequently the New Testament Greek form of the name, **Jonas** (the father of Simon Peter), has until recently always been much the commoner, although Jonah is currently now the more popular in the USA. This may be as a result of the popularity of the 1993 film *Sleepless in Seattle* which has a little boy called Jonah in it. Forms of Jonas are currently popular in many European countries.

Jonathan

Jonathan, in Hebrew *Yonatan*, means 'gift of God' (compare NATHAN). In the Bible Jonathan is the son of King SAUL and loyal friend of DAVID, whose lament on the death of Jonathan is justly famous. In the eighteenth century the name was thought of as typically American and 'Brother Jonathan' was as widely recognised a reference to Americans among the British they were fighting as 'Uncle Sam' is today. The short form is **Jon** and the name is sometimes spelt **Jonathon** and occasionally blended with John to give **Johnathon**. Jon is sometimes used for girls in the USA, but otherwise the name seems never to have developed a feminine form. However DOROTHY and THEODORA have the same meaning. Jonathan is once again very popular in the USA and in the Philippines, and is well used in England, Scotland and Ireland.

Jonelle see **Jane**

Jonquil

One of the flower names introduced in the twentieth century and briefly popular in the 1940s and 1950s, Jonquil is little used for children today.

Jools see **Julia**

Jordan

It is hardly surprising that the name of the River Jordan, which means 'flowing down', with its strong associations with baptism, became a Christian name. It is recorded as a man's name from the thirteenth century onwards, but is now well used for both sexes.

It can also be spelt **Jourdan**, **Jordin**, **Jordon**, **Jorden** or **Jordyn**, and there is a feminine form **Jo(u)rdana**. The name **Jordy**, while technically analysable as a form of GEORGE (usually spelt **Jordi**) is probably, in practice, a pet form of Jordan. The name is popular in the USA, but while still well used in the UK is declining from its peak in the late 1990s.

Jordi, Jorge, Jorja see **George**

Jordy see **Jordan**

Jos see **Josiah**

Joscelin, Joselyn see **Jocelyn**

Joseph
This is a Hebrew name meaning 'increase, addition (to the family)'. In the Old Testament Joseph is the best beloved of the twelve sons of the patriarch JACOB, by whom he is given the coat of many colours. In the New Testament, Joseph is the husband of the Virgin Mary. In the USA the Spanish form, **José**, is well used. Germanic countries use spellings such as **Josef**, and **Yosef** is the modern Hebrew form of the name. The feminine form of the name, **Josephine**, owes its popularity to Napoleon's wife, the Empress Josephine. Other feminine forms are **Josepha** and **Josephina** or **Josefina**. The pet forms **Jo** or **Joe**, **Jojo**, **Josie** or **Josey** are used for both sexes, but **Joey** is usually restricted to the masculine. **Fifi** is a French pet form of Josephine, **Pepita** the Spanish. **Josette** is another feminine form. In Arabic the name becomes **Yosef** or **Yusuf**. Forms of Joseph are currently widely popular throughout the world.

Joshua
A Hebrew name *Yehoshua* meaning 'the Lord is my Salvation', Joshua was the name of the great general who led the Israelites in the conquest of the Promised Land. **Josh** is used as a pet form. There are two Greek forms of the name JASON and **Jesus** popular with Spanish speakers, who also use the form **Josue**. Joshua has been a particularly popular name in recent years and both Joshua and Josh currently feature on the most popular lists of many Anglophone countries.

Josiah
Josiah was the name of one of the kings of Israel and means 'may the Lord heal'. Its most famous British holder was probably Josiah Wedgwood (1730–95), the founder of the china firm. The Greek form of the name, **Josias**, is also found, and pet forms are **Josh** and **Jos**.

Josie see **Joseph**

Joslyn see **Jocelyn**

Josse see **Joyce**

Josue see **Joshua**

Jourdan, Jourdana see **Jordan**

Journey
This is a new name, still rare but increasingly used for girls in the USA. It may be part of the trend for using vocabulary words as names, but it may be used sometimes with a religious implication. In such cases it is in an old American tradition, as **Sojourner** – one who only stays for a short time – was a well used Puritan (and earlier) name with strong Christian associations. Sojourner Truth (1797–1883) was a charismatic preacher, ex-slave and campaigner for women's rights and racial equality.

Jovan, Jovan(n)i, Jovan(n)y see **Gina, Javon, John**

Joy
An abstract noun used as a first name, Joy therefore has connections with the name JOCELYN. It is found as early as the twelfth century, but did not come into its own until the nineteenth. The French spellings **Joie** and **Joi** are sometimes found, and **Joya** is an elaboration.

Joyce

This name is of disputed, or perhaps mixed, origin and is used for both sexes. Some derive it from a Breton St Jodocus (giving the French name **Josse**), others from the same root as JOY. It has been in and out of fashion over the centuries, and is now very rare as a man's name, although the author Joyce Cary (1888–1959) shows its survival into the twentieth century.

Joycelin see Jocelyn

Juan see John

Juana, Juanita see Jane

Jude

Until recently, Jude has never been a particularly popular name, although its use was given a boost by the Beatles song *Hey Jude*, and it was known in literature through Thomas Hardy's *Jude the Obscure* (1896), a story not likely to increase the name's popularity. **Yehudi** Menuhin shows a Hebrew form of the name, which means 'praise', and appears as the name of one of the sons of Jacob and founder of the tribe of Judah. It is found in the Bible as **Judah**, and the Hellenised form of the name is found in **Judas** Iscariot. Jude was the form of the name used for the apostle who was elected to replace Judas, but neither this nor the attractive fact that St Jude is the patron saint of lost causes, was enough to displace the taint to the name of the treacherous Judas. The recent increase in use in both the UK and USA may be influenced by the fame of the actor Jude Law. As a girl's name it is usually a short form of Judy (see JUDITH).

Judge see Justin

Judicaël see Gael

Judith

Judith means 'a Jewess' and Judith is one of the great heroines in the Bible. When the Israelites are under attack she gets herself invited to spend the night with the enemy general Holofernes, but instead, after getting him drunk, she cuts his head off with his own sword. Inspired by her return to her native city with the head, the Israelites then fall upon the enemy and are victorious. Pet forms of the name, often used as names in their own right and currently more popular than the full form, are **Judy** or **Judie**, **Jodi**, **Jodie** or **Jody**. Jody is also used for boys. Its origin is unclear, but it may have been a pet form of JUDE or JACOB. Judith was one of the first Old Testament names to be widely used for women in western Europe, after Judith of Bavaria (895–843) became Queen of France on her marriage to Louis the First. However, the name was not much used by Puritans, despite their penchant for Old Testament names. This may have been because they did not feel that the biblical Judith matched their ideal of womanhood. The popularity of Judy in the mid-twentieth century may have been influenced by the singer Judy Garland. However, Judy is not much used now, and in the UK and Ireland Jodie, brought to the world's attention by the actress Jodie Foster, is by far the most popular form of the name.

Julia, Julian

The ancient Roman clan of the *Julii* claimed direct descent from **Venus** or **Aphrodite**, the goddess of love and generation, through her son Aeneas (see under ANGUS). We are told by the poet VIRGIL that Aeneas' son Ascanius had his name changed to *Iulus*, meaning 'the first down on the chin', because he had not yet reached the age of a full beard when he killed his first man. From him the *Julii* derived their name. Modern scholars have doubted this story, and have suggested that the name might be from the Latin *deus* ('god'). Julia is the feminine form of the name, and **Julie** is both its pet and the French form of the name, now as much used in its own right. **Juliet** and **Juliette** reflect the Italian form of the name, and their use derives from Shakespeare's heroine. **Julius**, the masculine form of the name, is regularly used in the USA as is **Caesar** in the Spanish form **Cesar**, but **Julian**, from the Latin adjective meaning 'connected with the Julii', is much more common, and is sometimes shortened to **Jule** or **Jools** (influenced by the French form **Jules**, and now sometimes found for girls). **Jolyon** is a form of the name from the north of England, given publicity by Galsworthy's use of it in his *Forsyte Saga* novels along with its pet form **Jolly**. **Julio** is the Spanish form. **Juliana** (**Yuliana** in Russian) is the feminine form of Julian, and this was corrupted in the Middle Ages to GILLIAN or Jillian, which later developed into **Jill** or **Gill** and its pet form **Jilly**. In the nineteenth century Juliana or **Julianne** developed in France into **Lianne** with its many variants such as **Leanne, Lian, Lean(n)a** and **Lianna**, although some parents prefer to interpret this as a blend of the names LEE and ANNE. **Julissa** is a modern American coinage based on the name.

Julie is recorded in France from the Middle Ages, and became very popular there in the eighteenth century after the publication of Rousseau's novel *Julie or the New Heloise* in 1761. Neither Julian, Julia or Julie is much used in the UK at present, but Julia is a bit more popular in Ireland, and is well used in the USA, and all forms of the name are popular in France and a number of other Continental countries.

Jumaina, Jumana see Pearl

June

This is the name of the month used as a first name. It may be given because a girl is born in that month, or because of the happy feelings associated with the beginning of summer. It has only been used as a name since the twentieth century, but the name for the month is very old, going back to the Latin meaning 'month sacred to JUNO'.

Junior

Junior was originally just an affectionate nickname or more specifically used of a child who had been given the same name as his father. This habit is more common in the USA than is other countries, and Junior is now given there as an independent name on occasion (compare TREY).

Juno see Oonagh

Justin

Derived from the Latin word meaning 'just', Justin was the name of a Christian martyr and theologian who died c. AD 165. **Justus** and **Justinian** are rare forms of the name. In the form **Iestyn** or **Iestin** it has been used in Wales since at least the sixth century. **Justina** is the older feminine form, but since the success of Lawrence Durrell's novel *Justine* (1957) and of the film made from it, this has been the more frequently used form. Occasionally the masculine form of the name is found used for a woman. In the USA **Justice** has been used for both sexes since the 1990s, replacing **Judge**, which was in use in the nineteenth century, but died out in the 1930s. The actor Judge Reinhold has Edward as his given name, Judge being a childhood nickname.

Jyoti

This is a girl's name from the Sanskrit for 'light'. **Jyotsna** or **Jyotsana** mean 'moonlight'.

K

Kaci see **Casey**

Kade, Kaden see **Cade**

Kadence see **Cadence**

Kadin see **Cade**

Kady

A recent girl's name, Kady appears to be a development of Kay, or to derive from the initials K.D., in the same way that Jacy relates to JAY. It is also found as **Kaydee** and **Kadi**, and with a spelling beginning with 'C'.

Kadyn, Kaeden, Kaiden see **Cade**

Kaelyn see **Kay**

Kai

Kai is a name with a multitude of origins. The oldest is from **Caius** or **Gaius**, a Roman first name which comes from the Latin *gaudere* ('to rejoice'). The name seems to have passed into use among native Britons during the Roman occupation, for it is the source of Sir **Kay** or **Kai**, King Arthur's foster-brother and steward in the legends. His is one of the earliest names associated with King Arthur and it is still used in Wales in the forms **Cai**, **Caio** and **Caw**. There is also a German name Kai which either comes from Caius as well, or else is a form of **Gerhard**, the German form of GERARD (*see* **Gerald**). This is the probably source of the name usually printed as Kay in Hans Christian Andersen's story *The Snow Queen* (see also GERDA). There is also a Swedish girl's name Kai, which like KAY, is a pet form of Katherine. Finally there is a Hawaiian name Kai, which can be used for both girls and boys, which means 'sea'. When Kai became a fashionable name in the late Seventies, it was probably from this source. However, it should be pointed out that Kai has also been used extensively in recent fantasy contexts from computer games to *Star Trek*. Wikipedia lists 10 fictional Kais from fantasy contexts. This is an unusually high number, and it may be that these uses have helped spread the name.

Kai had moved into the top hundred names in Scotland and England by the beginning of the twenty-first century, and is also in that category in Australia. It is not quite so popular in the USA, but is rising and has been used there longer. The feminine name **Kaia** or **Kya** is probably based on it. See also KAY

Kaila, Kailyn see **Kay**

Kaine see **Keenan**

Kaitlin, Kaitlyn see **Caitlin**

Kale, Kaleb see **Caleb**

Kalie see **Kayleigh**

Kalin see **Caleb**

Kama

Kama is the Hindu god of love. He is the son of the goddess LAKSHMI and his name means 'love, desire' in Sanskrit.

Kamal see **Kamil**

Kamari

This is a recent boy's name, which does not seem to have any history or background, but to have been coined from the fashionable Ka- sound combined with other fashionable sounds.

Kamden see **Camden**

Kamel see **Kamil**

Kameron see **Cameron**

Kami see **Camilla**

Kamil, Kamila

These names, respectively male and female, come from the Arabic for 'complete, perfect'. Kamil is one of the titles of Mohammed. The name is also spelt **Kamel**, while **Kamal** means 'perfection'.

Kamron, Kamryn see **Cameron**

Kane see **Keenan**

Kanisha

A fairly recent Black American name, blending the fashionable elements Ka- and -isha. It is also found as **Kaneesha**, **Kaneisha** and in forms such as **Kenisha**, when it may be thought of as a feminine equivalent of KENNETH.

Kanye

Kanye has come in to use as a boy's name in the last few years as a result of the success of the rapper Kanye West. Kanye is the name of a town in Botswana, but this may be coincidental.

Kara see **Cara**

Kareem

Kareem or **Karim** is an Arabic name meaning 'generous, noble'. The feminine is **Karima**. 'The most Generous' is one of the titles of Allah. The related name **Karam** 'generosity, bounty' is used for both sexes. The name is current among African-Americans inspired by such holders as the basketball player Kareem Abdul-Jabbar.

Karel see **Charles**

Karen

Karen is pet form of Katerina, the Swedish form of KATHERINE. **Karena** (although this may owe something to Carina – see under CARA), **Karin** and ultimately their variants **Caryn** and **Caron**, are further Scandinavian forms of the name, although Caron can also be a Welsh masculine name.

Karenza see **Kerensa**

Kari see **Caroline**

Karin, Karina see **Cara, Karen**

Karis see **Charis**

Karissa see **Cara**

Karl, Karla, Karlee, Karley, Karly see **Carl**

Karma

This concept, found in Buddhism and other religions, of the consequence of actions in spiritual enlightenment, from a Sanskrit word that means both 'work' and 'fate', has very recently come to be used as a first name. With its typically feminine -a ending, it is usually used for girls.

Karol, Karoline see **Carol**

Karson see **Carson**

Karter see Carter

Kasandra, Kassandra, Kassidy see Cassandra

Kasey see Casey

Kasia see Keziah

Kasimir see Casimir

Kason see Carson

Kasper see Jasper

Katarina, Kate, Katharine see Katherine

Katelyn, Katelynn see Caitlin

Katherine

Although it is a name of unknown meaning, Katherine was early on associated with the Greek word for 'pure' (an appropriate sense for the name of so many virgin saints) and this is frequently given as its meaning. It is a name spelt in a variety of ways. This is partly due to the fact that the original Greek form of the name was *Aikaterine*, giving the spellings with 'e' in the middle, while the Greek word for 'pure' was *katharos*, which led to these being 'corrected' to the 'a' spelling. The commonest forms are **Katherine, Katharine, Catherine, Catharine** and, more recently, **Kathryn**. A wide variety of forms from other languages have also been adopted by English speakers. **Caterina** and **Catherina** show the Italian forms, KAREN the Scandinavian, and **Katja** or **Katia** is a little-used Russian form. The Spanish forms **Catalina** and **Katarina** are well represented in the USA. There is an important group of names from the Celtic areas of Great Britain: **Kathleen** is the Irish form of the name, with CAITLIN showing its Gaelic form; **Catriona**, given wide currency by R.L. Stevenson's 1893 novel of that title, is the Scottish Gaelic form, with **Catrina, Katrina** and **Katrin(e)** as variants; Wales gives us **Catrin, Cadi** and **Cati**. Short forms of these names include **Cathie, Cathy, Kate** (occasionally **Cate**), **Katie, Katy, Kathie, Kathy,** KAY (which can be used for any name beginning with 'K'), **Kit, Kittie, Kitty** and, less frequently, **Trina**. KERRY is said by some to be an Irish or Irish-American pet form, and the name is the main source of KAY.

Currently Katie is very popular in England, Scotland and Ireland, with Kate rather less used. Katherine is the most used of the names in the USA, and is also used in England and Scotland, although Catherine is the more popular spelling there, as it is in the Irish Republic. The Scots also like Kathryn and use their native Catriona. The spelling Catharine seems to be out of favour everywhere.

Katlyn see Caitlyn (*see* Caitlin)

Katrin, Katrina, Katrine, Katy see Katherine

Kay, Kayla

Kay is primarily a pet form of Katherine, but can be a shortening of any other name beginning with K. There are many variations on this theme. Kay can become **Kaya** (and cases of Kya and Kaia may belong here rather than as KAI), there are the KADY group of names, and names such as Kayla (**Kaila, Kaylah, Cayla, Keyla**) which is very popular in the USA and growing in use in Scotland and the Irish Republic. This, however is as much a shortening of Michaela (see MICHAEL) as an elaboration of Kay. Others include **Kaylin** also found as **Kailyn, Kaelyn, Kaylyn, Kaylynn** and **Kaylen** and KAYLEIGH, below.

Kaycee see Casey

Kaydee, Kaydi see Kady

Kaydence see Cadence

Kayleigh, Keely

Kayleigh is probably best analysed as a blend of KAY and LEIGH, although it has been suggested that it comes from the Irish surname **Kayley**, which ultimately comes from the word *caol* ('slim'), just as the name **Kaylyn** has been derived from the Irish

Caelainn ('slender lady'), or *Caoilfhinn* (see CAOLAN) rather than the more obvious blend of Kay and Lyn, while **Keely** (also **Keylee**, **Keeley** and **Keelie**) is derived from *cadhla* ('graceful'). As with so many recently fashionable names, the sound of these names is probably more important than the sense, for they complete a set with the other recently fashionable names KELLY and KYLIE. Kayleigh is found in numerous spellings, such as **Kaylee**, **Kalie**, **Caley** and **Caleigh**. Use of the name took off after the group Marillion had a hit with a song called *Kayleigh* in 1985. Kayleigh is well used throughout the English-speaking world.

Kayne, Kean see **Keenan**

Keagan see **Keegan**

Kealan see **Caolan**

Keanu
Virtually unknown before the actor Keanu Reeves made the name famous, this is a Hawaiian name meaning 'cool breeze over the mountains'

Keaton
This is a surname, which probably comes from the Old English for the scavenging bird the kite. It has recently come into use as a first name for boys.

Keavy see **Caoimhe**

Keefer see **Kiefer**

Keegan
Keegan or **Keagan** is an Irish surname from the Irish *Mac Aodhagáin*, with *Aodhagáin* being a pet form of Aodh (see AIDAN). It is now being used as a first name for boys.

Keelan see **Caolan**

Keelie, Keeley see **Kayleigh**

Keelin see **Caolan**

Keely see **Kayleigh**

Keenan, Cian, Kane
The Irish surname **Keenan** comes from **Kenan**, the pet form of the name **Cian** ('ancient'), which was usually anglicised as **Kean** but is now found as **Kian** (occasionally **Kyan**). Variations of these names are not always easy to sort out from **Kane** (also found as **Kaine** and **Kayne**), which was popular in Australia in the 1960s and which usually comes from the Irish name **Cathan** meaning 'warrior', although as a surname Kane can also indicate someone from the French town of Caen. Cian is currently very popular in Ireland, where it is also found as Kian, and Kian is also well used in both England and Ireland. The other forms are more likely to be found in the USA.

Keesha see **Keisha**

Keeva see **Caoimhe**

Keir
The use of this surname, from the Norse word *kerr* for a patch of wet ground overgrown with brushwood, as a boy's name in Scotland is most likely due to the fame of Keir Hardy (1856–1915) Scottish socialist leader, and one of the first Labour party members of Parliament.

Keira, Keiron see **Kieran**

Keisha
The origin of this modern name is not known. It has been suggested that it could be from the Bobangi language of Central Africa, where the word *nkisa* means 'favourite', but this is likely to be wishful thinking; or that it is a blend of the fashionable K- beginning of a name with **Aisha**. However, it is spelt in a wide variety of ways, one of which is **Keshia**, which is also recorded as a form of KEZIAH, so Keisha could also be a

development of that. Other spellings of the name include **Keesha**, **Kiesha** and **Kesha**, and it is often found prefixed with La- to give forms such as **LaKeisha**.

Keith

Keith is a Scottish place and surname, meaning 'a wood'. It was not adopted as a first name until the twentieth century. It was popular in the mid-twentieth century. Its most famous bearer is probably the guitarist Keith Richard.

Kel see **Kelvin**

Kelan see **Caolan**

Kelly

This is an Irish surname, which probably means something like 'war, strife', used as a first name for both sexes, but now more commonly for girls. In the form **Kelley** it was well established in the American Bible Belt by the 1950s, but the form Kelly seems to have come into use rather later in the UK. Kelly is currently well used in Ireland and the USA. The masculine name **Kellen**, in use in the USA since the 1980s, may represent a new masculine form.

Kelsey

The surname from which this name comes derives from a place name in Lincolnshire meaning 'Cenel's Island', Cenel being a personal name derived from the Old English word for 'fierce'. It was at first a boy's name, then used for both sexes, but is now mainly female. Spellings such as **Kelsie** and **Kelsee** are also found. Kelsey Grammer the actor is an early male example. Kelsey has been very popular in the USA in recent years, but is in decline; but it is still well used in Scotland

Kelton see **Colton**

Kelvin

Attempts have been made to link this name with the Old English name **Kelwin**, meaning 'keel-friend', but it is far more likely that a bearer of this Scottish first name has connections with Glasgow, through which the river Kelvin flows, and which has a Kelvingrove Park, a Kelvin Hall and a benefactor in the scientist Lord Kelvin (1824–1907), who chose the river name as his title. The exact meaning of the river name is debated, but probably means either 'wooded river' or 'narrow river'. The name is sometimes shortened to **Kel**.

Kenan see **Keenan**

Kendall

This is a surname used as a first name for both sexes, particularly in the USA. The surname comes from either of two place names in the north of England, one meaning 'valley of the river Kent', the other 'valley with a spring'.

Kendra, Kendrick

Kendra is a blend of one of the many names beginning Ken- with the ending found in names such as Sandra. Some commentators regard it as the feminine version of the name Kendrick. This comes from a surname which has various sources depending on whether the original holder was English, Welsh, Scottish or Irish.

Kenelm

An Old English name meaning 'brave-helmet', Kenelm was the name of an Anglo-Saxon saint. It is not a common name, but had a famous bearer in Sir Kenelm Digby (1603–65), who in his varied life was a diplomat, privateer, writer and a scholar who left behind a magnificent collection of important manuscripts, as well as being the devoted husband of VENETIA Stanley. The name is said to have remained traditional in his family.

Kenia see **Kenya**

Kenisha see **Kanisha**

Kenna see **McKenna**

Kennedy

Kennedy is an Irish surname, originally *O Cinnéidigh* formed from *ceann* 'head' and *éidigh* 'armoured'. This was the name of the nephew of the great Irish warrior king Brian Boru, and seems to have been given to him not because he had an armoured head, but because it was misshapen in some way. It started to be used for boys in 1960, when John F. Kennedy was running for President, and was used throughout the 1960s, only to drop out of the records thereafter until the 1990s, when it started to be used for both sexes. It is currently more used for girls (when it sometimes appears as **Kennedi**) than for boys.

Kenneth

The Gaelic name **Cinaed**, meaning 'born from fire', was a common one in the MacAlpine family and when one of their clan became the first king of Scotland in the ninth century the name was anglicised to Kenneth. There was another Gaelic name, **Coinneach**, meaning 'fair, handsome', from which the MACKENZIEs get their surname, which was also anglicised as Kenneth. Short forms are **Ken**, **Kennie** and **Kenny**. **Cenydd** is the Welsh form of the name, which goes back to the Dark Age King of the Gododdin, Cunneda, founder of the dynasty of Powys and celebrated in verse by the great medieval Welsh poet ANEIRIN.

Kent

Kent is a masculine name which comes from the surname, which is in turn derived from the county name. This in its turn means 'coastal district'.

Kenya

The name of this African country has been used as a first name for girls since the 1960s. It sometimes appears as **Kenia**. **Kenyon**, an English surname from a place of unknown meaning, which is used for boys, may function as the masculine equivalent, while Kenya itself may be used as a female equivalent of names such as Kenneth.

Kenzie see Mackenzie

Keon see Kiana

Keren

This is the short form of **Kerenhappuch**, one of the three daughters of JOB (see also JEMIMA and KEZIAH). The name means 'horn (i.e. container) of antimony', which refers to the kohl used even then to enhance the eyes. Although not a common name, it has been used quietly but steadily since at least the seventeenth century, and there are even recorded cases of three daughters being given the names of Job's three. Keren may sometimes be used as an alternative form of KAREN, although the names are unrelated.

Kerensa

A traditional Cornish girl's name meaning 'affection, love', Kerensa is also found in the forms **Kerenza** and **Karenza**.

Keri see Cerys, Kerry

Kermit see Dermot

Kerry

The Irish county name is the obvious source of this name, but its popularity may have been helped by the existence of the Welsh name Ceri (see CERYS) which is pronounced in the same way, and by the fact that Kerry has been used, particularly among the Boston Irish, as a pet form of KATHERINE. The name first became popular in Australia in the 1940s, when it was primarily thought of as a masculine name, as in the case of the businessman Kerry Packer, but it is now mainly used as a feminine name. It can also be found in forms such as **Keri**, and **Ker(r)yn** should probably be thought of as an elaboration or as a blend of Kerry and Karen.

Kersten see Christine

Kesha, Keshia see Keisha, Keziah

Kester see Christopher

Keturah

This is the name of the second wife of Abraham and was adopted by the Puritans. It has been used regularly since then, although more frequently in America than Britain, but it declined in popularity in the twentieth century. The name means 'fragrance' or 'incense'.

Kevin

Kevin, **Caoimhín** in Irish, was the name of a seventh-century Irish saint who founded an important school at Glendalough, which became equally famous for its learning and the beauty of its situation. The name was restricted to Ireland until the 1920s, but in the second half of the twentieth century it became enormously popular throughout the English-speaking world. Kevin means 'comely birth'. The spelling **Kevan** is often treated as a variant, but strictly speaking is a separate name meaning 'little handsome one'. Kevin is currently popular in the USA, Ireland, France and Estonia.

Keyla see Kay

Keylee see Kayleigh

Keyon

This is a modern coinage used for boys in the USA since the 1990s.

Keyshawn see Sean

Keziah, Kezia

This is the Hebrew word for 'cassia', a type of shrub much admired for its fragrance. It was the name of the middle of Job's three beautiful daughters, the others being JEMIMA and Kerenhappuch (see KEREN). The fame of these three must have been great, for, unusually for the Bible, we are given his daughters' names, but not his sons'. Keziah was the name of one of John Wesley's sisters, who was known by the pet form **Kissy**. She took the name to America, where along with WESLEY it became a popular Black name. It is also found as **Keshia** (see KEISHA) and **Kasia** (although this is also a Polish form of the name KATHERINE) and has the further pet forms **Kizzie**, **Kissie** and **Kezie**.

Khadija

This is an ancient Arabic name, indicating a premature baby. It is widely used in the Islamic world because of Khadija, the first wife of Mohammed and the first woman to adopt Islam. She has the title 'the best of women'.

Khaled

Khaled or **Khalid**, **Khaleda** or **Khalida** in the feminine, is an Arabic name meaning 'immortal, eternal'. Kaled ibn-al-Walid was one of Mohammed's generals, who is known as 'The Sword of God'.

Khalil

Khalil is the Arabic for 'friend'. It is one of the Arabic names well used in the USA. It is found as **Khaleel** in the Indian subcontinent, and there is a feminine **Khalilah**.

Kian see Keenan

Kiana, Kiara, Kierra

Kiana, well used in the USA for girls and also used in Australia, has two sources. When it first appeared in mainland USA it was respelling of the trade name Qiana, the brand-name of a type of silk-like fabric. This in turn was chosen from a computer-generated list, so has no further significance. By 1988 there was a new source of the name. It is also the Hawaiian form of the name DIANA, and this was made widely known through the fame of the exercise expert Kiana Tom, and many subsequent uses of the name were influenced by this. More significant, perhaps, is the sound of the name. It not only uses the immensely fashionable k- sound, but fits in with other new names, those listed under KEISHA and on the surrounding pages, and it blends imperceptibly with names derived from Kiera, particularly as it is impossible to tell from the page when a name like **Kiara** is pronounced with two or three syllables. It has been suggested that the boy's name **Keon** or **Kion** is the masculine equivalent of Kiana.

Kiefer

This has come into use, sometimes spelt **Keefer**, as a result of the fame of the actor Kiefer Sutherland. In origin it is a German surname either meaning a barrel-maker, the equivalent of the English surname COOPER, or else it comes from the German word for 'a pine tree'. Kiefer Sutherland was named after a family friend with this surname.

Kieran

Derived from the Irish word *ciar* ('black') Kieran means 'little dark one'. There are as many as 15 Irish saints of this name, one of whom, St Kieran of Saighir, is said to have been a missionary in Ireland even before St Patrick got there. Another, St Kieran of Clonmacnoise, is said to have used parchment made from the skin of his favourite cow to write down the great Irish national epic of *The Tain*. A twelfth-century copy of this sixth-century manuscript has come down to us as *The Book of the Dun Cow*. The correct Irish form of the name is **Ciaran**, although the K- form has been commoner elsewhere as it makes the pronunciation clearer. However, in a reversal of the trend to spell C names with a K, there is currently something of a return to the C form. The name can also be spelt as **Kieron** or **Keiron** and there are feminine forms **Ciara**, **Kiera** and **Keira**. The success of the actress Keira Knightly has led to the spread of this spelling. However, in the USA Ciara (**Cierra**, **Ciera**) is a name taken from a brand of perfume, given a soft 'c', and often pronounced identically with SIERRA. **Kira**, popular for some years in the USA, is probably also a form of the name, although it can also be seen as a form of Kyra, a feminine of CYRUS. In England Keira is currently the most popular form of the name, followed in popularity by Kiera and Kieron; in Scotland Keira is also the most popular, followed by Kiera then Ciara. In Ireland Ciara and Cianan are the dominant forms, but Kieran is also well used. In the USA Ciara is the best used (probably in the unrelated form as there is a popular singer of this name), followed by Keira and Kira with Kieran lagging well behind.

Kierra see Kiana

Kiersten see Christine

Kiesha see Keisha

Kiley see Kylee (*see* Kylie)

Killian, Kilian

Killian is an Irish saint who went as a missionary to Germany in the late seventh century and was martyred at Würzburg, where a cathedral was later built in his honour. The survival of the name into modern times may owe something to its use by Sir Walter Scott in *Anne of Geierstein* (1829). The name is a diminutive of the Irish word meaning 'strife' and is spelt **Cillian** in Irish. The name is most used in France, where both Cillian and Killian are well used, and where the spellings Kilian and Kylian are also found.

Kim, Kimberly

The name Kim comes primarily from Rudyard Kipling's novel of that name, published in 1901. His child hero, the 'little friend of all the world', was known as Kim in the Indian bazaars, but his full name was **Kimball** O'Hara. The success of the book led to Kim being used occasionally as a boy's name, and more often as a pet name, but the full form of the name does not seem to have been used much. Within a few years Kim was being used for girls, and has remained predominantly a female name. The spy 'Kim' Philby (real name Harold) is an example of the name used as a masculine nickname. When he got to Russia, Philby would have found that the name was also in use there as a quite common masculine name, invented in post-revolutionary fervour from the initial letters (in Russian) for 'Communist Youth International'.

Kim is also used as a short form of **Kimberly**, the commoner spelling as a first name for **Kimberley**, the South African diamond town. This came into use at about the same time as Kipling's book was published. Soldiers used to have a custom of naming their children after the garrison in which they were born, or after battles, and at the turn of the century there were many British soldiers around Kimberley, fighting in the Boer War. (This custom is well illustrated in Kipling's short story 'Daughter of the Regiment', where Colour-Sergeant McKenna's children are called Colaba, Muttra and Jhansi from the cantonments where they were born). Kimberley was at first mainly masculine, and is still sometimes used as a man's name, but is now predominantly female. It was well established in America by the 1950s and has been very popular ever since, often shortened to **Kimmy**. **Kimora**, publicised by the model Kimora Lee, may be used as a variant of Kimberly.

Kinsley, Kinsey

These two surnames, the first a form of Kinsella, an Irish surname for descendants from someone known as 'proud', the second from an Old English name formed from elements meaning 'royal victory', are starting to be used for girls in the USA. The sound is probably more important than any associations.

Kion see Kiana

Kira see Kieran

Kiran

Kiran is a Hindu boy's name meaning 'sunbeams'.

Kirk

Kirk is a Scandinavian name meaning 'a church'; it was brought to public notice by the film star Kirk Douglas. It is sometimes spelt **Kirke**.

Kirsta, Kirstie, Kirsty, Kirsten, Kirsteen, Kirstine see Christine

Kissie, Kissy see Keziah

Kistna see Krishna

Kit see Christopher, Katherine

Kittie, Kitty see Katherine

Kizzie see Keziah

Kobe

This name has come into use from the fame of the American basketball player Kobe Bryant. It is interpreted as either the name of an African tribe, or from the Swahili for 'tortoise'. It is sometimes found as **Cobe** or **Coby**.

Konner, Konnor see Conor

Konrad see Conrad

Krishna

Krishna meaning 'dark, black' is the name of a very popular Hindu god. There are various regional variations of the name including **Kishnan**, **Krishan** and **Kistna**.

Krista see Christine

Kristel see Crystal

Kristin, Kristina see Christine

Krystal see Crystal

Krystyna see Christine

Kurt see Conrad

Kya see Kai, Kay

Kyan see Keenan

Kyle

This is the name of a district in Scotland, used first as a surname, then as a first name, mainly for men, but occasionally for women, although **Kyla** is usually used for girls. It has been in use since at least the later part of the nineteenth century. Tradition links the district of Kyle with the name of Old King Cole, but less romantic place-name experts derive it from the river Coyl, which means 'narrow'. It is particularly popular in Scotland at the moment, as so many local place names are, and is also well used in England, Ireland and the USA. There we also find the elaborations **Kyler** (possibly a shortening of SKYLER) and **Kylan**.

Kylian see **Killian**

Kylie

Kylie is the word in an Aborigine Noongar language for a boomerang, and was given as a childhood nickname to the Australian writer Kathleen Tennant (1912–88). She used it as a pen name, and as she was a very successful novelist, the name began to be used by other Australians. The huge success of the Australian actress and singer Kylie Minogue spread it to the rest of the world. It is currently best used in the USA where it also appears as **Kylee**, **Kiley** and forms such as **Kyleigh** that overlap with names such as KAYLEIGH and other K+l names.

Kyra see **Cyrus**

Kyree, Kyrie see **Cyril**

L

Laban see **Leah**

Lacey

Lacey is a surname, originally belonging to someone from the village of Lassy in Normandy, used as a girl's first name. However, the fashion for the name probably owes much to the attractive associations it has with lace, particularly as the name is also spelt **Lacy** along with **Laci** and **Lacie**. The form Lacy was used regularly as a boy's name from the 1880s to the 1960s.

Lachlan

This Scottish Highland name comes from the Gaelic name for Norway, *Lochlann*. It is the origin of the surname MacLachlan. It can also be spelt **Lachlann** and **Lachunn**, and has pet forms **Lachie**, **Lachy** and **Lauchie**. Its popularity in Australia may perhaps owe something to a memory of General Lachlan Macquarie, who was an exceptionally liberal governor of New South Wales (1809–21), and whose encouragement of building projects led to the local late-Georgian style of architecture being called Macquarie style.

Lacy see **Lacey**

LaDarius see **Daria**, **Laetitia**

Ladonna see **Donna**

Laetitia, Letitia

This is the Latin word for 'joy, delight', used as a girl's name. It has been in use in England since the twelfth century, and was early on anglicised to **Lettice**. It is shortened to **Lettie** or **Letty**, and **Laeta** is an alternative form of the name. Another shortening, **Tiesha**, **Teesha** or **Ticia** is used as a name in its own right. Laetitia was influential in the explosion of names beginning La- among Black Americans since the 1970s, although names based on the French forms of 'the', *la* and *le*, did already exist and the use of names beginning with La- goes back to the nineteenth century (see further at LAMAR and LAVINIA). Laetitia became the more phonetic **Latisha** (shortened to **Tisha**), and from this developed names such as **Latasha** (as if La + Natasha), **LaToya** (perhaps from **Toya**, a Mexican pet form of Victoria), an increase in the use of **Larissa** (see LARA) and even some boys' names such as **LaDarius**.

Lafayette see **Lamar**

Laia see **Eulalia**

Laila, Lailah see **Leila**

Lainey see **Delaney**, **Elain (see Elaine)**, **Lane**

LaKeisha see **Keisha**

Lakshmi

Meaning 'sign, mark indicating a lucky birthmark', this is the name of the Hindu goddess of luck and prosperity whose symbol is the lotus. The name is used for both sexes. It can also be spelt **Laxmi**. See also INDIRA, KAMA.

Lal

Lal is the Sanskrit for 'to play, caress', and is used as a term for 'darling'. It is a boy's name, as is **Lalit** 'playful, charming'; with **Lalita**, in myth one of KRISHNA's playmates, used for girls.

Lalage

This come from the Greek word for 'to babble, prattle'. The name was used in the first century AD by the Latin poet Horace for the woman addressed in his love poems, and has been similarly used by a number of English poets since then. **Lallie** or **Lally** are short forms.

Lalit, Lalita see **Lal**

Lallie, Lally see **Lalage**

Lamar

A surname from the French for 'the pond', Lamar is used as a masculine name in the United States. Use was probably inspired by either Mirabeau Buonaparte Lamar (1798–1859), 2nd president of the Republic of Texas, or Lucius Quintus Cincinnatus Lamar (1825–93), Confederate politician and associate justice of the US Supreme Court. Both were members of a prominent Georgia family. Lamar was one of the early names beginning with La- that has been in use from at least the 1880s. Another was **Lafayette**, the name of the French general who came to help the American colonists in their fight against the British. These, alongside the names under LAVINIA, may lie behind the more recent uses of La- as a name form among African-Americans.

Lambert

This is an old Germanic name meaning 'land-bright', which should perhaps be interpreted as 'pride of the nation'. It was the name of a seventh-century saint and was popular in the past, but is rarely used today, although a knowledge of the name is kept alive by the fame of Lambert Simnel, the pretender to Henry VII's throne.

Lana see **Alan**

Lance, Launce

These are both used as independent names from the surname and as short forms of **Lancelot** or **Launcelot**, the great knight of King Arthur's court. Despite his fame, we do not really know where the name comes from. Lancelot first appears in French Arthurian literature, and the name may come from the words *L'ancel*, diminutive *L'ancelot*, meaning 'the servant' (perhaps a reference to his humility or to his time spent learning from the Lady of the Lake).

Landon, London

Landon is a surname from an Old English place name meaning 'long hill'. It has been used quietly for generations as a first name, but increased in popularity from the 1980s, and is now among the top fifty names for boys in the USA. The success of, and affection felt for, the actor Michael Landon (1936–91) may have been an influence in this. The name has a number of variants such as **Landen** and **Landyn**, and mutates into the place name **London** which has been used increasingly for both boys and girls.

Lane

This surname, used as a first name for both sexes but mainly for boys, can come from various sources. The commonest is as an English surname from someone who lived in a lane; but it can also be from the French *laine* 'wool' or from the Irish surname O Luain 'descendant of Luan' a name meaning 'warrior'. It is also found as **Layne**. **Laney** (see ELAINE, DELANEY) may be used as a feminine equivalent.

Lanna see **Alan**

Lanty see **Atalanta**

Laoise

This Irish girl's name means 'radiant girl', a form of the name **Luigsech**. It is pronounced, and sometimes spelt **Leesha**.

Lara, Larissa

Lara is the pet form of the Russian Larissa, which is of uncertain origin. The ancient Greek city of Larissa has been suggested as a source, but so has the Latin *Hilaria* (the source of HILARY). Lara is the tragic heroine of Boris Pasternak's *Doctor Zhivago* (1957), and the name became widely known as a result of the success of the 1965 film of the novel. Some parents may use it as a variant of LAURA. Lara is used steadily in England, Scotland and Australia; Larissa is preferred in Switzerland and the USA.

Laraine, Larraine see Lorraine

Larissa see Lara

Larry, Lars see Laurence

Latasha see Laetitia

Latif, Latifa

These are the masculine and feminine forms of an Arabic name meaning 'kind, gentle, courteous'. The All-Gentle is one of the names of Allah. In the Arabic world Latifa al-Zayat is a distinguished novelist. The name is better known in the USA from the hip-hop singer and actress Queen Latifa.

Latisha see Laetitia

LaToya see Laetitia, Toya

Lauchie see Lachlan

Launce, Launcelot see Lance

Laura, Lauren

The Latin equivalent of the Greek DAPHNE, Laura comes from the word for a laurel tree. To be crowned with a wreath of laurels was an honour given in the ancient world to those triumphant in war, sport and the arts; a vestige of it survives in our term 'poet laureate'. Although the name comes from Latin, the Romans did not use it; but it was in use in the Middle Ages, probably with the idea that the bearer was of such excellent qualities or beauty that she deserved the laurel crown. In the fourteenth century, the Italian poet Petrarch made it famous by using it for the name of his beloved in his sonnets. The name is also spelt **Lora**, and has pet forms **Lori** and **Lolly**. It has a number of derivative forms, the most widely used of which at the moment is **Lauren**, a name that seems to have been coined for the film actress Lauren Bacall. The alternative form **Loren** is used for both boys (see under LAURENCE) and girls. The singer **Lauryn** Hill has popularised this alternative spelling. The plant name **Laurel** is also used, along with diminutives **Lauretta** or **Loretta**, as well as such elaborations as **Lorana** and **Lorinda**. Another form is found in the name of Ella **Lorena** Kennedy, the daughter of Scarlett O'Hara and Frank Kennedy in *Gone with the Wind*. **Lowri** is the Welsh form of the name, and **Laure** and its elaboration **Laurine** are used in France. These names may sometimes be used as feminine forms of LAURENCE. Lauren is the preferred form for girls at the moment in England, Scotland Ireland and the USA, although Laura is also well used. Laura is also widely popular on the Continent.

Lauraine see Lorraine

Laure, Laurel, Lauren see Laura

Laurence, Lawrence

This name shares with LAURA a derivation from the word for a laurel, probably via the name of the Roman town of *Laurentium*. It came into use because of the popularity of the third-century saint, a librarian who was martyred by being roasted on a grid-iron because he would not hand over the money which had been entrusted to him to distribute to the poor. The pet form **Larry** is sometimes used as a name in its own right. Other short forms are **Laurie** and **Lawrie**, and in Scotland **Lowrie**. **Laurent** is the form of the name used in France and sometimes used by English speakers (confusingly, Laurence is the French feminine form), and **Lorenzo**, the Italian and Spanish form of the name, is sometimes used in the USA. This gives a short form **Loren**, which is not uncommon, but can also be a form of LAUREN. **Lars** is the Scandinavian form. In Ireland Lawrence became popular because of St Lawrence O'Toole, bishop of Dublin and a man deeply involved in caring for his people at the time of the twelfth-century Norman invasion of Ireland. In his case, Lawrence was used as a substitute for the native Gaelic name **Lorcan** ('little fierce one'). One of the surnames that come from Laurence is **Lawson**, currently being used for boys in the USA.

Lauretta, Laurine, Lauryn see Laura

Lavada see Lavinia

Lavender see Flora

Lavenia, Lavera see Lavinia

Laverne

Laverne seems to be an American respelling of the French surname Lavergne. The family was an important one in France; Marie-Madeleine, Comtesse de la Fayette, the author of *La Princess de Clèves*, which is commonly considered the first novel in French, was from this family. Lavergnes were among the early settlers in Canada, and were among the Acadians expelled from Canada in 1755 who settled in Louisiana. In the form Laverne or **Lavern** the surname was being used as a first name for both sexes by 1880 and remained in regular use until the 1970s. The name later came to be thought of as typically African-American, and as a result was a major influence in the creation of the La- suffix now thought of as typical of many African-American creations.

Lavinia

In Roman mythology, Lavinia was the daughter of the king of Latium, and wife of Aeneas (see ANGUS), the Trojan who became the founder of the Roman people. It was not used by the Romans as a name, but was taken up in the fifteenth century with the Renaissance revival of interest in things classical. It was particularly popular in the eighteenth century after the success of a poem by James Thomson called 'Lavinia and Palemon' (basically a retelling of the biblical story of RUTH and Boaz), but is now only quietly used. **Vina** is a short form of the name. The name seems to have mutated early on in the USA. As early as 1880 alongside Lavinia we find **Lavina**, **Lavenia** and **Lavonia**. Lavina remained in regular use up until the 1940s. This set up a pattern of new names formed from the letters l, v and n or another consonant, so that we find **Lavada** in use by 1881 and used well into the 1940s; **Lavera** in use by 1903 and used into the 1930s and **Lavonne** and its variants from 1902 and in use into the 1970s. Lavon was in use for men by the 1920s and is found as **Levon** by the 1930. By the 1930s also, namers were beginning to break away from the v as the second consonant and forming names such as **LaWanda** and **Ladonna** (see further at LAETITIA). This, combined with the Southern surnames of French origin beginning with La or Le such as LAVERNE, above, lies behind the use of La and Le as a modern name element attachable to almost any name.

Lawrence, Lawrie, Lawson see Laurence

Laxmi see Lakshmi

Layla see Leila

Layne see Lane

Layton

Layton is a surname, from an English place name meaning 'leek field' which has been used as a boy's name in the USA for the last few years.

Lea see Lee

Leah

Leah is the name of one of the more hard-done-by women in the Bible. According to the story (Genesis 29), Jacob fell in love with his cousin RACHEL and served her father Laban for seven years to win her, but her elder sister Leah was secretly substituted on the wedding night. Although Jacob was later given Rachel to be Leah's co-wife, he hated Leah, but God compensated her with numerous sons. **Lia**, the Italian form of the name (also used as a short form of various names ending with those letters), and **Léa**, the French, are sometimes used as variants. Despite her sad history, Leah is currently a popular name throughout Europe and North America.

Leala see Leila

Leana, Leanne see Julia

Leander

In mythology, Leander swam the Hellespont every night in order to be with his beloved, Hero, until one night he was caught in a storm and drowned. In 1810 the Romantic poet Byron, who was always keen to show that his club foot did not prevent him being a sportsman, proved it was possible to swim this strait between Europe and Asia, but only at the cost of making himself ill. Afterwards he wrote a set of verses in which he wondered how on earth Leander had managed the swim *and* spent the night with his lover. He concluded cynically, 'Ye mortals, how the gods do plague you!/ He lost his life; and I've the ague'. Leander comes from the Greek meaning 'lion-man', which perhaps answers Byron's question. Spanish-speakers use the name in the form **Leandro**. It has also been used for girls, and there is a feminine form, **Leandra**. Some parents may use these names as an elaboration of LEE and ANNE.

Leanna see Julia

Leanora see Eleanor

Lee, Leigh, Lea

Lee comes from the common surname, which means 'a meadow'. Its popularity in the southern United States probably stems from the once common practice of naming children after people admired by the parents, in this case after the Confederate general Robert E. Lee (1807–70). From there it spread, developing variant forms, throughout the USA, and then to other English-speaking countries. At the moment Lee is well used as a boy's name in Scotland and the Republic of Ireland.

Leesha see Laoise

Leila, Leilani

Leila is a Persian name meaning 'darkness' or 'night' and thus a type of dark beauty. She is the heroine of a popular romance called *Leila and Majnun*. The name was made widely known in England by Lord Byron, who used it both for the Turkish child brought to England in *Don Juan* and for the tragic heroine of *The Giaour* (1813). It was subsequently used by other writers as a name for Eastern beauties. Variant forms are **Laila, Lailah, Leala, Leilah, Leyla, Lyla, Lila** and **Lilah**, and, particularly after Eric Clapton used it for his 1972 hit, **Layla**. **Leilani**, which looks like an elaboration is actually a Hawaiian name meaning 'heavenly flowers', while Lila or Leela can also be an Indian name meaning 'play, amusement'.

Leland

Leland is an English surname meaning 'fallow land' now being used for boys in the USA. The Governor of California, Leland Stanford founded what is officially Leland Stanford University in 1885 in memory of his son Leland Jr. The name has been used in a number of American television shows recently, which may account for the growth in its use.

Len, Lennie, Lenny, Lennard see Leo

Lena

Lena, is a short form of names such as Helena (see HELEN) and Magdalena (MADELINE), now used as a independent name. Lena is currently a popular choice in Austria, Germany and France.

Lennon

The surname Lennon, from the Irish *O Leannain* 'descendant of Leannan', a name meaning 'lover', has recently become a well-used choice for boys in Scotland. The singer Liam Gallagher named his son Lennon in honour of the Beatle John Lennon, and it is likely that others do so for the same reason.

Lenore, Lenora see Eleanor

Leo, Leonard, Leonie

There is a large group of names containing the element 'Leo' meaning 'lion'. Leo was the name of 13 popes, and was popular in the Middle Ages. Leonard, sometimes spelt **Lennard** (and **Leonardo** in both Spanish and Italian), is an old Germanic name meaning 'brave as a lion', and is shortened to **Len**, **Lennie** or **Lenny**. **Lionel**, the name of one of King Arthur's nobler knights, also belongs in this group since it means 'little lion', and it occasionally gets changed to **Leonel** to conform with the other names. **Leopold** looks as if it also belongs with the lion names; in fact, it comes from the Old German name *Leutpold*, formed from words meaning 'people' and 'bold', but it changed its form under the influence of Leo- names. (See also LLEWELLYN.)

The feminine forms of the name mostly come from the French form of Leo, **Leon**. They include **Leonie**, **Leontia**, **Leontine**, **Leola** and **Leona**. **Leonora** is not a lion name, but a form of ELEANOR.

Leo and Leon are both currently well used in England, Scotland and the Irish Republic; Leonie and Leon are popular in Germany and France. Léo and Lenny are also well used in France. In the USA Leonardo is currently the most popular of these names, probably under the influence of the actor Leonardo DiCaprio.

Leroy

The old French for 'the king', Leroy may have been used originally as a surname used to describe those who were servants to the king of France. It is a name particularly associated with the United States, and is sometimes found in the form **Elroy**. It has been recorded from the late eighteenth century in the USA and was at its most popular in the first half of the twentieth century.

Leslie, Lesley

This name comes from the Scottish place and surname, which probably means 'garden of hollies'. From the evidence of Robert Burns's poem to 'Bonnie Lesley' it seems to have come into use as a girl's name before being used as a boy's in the second third of the nineteenth century. This is a reversal of the usual pattern of boys' names becoming girls'. There used to be a careful distinction made between Lesley as a feminine form and Leslie as the masculine, but the distinction is no longer made, at least for girls. It can also be found in spellings such as **Lezlie** and **Lesly**.

Lester

This surname is a modified spelling of the place name Leicester, meaning 'dwellings on the river Legra'. It has been used for the last 100 or so years, well-known holders being the Canadian statesman Lester Pearson and the jockey Lester Piggott.

Letitia, Lettice, Lettie see Laetitia

Letty see Alethea, Laetitia

Levi

In the Bible, this is the name of the third son of LEAH and JACOB, whose descendants were to become the priests of Israel. His name means 'joined, attached'. However, in many people's minds the name is most strongly associated with jeans. There are records of the name being used for girls as well as the usual boys.

Levon see Lavinia

Lewis, Louis

When the barbarian Franks invaded France in the Dark Ages, they brought with them a name meaning 'famous battle' that was written down by the literate, but conquered, Gauls as *Hludowig* or *Chlodowig*. This name developed into **Clovis**, the name of the first Merovingian king (481–511), and later lost its first sound to become **Louis**, a name almost synonymous with French kingship. **Ludovic** comes from the Latin form of the name, and **Aloys** and **Aloysius** – the name of a Spanish Jesuit saint, but probably best known as the name of Sebastian Flyte's teddy-bear in Evelyn Waugh's *Brideshead Revisited* (1945) – was a form which developed in Provence, and spread to Spain and Italy. The English form of the name is **Lewis**. **Luis** is the usual Spanish form of the name, well used in the USA. Pet forms of the name include **Lou**, **Louie**, **Lew** and **Lewie**. LOUISE is the main feminine form. **Loïc** is a Breton pet form that is currently well used as an independent name in France.

Lewis has been used in England since the Middle Ages – it appears to have been the name of one of Chaucer's sons, for whom he wrote an astronomy primer – and is popular once again in the UK. (Louis is also well used). Lewis is particularly popular in Scotland. Scottish use may sometimes be with reference to the Isle of Lewis, as Scottish place names are a popular current source of first names. The growth in recent years of the name Lewis may owe something to the character in the *Inspector Morse* television show usually just referred to by his surname, Lewis. In the USA where Louis is the usual spelling there are two pronunciations current. Louis Armstrong, despite coming from French influenced New Orleans, always insisted that his name be pronounced Lewis. However, the three rhyming nephews of Donald Duck, Louie, Hughey and Dewey, show the alternative, French pronunciation.

Lex, Lexie, Lexus see **Alexander**

Leyla see **Leila**

Lezlie see **Leslie**

Lia see **Leah**

Liadan

This is an Irish name meaning 'grey lady'. In Irish legend Liadan plays a role similar to that of HELOISE, having been a nun and poet who fell in love with a monk and dies grieving for him.

Liam

Liam is an Irish shortening of WILLIAM, which has become an independent name. It is currently popular in the UK, Ireland and the USA.

Lian, Lianna, Lianne see **Julia**

Libby see **Elizabeth**

Liberty

Liberty is the vocabulary word for freedom used as a first name for girls in the USA. It had had a brief popularity in 1918 at the end of the First World War, but then disappeared until 2001, the year of the 9/11 attack on the World Trade Center Twin Towers, when it suddenly came back into use, peaking in 2004, the year after the invasion of Iraq.

Liesel see **Elizabeth**

Lige see **Elias**

Lila, Lilah see **Leila**

Lili, Lilian, Liliana, Liliane, Lilias see **Lily**

Lilith

A name from Jewish mythology, Lilith has been variously interpreted as 'a serpent', 'a screech-owl' or 'a vampire'. According to legend, she was the first wife of Adam, before the creation of EVE, but refused to submit to him, and as a result was expelled from the Garden of Eden. She became an evil spirit particularly dangerous to new-born children, and one tradition says she took her revenge by becoming the serpent of the Tree of Knowledge. The name is rarely given to children, but in recent years Lilith has been used as a symbol by some sections of the feminist movement.

Lily

Use of this flower name as a first name may owe something to Christian symbolism, both to the association of the Madonna lily with the Virgin Mary as a symbol of purity, and to the recommendation of the Sermon on the Mount to 'consider the lilies of the field'. Historically, it has also been used as a pet form of ELIZABETH (German **Lili** is still used in this way), and it is impossible to distinguish between these two uses. The name is also spelt **Lilly**. **Lilian** (or **Lillian**) comes from the Spanish form of the name, **Liliana**, and in Scotland this was transformed into **Lilias**, **Lillias** or **Lillas**. Lilian may have influenced the development of the name Lianne (see JULIAN). Occasionally, as in the case of the French national-team footballer Lilian Thuram, Lilian has been used for a man. As a result of his fame, Lilian is now established as a masculine name in France, where it fits with other popular boy's name ending in -an, such as DYLAN. Liliane is the feminine form in France. SUSAN is the Hebrew equivalent of Lily.

Lily was one of the flower names that came into use in the mid-nineteenth century, and Lillian was popular in the 1920s and 30s. As a result the names were felt to be old-fashioned by the middle of the twentieth century. However, there has recently been a marked fashion for Lily, and it is now popular in the UK and Ireland, while Lillian is popular in the USA. The model Kate Moss has called her daughter **Lila**.

Lina

This is a short form of a number of names ending in -lina, such as Angelina (ANGELA), Paulina (PAUL) and SELINA, which has come to be used as a name in its own right, just as **Line** is used in France and other countries from names such as CAROLINE and JACQUELINE. In Arabic Lina is a girl's name which means 'gentle, tender' and in India it can be a Sanskrit name meaning 'united'.

Lincoln

The surname, Lincoln, comes from the English place name, which means 'colony by the pool'. It has been in regular use in the USA as a boy's name since the Presidency of Abraham Lincoln. There has recently been an increase in use, perhaps in line with other patriotic names such as LIBERTY.

Linda

Linda started life as a short form of names ending -linda, such as BELINDA. These were old Germanic names where the *-linda* means 'serpent'. However, a much more obvious meaning for *linda* is the Spanish adjective meaning 'pretty', and most users of the name probably think of it in this sense. It is also found in the forms **Lynda** and **Lindy**. The shortenings **Lyn** and **Lin** are shared with a number of other names.

Linden

Used for both sexes, this appears to be the old English word for the lime tree, and is thus another plant name; but use, particularly for girls, owes much to the popularity of other Lin- names. The water is further muddied by the surname **Lyndon**, which is sometimes used as a first name, most prominently by the American president Lyndon Baines Johnson (1908–73). This comes, ultimately, from the same root, being from a place name meaning 'the hill with linden trees'. **Lynden** is an alternative form.

Lindsay

An aristocratic Scottish surname used as a first name, Lindsay probably comes from family connections with the district of Lincolnshire called Lindsey. When used for men it is usually in the form Lindsay, but for girls, now the more frequent use, it also occurs as **Lindsey**, **Linsey**, **Linsay** and various other spellings including **Linzi**. Lindsay has always been very rare as a masculine name in the USA. The actress Lindsay Lohan is a prominent current user.

Lindy see Linda

Linet, Linette see Lynette

Linnea

The Swedish botanist Linneaus, who established the modern form of plant classification, used his own name in the form Linnea as the Latin name of his favourite flower, the borage or starflower. This became a popular name for girls in Sweden, which has since spread to other countries. The short form is **Nea**.

Linsay, Linsey see Lindsay

Linus

A Greek name meaning 'flax', Linus is found in the New Testament (2 Timothy 4:21), where St Paul sends greetings from Linus and CLAUDIA. It was also the name of a saint and a Pope. There is an unsubstantiated tradition that Linus and Claudia were brother and sister, and British, and invited some of the first missionaries to Britain. There is, coincidentally, a Welsh feminine name **Llian**, which also means 'flax'. Linus is probably best known as the name of a cartoon character in the *Peanuts* cartoon, but the name is used in real life, as in the double Nobel Prize-winning scientist Linus Pauling and the actor Linus Roach.

Linzi see **Lindsay**

Lionel see **Leo**

Lisa, Lisbeth, Lise, Lisette see **Elizabeth**

Lito[1] see **Angel**

Lito[2] see **Angela**

Litzy

Litzy La Rosa is a Mexican singer and soap opera star whose success has led to use of the name in the USA. It appears to be a variant of Lizzy (see ELIZABETH).

Livia, Livy see **Oliver**

Liz, Liza, Lizbeth, Lizeth, Lizzie see **Elizabeth**

Lleucu see **Lucy**

Llewellyn

This is a Welsh man's name, traditionally interpreted as meaning 'lion-like', but which probably derives from the word for 'a leader'. It is also spelt **Llywelyn**, and is shortened to **Llew**, **Llelo** and **Lyn**, which last is often used as a name in its own right. It has been anglicised to **Leoline** or LEWIS.

Llian see **Linus**

Llinos, Llio see **Lynette**

Lloyd

This is a Welsh name usually described as meaning 'grey', but in fact the word covers a range of colours including browns and greys. The correct Welsh spelling of the name is **Llwyd**, and it is also found as **Lhuyd**, **Loyd** and, particularly in America – as in the case of the boxer Floyd Patterson – as **Floyd**.

Llywelyn see **Llewellyn**

Logan

As a surname this comes from a number of Scottish and Irish place names which come in turn from the Gaelic for 'little hollow'. A famous earlier holder of the name was the American-born British writer Logan Pearsall Smith (1865–1946). It is currently very popular in the USA as a boy's name and is beginning to be used for girls. It is also among the top boy's names in the UK, Canada, Australia and France.

Loïc see **Lewis**

Lois

Lois is another New Testament name: she was the grandmother of TIMOTHY, and is praised in St Paul's second Epistle to Timothy for her great faith. The name came into fashion, along with other biblical names, among the Puritans, and they took it to America, where it is still more common than elsewhere. The name is thought to be Greek, but its meaning is not known. The use of the name has been reinforced by Lois also being a form of HELOISE, via a contraction of the Provencal form **Aloisa** or **Aloys**. The name is probably best known as the name of Superman's girlfriend, Lois Lane.

Lola, Lolita see **Carl, Dolores**

Lolly see **Laura**

Lon, Lonnie see **Alfonso**

Lona

As a Welsh girl's name this was originally a short form of Moelona. This was the pen name of Elizabeth Mary Mones (1878–1953), Welsh language novelist and children's writer. She took her name from the farm where she lived *Moylon* which came from *moel* 'bare' (see MOELWYN). Lona can also be a short form of various other names.

London see **Landon**

Lora see **Laura**

Loraine see **Lorraine**

Lorana see **Laura**

Lorane see **Lorraine**

Lorcan see **Laurence**

Lorelei

The meaning of Lorelei is not entirely clear. The *ley* at the end is quite securely interpreted as 'cliff, rock', but the first part can be interpreted 'to lure' or 'to watch out for'. The Lorelei Rock is a headland on the River Rhine where legend says a beautiful woman, the Lorelei, lured sailors to their death in the treacherous current beneath her rock. The name is used in France and has recently been revived in the USA. Lorelei Lee was the name of the heroine of Anita Loos 1925 comic novel *Gentlemen Prefer Blondes*.

Loren see **Laura, Laurence**

Lorena, Loretta see **Laura**

Lorenzo see **Laurence**

Lori, Lorinda see **Laura**

Lorraine

This comes from the district of France which gets its name from the Latin *Lothari regnum* 'kingdom of Lothair' (see LUTHER). The reason it is used has been much discussed. In the form **Lorane** it is found in the USA by 1820, and has been suggested that it may initially have been a blend of LAURA and ANNE. It has also been claimed it is a Scottish name introduced via the mother of Mary Queen of Scots who was Marie de Lorraine. There can be little doubt that from the late nineteenth century it was used with reference to the Franco-Prussian war and in memory of fighting in the area in the two World Wars. It is also used with reference to Joan of Arc, who was known as the Maid of Lorraine as well as the Maid of Orleans. However, she was not made a saint until 1920. The name was not used in France until well into the twentieth century, but has been well used in England and America. There are numerous variants of which the most common are **Loraine**, **Laraine**, **Larraine** and **Lauraine**.

Lotfi see **Lutfi**

Lothair see **Luther**

Lotte, Lottie see **Charlotte**

Lou see **Lewis, Louise**

Louanne, Louella see **Luella**

Louie, Louis see **Lewis, Louise**

Louise

Louise is the feminine form of the name LEWIS. It is also found as **Louisa** and has the Spanish form **Luisa**. Pet forms are **Lou**, **Louie** and **Lulu**. Clovis, the alternative form of Lewis, has recently developed the feminine form **Clova**, although this may owe something to the flower name CLOVER, found in Susan Coolidge's 'Katy' books. Louise is currently well used in England, Scotland and Ireland.

Lourdes see **Dolores**

Lowena

Lowena or **Lowenna** is a Cornish name, meaning 'joy', that is being increasingly widely used.

Lowri see **Laura**

Lowrie see **Laurence**

Loyd see **Lloyd**

Luana, Luanna see **Luella**

Luca, Lucas see **Luke**

Lucasta

This was a name coined by the seventeenth-century poet Richard Lovelace for his poems addressed to LUCY Sacheverell. It is said to have been formed from the Latin *lux casta* ('chaste light'). His poem 'To Lucasta, Going to the Wars', contains the famous lines: 'I could not love thee (Dear) so much,/ Lov'd I not honour more'. (See also ALTHEA)

Lucca see **Luke**

Lucia, Lucian, Luciano, Lucien, Lucilla, Lucille, Lucinda, Lucius see **Lucy**

Lucretia

In Roman traditional history, Lucretia was a model of feminine virtue and modesty. According to the story, Lucretia is raped by Sextus, the son of TARQUIN, the despotic king of Rome. Unable to live with the shame, she summons her husband and her father, and, begging them to take vengeance, commits suicide in front of them. The outrage of her family and all who heard of what had happened is said to have led to the overthrow of the kings and the foundation of the Roman Republic. Shakespeare tells the story in his poem *The Rape of Lucrece* (1594). **Lucretius**, the male form of the name, was occasionally used in the past in honour of the great first-century BC poet and philosopher of that name.

Lucy

Lucy comes from the Latin word *lux, lucis*, meaning 'light'. It is because of this association with light that St Lucy, the fourth-century virgin martyr, is invoked against blindness and eye trouble. (St CLARE, whose name means 'bright, clear', is invoked against eye trouble for the same reason.) **Lucia** is the Latin and Italian form of the name, and **Lucilla** and **Lucille** Latin and French diminutives. **Lucinda** is another diminutive, particularly popular for fictional characters in the seventeenth and eighteenth centuries. Its pet form CINDY or **Sindy** is now a name in its own right. The Welsh name **Lleucu**, generally regarded as a translation of Lucy, can also be interpreted as from the word for 'light' combined with *cu* ('dear'). **Luz** is the Spanish form of the name.

The masculine forms **Lucius, Lucian** or **Lucien** come from the same root, via the Roman names *Lucius* and *Lucianus*. **Luciano** is the Spanish form of the name. Lucius was the name of two Roman kings and three Popes. Lucy is currently popular in the UK and Ireland.

Ludmila

Ludmila or Ludmilla is a Russian girl's name, made up from the Slavic elements *lud* 'people' and *mil* 'loved, dear'. It was the name of a popular tenth century saint, who is the patron saint of Bohemia. **Mila** or **Milla** is a short form.

Ludovic see **Lewis**

Luella

A blended name formed from LOUISE and ELLA, Luella is also spelt **Louella**. Similarly, **Louanne, Luanne, Luana** are formed from LOUISE and ANNE.

Luigi, Luigina see **Gina**

Luigsech see **Laoise**

Luis see **Lewis**

Luisa see **Louisa (*see* Louise)**

Luke

The fame of St Luke the Evangelist has made this a steadily popular name since the Middle Ages. St Luke was a physician and was also traditionally supposed to have been a painter and to have made portraits of the Virgin Mary, and he is the patron saint of both professions. He was a Greek, and his name simply means 'man from the district of Luciana'. The Greek form of his name, **Lucas** (occasionally **Lukas**), is occasionally used, and the Italian form, **Luca** (or **Lucca**, rarely **Luka**), has become fashionable in the UK, and is occasionally used as a feminine. Luke is currently widely popular.

Lulu see **Louise, Pearl**

Lulua see **Pearl**

Luna see **Selina**

Luned see **Lynette**

Lutfi

This is an Arabic masculine name meaning 'kind, gentle, courteous'. It is sometimes spelt **Lotfi**.

Luther

The use of Luther as a first name is due to the fame of the sixteenth-century religious reformer Martin Luther, although its use has been given a boost in honour of the civil rights campaigner named after him, Martin Luther King (1929–68). The name is a form of the German first name **Lothair**, meaning 'famous army' or 'warrior' (see also LORRAINE).

Luz see **Lucy**

Lydia

Lydia simply means 'woman of Lydia' (now western Turkey). It has strong literary associations. There is an anonymous Latin poem, once thought to be by VIRGIL, lamenting a lost love, addressed to a Lydia, but the name is given respectability by a brief mention in the Acts of the Apostles. Greater fame was given to it by its use by Ariosto in *Orlando Furioso* (1532) for a beautiful but cruel daughter of the King of Lydia, and it was a popular literary name in the eighteenth century, as in the case of Lydia Languish in Sheridan's *The Rivals* (1775). The name has had something of a revival in recent years and is now well used in England and the USA.

Lyla see **Leila**

Lyn see **Linda, Lynette, Llewellyn**

Lynda see **Linda**

Lynden, Lyndon see **Linden**

Lynette

Lynette comes from the Welsh name **Eluned** or **Eiluned**, which means 'idol, icon', so the name probably has some connection with ancient religion. **Luned** is the short form of Eluned, and this became **Linet** or **Linette** in the medieval French Arthurian romances in which she features as a heroine. The name was given what is now its commonest form, Lynette, by Tennyson in his story of 'Gareth and Lynette' in the *Idylls of the King*. **Lyn, Lynn, Lynne** are used as short forms. The name is only coincidentally like that of a bird, the linnet, although some parents may have used it for that association, and **Linnet** has been used as a first name. There is also a Welsh name **Llinos** or **Llio**, which means 'linnet', the bird being used as the symbol of a pretty woman.

Lyric

This vocabulary word has been in use as a girl's and occasionally boy's name in the USA since the mid 1990s. Since it can mean 'songlike' it probably belongs with the musical group of names that are becoming popular such as MELODY. With the filming of Philip Pullman's *His Dark Materials* books we can expect the related **Lyra** to start appearing.

M

Mab see **Mabel, Maeve**

Mabel

This name started life in the Middle Ages as a pet form of **Amabel**, meaning 'loveable' (see AMY), but has all but replaced its original. In its turn it developed into such forms as **Maybelle** and **Maybelline**, although these can also be thought of as developments of MAY; in turn, May, along with **Mab** and **Mabs**, is sometimes a pet form of Mabel. There is a Welsh form, **Mabli**, and Mabel can also be spelt **Mable**. At the start of the twentieth century Mabel had a brief spell as a boy's name.

Macaulay

This is a Scottish surname which can mean either 'son of Auley' or 'son of Olaf' (see OLIVER for both). It came into general use with the fame of the actor Macaulay Culkin, who became a star at the tender age of ten in 1990. It has been adopted as a girl's name, when it can appear as **Macaulee**.

Mackenzie

Mackenzie is a Scottish surname, meaning 'son of KENNETH'. It is used for both sexes, but is now primarily a girl's name. It has been in use in the USA since the 1970s for girls and is currently fairly popular there. It is also found as **Mckenzie** and many other variants – one researcher has counted 45, and the shortening **Kenzie** is used as an independent name. Mackenzie has also spread to Australia, and both Mackenzie and Kenzie are well used in Scotland. The British actor Mackenzie Crook is an example of the masculine use, while the author J.K. Rowling has called her daughter Mackenzie.

Macy

Macy has been recorded as a girl's name since the nineteenth century, but only came into regular use, in the USA, in the 1990s. It sometimes in the form **Maci(e)** or **Macey**. Although chiefly associated with the department store, it is a surname that comes from a French place name originally meaning 'Maccius' estate'. Its rise most probably owes something to the popularity of MASON as a boy's name. The singer Macy Gray has given the name publicity.

Madeline

Madeline, with its various spellings such as **Madeleine**, **Madaline**, **Madaliene**, **Madaleine** and **Madalain**, comes from St Mary Magdalen, the reformed sinner who anointed Christ with costly perfume and washed His feet with her tears and hair. Her second name means 'woman of Magdala', a village on the Sea of Galilee. Other forms of the name include **Magdalen(e)**, shortened to **Magda**, and **Madelena** or **Madalena**, shortened to **Lena** and the Scandinavian form **Malin**. From the old pronunciation of the name, **Maudlin** (which also gives us the adjective, from her tears of repentance), comes the occasional short form **Maude** or **Maud**, which properly belongs to MATILDA. **Madge**, properly belonging to MARGARET, can also be found as a pet form. **Maddie** or **Maddy** is, however, the usual short form. Madeleine is currently the most popular spelling in the UK, Madeline in the USA.

Madge see **Margaret, Madeline**

Madison

As a surname Madison can either mean 'Matthew's son' or 'Maud's son'. It came into popular use as a girl's name in the USA after the 1984 film *Splash* in which the mermaid heroine adopted it as her name after seeing a sign for Madison Avenue in New York. It had previously been used for boys often with reference to the surname of the fourth president of the USA. It is currently very popular for girls in the USA (sometimes as **Madyson** or **Maddison**), in Canada and Australia and is well used in England and Scotland.

Madiyya see Mehdi

Madoc, Madog

This Welsh masculine name means 'fortunate, good'. A certain Madog ap Owain Gwynedd is supposed to have discovered America ahead of everyone else from Europe in about 1150, and from this story come legends of blue-eyed, Welsh-speaking Native Americans. The name **Marmaduke**, with its short form **Duke**, is said to derive from the Irish *Maelmaedoc* ('servant of Madoc'). **Maddox** is a surname which comes from Madoc and which is used as a first name for boys. Use has risen notably in the UK since the actress Angelina Jolie adopted a son called Maddox.

Madonna see Donna

Madur

This one of a group of names based on the Sanskrit for 'sweet'. **Madhu** means 'sweet, honey' and is a name for the first month of the Hindu year. Like Madur it is used for both sexes. **Madhukar** 'bee, honey-maker' is masculine and **Maduri** 'sweetness, sweet girl' is feminine, as are **Madhubala** and **Madhumita** which have much the same sense.

Madyson see Madison

Mae see May

Maegan see Megan

Maelmor see Miles

Maeve

Maeve, also spelt **Meave** and **Maev**, comes from Irish mythology, where she appears in two forms, one as the powerful and forceful queen of Connacht, the other as the queen of the fairies, the origin of Shakespeare's Queen **Mab**. The name probably means 'she who intoxicates'. **Meaveen** is a pet form. Maeve is currently well used in Ireland. **Maéva**, which is popular in France, looks as if it is a form of this name, but is actually a Polynesian name meaning 'welcome', popularised in France by a 1972 children's book *Maéva, la petite Tahitienne* by Jacques Chegaray.

Magda, Magdalen, Magdalene see Madeline

Maggie see Margaret

Magnus

Stories of Charlemagne, whose name means 'Charles the Great', the king of the Franks and defender of the Christian faith against the heathen, were popular throughout Europe in the Middle Ages. The name translates into Latin as *Carolus Magnus*, and the second half of the name was given to the son of St Olaf, king of Norway (995–1030), a convert from paganism. This Magnus later became king of Norway and Denmark and Magnus became a traditional royal name, whence it spread to the general population. Among the Viking settlers of Ireland the name was softened to **Manus**. Although the television appearances of Magnus Magnusson and Magnus Pyke have made the name better known, it is still not often found outside Scotland and Ireland, although it is popular in Scandinavia.

Mags see Margaret

Mahalia

Best known from the singer Mahalia Jackson, this is a form of the (masculine) Hebrew name **Mahala** ('tenderness').

Mahbub, Mabuba see **Habib**

Mahdi, Mahdiya see **Mehdi**

Mahmud

Mahmud is a name related to Mohammed, and also means 'praised'. It is also spelt **Mahmoud**. The feminine is **Mahmuda**.

Mai, Maia see **May**

Mair, Maire see **Mary**

Maisie see **Margaret**

Maja see **Mia**

Makaela, Makai, Makayla see **Michael**

Makena, Makenna see **McKenna**

Makhi see **Mark**

Malachy

An Irish name, Malachy was used by two high kings of Ireland and by a popular saint, and early on it became identified with the Old Testament prophet **Malachi** ('messenger'). While Malachy is not usually found outside Ireland, Malachi has become fashionable in the USA, where it can also appear as **Malakai** or **Malaki**.

Malati

This is an Indian name which means JASMINE.

Malaya see **Mary**

Malcolm

Malcolm is a Scottish name, from the Gaelic *Mael-Colum*, 'follower of St **Columba**', also known as **Colmcille**. St Columba, whose name means 'dove', was an Irish noble who founded the monastery on IONA in 563 which became the centre for Celtic Christianity and the base for the conversion of Scotland. The Gaelic form of his name gives us the popular names CALLUM. Although a traditional Scottish name, it is not much used there at the moment.

Maleah see **Mary**

Maleek see **Malik**

Malia see **Mary**

Malik

This is the Arabic for 'king' and is one of the names of Allah. The feminine is **Malika**. Malik is popular with Black Muslims, when it can take forms such as **Maleek** and **Malique**. The Hebrew form is **Melek**.

Malin see **Madeline**

Maliyah see **Mary**

Mallory

This surname, originally meaning an unlucky person, has become a fashionable girl's name in the United States. Use seems to have spread in the 1980s after a character called Mallory Keaton appeared in the television series *Family Ties*.

Mally see **Mary**

Malvina

In the mid-eighteenth century, Europe was swept by an enthusiasm for the poems of OSSIAN. Supposedly ancient Gaelic epics, they were in fact largely the work of James Macpherson (1736–96). Macpherson seems to have invented the name Malvina (which may be meant to represent the Gaelic for 'smooth brow') for the name of the betrothed of the hero OSCAR. Many of the poems are dedicated to her. The enthusiasm for things Ossianic was particularly strong in Scandinavia, and it may be immigration from this area that led to the name being more common in the United States than in other English-speaking areas. Variants are **Melvina** and **Malvena**. (See also MELVIN)

Mamie see Mary

Mandy see Amanda

Manju

Manju is one of a group of Indian first names from the Sanskrit meaning 'pleasant, charming'. These include **Manjula** 'lovely, charming', **Manjubala** and **Manjulika** 'charming, girl', and **Manjusha** 'girl with a lovely voice'

Manny, Manuel see Emanuel

Manon see Marian

Manus see Magnus

Mara

Mara means 'bitter' in Hebrew. It was the name taken by Naomi on her return to Bethlehem (see Ruth 1:20).

Marc, Marcel, Marceline, Marcella, Marcelle, Marcelline, Marcello, Marchell, Marcia, Marcine, Marcus, Marcy see Mark

Maredudd see Meredith

Maren see Marina

Margaret

Margaret comes from the Latin word for PEARL. However, the French form **Marguerite** is also French for 'a daisy', and the name **Daisy** started life as a pet form of Margaret. Margaret owes its early popularity throughout Europe to the fame of St Margaret of Antioch, a legendary early martyr who was swallowed alive by Satan in the form of a dragon, but on making the sign of the cross burst through the monster's side, thereby saving her life and killing the dragon. In Scotland, this popularity was reinforced by another saint who was queen of Scotland from 1070 to 1093. The name was so popular in Scotland that it took on a number of different forms: **Margery** (**Marjory**, **Marjorie**, pet forms **Marge**, **Margie**, **Madge**), **Maisie**, **Mysie** and MAY. Pet forms of Margaret include **Maggie**, **Mags**, **Meg** and **Meggie**, and by alteration of the first letter **Peg**, **Peggie** or **Peggy**. MEGAN (or **Marget**) is the Welsh form of the name. From the Continent we get **Margarita**, **Marghanita**, **Margaretta**, **Margoletta** and pet forms **Greta**, **Gretchen**, **Grethel** or **Gretel**, **Meta** and **Rita**. **Margot** is the French pet form; the variant **Margaux** has recently come into fashion as an alternative, but the model Margaux Hemingway, who probably started the fashion, was named after the wine. Maisie is currently well used in England and Margot and Margaux in France.

Mari, Maria, Mariah, Mariam, Mariamne see Mary

Marian

Originally a pet form of Mary, Marian came to be analysed as a combination of MARY and ANNA, hence the variants **Marianne** and **Mary-Ann**. **Marianna** is a form used in Shakespeare's *Measure for Measure*. **Manon** is a French pet form of the name. The form **Marion** is also used in the United States as a man's name (it was, for example, the true first name of the actor John Wayne). In this case it comes from the surname with the same etymology as the first name, and probably owes its use to Francis Marion (d. 1795), who won fame fighting in the American War of Independence.

Maribel, Marie, Marie-Claire, Mariel, Mariella, Marietta, Mariette see Mary

Marigold

A marigold was the symbol of the Virgin Mary, the name coming from Mary + gold, the flower originally being simply called 'a gold', from its colour. Because of its healing properties, the flower was also chosen as the symbol of the apothecaries and can still be seen in use as a symbol by many herbalists. It was particularly popular as a girl's name at the turn of the nineteenth and twentieth centuries.

Marilyn see Mary

Marina

This is the name by which St MARGARET of Antioch is known in the eastern Mediterranean. Although it may not be the true derivation, Marina is usually taken to come from the Latin meaning 'of the sea'; and in this sense was used by Shakespeare for the sea-born heroine of *Pericles*. The name became more popular in England after 1934, when Princess Marina of Greece became the Duchess of Kent. She became so popular that her favourite shade of blue-green became known as 'Marina blue'. **Marin** (**Maren, Maryn**) is a variant that can be used for either sex. In France the name becomes **Marine**. This has been a popular choice for girls in France, but not as popular as the related **Océane**, which was top name for girls in 2000. The history of this name is cloudy. Many try to link the name to a St Ocean, a fourth century Turkish saint who is so obscure that no two sources can agree on his feast day. Others link it back directly to the embodiment of Ocean in Greek myth, which tells us nothing about why the name should be chosen. One convincing suggestion is that the A11 French motorway taken by many on their way to the sea for their holidays is known as the Autoroute Océane, and would have been new when the name started to be used at the end of the 1970s. Whatever the reason, the French are so fond of sea-connected names that there are even records of girls being given the tautological name Marine-Océane.

Marion see Marian

Marisa, Marisol, Marissa see Mary

Marius, Mario

Marius was a Roman family name, based on the name of the god Mars. Marius was the name of a remarkably successful but controversial Roman politician and general, which brought the name into use. However, in the Middle Ages it was regarded as a masculine form of MARY, and may still be used in this way today. The Spanish form is **Mario**. **Mariano** is from a related Roman name, and is used as a pet form. The combined for **DeMarius** is one of the more widely used De- names.

Marjorie, Marjory see Margaret

Mark

Mark is the English form of **Marcus**, a Latin name probably derived, like MARIUS, from the Roman god of war, Mars. **Marcos** is the Spanish form. **Marc**, the French spelling of the name, has become popular in recent years, while in the United States Marcus has been elaborated into **DeMarcus**. The pet form is **Markie** (sometimes in the USA **Makhi**, with **Markus** and **Markell** as further variants).The Latin pet form Marcellus became **Marcello** in Spanish and in French **Marcel**. The feminine forms of the name do not come directly from Marcus, but from the French Marc or from the related Latin name *Marcius*. From the latter we get **Marcia**, often found in the phonetic spelling **Marsha**. From the French come a number of forms: **Marcelline, Marceline** and their short form **Marcine, Marcella** and **Marcelle**. **Marchell** is the Welsh form, and is one of the earliest names borrowed from French into Welsh. **Marcy** is used as a short form of these names. (See also MARTIN.) Mark, Marc and Marcus are moderately well used in the UK and USA.

Marlene

A German pet form of Mary Magdalen (see MADELINE), Marlene was introduced into this country by the film star Marlene Dietrich and by the popularity with the troops on both sides of the German song 'Lili Marlene' in World War II. The variant form **Marlena** reflects the German pronunciation, but the name is now usually pronounced 'marleen' by English users. The -lene ending has been adopted for other, newly created names such as Charlene (see CHARLOTTE) and DARLENE. A shortened form, **Marlee** or **Marley** is currently more likely to be found used as an independent name than the full form is.

Marlon

This name is something of a mystery as it is not recorded in use before the actor Marlon Brando, except for his father who bore the name before him, and its spread is entirely due to him. It is assumed to be a surname used as a first name. Similar names have been found earlier, however. A Mahlon Pitney (1858–1924) was a member of the US Supreme Court, and there was a seaman called Marlin Ayotte present at Pearl Harbor, so time may throw more light on the history of the name. Mahlon was the name of the first husband of Ruth in the Bible, and may be from the Hebrew for 'mild'. Another interpretation is that since the Brando family claims to have French origins it may be a pet form of Marc with the French diminutive -on. However, Marlon is only known in France as a recent import from America.

Marmaduke

Marmaduke has strong associations with Yorkshire, where the name has always been more common than in the rest of the country. The name is often described as obsolescent, but Marmaduke Hussey, former chairman of the BBC, has shown this to be incorrect. See also MADOC.

Marquis

Marquis is the latest aristocratic title to have become fashionable as a boy's name in the USA, following in the steps of EARL, Duke and the less common King and Prince. Curiously **Marquise**, the French feminine form of the rank, is a not uncommon variant for boys. **Marques** and **Marquez** are also used. The similarity in sound to MARK and Markie probably influences the names survival.

Marsha see Mark

Marshall

This comes from the surname, which derives from German via French and originally meant a farrier or one who looked after horses. Its use as a first name may have been helped by the fact that the name of the Latin poet Martial (c. AD 40–104) has the same sound in standard English pronunciation. Marshall Mathers is the name of the rapper otherwise known as Eminem.

Martha

Martha is the name of the biblical woman who worked so hard to cater for Jesus and his disciples, only to be told that her sister had chosen the better course by sitting at His feet. Hence the name became popular from the sixteenth century onwards with those who wanted their daughters to grow up to be diligent housewives. Short forms shared with MATILDA are **Mat**, **Mattie** or **Matty**, and by a change in first letter (also found in other pet forms in 'm') **Pattie** or **Patty**, although this is also used for Patricia (see PATRICK). The name is Aramaic for 'lady'. The French form **Marthe** and the Spanish **Marta** are also occasionally used.

Martin

An old Roman name, Martin comes from Mars, the Roman god of fertility and war (see also MARK). Nowadays it is also spelt **Martyn** and has the short form **Marty**. It became part of the basic stock of European names because of the popularity of St Martin of Tours (c. 316–97), the Roman soldier who cut his military cloak in half in order to share it with a beggar, became a pacifist and left the army, and eventually became a missionary and bishop of Tours. Feminine forms include **Martina** or **Martine**, and more rarely **Martitia**, **Martita** and even **Martinella**. Martin is currently well used in Scotland and Ireland, and popular in a number of Continental countries.

Marvin see Mervyn

Mary

The Hebrew name **Miryam** became **Maryam** in the Aramaic spoken in the Holy Land in the first centuries. This becomes **Miriam** in English, and is the name of Moses' sister in the Old Testament. The origin of the name is uncertain, but it may be Egyptian and be based on a word meaning 'dear'. In the Greek of the New Testament the name becomes **Mariam** or **Maria**, which in turn passed into Latin (and Spanish) and became **Marie** in French and **Mary** in English. Miriam is found in forms such as **Maryam** and **Mariamne**. Maria is now often **Mariah**, after the singer Mariah Carey. These names have innumerable pet forms, including MAY, **Moll, Molly, Mally, Mamie, Minnie,**

Poll, Polly and **Ria**. Diminutives from the Continent include **Mariel** and **Mariella**, **Mariette** and **Marietta**, **Marisa** or **Marissa** as well as MARIAN. **Marilyn** or **Marylyn** is a derivative. In Welsh the name appears as **Mair** or **Mari**, while in Ireland it is **Mhairi** or **Maire**, which has developed into the phonetic forms **Moira**, **Maura** or **Moyra** and **Maureen** or **Moreen**. **Malia** is the Hawaiian form of the name, sometimes turned into **Maliyah** or **Maleah** as if blended with Leah, and which may also be the source of **Malaya** as a first name, rather than the country. **Marisol** is a Spanish name combining Mary with *sol* 'sun' and **Maribel** a blending of Maria and Isabel. Mary can be combined with others to form names like **Maryjane**, as in the heroine of the Spider Man series, or the popular French **Marie-Claire**. The name **Moriah** looks as if it might be a variant, but is also a place name in the Old Testament, the mound on which Solomon built his temple. Maria is the most popular of these names in the USA, Molly or Mollie in Scotland and England and Maria in Ireland.

Maryn see Marina

Mason

This surname from the occupation is a popular choice for boys in the United States and also well used in England. MACY seems to function as the feminine equivalent.

Mat, Mattie, Matty see Martha, Matilda, Matthew

Matilda

This is a Germanic name, from *maht* ('might') and *hild* ('battle'), the same element as in the name HILDA. It is puzzling to be told that **Maud** or **Maude** is a variant form of the name, but the transformation comes through the French, where the Germanic *Mahthilda* became something like *Maheud*, anglicised as Maud. Matilda would then be the Latin form of the name, the form written down by the chroniclers, while Maud would be the way ordinary people pronounced the name. Matilda was the name of the wife of William the Conqueror and was well used in England in the Middle Ages. Just as Mary became Molly which changed to Polly, so the short form **Mat** or **Matty** had its first sound changed to **Patty**, a short form shared with Patricia (see PATRICK), PATIENCE and MARTHA. **Tilly** and **Tilda** are also used as short forms. Matilda and Tilly are well used in England at the moment.

Matthew

This name means 'gift of God'. This is the commonest form of the name of the first Evangelist; **Matthias**, the Greek form of the name, is the alternative. **Mateo** and **Matias** are the Spanish forms of these names. The forms are found spelt with a single 't', and they are shortened to **Mat** or **Matt** and **Matty**. Matthew is currently popular on both sides of the Atlantic and in many other countries in the world.

Maud, Maude see Matilda, Madeline

Maudlin See Madeline

Maura, Maureen see Mary

Maurice

Maurice is the French form of the Latin *Maurus* ('a Moor'), which was used not only for those from North Africa, but for anyone with a dark complexion. The name gave us the surnames **Morris** and **Morse**, which have come in their turn to be used as first names. The Welsh form of the name, **Meurig**, gives us the surname **Merrick**, which is also found as a first name. In the USA, where the name also appears in the Spanish form **Mauricio**, Maurice tends to be pronounced in the French way with the stress on the final syllable, but in the UK Morris and Maurice are pronounced identically. (See also SEYMOUR)

Maverick

The vocabulary word for someone who does not conform was originally used to mean an unbranded calf, named after Samuel A. Maverick (1803–70) an unconventional Texas rancher who refused to brand his animals. In 1994 a film called *Maverick*, based on a much older television series or the same name, starring Mel Gibson and Jodie Foster was released, and the name started being used for boys soon after.

Mavis

An old dialect word for a song thrush, Mavis does not seem to have been used as a girl's name before the end of the nineteenth century. At the same time a similar name, **Merle**, the French for 'a blackbird', came into use. It was a well-used name for American boys in the first half of the twentieth century, as in the case of the country singer Merle Haggard, only dropping out of the records in the 1970s, but thanks to the actress Merle Oberon is now primarily a female name. It has never been a boy's name in the UK. **Merlene** is an elaboration of the name, probably influenced by MARLENE.

Maximilian

This is one of the best-known 'invented' names, having been made up by the Emperor Frederick III (1415–93) for his son. The name is a blend of the names of two admired Romans, Fabius Maximus and Scipio Aemilianus, whose qualities Frederick hoped his son would inherit. However, it is worth noting that *Maximilianus* already existed as a Roman name, based on the word for 'great'. The short form of the name, **Max**, often an independent name, is shared with the totally unrelated name **Maxwell**, which comes from a Scots place name meaning 'Mack's well'. However, the French name **Maxime**, used for either sex, does come from the word meaning 'great'. English speakers have used **Maxim** for the masculine, uncomfortable with the feminine feel of the final 'e' in the French form. **Maxine** seems to be a modern coinage, a female version of Max. There is also a feminine form of Maximilian, **Maximilienne**, or **Maximilianne**. Max is a popular name in England, Scotland and Ireland.

May, Maya

As well as being a pet form of MARGARET and MARY, May is used as an independent name, associated either with the other month names or the other flower names. **Mai** is the Welsh form of the name, while **Mae** is a common form in the United States. **Maia** and Maya, which have appeared in recent years, seem to be variants, rather than the name of the Central American people or a use of the obscure Roman earth-goddess or the legendary Greek mother of Hermes. Maia and Maya are also found as pet forms of Maria. In addition Maya is a popular name in India, from the Sanskrit word meaning 'illusion'. It was, according to tradition, the name of the Buddha's mother. It is also an alternative name for the goddess Durga. Maya can also be a Jewish name meaning 'water'. The American author Maya Angelou, who has done so much to spread the name, gets her name from yet another source discussed at MIA. A new name, **Myesha**, has been formed by blending Maya, currently popular in the USA, with AISHA. In the nineteenth century in the USA May was a popular choice for blended names such as Idamay and Ellamay.

Maybelle, Maybelline see Mabel

Maygan see Megan

Mayra see Myra

Mckayla see Michael

McKenna

McKenna is an Irish surname meaning, like Mackenzie, descendant of Kenneth, now used for girls. It is found in various spellings such as **Makenna**, **Makena** and the shortening **Kenna** is used as an independent name.

Mckenzie see Mackenzie

Meadow

This girl's name from the vocabulary word came into use after the tremendous success of the television series *The Sopranos* which has a character called Meadow.

Meagan see Megan

Meav, Meave, Meaveen see Maeve

Meena

This is an Indian girl's name also found as **Mina**. While it literally means 'fish' it refers to the constellation of Pisces.

Meera

Meera or **Mira** is an India name meaning 'sea, ocean'. Meera Syal is a well-known British writer and actress.

Meg see Margaret

Megan

Megan was originally a Welsh pet form of Margaret, but it has now become an independent name, popular throughout the English-speaking world. It has become so separated from its origins that, in the United States at least, spellings such as **Maegan** or **Maygen** suggest that it is being analysed as an elaboration of May; while forms such as **Meghan** or **Meagan** suggest that some users regard it as Irish. The name is currently popular in England, Scotland (which also uses the 'h' spelling), Ireland, Canada (it appears in the French spelling **Megane** in Quebec) and the USA.

Meggie see Margaret

Meghan see Megan

Mehdi

Mehdi or **Mahdi** is the Arabic for 'rightly guided'. Al-Mahdi, 'The Rightly Guided' is one of the titles of Mohammed. **Muhtadi** is a closely related name, and RASHID has the same meaning. **Mahdiya**, **Madiyya** or **Madia** are feminine forms. Mehdi is one of the most popular Arabic names in France.

Meir, Meira

These are the masculine and feminine forms of a Hebrew name meaning 'giving light'.

Meirion

Meirion was an early British prince who gave his name to the district of Merioneth in Wales. There are feminine forms **Meiriona** and **Meirionwen**.

Mel see Melvin

Melanie

This comes from the Greek word for 'black'. *Melaina* was one of the titles of the goddess Demeter (see DEMETRIUS) in her winter aspect, mourning for the loss of her ravished daughter **Persephone**. **Melany** is a variant, and **Melony** is said to be an old Cornish form. (See also CHLOE.) Melanie is one of the names made popular by Margaret Mitchell's 1936 book *Gone with the Wind*.

Melchior see Jasper

Melek see Malik

Melicent, Melisanda, Melisende see Millicent

Melissa

The Greek for 'honey bee', Melissa was the name of a nymph who is said to have introduced the use of honey to mankind. She is probably the remnant of an earlier earth or fertility goddess, for there is evidence of an important goddess associated with bees in Minoan Crete and in even earlier cultures. Associated names which come from the word for 'honey' are **Melita** and **Melina** and **Melinda** (the pet form of which is **Mindy** or **Mindie**). Some see Melinda as a blend of MELANIE and LINDA, but as it was in use by the eighteenth century this seems unlikely. Melissa is currently used regularly in both the UK and the USA.

Melody

Melody is simply the word for a tune used as a first name. It was used occasionally from the eighteenth century and interest was shown in the name in the middle of the twentieth century, and is growing in use again now, alongside other musical names such as LYRIC and those listed under HARMONY.

Melony see Melanie

Melvin

With its variant **Melvyn**, this comes from a Scottish surname with various sources, the most important of which is a form of **Melville**, derived from a noble family taking its name from a place in Normandy, meaning 'poor settlement'. It has also been explained as a masculine form of MALVINA via the variant Melvina. **Mel** is the short form.

Melvina see Malvina

Mercy

Mercy is the Christian virtue used as a first name, and as such was popular with the Puritans. **Mercedes** (see DOLORES) is the Spanish equivalent. **Merry** is said to be a pet form of Mercy, but nowadays is probably more often used as an independent name or as a short form of MEREDITH. **Mercia**, the name of an Anglo-Saxon kingdom which came into use at the beginning of the twentieth century when Old English names were popular, can also be used as a Latinate version of Mercy.

Meredith

This was originally a Welsh masculine name, also found as **Meredydd** and **Maredudd**, which has been in use since the sixth century and means 'magnificent chief'. Its use as a girl's name, which probably started in the United States from the surname, was a twentieth-century development. **Merry** is used as a short form.

Merfin see Mervyn

Merial, Meriel, Merille see Muriel

Merle, Merlene see Mavis

Merlin, Merlyn see Mervyn

Merna see Myrna

Merrick see Maurice

Merril, Merrill see Muriel

Merry see Mercy, Meredith

Mervyn, Marvin

The Welsh name **Myrddin** or **Merfin** has been anglicised as both Mervyn and **Merlin**, the wizard from Arthurian legend. Although the town of Carmarthen is traditionally said to take its name from Merlin, it seems probable that it was the other way round, and that the Welsh name for the wizard, Myrddin Emrys, means 'EMRYS from Carmarthen'. The town's name means 'fort by the sea'. There is a variant spelling, **Merlyn**, which is sometimes used for girls (and then perhaps thought of as an elaboration of MERLE). **Marvin** is an old variant of **Mervin**, an alternative spelling.

Meryl see Muriel

Mesach see Misael

Messiah see Salvador

Meta see Margaret

Meurigs see Maurice

Mhairi see Mary

Mia

Mia is a Scandinavian short form of the name Maria (see MARY). Mia Farrow, whose success as an actress has done so much to spread the name, was originally a Maria. **Maja**, serves the same function in a number of European countries. Mia coincidentally means 'my' in Spanish and Italian. The author MAYA Angelou did get her name from the way her younger brother said 'my sister', and these two sources seems to have blended together to produce names such as **Mya**, **Miah** and **Miya**, while **Myah** has been recorded for boys. The singer Mya Harrison may have led to the spread of this spelling. Mia is popular in England, Scotland (where Mya is also used) and the USA and well used in Ireland and in a number of European countries.

Michael

This name comes from the Hebrew meaning 'who is like God?' The name also appears in the Old Testament in the form of the name of the prophet **Micah** (now found used for both sexes). The popularity of the Archangel Michael, the defeater of Satan and weigher of souls, guaranteed the early spread of the name throughout Europe in various forms. **Miguel** is the Spanish form of the name. Michael also became a surname and, as **Mitchel**, is re-used as a first name. Traditional pet forms are **Mick**, **Micky** and **Mike**. **Misha** or **Mischa** is a Russian masculine pet form, which, because of its apparently feminine ending, is sometimes used in the UK as a girl's name (see also SASHA). The French feminine forms **Michelle** or **Michèle** have been well used and the German **Michaela** has also been popular. The name SHELLEY seems to have started life as a pet form of Michelle.

Since the late 1980s a whole raft of new names have come into use based on Michael and its variants. Michaela was respelt **Mikayla**, and spawned both spelling variants such as **Makaila** (currently the favourite form), **Makaela**, **Mckayla**, **Micaela**, **Mikalah**, but also the independent name KAYLA. Michael itself has been respelt **Micheal** or **Mikal** and **Mikey** turned into **Mikhi** or **Makai**. These transformations are not surprising when you realise that Michael has been either the most popular or second most popular name in the USA every year since 1954. It is also in the top ten in Ireland, and although not as popular, well used in the UK

Mignon

This is a French term of affection, used to children, something like 'little one'. Mignon came into use as a first name after it was used by Goethe in his story *Wilhelm Meister* and particularly after the story was turned into an opera called *Mignon* by Ambroise Thomas in 1866.

Miguel, Mikal, Mikalah, Mikayla, Mike, Mikey, Mikhi see **Michael**

Mila see **Ludmila**

Mildred

Mildred is a form of the Anglo-Saxon name *Mildthryth* ('gentle strength'). St Mildred was a seventh-century abbess who seems to have been well named, for she had a reputation for kindness and as a great comforter of the afflicted. The short forms **Millie** or **Milly** are shared with MILLICENT and AMELIA.

Milene see **Mylene**

Miles

Miles is an old name of disputed meaning, although it is generally agreed that the name being the same as the Latin word for 'soldier' is pure chance. In Ireland the name is used as an English version of **Maelmor** ('servant of the Virgin Mary'). **Myles** and **Milo** are variants. Because Miles Standish was prominent among the early settlers in Virginia in real life, and given a fictional life in Longfellow's poem *The Courtship of Miles Standish*, Miles is often thought of as a typical Puritan name, but it was, in fact quite unusual at that date. Miles is regularly used in the USA and interest in the name is growing.

Milla see **Camilla, Ludmila**

Millicent

Millicent is the English form of the French **Melisande**, itself from a Germanic name either from *(a)mal* 'work' + *swinth* 'strength', or as some suggest *mel* 'merciful' + *sind* 'journey'. **Melicent** and **Melisenda** are variants. The short form **Millie** or **Milly** is shared with AMELIA and MILDRED, but is the primary source of the short form. Millie has been steadily popular in England and Scotland for some years.

Millie, Milly see **Amelia, Camilla, Mildred, Millicent**

Milo see **Miles**

Milton

This English surname is made up of the elements 'mill' and the old word for 'an enclosure'. It is used as a first name in honour of the Puritan poet John Milton (1608–74), and is more common in the United States, where there is a stronger tradition of using the surnames of the famous as first names. **Milt** is the short form.

Mima see Jemima

Mina see Meena, William

Mindie, Mindy see Melissa

Minella see William

Minerva see Athene (*see* Athena)

Minna see William

Minnie see Athene (*see* Athena), Mary, William

Minta, Minty see Araminta

Mira see Meera, Myra

Miranda

Miranda is the Latin for 'worthy to be admired, deserving admiration', and was coined by Shakespeare for the heroine of *The Tempest*. **Mirabel** or **Mirabelle** is an older name from the same root, meaning 'admirable, lovely'. The French name **Mireille** and its Provencal form **Mirèio** also come from the same root. One account of the introduction of Mireille says that the Provencal poet and champion of Provencal culture Frédérique Mistral (1830–1914) found the name in local legend and used it as the title for a verse epic. He wanted to use the name for his god-daughter, but the priest refused to use a non-liturgical name, upon which Mistral emphatically stated that the name was a Provencal form of Miriam. As he was an expert in such things, the priest could hardly demur, and so the name came to be officially accepted in France, despite the fact that the name actually comes from the Provencal *mirar* ('to admire'). There is a Welsh name **Mirain**, which means 'wonderful'. From the same root come Admire, recorded as a first name in the seventeenth century, and Miracle, which has been in use from the mid 1990s and belongs with the trend for religious names such as HEAVEN. **Mira** can be used as a short form of these names or as a form of MYRA, but is also a shortening of Slavic names formed from the element *mir* 'peace' and an Indian name from the Sanskrit for 'sea'. For the related Mirabelle see under PEACHES.

Mireya see Myra

Miriam, Miryam see Mary

Misael

Misael is the Spanish form of the name **Mishael**, the original name of the biblical **Meshach** who in the *Book of Daniel* shared the fiery furnace with Shadrak and Abednigo. It is not uncommon among Spanish speakers.

Mischa, Misha see Michael

Misty

Misty has recently become fashionable as a girl's name in the USA, probably not so much in its sense of 'a light fog' as in 'misty eyed, sentimental'. **Mistie** and **Mistee** are also used. Use may have been encouraged by the 1954 song *Misty* by Johnny Burke and Errol Garner. It peaked as a girl's name in the 1970s, and it may be no coincidence that this was after the 1971 release of the Clint Eastwood film *Play Misty for Me* in which the song played a major role. The similar **Cloudy** has also been recorded.

Mitchel see Michael

Mitra see Aditya

Miya see Mia

Moelwyn, Moelwen

Moelwyn is the name of a mountain near Ffestiniog, used as a first name for boys. The name comes from *moel* 'bare' but often indicating steep hill, and *gwyn* 'white'. **Moelwen** is the feminine form. For Moelona see LONA.

Mohammed

This is the most widespread name in the Islamic world, used in honour of the Prophet. The name means 'praised, praiseworthy'. Because it is so widespread it has been transcribed in a number of different ways. In the UK **Mohammed** is the commonest spelling, but **Muhammad** and **Mohammad** are also very common. **Mohamed** is the commonest form in the USA, followed by Mohammad, **Muhammed** and **Muhamad**.

Moira see Mary

Moises see Moses

Moll, Molly see Mary

Mona

An Irish name, Mona comes from a word meaning 'noble'. However, in Wales it is sometimes used as the Welsh name for Anglesea, Môn, with a feminine ending. It can also be a short form of MONICA. In Arabic **Mona** or **Muna** means 'wishes, desires', which also has the singular form **Munya** or **Mounia**.

Monica

St Monica was the mother of St AUGUSTINE (*see* **Augustus**). We learn a lot about her in his autobiographical writings. She must have been a rather overwhelming as well as loving mother, combining ambition for her favourite son with a determination to save his soul. Because she was instrumental in his conversion to Christianity, her name was early on derived from the Latin *monere* ('to warn'), but the true source of her name is unknown, and may be Phoenician, as she was a native of Carthage. **Monique**, the French form of the name, is also used.

Montague, Montgomery

These two, which share the short form **Monty**, are both French baronial names brought over by the conquering Normans. Montague ('pointed hill') is a commonplace name in France, but the surname comes from the place in the district of La Manche in Normandy. Montgomery is a more complicated place name, being 'mount' plus the name of an earlier German invader made up of the elements *guma* ('man') and *ric* ('power'), and is a place in Calvados, a region of Normandy. In the USA Montgomery came into use as a first name in honour of General Richard Montgomery, the American commander killed in the attack on Quebec in 1775.

Montserrat see Dolores

Morag

Morag is a Scots name, probably made up of the Gaelic element *mor* ('great') with a feminine ending indicating a pet form. However it has been suggested that it shares with MURIEL a derivation from the word for 'sea'.

Morcant see Morgan

Mordecai

This is a biblical name, ultimately of Persian origin, meaning 'a follower of the god Marduk'. It is now very rare, but is kept before the public by the writer Mordecai Richler.

Moreen see Mary

Morfydd, Morfudd see Morwenna

Morgan

This is a Welsh name of disputed meaning. It seems likely that it is actually a conflation of several names, made up of the Welsh *môr* ('sea') or *mawr* ('great'), coupled with *can* ('bright') or *gen* ('born'). The sense 'sea-born' is supported by the Latin name **Pelagius**, also meaning 'sea-born', which probably translates Morgan, and was the name of the only notable early British heretic (born c. 370), whom St Germanus was sent to preach against (see GERMAIN). On the other hand, another early form of the name, **Morcant**, would support a sense 'great and bright'. It was originally a masculine name, but the appearance of Morgan, **Morgane** or **Morgana** Le Fey in Arthurian legend as Arthur's magic-working half-sister and implacable enemy has led to its use as a feminine, which is now well used on both sides of the Atlantic.

Moriah see Mary

Morna see Myrna

Morris, Morse see Maurice

Mortimer

Another Norman baronial name, Mortimer derives from a French place name which comes from *mort mer* ('dead sea or pond'). There are traditions associating the adoption of the name with Crusaders and the Dead Sea in the Holy Land. It came into fashion along with other aristocratic names in the nineteenth century, but to some extent its use as a first name is influenced by the Gaelic name **Murtagh** ('sea man') being translated as Mortimer.

Morven

Morven is a Scottish first name from the eighteenth century. In James Macpherson's *Fingal* poems **Morvern**, now usually Morven, is a mythical kingdom. It is thus, like SELMA, a literary place name used as a girl's name. It appears to have been formed form the Gaelic for 'the big gap'. The name has received some publicity recently from Alan Warner's book, filmed in 2002, *Morvern Callar.*

Morwenna

This comes from the Welsh word *morwyn* ('a maiden'). **Morwena** is a variant spelling, and there are the names **Morwyn** and **Morwen** as variants. **Morfydd** or **Morfudd**, the name given to his beloved by the great medieval Welsh poet Davydd ap Gwilym, probably comes from the same root. It was the name of a sixth-century princess, daughter of Urien Rheged and sister to the heroic Owain (see EWAN). It was a popular Welsh name throughout the Middle Ages.

Moses

This is a biblical name of disputed meaning. In the Bible we are told that Pharaoh's daughter called her adopted son Moses because she drew him out of the water, implying that the name comes from the Hebrew for 'to draw'. But as has been pointed out, an Egyptian princess was hardly likely to have been speaking Hebrew. It is likely that the name is Egyptian, like that of his brother AARON. Moses was regularly used until the eighteenth century, but then largely went out of use in the UK, although it was more likely to be found in the USA, where the Spanish form **Moises** is also used. The Hebrew form **Moshe** remained in use. **Moss**, both as a first name and surname, started as a diminutive of Moses.

Mostyn

This is a Welsh place name meaning 'field-fortress', which was adopted as a surname in the sixteenth century and then became a masculine first name.

Mounia see Mona

Mourad see Murad

Moustafa see Mustafa

Moyra see Mary

Muhamad, Muhammad, Muhammed see Mohammed

Muhtadi see Mehdi

Muirne see Myrna

Muna, Munya see Mona

Murad

Murad comes from the Arabic root meaning 'will, intention' which has strong religious overtones. It is also found as **Mourad**.

Murdo, Murdoch

Murdo is the phonetic spelling of the Scottish masculine name Murdoch, which is in turn the English form of the Gaelic **Murchadh** ('seaman'). It is thus the equivalent of the Irish Murtagh (see MORTIMER), as well as being the source of the common surname. There is a rare feminine, **Murdina**.

Muriel

This is an ancient Celtic name meaning 'sea-bright' which came back into use in the nineteenth century. It was revived in two main forms, Muriel and **Meriel**, and has since developed a large number of variants including **Merial**, **Meryl**, **Merille**, **Merrill**, **Merril** and **Muryell**.

Murray

A surname, now used as a first name, Murray comes from Moray in north-east Scotland. This area got its name from the old Celtic meaning 'settlement by the sea'. **Murry** is the Irish spelling. As might be expected, it is most likely to be found used in Scotland.

Murtagh see Mortimer

Muryell see Muriel

Mustafa

Mustafa, **Mustapha** or **Moustafa** means 'chosen' in Arabic, and is one of the titles of Mohammed.

Mya see Mia

Myesha see May

Myfanwy

This is a medieval Welsh girl's name meaning 'my rare or fine one', which was revived in Wales in the nineteenth century. **Myf**, **Myfi** and **Myfina** are all used as short forms.

Mylene

In French the double name Marie-Hélène can be shortened to Marylène, which in turn is shortened to Mylène or Milène. Mylène Farmer is a Canadian-French singer whose success has made the name well known through the Francophone world. In the UK the singer and presenter **Myleen** Klass has introduced a new form.

Myles see Miles

Myra

This is a poetic name invented in the seventeenth century by Fulke Greville, Lord Brooke (1554–1628), which remained a purely literary name until the nineteenth century. Its intended meaning is not clear, but if it meant to include the sense of the Latin *mirare* ('to admire'), as seems likely, then the name would be similar to MIRANDA. In the United States it has been used as the female equivalent of MYRON. **Mira** is a variant, and **Mayra** and **Mireya** are used in the United States. The notoriety of Myra Hindley has put the name out of general circulation in the UK.

Myrddin see Mervyn

Myrna, Morna

These two names are both forms of the Irish name **Muirne**, meaning 'beloved'. **Merna** is a rare, further variant. The actress Myrna Loy brought attention to the name in the 1930s.

Myron

Although this name is hardly used in the UK, it is not uncommon in the United States, where it belongs to the group of first names adopted from the names of the famous, in this case the fifth-century BC Athenian sculptor of the 'Discus Thrower'. In Greek, the name meant 'fragrant'.

Myrtle

This plant was probably adopted as a girl's first name because the plant has been used to symbolise love and fidelity. Until quite recently it was worn or carried by brides at weddings in the same way as orange blossom, and women would try to grow the plant from cuttings taken from their wreath or bouquet. It is one of the group of plant names introduced in the nineteenth century.

Mysie see **Margaret**

N

Naasir, Naasira see **Nasir**

Nabil
Nabil or **Nabeel** is a boy's name which means 'noble' in Arabic and has a feminine **Nabila**.

Nadia
Nadia is the pet form of the Russian name **Nadezhda** ('HOPE'), although only the pet forms of the name seem to be much used outside Russia. **Nadine** is a French variant, and in the past the form **Nadège** was also used in France.

Nahum
A prophet in the Old Testament, Nahum wrote in the seventh century BC. As well as the usual oracles about the rewards of respecting God, and the vengeance that awaits those who do not, his book gives a vivid description of the fall of Nineveh. The name means 'full of comfort', and is probably a short form of a name describing God as comforter. It is rarely used, but an awareness of it is kept alive by the hymn writer Nahum Tate.

Naim, Naima
These are Arabic names meaning 'happy, peaceful'. In Islamic tradition it is the name of one of the gardens of Paradise and the word used in the Koran to describe the state of those in Paradise. **Nima** and **Nimat** are related girls' names. The Hebrew equivalent is NAOMI.

Nais see **Anaïs**

Nan, Nana, Nanette, Nanna, Nanny see **Anna**

Nance, Nancy, Nansi see **Anna, Agnes**

Nandy see **Ferdinand**

Nanty see **Antony**

Naomi
The Hebrew word *no'ami* 'joy' becomes the name *No'omi* 'pleasantness', which appears in English translations of the Bible as Naomi. Naomi is the model mother-in-law of the Old Testament. When she and her daughter-in-law RUTH were left widows, Naomi wanted to travel back to her own land. Such was the love Ruth had for Naomi that she refused to be separated from her, even though it meant leaving her own people. In the past the name was usually pronounced 'nayer-me', but pronunciations such as 'nay-oh-me' are more prevalent now. The confusion over the vowel sound has led to variations in spelling such as **Noemi**. The name has been well used in both English-speaking countries and French-speaking ones, where **Noémie** is the standard form of the name.

Narayan
Narayan or **Narayana** means 'path of man' in Sanskrit, and is one of the titles of Vishnu. Another boy's name based on *nar* 'man' is **Narendra** or **Narinder** 'lord of men'.

Naseer, Naser see **Nasir**

Nash

This surname, originally given to someone who lived near an ash tree, came into general use as a boy's name in 1997, the year after the launch of the successful television show *Nash Bridges*.

Nasim

Nasim or **Nassim** means 'breeze, fragrant air' in Arabic. Nasim is used for both sexes, and **Nasima** can also be used for girls.

Nasir

Nasir, also found as **Nasser, Naser, Naseer**, and **Naasir**, is from the Arabic for 'helper', one of the titles of Mohammed. **Naasira** and **Nasira** are feminine equivalents.

Nastasia, Nastassja see Anastasia

Nat see Nathan

Natalie

Dies Natalis is the Latin for 'birthday'. In early Christian Latin *natalis* was the term used for the anniversary of the day on which a saint was martyred. This gave rise to the Latin Christian name **Natalia**, better known now as the Russian form of the name. Natalia became **Nathalie** in French and **Natalie** in English (now found in forms such as **Natalee**). In Russia Natalia (occasionally found as **Natalya** and shortened to **Talia**) has a pet form **Natasha** (sometimes spelled **Natasja** or **Natassia,** and shortened to **Tasha**). NOEL is a related name. Natalie is currently popular in the USA and well used in Scotland. Natasha is well used in both England and Scotland.

Nathan, Nathaniel

A Hebrew name meaning 'gift of God', Nathaniel was the name of one of the apostles, probably the same as BARTHOLOMEW. **Nathan** ('gift') was the name of a character in the Old Testament who was a prophet, and counsellor and critic of kings David and Solomon. Nathan is sometimes used as a short form of Nathaniel, and they share the short form **Nat** and more rarely **Nath** and **Nate**. Nathan is currently popular throughout the English-speaking world. It is sometimes respelt **Nathen**, and Nathaniel can appear as **Nathanael** or **Nathanial**. There is a rare female form **Nathania**.

Natividad see Belén

Nayeli

Nayeli is a Mexican girl's name that has spread to the USA. It comes from the Central American language Zapotec, where it means 'I love you'.

Nea see Linnea

Neal, Neale see Neil

Ned, Neddie, Neddy see Edgar, Edmond, Edward, Edwin

Neela, Neelam see Blue

Nehemiah

In the Old Testament Nehemiah is a Jew in captivity in Persia who is responsible for the rebuilding of Jerusalem after its destruction by the Persians. It was used occasionally in the later nineteenth century. It started being used again in the USA in the late 1990s and has been used increasingly ever since.

Neil

The true Irish form of this name is **Niall**, correctly pronounced the same way as the English form, but often given a spelling pronunciation. **Neal** or **Neale** is a common alternative form. The name is also the source of **Nigel**, which comes from *Nigellus*, the written form given to the name in medieval Latin. This was not at first a spoken form, but the Latin was later misunderstood, and the name Nigel born, and mistakenly linked with the Latin word *niger* ('black'). **Niles** is the Scandinavian form of the name. Admiral **Nelson** probably inherited his surname from a 'Neil son', and this is now used as a first name in memory of him, and more recently of Nelson Mandela. There have been attempts to form feminine forms of the name: **Nelda** from Neil and **Nigella** and

Nigelia from Nigel, but none of them is very common. The name, the origin of which is obscure, came into use because of the fame of Niall of the Nine Hostages, a fifth-century Irish warrior-king around whom many legends have collected.

Neirin see Aneurin

Nell, Nellie, Nelly see Eleanor, Helen

Nelson see Neil

Nerissa

This is the name of the delightful and witty maid and companion to PORTIA in Shakespeare's *Merchant of Venice*. Not as common as some other Shakespearean girls' names, it is nevertheless steadily if quietly used. The name comes from the Greek sea nymphs, the Nereides, daughters of Nereus, the Old Man of the Sea, who also give us the rarer **Nerida** and **Nerina**.

Nerys

This Welsh girl's name is usually interpreted from the Welsh word *ner* ('lord'), plus a feminine ending, but a recent writer has suggested that it may be a shortening of **Generys**, a name popular in medieval Wales; or derived from the same root as NERISSA. It is a recent name, given fame by the actress Nerys Hughes.

Nessa, Nessie, Nest, Nesta see Agnes, Vanessa

Nestor

Nestor is the Greek king of Pylos in Homer's epics, whose great age has brought with it great wisdom. In the past Nestor has, consequently, been used as a byword for wisdom. The name is better used in Spanish-speaking countries than English-speaking ones, which may explain a revival in its use in the USA since the 1970s. The meaning of the name is not known.

Net, Netta, Nettie, Netty see Agnes, Antony, Jane

Nevaeh, Neveah see Heaven

Neve see Niamh

Neville

Neville or **Nevil** is a noble surname used as a first name. The fifteenth-century earl of Warwick, known as 'Warwick the Kingmaker', was the first of the Neville earls of Warwick. Three of his five paternal uncles were earls, and all four of his aunts married dukes, so the family name spread through the aristocracy. The name, which means 'new town', came into use as a first name in the seventeenth century, but only became popular in the nineteenth century.

Niall see Neil

Niamh

Niamh (**Neve** or **Niav** in its anglicised spelling reflecting its pronunciation) is an Irish name meaning 'bright', originally the name of a goddess. In Irish mythology, a woman of this name takes the poet OSSIAN to the otherworld Land of Promise where she is a princess. A pet form, **Nia**, has become very popular in Wales. This popularity was inspired by a poem by T. Gwynn Jones in praise of *Nia Ben Aur* ('Nia of the golden head'). African-Americans also use Nia or **Nya** as a first name, in this case from the Swahili word meaning 'intention, purpose'. Niamh is very popular in Ireland and well used both in England and Scotland, where Neve is also used.

Nic see Dominic

Nicholas

Nicholas comes from a Greek name meaning 'victory of the people'. **Nicolas** was the original form of the name, the insertion of the 'h' being a hypercorrect form, like the 'h' in Anthony. **Nicol** or **Nichol** is an old pet form, while **Nick**, **Nicky** and **Nico** are more common today. The old form was shortened to **Col**, the pet-form ending -in was added, and thus the now separate name COLIN developed. St Nicholas was a fourth-century bishop in Asia Minor, who, according to legend, secretly supplied three destitute girls with dowries by leaving the money at their windows. As his feast day is 6 December, this deed became associated with Christmas. The feast day of St Nicholas, or Santa **Claus** as he is known in Dutch, is still celebrated in many parts of Europe as the beginning of the Christmas season, or as a time for giving presents. Dutch settlers took the tradition to the United States, where it became more firmly associated with 25 December, and from there it spread to other parts of the world. **Nichola** is the commonest feminine form of the name along with the French **Nicole**; the latter has the diminutive **Nicolette**, which in turn leads to **Colette** (see COLIN). The short form of the name is spelt variously **Nicky**, **Nickie**, **Nikki** or **Nicci**. **Nikita** is strictly speaking a Russian masculine name, from a Greek name meaning 'unconquered', but is used, particularly in the United States, as a form of Nicola.

Nigel, Nigelia, Nigella see Neil

Nikhil
Nikhil is an Indian boy's name, which comes from the Sanskrit for 'whole, entire'. It is a common name in India, and well used by Americans of Indian ancestry.

Nikita see Nicholas

Nila, Nilam see Blue

Niles see Neil, Nyla

Nilima see Blue

Nima, Nimat see Naim

Nina, Ninette, Ninon see Anna

Ninian
St Ninian was a fifth-century Briton who became a missionary to the Picts in Scotland. This led to the name being a popular one in Scotland in earlier times. There has recently been something of a revival of interest in this as well as other local names, possibly helped by the name being kept alive by its appearance in Scott's *The Antiquary*. **Ringan** is a dialect form of the name.

Nisha
Nisha is an Indian girl's name from the Sanskrit for 'night'. **Nishit(h)** 'midnight' and **Nishant** 'night's end, i.e. dawn' are used for boys.

Nita see Anna, Jane

Noah
Noah is a Hebrew name of uncertain meaning, but traditionally interpreted as meaning 'repose'. The story of Noah and his ark must be one of the best-known Bible stories, but despite this the name has not been much used historically, although it is in fashion at the moment. One bearer of the name, Noah Webster (1758–1843), had a considerable impact on the cultural history of the United States, being not only the creator of Webster's *Dictionary*, but also introducing the spelling reforms that distinguish American English from that of Great Britain. **Noé** is the French form. Noah is popular in the USA and increasingly used in the UK and Ireland.

Noel
Noel or **Noël** is the French word for **Christmas** (itself occasionally used as a first name). It comes from the Latin *dies natalis* 'birthday' which also lies behind NATALIE. It was originally given to children born on or about 25 December. **Noelle** or **Noëlle** is the French feminine form of the name, with **Noella** a variant. In English-speaking countries **Noele**, **Noleen**, **Noelena** and **Noeline** are also found.

Noemi, Noémie see Naomi

Nola see Fenella

Nolan
Nolan is an Irish surname, ultimately going back to the word *nuall* ('famous'), now increasingly used as a boy's name in the USA. It does not seem to have had much success in the UK, but is well used in France.

Noor see Nur

Nora

Nora or **Norah** started life as a pet form of such names as HONORIA, LEONORA (*see* **Leo**) and ELEANOR, but has long been used as an independent name. Honoria was a particularly popular name in Ireland, and was frequently reduced to Nora. It then acquired a diminutive suffix, and **Noreen** was formed. This name has been further elaborated to **Norlene** and **Noreena**. **Nonie** is a pet form. Nora is the name of the heroine of Ibsen's play *A Doll's House* which might explain why it is particularly popular in Norway.

Norman

Norman means 'man from the north', and was in use in England for Scandinavian settlers even before the country was invaded by the Normans, who were themselves Scandinavian settlers in France. In Scotland the name was used to anglicise another Viking name, **Tormod**, adopted by Gaelic speakers from their Norse conquerors. This is formed from the name of the pagan god Thor, and *mod* ('mind, courage'). (For other Thor names see THORA). **Norma**, which is used as the feminine form of the name, seems to have been invented by Felice Romani, the librettist of Bellini's opera of that name, which was first performed in 1832. Some would derive it from the Latin *norma* meaning 'rule, standard, measure'.

Normandie, Normandy see Brittany

Nour, Nouredine see Nur

Nuala see Fenella

Nur, Nour

Nur, **Noor** or Nour is an Arabic name used for both sexes. It means 'light, illumination' and is one of the titles of Allah. There are many related names. **Nuruddin**, or **Nouredine**, means 'light of the world; **Anwar** or **Anour** comes from the same root and means 'brighter' while the plural of Nur is **Anwaar**. MONA also comes from the same root.

Nya see Niamh

Nyasia see Nyla

Nye see Aneurin

Nyla

One has only to see the variety of explanations available to give a history to this new name, to realise that it is probably a coinage. Some claim it is a female form of Niles – the Scandinavian form of NEIL. Other that is it is a shortening of CORNELIA. The most probable explanation is that it is an invented name, with no previous history. The same probably applies to the name **Nyasia**.

O

Oberon see **Aubrey**

Océane see **Marina**

Octavia, Octavius

These are the Latin for 'eighth'. It was originally a Roman name given to an eighth child, but later it was associated with the imperial family. The first emperor, AUGUSTUS, was called **Octavius** or **Octavian** before he took his title. Octavia is shortened to **Tavy**, **Tave** or **Tavia**. Octavius is **Octavio** in Spanish. The boy's name **Davian** is probably a form of Octavius via the shortening **Tavian**.

Odette, Odile, Odo see **Otto**

Odharnait, Odhran see **Orrin**

Odysseus see **Ulysses**

Oighrig see **Afric, Euphemia**

Oilibhéar, Olaf, Olave see **Oliver**

Oisin see **Ossian**

Olga

Olga is the Russian version of the Scandinavian name **Helga**, meaning 'holy, blessed'. Although Helga was found in pre-Conquest England, its use today by English-speakers is a modern re-introduction. The predominance of Olga over Helga probably reflects the popularity of Russian literature.

Oliver, Olivia

ROLAND and Oliver were inseparable companions and the two greatest of Charlemagne's peers in the old French stories. Their friendship was so great that it became proverbial. The followers of Charlemagne in both fact and fiction were Franks, a Germanic people, and their names reflect this. Thus, although Oliver looks as if it is based on the olive, symbol of peace, and the French form of the name, **Olivier**, is identical with the French for 'an olive tree', the name most probably is a form of the Scandinavian name **Olaf**, formed from elements meaning 'ancestor' and 'heir, descendant', which in its old form *Olafr* (*Olvir* in many early texts) would have a very similar pronunciation to Oliver. The name was long out of fashion after the fall of Oliver Cromwell (whose nicknames illustrate the old pet forms Noll and Nolly), but time has reduced the close association of the Protector and the name. When Dickens named his character *Oliver Twist* it was part of the mockery of the poor to give him such a peculiar name. However, the book reintroduced the name, and the success of the musical version in the twentieth century may have started its return to fashion. **Ol** and **Ollie** are now the more common short forms. The name **Havelock** is said to be the Welsh form of the name. In Irish Olaf becomes **Amhalgaidh** or **Amhlaoibh** anglicised as **Auliffe** or **Olave** (sometimes **Awley** or **Auley** is treated as a form of this, although it is technically a different name). Another Irish form of the name is **Oilibhéar**. The Amhlaoibh form was taken directly from the Norse settlers and Olaf; the Oilibhéar from the Normans.

Feminine forms of the name are even more closely associated with the plant, being **Olive** and **Olivia**. Olivia is another Shakespearean introduction, used for the noble lady beloved by the duke in *Twelfth Night*. The name is sometimes shortened to **Livia** or **Livy**, although Livia is a name in its own right, being a Roman family name made famous by the wife of the emperor AUGUSTUS. **Alivia** is a variant.

Oliver and Olivia are currently very popular names. Olivia became the most popular name in England for girls in 2006

Olwen

Olwen is a character from the medieval Welsh story of *Culhwch and Olwen* in which her wise advice enables her lover to win her from her ogre father. She possessed outstanding beauty, and four white trefoils sprang up in her footprints wherever she trod, hence her name, which means 'white footprint'. **Olwyn** is a frequent variant of the name, and it is not surprising that this charming legend has made the name popular with Welsh parents.

Olympia

Mount Olympus was the home of the gods in Greek mythology. From this mountain the Greek name **Olympias** was coined. It was the name of the ruthless but admired mother of ALEXANDER the Great, and from there spread through the lands he conquered. It was given to a fourth-century AD Byzantine woman of equally strong but rather more attractive character who was later canonised, and as St Olympia the name spread through Europe. Both forms of the name occur early on in England, but now the name is rare, except among those of Greek descent. **Olympe**, the French form, and **Olympie** are also used.

Omar

As a boy's name, this can have three different sources. It is a well-known Arabic name meaning 'flourishing', also found as **Umar**. It can be a biblical name mentioned in the book of Genesis. Finally, some uses may be inspired by the fame of US general Omar Bradley (1893–1981), who distinguished himself as a commander in World War II. **Omari** is a variant, as is **Omarion**, publicised as the name of a singer. There is also a French name Omer or Omar from the Germanic name *Odomar* formed from elements meaning 'riches' and 'famous'. A saint of this name gave his name to the French city of St Omer.

Onyx see Jewel

Oonagh

Oonagh or **Oona** is an early Irish name, also found as **Una**. In the past it has sometimes been anglicised as **Juno**. Its meaning is not clear, but it has been argued that it is from the Irish word *uan* meaning 'lamb'. Another source of the name Una is Spenser's poem *The Faerie Queene* (1590–96), in which she is the heroine of Book I. Here the name is based on the Latin for 'one', for Una is truth personified and is so-called because Truth is one, while Error is multiform. However, it is probably no coincidence that Spenser was a resident of Ireland, and he was very possibly influenced by the Irish name. The sense of 'one' is found in another name, **Unity**, introduced as an abstract name by the Puritans but often regarded as a variant of Una. More recently another name with the same meaning has appeared in the name **Unique**.

Opal see Jewel

Ophelia

Another Shakespearean introduction, Ophelia is the tragic and rather ineffective heroine of *Hamlet*. Although this is not one of the commonest Shakespearean names, parents do not seem to have been put off by the story of her madness and suicide, and the name has a steady use. It was probably coined from a Greek root meaning 'help'

Oran, Oren see Orrin

Orfhlaith see Orla

Oriel, Oriole see Aurelius

Orin see Orrin

Orion

This is a name from Greek mythology of unknown meaning. Orion was a great hunter beloved of the goddess who was Mistress of the Beasts, Artemis. After his death she put him in the sky as the constellation Orion. The name has been used for boys in the USA since the 1990s, perhaps influenced by the popularity of RYAN.

Orla

An Irish name meaning 'golden lady', Orla thus has the same meaning as the AURELIAN (*see* **Aurelius**) group of names. In Irish it is spelt **Orlaith** and **Orfhlaith**, and it can also be found in the form **Orlagh**. **Aurnia** is a variant. There is also a masculine Orla who occurs in the poems of OSSIAN, but while this was used at the height of the European Ossianic craze in the nineteenth century, it is probably now obsolete. Orla is used in Scotland, Northern Ireland and the Irish Republic, where the form Orlaith is also well used.

Orlando see Roland

Orrin

Orrin or **Orin**, a name well represented in the United States and in use since at least the eighteenth century, is probably a form of the Irish name **Oran** or **Odhran** ('grey-brown, dark') and the name of a number of Irish saints. **Orna (Odharnait)** is the female equivalent. Orna is also the feminine form of **Oren**, a Hebrew name meaning 'pine tree'. Oran is well used in both Northern Ireland and the Republic, but the spelling Odhran is the preferred one in the north.

Orson

Orson means 'bear cub'. In medieval legend Valentine (see VALERY) and Orson were twins born to an exiled Byzantine Princess. The new-born Orson is stolen by a bear, who brought him up. Despite his rough behaviour and ursine appearance, his noble nature shows through in his fighting skills, and after many adventures he is finally reunited with his family and regains his rightful place in society. By no means a common name, it became well known in the twentieth century through the fame of Orson Welles (1915–85). URSULA is the feminine equivalent of the name.

Orville see Wilbur

Osama see Usama

Osbert

This is one of a group of Old English names containing the first element *os*, meaning 'god', combined with other common name elements. Thus we have **Osric** ('god' + 'rule') **Oswald** ('god' + 'power') and **Oswin** ('god' + 'friend'). They all share **Os, Oz, Ozzie** and **Ossy** as short forms. There was a revival of these names in the nineteenth century, but they are not popular at the moment, although Spanish speakers used **Oswaldo** and **Osvaldo**.

Oscar

Although some authorities give this name a German source meaning 'divine spear', it is much more likely to be an Irish name meaning 'champion warrior'. It has strong associations with Scandinavia, but despite its being a Swedish royal name, this is not evidence for a Germanic inheritance, for it comes from Napoleon Bonaparte's passion for the poems of OSSIAN. In 1799 Napoleon was godfather to the first son of his Marshal, Jean-Baptiste Bernadotte, who became king of Sweden as Karl XIV Johan. Napoleon chose to name his godson Oscar after the hero of Macpherson's poems, and this child became Oscar I of Sweden in 1844. From him the name spread to the general population, along with a number of other Ossianic names. King Oscar had as his court physician a certain Sir William Wilde, and it is probably this connection, rather than the Irish one, that led to his son being christened with two Ossianic names, Oscar FINGAL O'Flahertie Wilde. Oscar had been a popular name in the nineteenth century, but the scandalous trial of Oscar Wilde in 1895 led to a distinct fall in its popularity and it became rare in the UK, although it has now become popular again. Scandinavian immigration made sure that it never suffered the same fate in the USA. The name remains popular in Sweden, having reached number 1 in 2005, and is well used in English-speaking countries.

Osheen, Osian see Ossian

Osric see Osbert

Ossian

Ossian means 'fawn' and is the name of the legendary son of Finn (see FINLAY). The name is also found as **Ossin**, **Oisin** and in a phonetic spelling of the Irish form **Osheen**. According to legend, Ossian was the leader of the Irish Fenians who were defeated at the battle of Fabhra by King Carbery in 283. Ossian was left as the last survivor of the Fenians and after spending some years in fairyland (see NIAMH) he was converted to Christianity by St Patrick. In the eighteenth century James Macpherson created a great stir by publishing a series of poems associated with Ossian, supposedly ancient but in fact mainly his own work, and this led to a number of names which occurred in these poems, such as OSCAR, FINGAL, SELMA and MALVINA, coming into use. The form **Osian** is well used in Wales. A feminine form, **Ossia**, is also found. Oisin is currently moderately popular in Ireland.

Ossy, Osvaldo, Oswald, Oswaldo Oswin see Osbert

Otto

The Germanic name element *ot* or *od*, meaning 'riches, prosperity', has developed into a number of names. Otto is the German form which has not been much used by English speakers, despite the fact that the name came over with the Normans in the form of **Odo**, William the Conqueror's avaricious half-brother. The French feminine forms of the name, **Odile** and **Odette**, reflect this form in 'd', but the 't' forms are also to be found in **Ottilie**, **Ottoline** and **Ottilia**. The name **Otis** comes from a surname which developed from the same root. It came into use in America as a first name out of respect for James Otis (1725–83), a campaigner for American rights in the lead up to the Revolution.

Owain, Owen see Ewan

Oz, Ozzie see Osbert

P

Pablo see **Paul**

Padarn, Paddy, Padraic, Pàdraig, Padrig see **Patrick**

Padma

Padma, used for both sexes, is the Sanskrit for 'lotus', a name which has strong religious associations for Hindus. The model and author Padma Lakshmi has made the name better known in the West.

Pagan

In the Roman world you could be classified as either *urbanus* a town-dweller, or *paganus* a country-dweller. *Urbanus* developed into the name URBAN, used by a number of Popes, as well as giving us the word urbane, while *paganus* became pagan. The journey from country-dweller to unbeliever happened because the word developed the secondary sense of civilian, someone who was not in the army, and from that to someone who was not a member of the army of Christ. Despite its sense, Pagan was introduced into England by the Normans and was a popular name for both sexes in the Middle Ages, as can be seen by the frequency of surnames such as Paine and Payne that come from it. It shows signs of coming back, sometimes in the form **Paygan**. Pagan Kennedy is an American author.

Paige

This surname, originally given to someone who was a page, has been one of the most successful new names in recent years. It was well established in the USA in the late 1980s, but did not enter the British top 50 until the second half of the 1990s. It is still well used in these countries, as well as in Canada and Australia.

Pallav

This is a Sanskrit boy's name meaning 'young shoot, leaf bud' which is also found as **Pallab**. **Pallavi** is the female equivalent.

Paloma

This is the Spanish for 'dove'. It was used by Picasso for his daughter's name, and is occasionally found in other countries, probably as a direct result of Paloma Picasso's fame. For masculine names meaning 'dove', see under MALCOLM.

Pamela

Pamela was invented by Sir Philip Sydney (1554–86) as a name in his pastoral *Arcadia*. From the way his verse scans, he seems to have intended the word to be pronounced with the stress on the second syllable, and may have intended it to be understood as from the Greek meaning 'all honey'. It became a famous name with the success in 1740 of Samuel Richardson's long novel *Pamela: or Virtue Rewarded*. **Pamella** is a variant and **Pam** or **Pammie** the pet forms.

Pandora

In Greek mythology Pandora plays the same role as EVE in the Bible, bringing misfortune upon mankind. She was created by the gods on the orders of Zeus, to take vengeance for the stealing of fire for mankind's use. Each god gave her a gift of some desirable quality (the name means 'all gifts'), but she was also made inquisitive. Her husband had a sealed box which she had been forbidden to open, but she did so, and out flew all the ills which afflict mankind. HOPE had also been sealed in the box, which alone made the afflictions bearable. Despite this story, Pandora is now quite regularly used, and can be shortened to **Panda**.

Pansy

One of the less common flower names, Pansy has been in use since the end of the nineteenth century. The name of the flower comes from the French word *pensée* ('a thought'), from the way in which the markings on the flowers and the way they grow can look like a face bowed in thought.

Paola, Paolo see Paul

Paris

Although Paris was originally a man's name (see ALEXANDER, HELEN), it is now more common as a first name for girls. Although some male uses may hark back to the original Trojan hero (the name is also used in passing by Shakespeare), most parents who use it are probably thinking of the French city of Paris (which got its name from the ancient Gaulish tribe who lived there, the Parisi) and all the associations of culture and the good things in life that are associated with it. Paris Hilton is a well-known bearer.

Parker

Parker, or its shortened form **Park**, has been used as a boy's name in the USA since the nineteenth century. It went out of fashion in the 1950s but was revived in the 80s and has been used increasingly ever since. It is now being used for girls as well. It comes from a surname which would have been given in the Middle Ages to a gamekeeper.

Parnel see Peter

Parthalon, Partholon see Bartholomew

Parvati

Parvarti is the name of a Hindu goddess who is the wife of Shiva and the mother of Ganesh. Her name means 'daughter of the mountains'.

Parvin see Soraya

Pascal

Pascal means 'Easter' and was originally given to those born at that time of year, just as NOEL was given to those born at Christmas. The surname **Pascoe** comes from the Cornish form of the name. **Pascale**, **Pascalle** or rarely **Pascaline** are its feminines.

Pat see Patrick

Patience

Patience is one of the Christian virtues, and as such was brought into use in the seventeenth century by the Puritans, when it was used for boys. It is now a firmly feminine name.

Patrick

Patrick comes from the Latin *patricius* ('a nobleman') ultimately from *pater* 'father'. The Irish form of their patron saint's name is **Pádraig**, with **Padraic** and **Phadrig** as variants, but the name was not used in Ireland in early times, possibly out of reverence for the great saint. St Patrick was not a native Irishman, but a Briton, and his name has survived in Welsh as **Padrig**. **Pat** and **Paddy** are the commonest short forms of Patrick, with **Patsy**, once common, now more generally female. In Wales the name **Padern** comes from the same root, in this case via *paternus* 'fatherly'. It is the name of a sixth-century saint, and may go back to Roman times. **Patricia**, the feminine, comes from the Latin form of Patrick, and came into general use after Queen Victoria chose to name one of her daughters Patricia in 1886. It has a number of short forms such as **Pat**, **Patty**, **Patsy**, **Tricia** and **Tisha**. **Patrice**, used in France for both sexes, is usually feminine in English-speaking countries. Patrick is well used in the USA, and the UK, but is currently most popular in Australia and Ireland, where Padraig is also well used.

Pattie, Patty see Martha, Matilda, Patricia (*see* Patrick), Patience

Paul

This name comes from the Latin *paulus* ('small'), and was therefore a suitably humble name for SAUL of Tarsus to adopt after his conversion from persecutor of Christians to Apostle. **Pablo**, the Spanish form, and **Paolo**, the Italian, are found in the USA. **Paula** is the direct Latin feminine of the name, with **Pauline** a diminutive derived from the Latin alternative **Paulina**. **Paola** is the Italian form and **Paulette** a French pet form. **Polly** is occasionally a pet form of Pauline.

Paxton

Paxton, a surname from an English place name, is sometimes used as a first name for boys in the USA.

Paygan see Pagan

Payton see Peyton

Peaches

There is a slight, but growing trend for naming children not just after flowers, but after fruit. Peaches is probably the best-known and most used of these, after the media appearances of Peaches Geldof, followed by **Apple**, the name chosen for her daughter by Gwyneth Paltrow, after her husband's agent had used it for her own daughter. However, a radio broadcast in England on the subject turned up children named after practically any fruit, including Raspberry, Strawberry and Orange. There is a Japanese novelist called Banana Yashimoto. The French use **Cerise** (CHERRY), **Mirabelle** (a type of plum) and indeed, very occasionally **Prune** (plum, see also PRUNELLA).

Pearce see Peter

Pearl

Although it is one of the jewel names, Pearl has the same meaning as MARGARET, so is also found as a pet form of that name. **Perla** is the Spanish form of the name and it is **Perle** in Yiddish. **Jumana** and its pet form **Jumaina** mean pearl in Arabic, as does **Lulua** and its plural **Lulu**. Nathaniel Hawthorne used the name Pearl in his 1850 novel *The Scarlet Letter*, and this may have been responsible for its subsequent increased popularity.

Pedran, Pedr, Pedro see Peter

Peg, Peggie, Peggy see Margaret

Pelagius see Morgan

Penelope

In Homer's *Odyssey*, Penelope is the faithful wife of Odysseus (see ULYSSES), who successfully resists the wooing of the 50 suitors who wish to win the kingdom by marrying her, for the 10 years it takes for her husband to reach home after the fall of Troy. Her main ploy is to say that she will not choose a new husband until she has woven a shroud for her father-in-law. Although she diligently weaves all day, at night she unpicks her work. The meaning of the name is something of a problem. It appears to come from the word for 'a duck', but it is very difficult to see why the ancient Penelope should have been named after this bird. The name may be so early, possibly pre-Greek, that its meaning has been lost. **Pen** and **Penny** are its short forms.

Pepita see Joseph

Percy

The first of the Percys came over with the Conqueror and founded the great Northumbrian family of that name. The surname comes from the common French place name Percé, in his case probably from the village near St Lô. The village name, in its turn, comes from the Gallo-Roman name *Persius*. The surname came into use as a first name in the eighteenth century. Percy is also used as a short form of the name **Percival**, which comes from Arthurian romance. It was invented in the twelfth century by the French writer Chrétien de Troyes for his perfect knight. It seems to be made up of the elements *perce-val* ('pierce-valley'), although the reason for this is not clear, and it may be that the name is a corruption of the Welsh name for a hero who shares some of the same adventures, **Peredur**, whose name means 'hard spears'. Percival is sometimes shortened to **Val**.

Perdita

This name means 'the lost one' and was created by Shakespeare for the heroine of *The Winter's Tale*, who is abandoned as an infant. Despite the charming personality of the original, and the happy outcome of the play, this is not one of the commoner Shakespearean names, although it was certainly in use among the ruling classes by the early part of the twentieth century, for the name was given to the granddaughter of the prime minister H.H. Asquith in 1910.

Peredur see Percy

Peregrine

Peregrine comes from the Latin for 'a pilgrim, traveller', and was a common early Christian name, emphasising the transitory nature of life on earth against the eternity of heaven. Its only connection with the peregrine falcon is that they share a common root. Most birds used for falconry were taken from the nest, but the peregrine was captured while travelling to its breeding ground; hence its name. **Perry** can be used as a short form of Peregrine, but is also used as an independent name in the United States in honour of two Admiral Perrys, one of whom, Oliver Hazard Perry, defeated the British fleet on Lake Erie in 1812, while Matthew Galbraith Perry opened up Japan to foreign interests. However, the best-known Perry, the singer Perry Como, was originally Nick Perido, so got his stage name from his surname.

Perkin see Peter

Perla, Perle see Pearl

Pernel, Pernilla see Peter

Perry see Peregrine

Persephone see Corinna, Melanie

Perseus see Danaë

Persis

Persis means 'Persian woman'. It is now an unusual name, but was not uncommon in the seventeenth century, when obscure names from the Bible were in fashion. The biblical Persis is mentioned in the Epistle of St Paul to the Romans (16. 12), when he writes 'Salute the beloved Persis, which laboured much in the Lord'. Nothing else is known of her. The simple **Persia** is also occasionally used as a first name.

Peter

Peter means 'stone', and started life as a nickname, given to the Apostle SIMON by Jesus, who, punning on the meaning of the name, says 'thou art Peter, and upon this rock I will build my church' (Matthew 16:18). Peter is formed directly from the Latin *petrus*; but **Piers**, the alternative form of the name, comes via the French **Pierre**. Piers was the common vernacular form of the name in the Middle Ages, and gives us the surnames **Pearce** and **Pierce**, sometimes used as first names. **Pete** is now the common pet form, but in the past **Peterkin** and **Perkin** were used. In Welsh the name became **Pedr**, with the pet forms **Pedran** and **Petran**. **Pedro** is the Spanish masculine.

There are a large number of feminine versions of the name. According to legend, St **Petronilla** or **Petronella** was the daughter of St Peter (the name is actually a form of the Roman family name of the Petronii), and this was used as a feminine equivalent. It is shortened to **Petsy**. It was very common in medieval England, when it was shortened to **Petronel**, **Pernel** or **Parnel**. In Scandinavia it became **Pernilla**. **Peta**, **Petra** and **Petrina** are based more closely on the masculine.

Peter in its various forms is used steadily throughout the Western world.

Peyton

Peyton or **Payton** is a surname, from an English place name, now used as a first name for both sexes, although rather more for girls than boys. Surprisingly, Peyton came into use for girls in 1992 after the film *The Hand that Rocks the Cradle* was released. In this film there is a female character called Peyton who is a vicious killer.

Phadrig see **Patrick**

Phebe see **Phoebe**

Phelim see **Felicity**

Phemia, Phemie see **Euphemia**

Phia see **Sophy** (*see* **Sophie**)

Philip

A traditional name in the Macedonian royal family, Philip means 'loving horses'. It was spread by the conquests of Philip the Great of Macedonia's son, Alexander (see further under ALEXANDER), became common throughout the Middle East, and was the name of one of the Apostles and a number of saints, which guaranteed the spread of the name through Europe. It is sometimes spelt **Phillip**, as in the surname, and shortened to **Phil** and **Pip**. **Flip** is a contracted form of the name, and **Felipe** the Spanish. **Philippa** (sometimes **Phillipa**, **Phillippa** or **Philipa**) is the usual feminine and this is shortened to **Pippa**, which was originally an Italian form. The French feminine **Philippine** is occasionally found.

Phillida, Phillis see **Phyllis**

Philomena

Philomena means 'beloved'. In 1802 an inscription and some bones were discovered in the Catacombs at Rome, and a dedication to the bereaved's 'beloved' was interpreted as indicating that these were the bones of a St Philomena. In 1863 Charlotte M. Yonge could write, 'So many wonders are said to have been worked by this phantom saint, the mere produce of a blundered inscription, that … she is by far the most fashionable patroness in the Romish Church'. The name was particularly popular in Ireland, but has lost favour there since the saint was declared spurious. However, the name is still regularly used, with the French form **Philomène** occasionally found.

Phineas

This is the name of two minor characters in the Old Testament, where the name appears as **Phinehas**. Its meaning is obscure, but it may mean 'oracle'. Little used now, the name is kept alive by the stories about the showman Phineas T. Barnum (1810–91), and in literature by Trollope's novel *Phineas Finn* (1869).

Phoebe

Phoebe means 'the shining one' and was an epithet of the goddess **Artemis**, sister of Phoebus Apollo, in her aspect of moon goddess (see also DIANA, CYNTHIA). It is found in the Bible in the same chapter of Romans as PERSIS, in the form **Phebe**, and this justified it being adopted as a Christian name. Phoebe is also used as a short form of EUPHEMIA. It fell out of favour at the end of the nineteenth century, but is now decidedly popular in the UK

Phoenix

The phoenix, which gets its name from the Greek for 'dark red', is a mythical bird. According to legend there is only ever one phoenix. When it gets old it builds a special nest on which it bursts into flame and is reborn from the ashes. Thus the phoenix became a symbol of both resurrection and of uniqueness. The name is fashionable for both sexes.

Phyllis

This is a Greek name meaning 'leafy'. In mythology, Phyllis is a Thracian maiden who hangs herself when her lover does not return from his own country, where he has gone to settle his affairs, within the promised time, and is transmogrified into an almond tree. When her delayed lover finally returns he embraces the almond tree, and the plant, hitherto barren, puts forth green leaves. **Phyllida** is a literary elaboration of the name. Other forms are **Phillis**, **Phylis** and **Phillida**.

Pia

The Latin feminine for 'pious', Pia is an Italian name which has only recently come into use in anglophone countries, although the masculine, **Pius**, has long been familiar as the name of numerous popes.

Pierce, Pierre, Piers see Peter

Pip, Pippa see Philip

Piper

Piper is a surname from the occupation, used for a first name for girls. It has been given public exposure since the 1950s by the actress Piper Laurie, but the name only took off after it was used for a character in 1998 in the highly successful television show *Charmed*.

Pippa see Philip

Poll see Mary

Pollux see Cosmo

Polly see Mary, Paul

Poonam

Poonam is an Indian name meaning 'full moon' **Poornima** or **Purnima** is from the term for the night of the full moon.

Poppy

This is another flower name which became particularly popular at the end of the nineteenth century and the beginning of the twentieth. It then fell out of use, but is once again well used in the UK

Porter

This is the surname, from the occupation, used as a first name for boys.

Portia

A Roman family name, coming from the word for 'pig', Portia has become dissociated from its roots thanks to Shakespeare. He has two Portias in his plays. One, Cato's daughter and Brutus' faithful and stoical wife in *Julius Caesar*, is a Roman matron who really existed. The other, the heroine of *The Merchant of Venice*, combines charm with wit and wisdom, and it is after her that most Portias are named. The name has been fashionable in recent years, and in the United States many phonetic forms have developed, the most common of which is **Porsha**. Since the pronunciation of the name and that of the German Porsche car is all but identical, one name blends imperceptibly into the other, and as well as **Porsche**, spellings such as **Porchia**, **Porscha** and **Porshia** are found.

Pranav

Pranav is the name of the symbol, pronounced 'om' or 'aum' that is placed at the beginning of Hindu sacred texts, which has similar functions as 'amen' in Judea-Christian religion. It means 'to shout praise'. It is used as a boy's name.

Precious

This name, generally a term of affection, is now being used as a girl's given name, and is also occasionally used for boys

Presley

The surname Presley, meaning a clearing where a priest lived, and made famous by Elvis Presley, has been used as a girl's name in the USA since the end of the 1990s.

Preston

This surname comes from a place name that can either be interpreted as 'village with a priest', or 'village on land owned by the church'. It has been in regular use in the USA since the nineteenth century and use has recently increased. It has also increased sharply in the UK, after the singer of the group The Ordinary Boys, known just as Preston, appeared on *Celebrity Big Brother*.

Primrose

Primrose, like POPPY, was a very popular name at the turn of the nineteenth and twentieth centuries but there does not seem to have been the same return of interest in it. **Primula**, the Latin name for the plant, has also been used.

Prince, Princess

Prince has been in the public eye for some years as the name of a highly successful singer, but use of both Prince and Princess has become more usual in recent years.

Priscilla

This is a biblical name. Priscilla was very active in the early Church, being both a supporter and follower of St Paul. She is mentioned in various books in the New Testament, including the chapter of Romans that gives us PHOEBE and PERSIS. Priscilla is an old Roman family name meaning 'ancient'. **Prissy** and **Cilla** are the short forms.

Prudence

Like other virtue names, Prudence was much loved by the Puritans. An earlier form of the name is **Prudentia**, a saint's name, probably in its turn modelled on **Prudentius**, a much admired early Christian poet of the fourth century. **Prue** is the short form.

Prunella

Prunella may be a diminutive of the Latin *prunus*, both the word for 'a plum tree' and for the group of winter-flowering trees that do so much to lighten winter gardens. Prunella is also the name for a kind of silk and the Latin name for both the wild flower self-heal and the hedge sparrow, but this is probably coincidental. An alternative suggestion is that it is a variant of **Brunella**, a feminine form of BRUNO dating back to the Middle Ages, which is also used to indicate a brunette. It is an unusual choice, but well known from the actress Prunella Scales. See also under PEACHES.

Purnima see Poonam

Q

Queenie see **Rex, Victoria**

Quentin

Quentin comes from the Latin name *Quintus* ('fifth'), traditionally given to a fifth son. St Quentin was a third-century missionary and martyr who met his death at the French city now named after him. There is a similar surname, **Quinton**, which comes from a place name meaning 'queen's settlement'. Other forms used are **Quintin** and **Quinten**. The martyr is the main source of the name, which was used in the Middle Ages in England, fell out of use thereafter and was revived after the publishing of Sir Walter Scott's *Quentin Durwood* in 1823. The director Quentin Tarantino is a well-known holder.

Quincy

An aristocratic surname, Quincy comes from the French place name of Cuinchy (north of Arras). This, in its turn, comes from a Roman personal name *Quintus*, so the name has the same root as QUENTIN. Quincy (sometimes **Quincey**) is used more frequently in the United States than elsewhere, where it came into use in honour of John Quincy Adams (1767–1848), the 6th president of that country.

Quinn

This boy's name comes from an Irish surname meaning 'descendant of Conn', CONN meaning 'chief, leader'. Quinn is traditionally a masculine name, but started being used for girls around 1995 in the USA. It is probably no coincidence that two years earlier a long-running and very successful television show called *Dr. Quinn, Medicine Woman* started being shown.

R

Rab, Rabbie see **Robert**

Rachel

A Hebrew name meaning 'ewe', Rachel was a suitable name for a girl who kept her father's sheep (Genesis 29:6). The biblical Rachel was 'beautiful and well favoured' and dearly loved by her husband JACOB, although she did not get on with her sister and co-wife LEAH. The name is often spelt **Rachael** and has developed in a number of different directions. The variant **Rachelle**, with a 'sh' sound in the middle, has in turn developed the form **Rochelle** (also a place name meaning 'little rock'). This is a more likely source of the name than the Breton port meaning 'little rock', although it is worth noting that it is an American name, and Rochelle is also a transatlantic place name, for example Rochelle Park in New Jersey. Rachelle and Rochelle use SHELLEY as a short form. Rachel can be shortened to **Rae** or **Ray**, and this has been elaborated into **Raelene**. **Raquel**, the Spanish form of the name, has come into use since it was made famous by the actress Raquel Welch. **Rahil** is the Arabic form. Rachel is popular on both sides of the Atlantic and has been since the 1970s.

Rachid see **Rashid**

Rae see **Rachel, Raymond**

Raelene see **Rachel**

Raeven see **Raven**

Rafael, Rafaela see **Raphael**

Rafe see **Ralph**

Rafiq, Rafiqa

These are from the Arabic for 'intimate friend', the first masculine, the second feminine.

Raheem see **Rahim**

Rahil see **Rachael** (*see* **Rachel**)

Rahim

Rahim is the Arabic for 'merciful, compassionate, kind', one of the most used names of Allah. In the USA Black Muslims tend to use **Raheem**, which makes the pronunciation clearer. **Rahima** is the feminine form.

Raina, Raine see **Rex**

Raj

Raj means 'king' or 'prince'. **Rajesh** means 'ruler of kings', **Rajinder** or **Rajendra** 'lord of kings, **Rajneesh** or **Rajnish** 'lord of the night'. **Rajni** and **Rani** 'queen' and **Rajkamari** 'princess' are female counterparts.

Rakeem

This name was popular among African-Americans in the 1990s. It is regarded as a Muslim name, and may be a re-spelling of Rakhim 'sweet, sweet-voiced, pleasant'. There is a well-known rapper who has called himself, among other things, Prince Rakeem.

Ralph

This comes from an old Germanic name *Rad(w)ulf* made up of the elements meaning 'counsel' and 'wolf'. The spelling **Ralf** is closer to the original, the -ph form being an eighteenth-century 'improvement'. The variant **Rafe**, found since the Middle Ages, reflects the pronunciation which was the norm until the twentieth century. **Raoul** is the French form of the word, **Raul** the Spanish. **Rolf**, from *Hrodulf* ('fame' + 'wolf'), is a closely allied name, which was absorbed by Ralph in the Middle Ages, and obsolete until revived as a separate name in the nineteenth century. **Rollo** was the medieval Latin form of Rolf, while in Germany the name became **Rudolph** or **Rudolf**, with a short form **Rudy** or **Rudi**. **Rodolfo** is the Spanish form of the name. Rudolph gained tremendous publicity in the early twentieth century in the person of the film star Rudolph Valentino, but is now most associated with a red-nosed reindeer.

Ramiro, Ramon, Ramona see Raymond

Ranald see Reginald

Randolph, Randall

Randolph or **Randolf** is an Old English name meaning 'shield wolf'. It has two major variants, **Ranulf** (very occasionally **Renouf**), and **Randal** or **Randall**, which at the moment is probably more frequently given than the original form. The short form **Randy** is now treated as an independent name (and **Randi** is sometimes found as a feminine form), and is used in the United States where the vocabulary word which makes the name seem inappropriate to the British is little used, but the alternative **Dolph** is rarely heard now.

Rani see Raj

Raoul see Ralph

Raphael

The archangel Raphael's name means 'God heals', reflecting his role in the Apocryphal *Book of Tobit*, where he restores Tobit's sight. The name has in the past been less popular than the other archangels MICHAEL and GABRIEL, despite his being the patron of doctors and travellers, and for a long time it was regarded as a particularly Jewish name. Nowadays it is probably most closely associated with the Renaissance painter. **Rafael** is the Spanish form, and the Italian feminine **Raphaela** or **Rafaela** is sometimes found. Currently Raphael is particularly popular in France.

Raquel see Rachel

Rasha see Tabitha

Rashid

Rashid, sometimes **Rachid**, means 'wise, rightly guided' in Arabic. It is one of the titles of Mohammed, and is also used of the first four Caliphs. There are two confusingly similar masculine names **Rashed** 'right-minded, rightly guided' and **Rashad** 'right guidance, integrity of conduct'. Rashad has been well used by African-Americans is the USA, with the result that Rash- has been adopted into the corpus of name elements, leading to such coinages as **Rashawn**. **Rasheda** and **Rashida** are feminine forms of Rashid.

Rasmus, Rastus see Erasmus

Raul see Ralph

Raven

Recorded from as early as 1869, Raven (sometimes **Raeven** or **Ravyn**) has been fashionable as a girl's name in the USA since the 1970s, with use peaking in the 1990s, presumably because of its associations with glossy darkness shared with EBONY and Sable. It is by no means an exclusively African-American name.

Ravi
Ravi, which means sun in Sanskrit, is the name of the Hindu sun god. The fame of the Sitar player Ravi Shankar has led to some people using the name outside a Hindu context. **Ravindra** means 'lord of the sun'.

Ray see Rachel, Raymond

Raymond
The old Germanic name *Raginmund*, formed from *ragin* and *mund*, words meaning 'counsel' and 'protection', became *Raimund* in Old French and was brought over to England by the Normans, where it became Raymond or **Raymund**, with the short form **Ray** or **Rae**. When the Normans later conquered Ireland, they took the name with them, and there it became **Redmond** or **Redmund**, an increasingly popular name. In Spanish it became **Ramon**, well used in the United States, with a feminine **Ramona**, made famous as the title of a popular song published in 1927. The French feminine **Raymonde** is also occasionally found. The Spanish name **Ramiro** has a similar source, being formed from *ragin* + *mari* 'famous'.

Rayna see Rex

Reagan
This is an Irish surname, formed from *O Riagáin* 'descendant of Riagáin'. **Riagáin** was the name of a nephew of the great Irish king Brian Boru. The meaning of the name is not clear, but it may mean 'impulsive'. Many people, however, like to analyse Reagan as based on a pet form of the Irish *ri* and interpret it as meaning 'little king'. It is a recent introduction, not being recorded before 1975 and not in general use until the 1990s for girls, and not recorded before the mid 1990s for boys. It has always been more common for girls than boys. There are mixed reasons for using the name. Some cases, particularly for boys, are undoubtedly used on account of President Ronald Reagan. In many cases for girls it is used as a variant of REGAN.

Reanna see Rhiannon

Rebecca
The meaning of the name Rebecca is not clear and it may not even be Hebrew. She appears as **Rebekah**, a form that is increasingly used, in the Old Testament, Rebecca being the spelling used in the New. She was the mother of Esau and JACOB, the founder of the house of Israel. Jacob was her favourite son, and it was Rebecca who planned the scheme by which Jacob deprived his brother of his birthright (Genesis 27). Rebecca comes across as a strong-minded woman, used to giving orders and with no patience if contradicted; but also as a woman capable of great love. **Becky** is the usual short form but **Becca** or **Becka** and **Reba** are also used. The name is currently popular on both sides of the Atlantic, particularly in Ireland.

Redmond, Redmund see Raymond

Reece, Rees, Reese see Rhys

Reed see Reid

Regan
The background to this name is a bit of a mystery. There are two main sources. One is the Irish surname, which is the more common form of REAGAN. The other is the character of the cruel undutiful daughter in Shakespeare's *King Lear*. The name came into use in 1974 after it had been used as the name of a girl possessed by a devil in the 1979 film *The Exorcist*. It was in use through the 1970s, drops out of the record for most of the 80s, and then re-emerges in the 1990s, following much the same pattern as Reagan, although it is used more often. Unlike Reagan, Regan does not appear to be used for boys.

Regina, Regine see Rex

Reginald
Reginald, with its short forms **Reg**, **Reggie** and occasionally REX, comes from *Reginaldus*, the Latin form of the name **Reynold**, the Norman form of an old Germanic

name *Reginwald*, formed from elements meaning 'might' and 'rule'. **Ronald**, with its short forms **Ron** and **Ronnie**, is from the Old Norse form of the same name. **Reynaldo** and **Ronaldo** are the Spanish forms of the names. In Scotland, **Ranald** is found as an occasional variant.

Regis see Rex

Reid, Reed

These are surnames derived from the word 'red' that would have been given to someone with red hair, now used as boys' first names.

Reina, Reine see Rex

Remington

The surname Remington comes from an English place name which refers to a boundary stream. While for older people Remington is most closely associated with portable typewriters or shaving products, it seems likely that the name came into use for boys in the USA from the television detective series *Remington Steele*. The series was first shown in 1982 and the name first appears in the records in 1983.

Rena see Andrew

Renan see Ronan

Renée

Also found without the accent as **Renee**, this is the French form of the Latin name **Renata** ('reborn'), referring to Christian baptism. It can also be spelt **Rennie** or **Renie** (see also IRENE), **Rene** and **Renny**. The masculine form **René** from **Renatus** is common in France, but little used by English speakers.

Reuben, Ruben

The name given to the eldest son of JACOB, Reuben was interpreted in the Bible (Genesis 29:32) as meaning 'behold a son'. Reuben is the standard biblical spelling and the usual form in the UK, but Ruben is currently much preferred in the USA, and is the standard spelling in France. In nineteenth-century America Reuben became associated with country bumpkins, and was the source of the word 'rube' from the short form of the name.

Rex, Regina

Rex, the Latin word for 'king', came into use as a first name in the nineteenth century (see also REGINALD). The French equivalent of Rex is **Regis**, the inflected form of the Latin, although this was adopted as a first name in honour of St Jean François Regis, the apostle of the Vivarais region. There is a wide range of feminine equivalents. **Regina** (sometimes shortened to **Gina**) is the Latin for 'queen' and **Queenie** started life as a pet form of this name (although it was also used for VICTORIA, a name which only became popular during Queen Victoria's long reign). In French, the name becomes **Regine**. **Raine** and **Reine** are based on the French word for 'queen', while the Spanish form is **Reyna** (sometimes found as **Rayna**, **Raina** or **Reina**). The Irish name **Riona** has the same meaning, and ultimately the same root.

Reynold, Reynaldo see Reginald

Rhapsody see Harmony

Rhett

Rhett is one of the many names that came into use from Margaret Mitchell's novel *Gone with the Wind* (1936), where the love scenes between SCARLETT O'Hara and Rhett Butler are central to the book and subsequent film. Robert Barnwell Rhett was a well-known politician during the American Civil War during which the book is set, and Mitchell may have got her inspiration from his name. **Rhetta** has been recorded, but this is likely to be a shortening of Margaretta (see MARGARET)

Rhiannon

An important figure in early Welsh literature, Rhiannon's antecedents go back even before the earliest surviving legends, for she seems to be a survival of an ancient Celtic goddess, possibly having some connection with horses. Her name means 'nymph, goddess'. It is also spelt **Rhianon**, and use has spread to non-Welsh parents, perhaps as a result of the Fleetwood Mac hit single *Rhiannon* (1975). As a result, variants such as **Rhianna** and spellings without the 'h' have developed. There are a number of other Welsh girls' names which come from the same root. Another popular Welsh name **Rhian** (now also **Rhianne, Rhianna**) could be a short form of Rhiannon or from *rhian* ('maiden'), an interpretation backed by names such as **Rhianedd** and **Rhianydd**, which are based on the plural form of the word, and **Rhianwen** or **Rhiainwen**, which combines the word for 'maiden' with that meaning 'white' or 'fair'. **Reanna**, used in the USA, is either from Rhiannon or is a pet form of Adriana. Rhiannon is currently well used in Scotland and Northern Ireland, where Rianna is also well used.

Rhoda

Rhoda is from the Greek meaning 'rose' and is another example of an apparently pagan name being made 'respectable' by being that of a minor New Testament character (Acts 12). It was very popular at the turn of the last century, but is not much used now.

Rhodri see Roderick

Rhona, Rona

This is a name which presents problems. It may be from the Scottish island Rona, given an h to conform with names like RHODA, in which case it means 'rough island'; it may be a short form of ROWENA, or it may be a feminine form of RONAN or RONALD. St Ronan lived for a time on Rona. It has also been said to be a shortening of **Rhonwen** (see ROWENA). It seems to have been in use only since about 1870, and became fashionable in the 1930s when it was given glamour by the successful 'Rhona Roy' fashion clothes, but it is not much used now.

Rhonda

This is a comparatively recent name, probably a respelling of the Welsh Rhondda valley, which takes its name from its river. The word means 'noisy'. It is also interpreted as from Welsh *rhon* 'spear' as in Rhonwen (see ROWENA), and *da* 'good', or as a blend of RHODA and RHONA

Rhydderch see Roderick

Rhys

A Welsh masculine name, Rhys means 'ardour' and so implies 'fiery warrior'. It was the name of two twelfth-century warriors who fought successfully against the English invaders of Wales. It is frequently found in the forms **Rees(e)** and **Reece**, the more usual form for surnames. It was originally an exclusively masculine name, but success of the American actress Reese Witherspoon means that it is now used more for girls than boys in the USA. In the UK however, it is still primarily masculine. It is in the top ten names in Wales as Rhys, both Rhys and Reece are well used in England with Rhys the slightly more popular, and both are also well used in Scotland, but this time with Reece the more popular.

Ria see Mary

Riagáin see Reagan

Riana see Adrian, Rhiannon

Richard

Richard comes from a Germanic root meaning 'strong ruler'. It was in use among the Anglo-Saxons in the form *Ricehard*, but the modern form was introduced by the Normans. It has long been a popular name, as can be seen from the number of pet forms it has developed, which include: **Dick, Dickie, Dicky, Diccon** or **Dickon; Rick** and **Ricky** (see also ERIC, FREDERICK), **Rich** and **Richie**. In the USA, the Spanish form **Ricardo**, and its shortening **Rico**, are well used. Attempts at forming feminines have been less successful, but **Ricarda, Richenda** and **Richelle** are all used.

Rick, Ricky see Cedric, Eric, Frederick, Richard

Rigoberto see Herbert

Riley

This is an Irish surname, of obscure origin. It is used for both sexes. In the 1990s it was more used for boys than girls in the USA, but now the position is reversed, although it is still mainly a boy's name in the UK. It is also found as **Rilee**, **Rylie** and **Ryleigh**, and the occasional use of the surname **Ryland** may be a variant.

Ringan see Ninian

Rio see River

Riona see Rex

Rishi

Rishi is a Sanskrit name or obscure origin. It is a title used to indicate a sage or poet and often used much as the Christian 'saint'.

Rita see Margaret

River, Rio

River is the vocabulary word used as a first name and Rio the Spanish or Portuguese equivalent. Both are used for both sexes, but more often for boys. River came into use after the success of the actor River Phoenix, and Rio is well-known from a Duran-Duran song (where it is a girl's name) and from the footballer Rio Ferdinand.

Robert

A Germanic name, Robert is formed from elements meaning 'fame' and 'bright', and originally had the form *Hrodberht*. Like Richard, it has long been part of the basic stock of English names and has consequentially developed a large number of pet forms. Dod, Dobbin, Hob and Hobbie were all used in the past but are now obsolete, but that still leaves **Bert** and **Bertie**; **Bob** and **Bobbie** or **Bobby**; **Rob**, **Robbie**, **Robby**, **Robo**, and in Scotland **Rab** and **Rabbie**. **Robin** (sometimes **Robyn** in Wales) is now often used as a separate name, but started life as a French pet form of Rob. **Roberto** is the Spanish form. **Roberta** and **Robina** are the older feminine forms, and more recently **Robyn** (or **Robin**) and **Bobbie** have been well used for girls. In Germany, the 'o' of Robert became a 'u', the 'b' changed to 'p' and the name became **Rupert**. This name was introduced into England by Prince Rupert of the Rhine (1618–92), a romantic figure who combined a keen interest in science with great bravery displayed while fighting on the side of his uncle King Charles I during the English civil war. Although used steadily in the UK, Rupert is an unusual name in the USA and thought of as distinctively British. This is probably because the early English settlers in America were mainly Puritans who had been on the Parliamentary side in the English Civil War, and would not have had a high opinion of the Royalist Rupert.

Rocco

The Germanic name *hrok* mean 'rook, crow' (although some would derive it from a similar word meaning 'rest'). In France it became **Roch**, the name of a fourteenth century saint who while in Italy on pilgrimage, healed many of the plague. This led to the name's being used in Italy in the form Rocco. In 1923 Rocco Marchegiano was born in the USA to Italian American parents. When he was a professional boxer he went by the name of **Rocky** Marciano and his form of the name was taken up for the Rocky series of films about a boxer, the first of which was shown in 1976. The occasional use of **Stone** as a boy's name in the USA may be connected to Rocky. The singer Madonna has called one of her sons Rocco.

Rochelle see Rachel

Roderick

Roderick comes from two Germanic name elements meaning 'fame' and 'power' and has short forms **Rod** and **Roddy**. It is also used as the English equivalent of two ancient Welsh names, **Rhodri**, formed from 'circle' (possibly implying a coronet) combined with 'ruler', and **Rhydderch** ('exalted ruler'). The Welsh patronymic 'ap (son of) Roderick' developed into the surname **Broderick**, which is sometimes used as a first name. In Scotland, Roderick has also been used as the equivalent of the Gaelic **Ruairi** (see RORY). Sir Walter Scott published a poem in 1811 called *The Vision of Don Roderick* where he used Roderick for the Spanish form of the name **Rodrigo**. This poem led to a revival of the name Roderick in the UK

Rodge see Roger

Rodney
This is a surname which came to be used as a first name in honour of Admiral George Rodney (1718–92), an outstanding commander who was instrumental in bringing much of the West Indies under British rule. It has the same short forms as RODERICK.

Rodolfo see Ralph

Roger
Roger comes from the Germanic elements *hrod* 'fame' and *gar* 'spear' and is the French form of the name that appears in the great Anglo-Saxon epic *Beowulf* as *Hrothgar*. **Hodge** and Hodgekin were used as diminutives in the past and became the typical names of rustic labourers. **Rodge** is now sometimes used as a short form. The Spanish name **Rogelio** looks as if it might be from the same source, but is not. Saint Rogelio or Rogellus was martyred at Cordoba in 852 and his name may be a form of Rogatus 'prayed for', but this is uncertain.

Rohan
In most cases someone called Rohan is using the popular Indian name from the Sanskrit religious word meaning 'ascending'. This is a boy's name. However, there are recent records of it having been used for both sexes, but predominantly girls, as a name taken from the place name Rohan, meaning 'horse country', taken from J.R.R. Tolkien's *Lord of the Rings*.

Roisin see Rose

Roland
Roland or **Rowland** (the commoner form for the surname) is a Germanic name combining 'fame' with 'land'. It is sometimes shortened to **Roly**. The *Song of Roland* is the great epic of medieval France in which Roland, brave and honourable above all, but lacking the wisdom of his close friend OLIVER, is betrayed by his step-father Ganelon and killed by the Saracens, but is afterwards avenged by his uncle, Charlemagne. This character became the hero of later stories in Italy, where his name became **Orlando**, a form that has been growing in popularity in recent years. A feminine form, **Orlanda**, has been recorded. The name becomes **Rolando** in Spanish. The actor Orlando Bloom has brought this name to public attention recently.

Rolf, Rollo see Ralph

Romeo, Roma
This is a group of names connected with the city of Rome, although none of them is particularly common. Roma is simply the Italian form of the city's name. **Romaine** or **Romane**, more common on the Continent, is the feminine of **Roman** ('a citizen of Rome') or in its French form **Romain**, and the same name as the Italian **Romeo**. **Romola**, the heroine of George Eliot's novel (1863), is a feminine form of the name **Romulus**, the legendary founder of Rome. **Romilly**, a surname occasionally used as a name (now more often for girls than boys), comes from a French place name, but this in its turn would have come from a founder whose name derived from Romulus. Romain is currently popular for boys in France and Romane for girls. Romeo was rare in the UK although use has been increasing for some time in the USA, and use increased slightly in the UK after the Beckhams used it for one of their sons.

Romy see Rosemary

Ron see Aaron, Reginald

Rona see Rhona

Ronald, Ronaldo see Reginald

Ronan

Ronan is an ancient Irish name meaning 'little seal'. It was the name of numerous saints, one of whom worked as a missionary in Brittany, where the name can be found as both Ronan and **Renan**. The name was introduced to a wider public by Sir Walter Scott's novel *St Ronan's Well* in 1823. Ronan has been a popular name in the British Isles for some time, but has only been used in the USA since the start of the twenty-first century. It is currently well used in both Ireland and Scotland.

Ronee, Roni, Ronni see Veronica

Ronnie see Reginald

Rory

Rory or **Rorie** is the anglicised form of the Gaelic **Ruairi** or **Ruairdhri** ('the red-haired one'), originally a nickname. In Scotland it is still very much a Highlander's name, and its spread to England is probably from Ireland rather than Scotland (see also RODERICK). **Roy** is from the same root, the Gaelic *ruadh* ('red'). Rory is currently well used throughout Ireland, where it is also found as Ruairi, and well used in Scotland.

Rosa, Rosabel, Rosabella, Rosaleen, Rossalia, Rosalie see Rose

Rosalind, Rosamund

Rosalind is originally a Germanic name *Hrosmund* made up of the elements long interpreted as meaning 'horse' and 'serpent'; but now some the philologists seem to prefer the meaning 'shield, protection' for the second element. However, like BELINDA, the name has long been thought of as if it comes from a Romance language, and analysed as 'rose' + *linda* 'beautiful'. Variants are **Rosalyn**, **Rosaline**, **Roslyn** and **Rosalinda**. In the same way Rosamund ('horse (or fame)' + 'protection') has been thought of in terms of the Latin *rosa munda* ('pure rose') or *rosa mundi* ('rose of the world'), both of which are images that have been used to describe the Virgin Mary. It has **Rosamond** as a variant and the two groups of names share **Roz** as a short form.

Rosasharn see Sharron (*see* Sharon)

Rose

Historically, Rose may not be the simple plant name that it appears, but a Germanic name from the same root as ROSALIND and Rosamund. However, there can be little doubt that since the Middle Ages it has been thought of as a flower name, despite the fact that such names were unusual at that time. Because the rose is symbolic of so many things – the Virgin Mary, love, England and much else – it is hardly surprising that the name has enjoyed such long use. Although in recent decades the name has been out of favour, in the last few years it has enjoyed a sudden burst of popularity with parents in the UK, usually in the form **Rosie**. It has developed a large number of pet forms, compounds and elaborations, many of them based on the Latin form of the name, **Rosa**. Thus we find: **Rosabel**, **Rosabella**, along with **Rosetta**, **Rosie**, **Roseanna**, **Roseanne**, **Rosina** and **Rosita**. In Ireland the name became **Roisin** or **Rosheen** (a phonetic spelling), which is anglicised to **Rosaleen**. **Rosalia** and **Rosalie** are ancient names from the same root. Originally the rosalia was a religious ceremony in which roses were placed on the tombs of the dead in remembrance. Rosalia is also the name of a 12th-century recluse who is the patron saint of Palermo in Sicily. **Rosario** also has a religious origin, being from the Spanish *Neustra Senora del Rosario* 'our Lady of the Rosary', the word rosary being from the Latin for 'rose garden', used figuratively of prayers. Although Rosario is feminine in Spanish, it is masculine in Italian, giving a rare example of a boy's name in this group.

Rosemary

One of the nineteenth-century flower names, Rosemary is an obvious elaboration of ROSE. The plant's symbolism – rosemary for remembrance – is well known thanks to the mad Ophelia's speech in *Hamlet*. In the past this strongly scented herb was used to make crowns and garlands as well as to scent clothes and protect them from moths. The true meaning of the name has nothing to do with the rose, but comes from its Latin name *ros marinus* ('sea-dew'), so-called because the plant likes to grow near the sea, and from the misty bluish colour of its leaves. **Rosemarie** is a variant, and Rose is used as a short form. The name **Romy**, given publicity by the actress Romy Schneider, is a Germanic pet form of the name.

Rose-of-Sharon see Sharon

Roshan see Roxana

Rosheen, Rosie, Rosina, Rosetta, Rosita see Rose

Roslyn see Rosalind

Ross

Ross is a surname used as a first name. The surname has a number of different origins, but is particularly common in Scotland and Ulster, where it has also been used as a first name since at least the sixteenth century, and in these cases it comes from the Gaelic meaning 'a promontory'. Nowadays it is also used occasionally for girls. It is still most likely to be found in Ireland or Scotland. The actor Ross Kemp is a well-known bearer of the name in the UK, and in the USA Ross Perot.

Rotem

Rotem is a Hebrew name used for both sexes. It is the name of a desert plant.

Rowan

As a masculine name, this comes from the Irish *Ruadhán* ('little red one') and thus like RORY and RUFUS would have started life as a nickname for someone with red hair. As a feminine name it could be a transferred use of the masculine, but just as probably refers to the plant name, which is the alternative name for the slender and graceful mountain ash, a tree with strong Welsh and Scottish associations. As a boy's name its use is old, but for girls it is recent, and no doubt its similarity to the already well-established ROWENA has helped its spread. **Rowann** or **Rowanne** are also found, reflecting a second pronunciation, with the stress on the second rather than the first syllable. A famous bearer is the Welsh Archbishop of Canterbury Rowan Williams.

Rowena

According to the traditional history of Britain, Rowena was the beautiful daughter of the Saxon invader Hengist, who used her beauty (and some say witchcraft) to persuade the ruler of Britain, Vortigern, to give large areas of the country to the Saxons in return for marriage to Rowena. It is possible to construe the name as Anglo-Saxon, composed of such elements as *hrod* and *wynn* ('fame' and 'joy'); but the name appears in very early sources as *Renwein* or *Ronnwen*, and since most of the early accounts come from the British side, the name is most probably a form of the Welsh **Rhonwen**, made up of the elements *rhon* ('a pike or lance', thus figuratively 'tall, slender'), and *gwen* ('fair, blessed'). Rowena came into general use after Sir Walter Scott used it as the name of his heroine in the novel *Ivanhoe* (1819).

Rowland see Roland

Roxana

Also found as **Roxanne** or **Roxane**, this was the name of an Asian princess who was married to ALEXANDER the Great after he defeated her father in 327 BC. According to the Greek biographer Plutarch (c. 46–120), the marriage took place not for political ends but because Alexander had seen Roxana and fallen in love with her. Her son by him, Alexander IV, was at one time joint ruler of his father's empire, but both he and his mother were murdered in the power struggles that followed Alexander's death. Her romantic story was turned into a play in the late eighteenth century, which dealt with the rivalry between her and Statira, her co-wife, and stories circulated about how various actresses playing the two women carried the stage rivalry over into their own lives, so that the conflict between the two women became proverbial. The name was given a further boost by the publication of a novel called *Roxana* by Daniel Defoe in 1724, and more recently by Edmond Rostand's *Cyrano de Bergerac* (1897), in which the heroine is called **Roxane**. It is not clear where the name comes from. It is traditionally said to be from the Persian for 'dawn' or 'bright, star', also found in Persian as **Roshan**. **Roxy** or **Roxie**, used in the musical *Chicago*, is used as a short form.

Roy see Rory

Royce, Royston

Royce was originally an English surname from the Germanic name *Hrodhaidis* made up of elements meaning 'fame' and 'kind'. It was the surname of a man who joined with a Mr Rolls to produce the Rolls Royce car, and it is likely to be the prestige of the brand combined with the closeness to the name Roy that has led to its occasional use as a boy's name. Royston has similar sounds, but a very different origin. It is another surname, from an English place name first recorded in 1262 as Croyroys, from the Old French for 'Rose's Cross'.

Roz see Rosalind

Ruairdhri, Ruairi see Roderick, Rory

Ruben see Reuben

Ruby

Ruby is another of the gem names so popular in the nineteenth and first part of the twentieth centuries. This popularity dated bearers, and it was for a long time out of fashion, but is now very much back in fashion, having recently been the fourth most popular name for girls in England and in the top names for those in Scotland and Ireland.

Rudi, Rudolf, Rudolph, Rudy see Ralph

Rufus, Russell

Rufus comes from a Latin word used as a nickname for someone with red hair, and thus has the same meaning as the names under ROY and ROWAN. Two people with this name are mentioned in the New Testament. It is particularly associated with the assassinated Norman king William Rufus (William II), but his unsavoury reputation did not stop eighteenth-century parents adopting it as a first name, particularly in the USA. The Old French equivalent of Rufus was **Russell**, which became a surname, and later a first name. **Russ** is a short form also used as an independent name. Currently the names are particularly associated with the Australian actor Russell Crowe and the singer Rufus Wainwright.

Rupert see Robert

Russ, Russell see Rufus

Ruth

Ruth is a Old Testament name of uncertain meaning. It has been linked to the Hebrew for 'friend', but since Ruth was a Moabite her name may not have any Hebrew meaning. The Book of Ruth tells the charming story of Ruth's devotion to NAOMI, and of how Boaz, whom she later married, saw the poor widow gleaning in his field and ordered his men to drop grain on purpose, so that she could have more to collect.

Ryan

Ryan is from an Irish surname *O'Riain* 'descendant of Rian', of unknown meaning although it may have connections to the word *rí* 'king'. It has come into use as a first name, particularly since the 1970s when the actor Ryan O'Neal made it well known. It has remained among the most popular first names on both sides of the Atlantic since then. It is now used for girls as well as boys, and has taken on variations such as **Ryann**. **Rylan** is technically another surname, from the English meaning 'rye land', but its use is probably due to the popularity of Ryan. In Ireland **Rian** is well used, but Ryan is also in the top dozen boy's name, and it is also very popular in England, Scotland Australia, Canada, France and many other countries.

Ryder

Ryder is an English surname which would have been given either to a messenger or a knight. Its rapidly growing popularity for boys in the USA no doubt is connected with the prestige of the Ryder Cup golf tournament.

Ryker

Ryker is a re-spelling of the surname Riker, a Germanic surname given to someone who was rich. It is probably used as a first name form the character of Will Riker in the popular television series *Star Trek the Next Generation* who is usually referred to by his surname.

Rylie, Ryleigh, Ryland see **Riley**

S

Saalim, Saalima see Salim

Saami, Saamia see Sami

Sabah

This is an Arabic name, used for both sexes, meaning 'morning'. It is one of a number of related names where morning is transferred by association to ideas of light and beauty in the traditional interpretation of the names. Thus for boys we find **Saabih** 'coming in the morning', **Sabuh** 'shining, brilliant'; and for girls **Saabiha** 'coming in the morning', **Sabaha** 'beauty'; **Sabia** 'charming', **Sabih** 'pretty', **Sabiha** 'morning', **Sabuh** 'shining, brilliant'. Sabah is particularly popular for boys in Kuwait, and for girls is well-known throughout the Arab world as the name of a very popular Lebanese singer.

Sabina

Sabina and its German form **Sabine** (pronounced in the same way) mean 'Sabine woman'. In the legendary history of Rome told by the historian Livy, the neighbouring Sabine people refused to intermarry with the men of the newly founded Rome, where there was a desperate shortage of women. To avoid their city dying after one generation, the Romans invited the Sabines to a festival, ambushed them, and then carried off all the young women and married them by force. This became known as 'The Rape of the Sabine women'. It took a long time before the Sabines could organise their revenge. When battle was finally joined, the Sabine women found themselves faced with the prospect of losing either their parents or their husbands, now the fathers of their children. To escape from this situation they forced their way between the two armies and imposed peace. For this they were greatly honoured. The name is used in Ireland to anglicise the Irish name **Sadhbh**, **Sadb** or **Sive** ('goodness, sweet', rhymes with alive), which is also anglicised as **Sabia**. Sadhbh was a goddess who was turned into a fawn by the Dark Druid, but was able to visit Finn at night in human form, and by him became the mother of OSSIAN, the 'little fawn'. Sadhbh is regularly used in the Irish Republic

Sable see Ebony

Sabri, Sabria

These are the masculine and feminine forms of an Arabic name meaning 'patience'. Sabri Moudallal is a very popular Syrian singer.

Sabrina

According to the mythological history of Britain, Sabrina was the daughter of Locrine, the second king of Britain. Her stepmother Guendolen (see GWEN) rebelled, killed her father, took over the government and ordered her to be thrown into the nearby river, ever since called the Severn after Sabrina. She is probably best known as the nymph of the Severn in Milton's masque *Comus*, where she is addressed with the words: 'Sabrina fair,/Listen where thou art sitting/Under the glassy, cool, translucent wave,/In twisted braids of lilies knitting/The loose train of thy amber-dropping hair'. In 1954 the name was introduced to a wider audience by a film called *Sabrina* starring Audrey Hepburn, and became quite fashionable in the USA, sometimes in the form **Zabrina**. However, in the 1960s in the UK the name was most closely associated with a certain voluptuous actress, Britain's answer to the Hollywood starlet of the time. Sabrina is now closely associated with the television series *Sabrina the Teenage Witch*.

Sacha see Sasha

Sadb, Sadhbh see Sabina

Sade
This is the name of the British-Nigerian singer. It is actually a shortening of her full name, Folashade, which means, in the Nigerian Yoruba language, 'honour confers a crown'. She pronounces her name **Sharday** and parents often spell it this way or give it a similar twist to reflect the pronunciation.

Sadie see Sarah

Saeed
Saeed is an Arabic name meaning 'fortunate, blessed'. Saeeda is the feminine. The names are also found as **Saïd** and **Saïda**. Saeed Jaffrey is a well-known actor.

Saffron
This is the name of the autumn-flowering crocus, as well as of the flavouring and the colouring agent obtained from it. The plant was at one time extensively cultivated in Cornwall, but its use as a first name is modern, and it was probably not used before the 1960s. It probably received a boost in 1966 when it was used as a girl's name in the hit song *Mellow Yellow* by Donovan. **Saffy** is used as a pet form.

Safi, Safiya
This is the masculine and feminine form of an Arabic word meaning 'sincere friend'. Safiya or **Safia** was the name of a wife of Mohammed.

Safire see Sapphire

Safiya see Safi

Sage
The herb sage got its name from the reputation tea made from its leaves has for improving the memory, making the drinker more sage. Thus this name is both a plant and a virtue name. It has been fashionable for both sexes for a number or years, but is not a new name, having been well used in Wales in the fifteenth to seventeenth centuries. It is occasionally spelt **Saige**.

Sahara
This place name, with all its romantic associations, has been quietly but steadily used as a girl's first name for a number of years. One of the attractions is probably the form of the name. It not only ends in -a, like so many girl's names, but shares the sounds and form of a number of other new names, such as SAVANNAH, found on these pages. The Sahara desert gets its name from the Arabic word for 'deserts'.

Saïd, Saïda see Saeed

Saige see Sage

St John see John

Sal see Sarah, Salvador

Salam, Salama, Salema see Solomon

Salim, Salman
Salim means 'sound, safe, perfect, secure'. It is also found as **Saalim**, **Salem** and **Selim**. The feminine forms are **Saalima**, **Salima**, which can be shortened to **Salma**, and **Selima**, shortened to **Selma**. **Salma** can also be a separate woman's name meaning 'beloved, sweetheart'. **Salman**, meaning 'safe' is from the same root. The actress Salma Hayek, a Mexican whose father is Lebanese, is a famous bearer of the name.

Sally see Sarah

Salma see Salim

Salome see Solomon

Salvador

The Late Latin word *salvator* means 'Saviour'. This is taken directly into Spanish, and in Italian becomes **Salvatore**. Both of these can be shortened to **Sal**. The rare name **Savion** may be a coinage formed on Salvador with the fashionable ending -ion. There is an even rarer religious name with similar connotations, **Messiah**, which fits in with the current American trend for new but overtly religious names. All these are used for boys.

Sam see Samantha, Samuel

Samantha

The origin of Samantha is not known. It appears in the eighteenth century and it has been conjectured that it is meant to be a feminine form of SAMUEL. It really took off as a name after the 1950s when the song 'I love you, Samantha' and the character of Tracy Samantha Lord in the film *High Society* (1956) gave the name a great deal of exposure. This name was taken over from the original play and film *The Philadelphia Story*, filmed in 1940. It is obvious from the context that the names are meant to be as aristocratic as an American name can get. Use of TRACY seems to have increased at the same time. **Sam** and **Sammy** are used as short forms as they are for all Sam- names. Samantha is currently very popular in the USA and Australia and well used in Scotland and England.

Samara, Sameer, Sameera(h) see Samir

Sameen, Sameena see Samina

Sami

Sami or **Saami** is an Arabic name meaning 'exalted, eminent, sublime'. This is the masculine form, the feminine being **Saamia, Samiya** or **Samia**, which can have a pet form **Soumaya**.

Samina, Samin

These are the feminine and masculine forms of an Arabic name meaning 'precious, priceless'. They can also be found as **Sameena** and **Sameen**.

Samir, Samara

These are the masculine and feminine forms of an Arabic name based on the term for a friend with whom one can spend an entertaining evening in conversation. They are also found as **Sameer, Samira**, and **Samirah, Sameera(h)**. Not all uses of **Samara** are Muslim. Samara was a name used in the horror film *The Ring* (2002) and although the character with the name is not pleasant, the name has passed onto more general use in the USA.

Samiya see Sami

Sammy see Samantha, Samuel

Samson

Although the Bible claims Samson as one of the judges of Israel, he appears in the stories about him as a violent, vengeful and unrestrained folk-hero, notable chiefly for his strength, sarcastic sense of humour and weakness for Philistine women (see DELILAH). The name can be interpreted as a diminutive of the Hebrew for 'sun' or as meaning 'son of the sun god Shamash'; and this latter, with the similarities between his adventures and those of demigods of other cultures such as Hercules and the Babylonian Gilgamesh, has led to suggestions that he represents a reworking of the myths of a sun god. The name is not much used at the moment, but has been very popular at various times in the past. **Sampson** is an alternative form, most commonly found as a surname.

Samuel

One of the great judges and prophets of the Israelites, Samuel was instrumental in making kings of both SAUL and DAVID. The name is *Shemuel* in Hebrew and probably means 'name of God', and he was destined for a holy life from birth. His mother HANNAH, desperate to have children, had vowed to God that if she had a son he should be dedicated to His service. The infant Samuel was therefore taken to the Temple and given to ELI to bring up. **Sam** and **Sammy** are short forms and SAMANTHA functions as a feminine. The name is popular at the moment on both sides of the Atlantic, as well as in Australasia.

Sanaa

There are two different Arabic names used for both sexes spelt Sanaa. One, pronounced as spelt means 'brilliance, radiance, splendour'. The second, in which the 's' is softened to a 'th' sound means 'praise'.

Sanchia

This is a Spanish name meaning 'holy'. **Sancha** and the German form **Sancia** can also be found. The masculine is not used, but is famous thanks to the resourceful servant **Sancho** Panza in Cervantes' *Don Quixote* (1605–15).

Sander, Sandra, Sandy see Alexander

Sani, Saniyah

These are the masculine and feminine versions of an Arabic names meaning 'brilliant, majestic, exalted, splendid'. Saniyah is also spelt **Sania** and **Saniya**.

Sanjay

In the Indian epics Sanjay is the name of a famous charioteer. The name means 'triumphant'. Sanjay Ghandi was an eminent Indian politician. **Sanjit** or **Sanjeet** means 'invincible, complete victory'.

Sanjiv

Sanjiv or **Sanjeev** is an Indian boy's name from the Sanskrit for 'living, reviving'.

Santiago see James

Santos, Santino

Santos means 'saints' in Spanish and invokes the protection of the saints on the bearer. Santo, and its feminine **Santa**, is an Italian name meaning 'holy' (compare SANCHIA), and Santino was originally its pet form. In the film of *The Godfather* a character whose proper name is Santino is generally called **Sonny**.

Saoirse

This is an Irish girl's name using the Gaelic word for 'freedom'. Compare LIBERTY.

Sapphire

One of the rarer gem names, Sapphire was no doubt kept from popularity when other gem names were current by its associations with the biblical **Sapphira**, wife of the Ananias who in the Acts of the Apostles sells some of his goods to give to the Church, but keeps back a part of the proceeds for his own use. They are both struck dead for this deception. As a first name, the spelling is sometimes simplified to **Safire**. See also under BLUE.

Sarah

This is the Hebrew for 'princess' and the name of the wife of the patriarch ABRAHAM in the Old Testament. The name takes the form **Sara** in the Greek New Testament and in Arabic. **Sadie**, **Sal**, **Sally** and even **Sallie** are short forms. In Ireland the name has been used to anglicise the native **Saraid** ('excellent'), probably influenced by the similarity of the names and by the fact that Sarah was originally called by the even more similar-looking **Sarai** ('contentious'), before her name was changed as a sign of God's blessing. Sarah is currently popular in many countries around the world and Sara is well used in Scotland as well. There are two variants which are being used in the USA. **Sariah**, which is a name found in the *Book of Mormon*, and **Sarahi**.

Sasha

The Russian form of Alexander, Aleksandr has pet forms **Sasha** or **Sacha** and **Shura**. These are male names in Russia, but because English speakers think of names ending in -a as feminine, they are now often given to girls.

Saskia

This is a Dutch name, It was the name of Rembrandt's wife, who was painted by him in some memorable portraits. It was also used by John Buchan as the heroine of his 1923 adventure story *Huntingtower*, which would have made the name more widely known. Its origin is not clear, but it may mean 'Saxon woman'. There has been a marked increase in use of the name outside Holland in recent years, perhaps as a result of the fame of the actress Saskia Reeves.

Sati

Sati is used as an Indian girl's name. It means 'truthful' and is one of the names of the goddess Durga. The masculine equivalent is **Satish** 'lord of Sati'.

Saul

Saul is the Hebrew for 'asked for (child)'. The Old Testament Saul is elected the first king of Israel, but his sins lead to God's favour being taken from him and given to DAVID, at one time Saul's favourite, but whom he now persecutes. Saul was also the name of St PAUL before his conversion to Christianity (see further under STEPHEN). These rather negative role-models meant that the name was nothing like as popular as many other biblical names, although use did increase in the twentieth century.

Sausan see Susan

Savannah

As a term for 'a grassy plain', savannah comes from the Caribbean Taino Indian language word *zabana* ('meadow'). However, as a first name use is probably most influenced by the Georgian city of Savannah and the associations that go with it. Spellings such as **Savanna** and **Savanah** are also used. The name is currently popular in the USA.

Savion see Salvador

Savitr see Aditya

Sawnie see Alexander

Sawyer

This is a surname from the occupation, currently being used as a boy's name in the USA, and occasionally for girls. Its use probably owes something to the iconic status of Mark Twain's *Tom Sawyer* in American society. There is a character called Sawyer in the cult television series *Lost*.

Scarlett

This name, which has been fashionable for a number of years, is one of the many names brought to the attention of the public by the book (1936), and particularly the film (1939), of Margaret Mitchell's *Gone with the Wind*. In this Scarlett O'Hara is actually named from her grandmother's maiden name, and it is her middle name, although (like many other characters in the book) she is generally known by her middle name. The surname would have originated with someone who dealt with the costly cloth called scarlet in the Middle Ages: a cloth that was worthy of the expense of being dyed bright red, then a rare shade, and so transferred its name to the colour. The name has been well used in England for some years, and is popular in Australia. It has recently gained publicity through the success of the actress Scarlett Johansson.

Schuyler see Skyler

Scott

This name is simply a surname which would have been given to someone from Scotland, particularly a Gaelic speaker, transformed into a first name. The admired American novelist Francis Scott Fitzgerald (1896–1940), like Scarlett O'Hara above generally referred to by his middle name, may have been influential in the rise of the name, which has been steadily popular since the 1960s. The pet forms **Scottie** or **Scotty** are also used as independent names, perhaps influenced by *Star Trek*'s 'Beam me up, Scottie'. Scott is currently popular in Scotland and well used in Ireland.

Seamus

Seamus is the Irish form of JAMES. Celtic languages do not have a 'j' sound in native words, and when names beginning with the sound are adopted into these languages they are usually changed to begin with a 'sh' sound, written as an 's' followed by an 'e' or 'i'. The name is sometimes written phonetically **Shamus** with the form **Seumus**, or less commonly **Seumas**, used by Scots Gaelic speakers. The Nobel Prize winning poet Seamus Heaney is a well-known user.

Sean

Sean is the Irish form of JOHN (see SEAMUS, above, for why). **Shaun** or **Shawn** are phonetic spellings, while **Shane** is a regional variant. Shayne is another spelling that is on the increase. Shawn or Shaun has become a name element in the USA, combined with other sounds to produce names such as **Dashawn, Deshawn** or **Deshaun, Keyshawn,** or **Tayshaun**. In Welsh John becomes **Siôn**, with pet form **Sioni** and **Sionyn**. Sean and Shawn are beginning to be used for girls as well as boys, and **Seaneen** has been recorded as a girl's name. Both Sean and Shane are popular for boys in Ireland at the moment and well used in Scotland, while Sean is most likely to be used in England and the USA.

Searlait see Charlotte

Sebastian

This means 'man from Sebastia', a town (now Sivas) in central Asia Minor that got its name from the Greek translation of the name AUGUSTUS. St Sebastian was a martyr of unknown date. According to his highly dubious legend he was a Roman officer who was sentenced to be shot to death with arrows for his faith, a subject very popular with Renaissance artists. Left for dead, he was healed of his wounds by a pious widow, but on confronting his persecutors he was beaten to death. **Seb** is a short form, and **Bastian** is also used. There is a French feminine form **Sebastienne**, which can be shortened to **Bastienne**, the French masculine shortening being **Bastien**. Sebastian is regularly used in the UK and USA, and Bastien well used in France.

Sedrick see Cedric

Ségolène

A name that has been much in the news after the French politician Ségolène Royale attempted to become France's first female President, Ségolène is the French form of the Germanic name *Sigolind*, formed from *sig* 'victory' and *lind* 'gentle, soft'. In German the name became **Sieglinde**, mother of SIEGFRIED in Wagner's *Ring Cycle*.

Seisyllt see Cecil

Selah

In the Psalms *selah* is used as a term for a pause for reflection. It has just started to be used as a first name for girls, perhaps influenced by its used as a name by a Christian rock band.

Selim, Selima see Salim

Selina

This is probably originally a variant of CELIA and CELESTE, names meaning 'heavenly', a derivation which seems to be confirmed by the form **Celina** and the French **Céline**. In Spanish it is **Selena**. However, the name looks very like a Latinate form of **Selene**, the Greek moon goddess, who fell in love with the beautiful young man **Endymion**, and it is often understood in this way. **Luna**, the Latin, Spanish and Italian word for 'moon' is also used as a first name. It is found in Italy, Spain and Germany. It was used regularly in the USA in the nineteenth century and into the beginning of the twentieth, and then disappeared from the records. It reappeared in 2003, the year it was used as a character in one of the *Harry Potter* books. Celine Dione is a well-known singer and Selena Quintanilla Perez (1971–95) was a popular Mexican-American singer, murdered in 1995.

Selma

Selma is another of the names that came into use from the popularity of the poems attributed to OSSIAN. It is not a personal name in these poems, but the name of Fingal's castle (see FINN). However, when these poems were translated into Swedish it was not clear what 'Selma' was, and it was taken to be a feminine personal name. It then became popular in Sweden from the fame of the Selma poems of the Finno-Swedish poet Frans Mikael Franzén (1772–1849). More recently the name became well known through another Swedish writer, Selma Lagerlöf (1858–1940). The name spread from Scandinavia to the English-speaking world through Scandinavian immigration to the USA. It is also an American place name, the town from which Martin Luther King led a 50-mile civil rights march in 1965. **Zelma** is an occasional variant. Selma can also be a form of the names under SALIM.

Semaj

This is a boy's name found occasionally in the USA. It is JAMES spelt backwards, just as **Nevaeh** is HEAVEN backwards, and **Senga**, AGNES.

Senga see Agnes

Seonaid see Sheena

Septimus

A Latin name meaning 'seventh', Septimus was originally given to a seventh child (compare OCTAVIA and QUENTIN). The feminine is **Septima**.

Seren see Stella

Serena

Serena is the feminine form of an old Roman name meaning 'serene'. It was the name of a minor saint, but until the twentieth century its use in Britain was mainly literary. In Edmund Spenser's *The Faerie Queen* (1590–96), Serena is a character who is gathering flowers for a garland when she is attacked by the Blatant Beast, who seizes her in his mouth and carries her off, until her cries attract the attention of a wandering knight who comes to her rescue. **Serina** is a variant, used by the seventeenth-century playwright Thomas Otway in *The Orphan* (1680). Despite the success of the tennis player Serena Williams, the abstract noun, **Serenity**, is currently more popular in the USA than Serena.

Serge

The old Roman name **Sergius** became **Sergei** in Russian, but it is often found in its French form Serge, in part because at one time French was the dominant language in polite society in Russia. The enormous popularity of the name in that country is due to St Sergius of Radonezh, a fourteenth-century hermit who became the founding father of Russian monasticism. He lived in the woods and had a close relationship with nature not dissimilar to that of St FRANCIS. This and his reputation as a saint that embodied all the virtues associated with the Russian peasant – humble simplicity, gentleness, gravity and good-neighbourliness – has led to his being regarded as the embodiment of all that a Russian saint should be. The Spanish and Italian form **Sergio** is well used in the USA.

Seth

In chapter four of the Book of Genesis we are told 'And Adam knew his wife again; and she bare a son, and called his name Seth: For God, said she, hath appointed me another seed instead of Abel, whom Cain slew'. This has led to the name traditionally being interpreted as 'appointed', but it actually means 'a setting, a cutting', the pun being on the word translated as 'seed'. It was a popular name among the Puritans and remained in use in the USA, and has now come back into fashion.

Seumas, Seumus see Seamus

Severinus see Soren

Sextus see Cecil

Seymour
A masculine name, Seymour is taken from the surname of a noble family. This in its turn came from the French village (now a south-eastern suburb of Paris) of St-Maur-des-Fossés, where the saint's name is the local form of MAURICE.

Shaina, Shania
Shaina is a Yiddish girl's name meaning 'beautiful', used increasingly in the USA. However, many parents may use it because it fits in with names derived from Shane (see SEAN), a view reinforced by spellings such as **Shaine**, **Shana** and **Shayna**. The country singer **Shania** Twain's name is not a variant, but an Ojibwa Indian name meaning 'I'm on my way'. See also under SHANAE.

Shakil, Shakila
These are the masculine and feminine forms of an Arabic name meaning 'beautiful'.

Shakir, Shakira
This is an Arabic name meaning 'thankful, grateful'. Knowledge of the feminine form was spread by the beauty of the actress Shakira Baksh, now married to the actor Michael Caine, and it is now world famous as the name of a very successful Colombian-Lebanese singer.

Shalom see Solomon

Shameka
This appears to be a blend of TAMIKA and the fashionable Sha- found in names on these pages (see particularly under SHANAE). It was one of the wave of names coined by Black Americans in the 1970s to assert their identity, and remain in use until the end of the 1980s.

Shamus see James

Shana see Shaina

Shanae, Shanice, Shanika, Shaniqua
Sha- (also found as Cha-, pronounced with a soft 'ch' sound, as in CHANEL) has become a very active element in the creation of new names for some time. The sound first became popular in the name SHARON, which although recorded as a male name in the eighteenth century, as a popular name began life in the 1930s, reaching the 20s in the most-used names statistics in the 1940s in America, and being the tenth most popular name in the UK in 1965. The sound was then found in another new name, SHANNON, which first became really popular in the USA in the late 1960s but does not make significant inroads in the UK until the late 1990s. Evidence for the popularity of Sha-names, particularly for girls but also for boys, will be found in the surrounding entries. The ones grouped here are, like many of the new names, typically African-American, although many of these names are adopted by the more general population; and, like all new names, they come in a variety of spellings. They can be analysed as blends, but are best viewed as creations combining attractive, fashionable sounds. Thus while Shanae can be analysed as Sha- plus the ending of Renee, the -ee or -ae ending is a common one in names, as is the -ice of Shanice. Shaniqua and Shanika use a newly fashionable ending, perhaps inspired by TAMIKA. These names started to become popular in the 1970 and dropped out of the charts in the 1990s.

Shane see Sean

Shanel, Shanelle see Chanel

Shani see Sian

Shania see Shaina

Shannon
Shannon comes from the name of the longest river in Ireland and means 'the old one'. It is used for both sexes, but predominantly for girls. Like other recent names with strong Irish associations, such as ERIN, the name was initially little used in Ireland itself, but seems to have arisen from the sentiment of those of Irish emigrant stock. More

recently **Shanna** has appeared, either as a short form of Shannon, or from **Shannagh**, an Irish name coming from the same root, a word meaning 'old, wise'. Shannon is now steadily used in England, Scotland and Ireland.

Shantal see Chantal

Shante see Ashanti

Shara, Shari see Sharon

Sharday see Sade

Sharice see Charis

Sharlene, Sharley, Sharlotte see Charlotte

Sharma, Sharmila

These are the masculine and feminine forms of Indian names from the Sanskrit for 'comfort, protection, joy'.

Sharmaine see Charmaine

Sharon

Sharon means 'the plain' and in the Bible refers to the rich and fertile coastal plain of Palestine. In the *Song of Solomon* the 'rose of Sharon' is an image of beauty (although 'rose' is a mistranslation; the flower referred to may be the narcissus). The name was initially used for men – Sharon Turner (1768–1847) was a prominent English historian. The change to feminine use may have been influenced by the use of **Rose-of-Sharon** as a name. This appears as **Rosasharn** in John Steinbeck's novel *Grapes of Wrath* (1939). At one time the name was pronounced with its first syllable lengthened as in 'share' (still the pronunciation preferred by the actress Sharon Stone), but a pronunciation as in 'shan't' is now almost universal, and is reflected in the spelling **Sharron**. **Sharyn** is also found, while **Shara** and **Shari** are pet forms, with **Shaz** and **Shazza** used in the UK. **Sharona** is an elaboration.

Shasta see Flora

Shaun, Shauna, Shawn, Shawndelle see Sean

Shavon see Siobhan

Shay, Shaye, Shayla, Shaylee, Shaylyn see Shea

Shayna see Shaina

Shayne see Sean

Shaz, Shazza see Sharon

Shea

This is an Irish surname meaning 'descendant of the fortunate one', used more or less equally for boys and girls in the USA. It is also found as **Shaye** or **Shay**, which has been the base of a number of new blends used for girls, such as **Shaylee**, **Shaylyn** and **Shayla** (although some users may regard the latter as a form of SHIELA). These have somewhat taken over from the names under SHAINA. Shea is currently popular in Northern Ireland.

Sheba see Bathsheba

Sheelagh see Sheila

Sheena, Sinead

Sheena, also found as **Shona** and spelt **Sine** Gaelic and Irish, is a Celtic form of the name JANE. **Sineag** is a pet form. It differs from SIOBHAN because it comes from the French form *Jeanne* rather than *Jehanne*. Similarly *Jeanette*, which became Janet in English, became **Sinead** in Irish and **Seonaid** in Gaelic.

Sheila

In Irish CECILIA or Celia became **Sile**, which was in turn re-anglicised as Sheila. It is also found in a wide variety of spellings such as **Shiela** and **Sheelagh.**

Shelby

This is a surname now used as a first name. The surname, like the first name, is more common in the USA than in the UK, and can come from a number of sources, one of which is a place meaning 'hut-farm'. The similar-sounding **Sheldon**, mainly used for boys, probably contains the place-name element meaning 'shelf, ledge' combined with *don* ('settlement'). Shelby had been used for girls since the 1930s, but did not become really popular until after it was used in the 1989 film *Steel Magnolias*.

Shelley

This, with its variant **Shelly**, is a girl's name with a number of sources. The actress Shelley Winters, who made the name more widely known, is really a SHIRLEY, which is probably the most important source; but other names ending in the -shell sound such as Michelle (see MICHAEL) and Rachelle or Rochelle (see RACHEL) have also contributed. In addition the surname, reinforced by the fame of the poet, has contributed to the name, and the occasional masculine use of the name comes from this source.

Sheralyn, Sherel, Sherell see Cheryl

Sherise see Charis

Sherlyn, Sherrel, Sherrell, Sherri, Sherry, Sheryl see Cheryl

Sheyenne, Shianne see Cheyenne

Shiela see Sheila

Shiloh

This is a Hebrew word meaning 'he who has been sent', usually taken to refer to the Messiah, which on the rare occasions it has been used in the past has usually been given to boys. However, Angelina Jolie and Brad Pitt called their daughter Shiloh Nouvel Jolie-Pitt in 2006, and there has already been an increased interest in its use for girls.

Shirley

This is a place name made up of elements meaning 'shire' and 'meadow', which became a surname. Originally a man's name (and still occasionally found as one – the wrestler known as Big Daddy (1937–97) was christened Shirley Crabtree), it came into fashion as a girl's name in 1849 after Charlotte Brontë gave it to the heroine of her highly successful novel *Shirley*, a work which urged the public to accept a wider choice in life for women.

Shivaun see Siobhan

Sholom see Solomon

Sholto

This is a Scottish name, restricted at one time to the Douglas family, and still particularly used by that family. It has been derived from the Gaelic for 'sower', probably indicating fertility. It is spelt Sìoltach in Gaelic.

Shona see Sheena

Shoshana see Susan

Shreya

Shreya is a girl's name, formed from the Sanskrit word for 'auspicious, lucky'.

Shri

Shri is an Indian girl's name meaning 'radiance, beauty' and is one of the names of the goddess LAKSHMI. For boys Shripati 'husband of Shri', one of the title of Vishnu, can be used. Shri can also be spelt **Sri**.

Shura see Alexander

Shyann, Shyanne see Cheyenne

Si see Simon

Sian

The nearest the Celtic languages come to a 'j' is 's', pronounced 'sh', before 'i' or 'e', giving us **Sian** (**Sîan**) in Welsh, with pet forms **Siani** or **Shani** for JANE. Joan becomes

Siwan. Siwan was the name given to the illegitimate daughter of King John of England, who became the wife of Llywelyn the Great of Wales in the early thirteenth century. This Siwan was the subject of a play written by Saunders Lewis and performed in Welsh in 1954, and later translated and performed in English. This led to a great revival of the name in Wales. (See also under SHEENA and SIOBHAN).

Sib, Sibyl, Sibylla see **Sybil**

Sidney

Sidney and its alternative spelling **Sydney** is an aristocratic surname, traditionally derived from the French name Saint-Denis, used as a first name for both sexes. In the United States it did not suffer the rejection that many other aristocratic names did, because Thomas Townshend, Viscount Sidney had been a supporter of the Colonies during the Revolution. The 'i' spelling is now primarily male, the 'y' primarily female. It has been suggested this feminine use comes from the name **Sidonia** or **Sidony**, **Sidonie** ('woman of Sidon'), but Sidney has a long history of use as a woman's name, and there is no reason why it should not be from the surname. An early female bearer was Sydney Owenson, Lady Morgan, whose novel *The Wild Irish Girl* (1806), which passionately supports Irish nationalism, was considered by the authorities so dangerously subversive that she was put under surveillance at Dublin Castle. **Sid** is a short form of Sidney, **Siddy** of Sidonia. Not much used in the UK at the moment, Sydney is a popular girl's name in the USA, sometimes as Sidney or **Sydnee**.

Siegfried, Sigrid

Siegfried is a Germanic name, from the elements *sig-* and *frid* meaning 'victory' and 'peace', introduced to English speakers in the nineteenth century by admirers of Wagner's *Ring Cycle*. Other Germanic names which have the element meaning victory are **Sigurd** ('victory' + 'word'), the earlier name for the hero Wagner calls Siegfried, **Sigmund** ('victory' + 'protection'), the name of Sigurd's father; and its variants **Siegmund** (the German rather than Scandinavian spelling), and **Sigismund**, a name much used by the Polish royal family. **Sigrid** ('victory' + 'beautiful'), which is shortened to **Siri**, is the only well-known feminine name with this element. (See also SÉGOLÈNE). These names are well used in Scandinavian countries, but more rarely by English speakers.

Sienna

Sienna or **Siena** is the name of the Italian city used as a first name. The city gets its name from the Etruscan people, the Saina, who founded the city. The spelling Siena is the usual one for the city, the spelling Sienna the usual one for the artist's pigment which in turn gets its name from the city. The spelling with two ns is now the dominant one for names, and the name is spreading thanks to the fame of the actress Sienna Miller.

Sierra

This Spanish word for a mountain range, with its associations with the Wild West and the natural world, has become a well-used name for girls in the USA. The Sierra Club is the USA's most prominent environmental organisation. See also Ciara under KIERAN.

Sigourney

The actress Sigourney Weaver chose to change her first name when still a child, feeling that her given name of Susan did not match the striking nature of the names borne by the rest of her family, such as her brother Trajan. She chose Sigourney because it was the name of a favourite character, Sigourney Howard, in Scott Fitzgerald's novel *The Great Gatsby* (1925). A number of parents have since chosen to follow her lead. Fitzgerald seems to have chosen the name from the nineteenth-century author Lydia Huntley Sigourney.

Silas see **Silvia**

Sile see **Cecilia, Sheila**

Silvia

Silvia and its alternative spelling **Sylvia** mean 'of the wood', and would therefore be a suitable epithet for numerous goddesses and nymphs, such as DIANA. **Silvie** or **Sylvie** is the French form, also used as a diminutive of Silvia. An early use of the name is found in Rhea Silvia, the mythical mother of Romulus (see ROMA) and Remus. However, as a Vestal Virgin her associations are with the worship of the hearth and state, and in her case the name may have been changed from some earlier form that sounded as if it came from the Latin *silva* ('a wood'). The name was given Christian respectability by being the name of a saint, the mother of GREGORY the Great. There is a large group of less frequently used names which come from the same root. **Silvius**, the masculine of Silvia, does not seem to be used, and **Silvanus** is most often found in the New Testament short form of the name, **Silas**, although the feminine **Silvana** or **Silvania** is sometimes found. **Silvester** or **Sylvester,** 'of the woods', the name of an outstanding early pope, is more common, and has the feminine **Sylvestra**. It is sometimes shortened to **Sly**. Sylvester Stallone is a well-known user of the name.

Simon

Simon is a name that occurs frequently in the New Testament, the best-known holder being the apostle Simon Peter. It is the Greek form of the Hebrew **Simeon**, the name of one of the tribes of Judah, and of the 'righteous and devout' old man who took the infant Jesus in his arms when He was presented at the temple and blessed Him. It probably comes from the Hebrew word for 'to listen'. **Sim**, **Simmy** and **Simkin** are old pet forms of Simon, but **Si** is used now. **Simone** is a French feminine that has been gaining ground in recent years.

Sincere

This is the vocabulary word that has been used as a boy's name in the USA in the twenty-first century.

Sindy see Cindy, Cynthia, Lucy

Sine, Sinead, Sineag see Sheena

Siobhan

This is the Irish form of JANE (compare names under SHEENA). The Irish actress Siobhan McKenna (1923–86) brought the name to the attention of the world outside Ireland, and it has become well used elsewhere. Because its spelling is far from its pronunciation (shuh-vorn), a wide range of spellings have developed. The Irish author Sean O'Casey chose to anglicise it as **Shivaun** for his daughter, while in the United States it appears in a bewildering range of forms, most often **Shavon**, but including forms such as **Chavon** and **Chivonne**. The name is currently well used in Scotland.

Sioltach see Sholto

Siôn, Sioni, Sionyn see John, Sean

Siri see Siegfried

Siriol

Siriol or **Sirol** is a Welsh feminine name meaning 'cheerful'. It is a fairly recent name, but currently popular with Welsh parents.

Sis, Sisley, Sissie, Sissy see Cecilia

Sive see Sabina

Siwan see Sian

Skye

The name of this Hebridean island is one of the names currently making its mark as a new name. It is used for both sexes, but most often for girls. The island has a reputation for beauty and is a favourite holiday place, as well as having a reputation as a good place to seek an alternative life style. To these associations is probably added those that come from it having the same sound as 'sky'. Use may also have some overlap with SKYLER, below. The vocabulary word **Sky** is also used.

Skyler

This is a phonetic spelling of the old Dutch surname **Schuyler**, meaning 'scholar'. The Schuyler family were prominent in the eighteenth-century history of New York. Schuyler Colfax (1823–85) was the 17th vice president of the USA, serving under Ulysses S. Grant, and other nineteenth-century bearers of the name are found. The name is used for both sexes, with the spelling Skyler rather more common for boys and **Skylar** (and occasionally **Skyla**) for girls.

Slaine

Slaine, anglicised to **Slany**, is the Irish word for 'health', used as a first name for girls. It is sometimes found in France in the forms **Slania** or **Slanie**.

Sly see Silvia

Sofia see Sophie

Sojourner see Journey

Solomon

The name of the Old Testament king famous for his wisdom, Solomon comes from the Hebrew **Shalom** ('peace'), which, with the variant **Sholom**, has also been used as a name. **Sol** and **Solly** are short forms of Solomon. A feminine equivalent of Solomon is **Salome**, a name which was much used by the ruling family of the kingdom of Judea, but best known as the name of the girl who danced before Herod, and when asked to name her reward asked for John the Baptist's head. However, it was also the name of one of the women who stood at the foot of the cross during the crucifixion, and occasional uses of the name are probably inspired by her. The Arabic forms of these names are very similar. Solomon becomes **Sulayman**, **Sulaiman**, **Solaiman** or **Suleyman**; Shalom becomes **Salam** or **Salama** or **Salema**.

Somerled, Somhairle see Sorley

Sondra see Alexander

Sonia, Sonja see Sophia (*see* Sophie)

Sonny .

This is the nickname, used of a son or young boy, used as a first name. In at least one case it is a pet form of SANTINO. It may sometimes pun on **Sunny**, which has been used on occasion for both girls and boys. See also under SURINDER.

Sophie

This is the traditional English form of **Sophia**, which comes from the Greek word for 'wisdom', used to denote the holy wisdom of God, as in the great sixth-century church of Santa Sophia built in Constantinople (now Istanbul). Sophia is **Sofia** in some languages and sometimes shortened to **Phia**. Sophie is the French form of the name, sometimes appearing as **Sophy**. It is **Zofia** is a Polish form and **Sonia** (**Sonya**, **Sonja**) a Slavic pet form. Forms of these names, particularly Sophie and Sophia are currently enormously popular in numerous countries.

Soraya

Soraya, also found as **Surayya** and **Thurayya** is a girl's name from a Persian term for the constellation known in the West as the Pleiades. **Parvin** is a name with the same meaning.

Sorcha

This is an increasingly popular early Irish name meaning 'bright, radiant'. The actress Sorcha Cusack has made the name more widely known outside Ireland.

Sorel, Sorell see Sorrel

Soren

This is a Scandinavian form of the name **Severinus**, an ancient Roman family name and the name of a number of saints. Soren Kierkegaard was an important Danish philosopher. Soren is used occasionally for boys in the USA.

Sorley

Sorley, in Irish **Somhairle** and in the Scottish islands **Somerled**, despite being a Gaelic name, comes not from the Celtic language but from Old Norse, for it represents a form of the words *sumar* ('summer') and *lithr* ('warrior'), a term used for the Vikings who made regular raids on these areas during the sailing season. They later settled, founded new communities such as Dublin, and passed on some of their names, while at the same time Celtic names passed into the stock of Norse names.

Sorrel

This girl's name can be derived either from the plant name, or from the rich reddish brown colour found in the coat of some horses and of dogs such as red setters. The latter seems the more likely, as the plant is notorious for its sourness. It is also spelt **Sorrell** or **Sorell**, and Noel Coward used the name **Sorel** Bliss in his play *Hay Fever* (1925). This form is probably a direct allusion to the notorious Agnes Sorel (c. 1422–50), mistress of and procuress for the French king Charles VII, known as 'Dame de Beauté' from the estate at Beauté-sur-Marne, which he gave her. Her undoubted beauty has been preserved in a portrait where she is shown in the role of the Virgin Mary breast-feeding her child, but which has rather more to do with pornography than with religion.

Soumaya see Sami

Spencer

This surname, originally given to the steward of a medieval household, has come into fashion as a boy's name in the USA, sometimes in the form **Spenser**. It is well used in the USA and UK

Spring see Summer

Sri see Shri

Stacey

Stacey or Stacy is a short form of both ANASTASIA and EUSTACE. The use as an independent name can either be from these or from the surname. This in turn comes from the shortening of Eustace, which was a popular name in the Middle Ages. Stacey can be used for either sex. Use as a masculine name peaked in the USA in the 1960s, and a decade later for girls. This happened rather later in the UK, where the name has always been more common for girls.

Stanislaus

This is the Latin form of the Slavic **Stanislav**, a name made up of the verb 'to be' combined with a word meaning 'glory'. **Stanislas** is the French form of the word. It is occasionally used by English speakers – for instance it was the name of James Joyce's brother – but usually by those of Slavic descent, in honour of St Stanislaus of Cracow, an eleventh-century Polish bishop and martyr, probably murdered by his king, whom he had frequently rebuked for his irregular private life.

Stanley

As a surname, Stanley belongs to one of the oldest and most distinguished aristocratic families in England, with an ancestry going back to the Norman Conquest. It is the family name of the earls of Derby who were at one time kings of the Isle of Man, and who over the centuries have provided many famous politicians. The word means 'stoney field', and refers to property owned by the family. It had been used quietly from the eighteenth century as a first name, but became popular in the next century in honour of the journalist and explorer Henry Morton Stanley (1841–1904) of Dr Livingston fame. Stanley's background was anything but aristocratic, as he was born illegitimate, spent part of his childhood in a workhouse and ran away to America, where he was adopted by a family named Stanley. Despite these beginnings, he did in fact join the nobility when he became a knight of the Order of the Bath in 1899. In the USA some Stanleys of Central European descent may have been adaptations of Stanislavs (see above) via the common shortening **Stan**. For example, one suspects that Stanley Kowolski in *A Streetcar Named Desire* might have been one such.

Star see **Stella**

Steenie, Stefan, Steffan Steffi, Steffie see **Stephen**

Stella

The Latin for 'star', Stella seems to owe its use as a first name to Sir Philip Sidney (1554–86), who wrote a sonnet sequence called *Astrophel and Stella*, using the name to show how far above her lover Stella was. However, he was not the first to use the idea, for **Estelle**, which comes from the same root, was an Old French name. A St Estelle was a first century martyr, who was adopted in the nineteenth century as the patron saint of those trying to revive the literature of Province. Along with the Latinate **Estella**, Estelle became popular in the nineteenth century. **Estrella** is the Spanish form of the name. In Welsh **Seren**, a popular choice with parents, also means 'star'. **Star** itself is occasionally used as a name.

Stephen, Steven, Stephanie

St Stephen was the first person to be martyred for his Christian faith, stoned to death as a blasphemer after accusing the Jewish Elders of rejecting the Messiah. Among those who supported his execution was SAUL of Tarsus, the young man who was later to see the light on the road to Damascus, and on his conversion take the name PAUL. Stephen's name reflects the martyr's crown he won, for it comes from the Greek for 'crown'. St Stephen's feast day is 26 December, the day on which the Bohemian King **Wenceslas** (nowadays more usually found in central Europe in the forms **Vaclav** or **Wenzel**, a name that shares Stephen's meaning, being made up of a Slavic element also meaning 'crown' combined with 'glory') looked out and saw the poor man gathering winter fuel. Continental forms such as **Stefan**, **Steffan** or **Stephan** are sometimes found. The form Steven is simply a modern respelling of the Greek 'ph'. There is an old Scots form **Steenie** but **Steve** or **Stevie** are the usual pet forms. **Esteban** or **Estavan** are Spanish forms of the name. **Stefan** is used in various Continental languages.

Stephanie is the French feminine of the name which has been popular in recent years, and which has short forms **Steffi(e)** and **Stevie**, while there is an older, rarer form **Stephana**. The name becomes **Estafania** or **Estefani** is Spanish. Both the Stephen and Steven forms are well used in the USA and UK at the moment, with a slight preference for the 'v' spelling. However, the Irish Republic shows a distinct preference for the 'ph' spelling.

Sterling see **Stirling**

Steuart see **Stuart**

Steve, Steven, Stevie see **Stephen**

Stew, Stewart see **Stuart**

Stirling

This is the name of the Scottish city, of unknown meaning, used first as a surname and then as a first name. In America it is more frequently spelt **Sterling**.

Stone see **Rocco**

Storm, Stormy

These have been used as respectively boy's and girl's names since about the 1960s, although they only entered the charts in 1991. The associations are presumably not of cold and wet, but of romantic adventures and the sort of personality that could also be described as 'tempestuous'; indeed **Tempest** is, itself, occasionally used, and Storm sometimes used for girls. The fact that there is a character called Storm in the popular soap *The Bold and the Beautiful* may have influenced its growth.

Stuart

Stuart, **Stewart** and **Steuart** are all forms of the Scottish surname and royal name. The name means 'steward' and was adopted from the title of hereditary Steward of Scotland conferred by King David I on Walter Stewart (d. 1177). His great-grandson and great-great-grandson were both regents of Scotland, and the marriage of the son of the next generation into the royal family led to *his* son becoming King Robert II (1316–90).

Short forms are **Stu** or **Stew**. Both the -uart and -ew spellings are currently used regularly in Scotland.

Suellen see **Susan**

Sukie, Suky see **Susan**

Sulaiman, Sulayman, Suleyman see **Solomon**

Suleika see **Zuleika**

Sullivan
Sullivan is an Irish surname now fashionable as a boy's name in the USA. The surname comes form the Irish *O Suileabhain* formed from *suil* 'eye' and *abhain* 'dark' plus a diminutive affix. Although it has been suggested this might indicate 'blind eye', the name is usually glossed as meaning 'little dark eye'.

Summer
This is the season, used as a girl's name. In the UK Summer is currently the most popular of the season's names for girls, with AUTUMN lagging far behind, and no Springs or Winters in the last year for which there are records available. Summer is also well used in Australia. In the USA however, Summer has long been overtaken by Autumn in popularity.

Sumner
Sumner is a surname, sometimes used as a boy's name. The surname is from England, mainly from Lancashire, and would have been given originally to a Summoner, someone who was responsible for getting people to a law court.

Sunil, Sunila see **Blue**

Sunita
Sunita or **Suniti** come from the Sanskrit for 'well conducted, polite'. In Indian epic poetry this is the name of a Bengali princess.

Sunni see **Surinder**

Sunny see **Sonny**

Surayya see **Soraya**

Suri
This name received great attention in 2007 when it was chosen by the actors Tom Cruise and Katie Holmes for their daughter. It was said to be both a Yiddish form of SARAH and a Persian name meaning ROSE.

Surinder
Surinder or Surendra is an expansion of the name of the god Indra, and means 'mightiest of the gods'. It can be used for both sexes, but is usually used for boys, when it can be shortened to **Sunni**.

Surya see **Aditya**

Susan
In the Apocryphal story of Susanna and the Elders, **Susanna**, whose name means 'lily', is a very beautiful and virtuous woman. Two old men try to blackmail her into going to bed with them by threatening to say that they have seen her sleeping with a young man in a garden. Susanna defies them, and when they accuse her the judge DANIEL takes a hand in the case. He questions the old men individually, and when they differ in their accounts of what species of tree the couple were making love under, Susanna's innocence is proved, thus giving the tale a claim to be the earliest recorded detective story. **Susannah** and **Suzanna** are variants of the name; **Susan** is the English form and **Suzette (Susette)** the French pet form of **Suzanne**. **Sue**, **Sukie** or **Suky**, **Susie**, **Susy** and **Suzy** are the short forms. **Shoshana** is the Hebrew form of the name, which appears as **Sausan** in Arabic. In English the short form Sue is sometimes used in combinations such as **Suellen**, the name of SCARLETT O'Hara's sister, but better known from its *Dallas* television connections.

Sushila, Sushil

Sushila, which means 'good-tempered, well-disposed' is the name of the wife of the god KRISHNA. It is also found as **Susheela** and **Sushil** is the masculine.

Suzanna, Suzanne, Suzette, Suzy see Susan

Sybil

This is now the more usual spelling of **Sibyl**, the title given to the women who spoke the oracles in various religious centres in the ancient world. Collections were made of these prophecies, and in the Middle Ages some of these were interpreted as foretelling Christ, so that sibyls became associated with the biblical prophets, and it became possible for Christians to use the word for a pagan priestess as a first name (this also explains the presence of sibyls in such otherwise incongruous places as Michelangelo's ceiling in the Sistine Chapel). **Sib** is a short form and variants include **Sibylla**, **Sybilla** and **Sybella**, while the actress **Cybill** Shepherd has introduced another spelling of the name.

Sydnee, Sydney see Sidney

Sylvester, Sylvestra, Sylvia, Sylvie, Sylvius see Silvia

Symphony see Harmony

Syril see Cyril

T

Tabitha

This comes from an Aramaic word meaning 'gazelle'. **Dorcas** is the Greek translation of the name. In the Bible we are told 'there was at Joppa a certain disciple named Tabitha, which by interpretation is called Dorcas' (Acts 9:36). She died, and the Apostle Peter was summoned. He went to the body and said 'Tabitha, arise. And she opened her eyes: and when she saw Peter, she sat up'. The trouble taken in this account to give the Aramaic as well as the Greek form of the name probably arises from a desire to echo Jesus' words in Mark 5:41, when He performs a similar miracle: 'And he took the damsel by the hand, and said unto her, Talitha cumi: which is, being interpreted, Damsel, I say unto thee, arise'. **Talitha** ('damsel') is sometimes used as a first name. Although Tabitha is now the more frequent form of the name, Dorcas was popular in the past and Dorcas Societies were formed where women would meet to make clothes for the poor, inspired by the biblical Dorcas, who was 'full of good works and almsdeeds'. Arabic also has two names meaning 'gazelle', **Ghazal** or **Ghazala**, and **Rasha** which means 'young gazelle'.

Tacey

Tace or Tacey was a name coined by the Puritans from the Latin meaning 'be silent', as a reminder to women that the New Testament says that they should be silent in church (and no doubt hoping for silence elsewhere). It was sometimes used in its English translation – for instance, Conwy parish church has a seventeenth-century plaque commemorating a Silence Jones. Despite a meaning that might be expected to be too sexist for modern use, the name is still regularly encountered.

Tad see Thaddeus

Tadhg

Tadhg is an Irish name meaning 'poet'. It is also found as **Tiegue**, and has pet forms **Tadleigh**, **Tadhgan** and **Taidhgin**. It was often anglicised in the past as **Thady**. It is generally pronounced Tyeg or Thyg. Tadhg is currently popular in Ireland.

Taffy see David

Tahir, Tahira

Tahir means 'virtuous, pure' in Arabic. The feminine form Tahira is an epithet attached to both KHADIJA, the first wife of Mohammed, and his daughter FATIMA.

Talia see Natalie

Taliesin

The name of an ancient Welsh bard, supposedly from the sixth century, Taliesin's name means 'radiant brow'. Much of the tradition about him is mythical, but the very earliest manuscripts of Welsh poetry have works that are said to be by him. (See also EUGENE, CERIDWEN)

Talitha see Tabitha

Tallulah

This name was introduced to the general public by the American actress Tallulah Bankhead (1903–68), who was named after her grandmother, who had in turn been named after Tallulah Falls in Georgia. The place name is said to come from a Native

American Choctaw word meaning 'leaping water'. The name got a further boost after the success of the film of the musical *Bugsy Malone* (1976), where the female lead, called Tallulah, was played by the young Jodie Foster. There is a very similar Irish name **Talulla** (**Tuilelaith** in Irish), which is an old name meaning 'lady of abundance' and is sometimes spelt to conform with the more familiar Tallulah.

Talon

It is impossible to say whether parents are using this as the surname or the vocabulary word, or even analysing their choice in these terms. No doubt the vocabulary sense makes the name sound suitably masculine – the name is exclusively masculine at the moment – and use has been growing steadily since the 1990s. Its spread may be helped by its use as a name in a number of fantasy contexts.

Tam see Tammy, Thomas

Tamara

This is the Russian form of the biblical name **Tamar**, which means 'date palm'. **Thamar** or Tamara was a highly successful, twelfth-century queen of Georgia in Russia and her fame helped to spread the name throughout the country. Tamara, along with TAMSIN, is one of the sources of the name TAMMY.

Tamika

In 1962, a film called *A Girl Called Tamiko* was shown in the USA. Tamiko is a Japanese name formed from the elements *ta* 'many', *mi* 'beautiful', and *ko* 'child', although the name is sometimes interpreted as meaning 'beautiful flower'. The name obviously struck a chord, but the Japanese name endings -o for women and -a for men are counterintuitive to Western ears; the name was changed to Tamika, and widely adopted by African-Americans. Not only did this introduce a new name and new variants such as **Tamisha**, but it is probably also the source of -ika as a fashionable ending for names. Tamiko Jones is an American jazz singer.

Tammy, Tamsin

Tammy is a girl's name which started out as a pet form of either TAMARA or **Tamsin**, and more recently TAMIKA. It can in turn be shortened to **Tam**. **Tamsin** is a Cornish form of **Thomasina**, the feminine form of THOMAS. It is also found as **Tamzen** or **Tamzin**, while Tammy can also be spelt **Tammie**. Tammy was a particularly popular choice in the 1960s and early 70s. Tam and Tammy can also be Scottish forms of the boy's names Tom and Tommy. Tammy Wynette is a popular and influential country music singer.

Tania

Tania or **Tanya** is the Russian pet form of the name **Tatiana**. This popular Russian name comes from ancient Rome; it means 'belonging to the house of Tatius', a Roman family name which seems to go back to the Roman baby word for 'daddy'. Tatiana spread to Russia as the name of a martyr venerated by the Eastern Church who died c. AD 228. **Tonya** can be viewed as a variant of this, or as from Antonia, and there are other developments of the name such as as **Taniya** and **Taniyah**. Similarly, Tatiana is sometimes respelt **Tatyana**, and can be shortened to **Tatty**.

Tanisha

This widely used African-American name may be a modern blend of a name like Tania and the fashionable -isha, but it can also be linked to the name *Tani*, used by the Hausa of Nigeria, meaning 'born on Monday'. Tanisha is also a Hindu girl's name meaning 'ambition', which is **Tanish** for boys.

Tanith

The Phoenician goddess of love and fertility, Tanith was worshipped in Carthage as the Great Goddess under the name **Tanit**. The name has come into limited use in recent years, mainly in a literary context.

Taniya, Taniyah see Tania

Tanner
This is a surname which would originally have been given to someone who had that job, now used as a boy's name.

Tansy see **Anastasia**

Tanya see **Tania**

Tara
This is the hill in County Meath in Ireland where the ancient high kings of Ireland were crowned. The remains of prehistoric earthworks can still be seen there today. Although the name was certainly in use by the end of the nineteenth century, it was widely used only in the last half of the twentieth century, due largely to its use for the name of the house in *Gone With the Wind* (see further SCARLETT). It has been used for both sexes, but is predominantly female. Tara is also an Indian girl's name, from the Sanskrit for 'star'. Tara is well used in both parts of Ireland.

Tariq
Tariq is the Arabic name of the morning and evening star. It is sometimes found as **Tarik** or **Tarek**. Tariq Ibn Zayad was the general who captured the Rock of Gibraltar (*jabal tariq* 'Tariq's Rock' in Arabic) in 711, which led to the Muslim conquest of Spain. Tariq Ali is a well-known British author and politician.

Tarquin
Tarquin was the name of two semi-legendary kings of Rome in the sixth century BC. The second of these, Tarquin the Proud, was a murderous tyrant who tried to reverse many of the reforms that had recently been made. His conduct, together with his son's rape of LUCRETIA, led to revolt and the institution of the Republic. Despite the name's reputation, it is in limited use (for example Sir Laurence Olivier gave it to his first child), although it is more frequent as a literary name.

Tarrin, Taryn see **Tyrone**

Tasha see **Natalie**

Tate, Tatum
Tate is an English surname of uncertain origin, now used as a boy's first name. Tatum is Old English surname, meaning 'Tata's Homestead' It was introduced to the general public as a girl's name in 1963 when the American actor Ryan O'Neal named his daughter Tatum after the jazz musician Art Tatum.

Tatiana, Tatty, Tatyana see **Tania**

Tave, Tavia, Tavian, Tavy see **Octavia**

Taylor
For some reason this surname, from the occupation, has become enormously popular in the USA as a first name, and has spread from there to other countries. It is also found as **Tayler** and **Tayla**. It is now primarily given as a girl's name in the USA and Canada; slightly more often for girls than boys in Scotland, but currently is mainly for boys in England, although this can be expected to change. Taylor and TYLER is a popular combination for twins in the USA.

Tayshaun see **Sean**

Teah, Teia see **Tia**

Tearra, Teaira see **Tiara**

Tecla see **Thekla**

Ted, Teddie, Teddy see **Edgar, Edmond, Edward, Edwin, Theodore**

Teesha see **Laetitia**

Tegan, Tegwen
Tegan is a Cornish name based on the word *teg* ('beautiful'). In Australia it tends to be spelt **Teigan**, and has been used as **Teagan**. It is a girl's name, although Teagan is also

used for boys in the USA. Tegwen is a Welsh woman's name which means 'fair and white (or blonde)'. The masculine equivalents are **Tegwyn** and **Tegyd** or **Tegid**.

Tel see Terence

Telma see Thelma

Tempest see Storm

Terence

This is the anglicised form of the name of a Roman comic playwright of the second century BC. He is said to have been a Carthaginian who was brought as a slave to Rome, where his owner freed him. There is an obscure saint of the same name, which may have helped make the name more popular, but it seems likely that the short form of the name holds the key to its spread. **Terry** is also a form of the group of names that give us DEREK, and it may well be that many a Terry was interpreted as a pet form and 'corrected' to Terence. Terence occurs in variants such as **Terrance** (the most popular form in the USA), **Terrence** and **Terance**. **Tel** is a recent short form of Terence. Terence is a name particularly associated with Ireland, where it was used to anglicise a number of names, particularly Turlough (see THORA). **Terrel** or **Terrell** is a variant. It seems to have arisen in the United States, was in use by the beginning of the twentieth century, and may owe something to the city of Terrell in Texas. **Tyrrel**, a surname of uncertain origins now used as a boy's name, could have evolved in turn from Terrel, as some forms blur the distinction. **Terron** seems to be a blend of Terrance and DARREN.

Teresa see Theresa

Terrie, Terry see Terence, Theresa

Tessa, Tess, Tessie see Theresa

Tevin

Well used as a first name for boys in the USA in the 1990s, but since dropping out of favour, this is of obscure origin. It may be from a French surname which was in turn based on a medieval French form of STEPHEN, but it may well simply have been made up, attractive because of its echo of the popular name KEVIN.

Tewdwr see Theodore

Thaddeus

Thaddeus or **Thaddaeus** was the name of one of the Apostles. He may be the man identified elsewhere as 'Judas, not Iscariot', and so identical with St JUDE. Thaddeus would therefore be a surname to distinguish him from the treacherous man of the same name. Its meaning is disputed. It may be from the Aramaic meaning 'praise' or 'desired', or it may be a local variant of THEODORE. In the past it was used in Ireland to render the native TADHG, but was not much used elsewhere among English speakers. However, it was well used in Eastern European countries and immigrants would have introduced the name into the USA. Knowledge of it was also kept alive in the nineteenth century through Jane Porter's popular 1803 novel *Thaddeus of Warsaw*. Thady (see also TADHG), **Thaddy** or **Thady** are sometimes found as short forms, but **Tad**, sometimes used independently, is the most common form.

Thalia

Thalia is the Greek Muse of comedy and pastoral poetry. The name is quietly used in the USA for girls. It seems to have been taken up as a result of the success of a Mexican singer and actress who goes by the name of Thalia, as it appears in the US charts first in 1992, the year she had a very successful hit song and started to appear in a successful telenovella, with use peaking the next year.

Thamar see Tamara

Thandie

The actress Thandie Newton who has made this name well known is from an Anglo-Zambian family. Her full name is Thandiwe, which means 'beloved' in Ndebele.

Thea see Dorothy, Theodore

Thekla

This means 'god's glory' and is the name of the first female martyr. Unfortunately, unlike the protomartyr St STEPHEN whose story is well authenticated, little is known for sure about Thekla, as most of her legend is highly romantic and thus dubious, and even her existence has been doubted. However, in the fourth century St Thecla's church in Milan was one of the largest buildings in the Western World. There was a later St Thekla, an Anglo-Saxon Abbess who worked as a missionary in Germany in the eighth century, so it is surprising that this name has not been more widely used in the UK. **Thecla** and **Tecla** are variants.

Thelma

This is a name invented by the writer Marie Corelli for the heroine of a novel *Thelma, A Norwegian Princess*, published in 1887. There is no evidence that there was such a Scandinavian name. Nevertheless the form **Telma** is currently popular in Iceland.

Theobald

Theobald is a Germanic name made up of elements meaning 'people' and 'bold'. It is one of a number of Germanic names starting with the element *theo-* ('people'), which have at times been confused with those names from the Greek *theo-* 'God' (see THEODORE below). Shakespeare's **Tybalt** shows an early form of the name, reflecting the old pronunciation, and it was also found as Tibald, a name which was once traditional for cats, but which is now best known as a surname.

Theodore, Theodora

Of the many names that contain the Greek element *theos* ('God'), the most common are Theodore and Theodora ('gift of God'), although the latter is more likely to appear in its reversed form of DOROTHY or Dorothea, both forms using **Thea** and **Dora** for short. **Theo** and **Teddy** are the commonest male short forms. Although the associations of Theodora are nowadays Christian, it is a very ancient name, a form of it having been found on a Minoan Linear B clay tablet from Knossos in Crete. The Russian form of the name is **Feodor** or **Fedor**, and the feminine **Fedora** is occasionally found. The Welsh **Tudor** (**Tudyr**, **Tewdwr**), an ancient name which eventually became the surname of the ruling family of Britain, is traditionally supposed to be a form of Theodore, but may owe something to the Welsh word *tud* ('country, tribe'). **Theodosius** and **Theodosia** are related names, meaning 'given by God'. **Theophilus** ('beloved by God' or 'loving God') and its even rarer feminine **Theophila** are little used by English speakers, but in France **Théophile** is not uncommon. Although *theos* names were in use in the pagan world, they were particularly popular with early Christians, and most of the names were used by a number of saints. Since the meaning of the names is quite transparent, this group of names is found translated literally into other languages. Thus the sense of Theodore is found in Latin as **Deodatus**, and in French as **Dieudonné**, while **Theophilus** is the Greek form of Mozart's middle name, **Amadeus**, or in German, **Gottlieb**. The feminine **Amadea** has also been recorded, perhaps used by admirers of Mozart for their daughter.

Theodoric see Derek

Theophania see Tiffany

Theresa

This is a name of unknown meaning. The name has been derived from the Greek for 'to reap' and from the Greek island of Thera (Santorini), but since it seems to have arisen in Spain, neither of these seems very likely. The spread of the name owes much to the popularity of St Theresa of Avila, the sixteenth-century nun. Her complex and engaging personality, said to be a combination of 'the eagle and the dove', has led to many being devoted to her. She was a gifted writer and combined great practicality with being a mystic. She has the distinction of being one of the first two women ever to be officially declared doctors of the Church, in 1970. **Teresa** is an alternative spelling; the German form is **Theresia**, and the name is shortened to **Terry** or **Terri(e)**, **Tess**, **Tessie** and **Tessa**. **Tracy** or **Tracey**, now an independent name, started out as another pet form of

Theresa, helped by the use of the surname as a masculine first name. The surname comes from a village in the Calvados region of France, which would have come from a Gallo-Roman personal name meaning 'an inhabitant of Thrace'. The name **Trace** is a short form of Tracy; it is currently also being used as an independent masculine name, perhaps under the influence of the singer Trace Adkins.

Thierry see Derek

Thomas

This is the name of one of the 12 Apostles. The word is Aramaic for 'twin', and sometimes appears in the Bible in its Greek equivalent, *Didymus*. It was probably a nickname, and although no other name for him is mentioned in the Bible, there is a tradition that his name was really Judas, in which case Thomas would have been used to distinguish him from the other Judases – Judas Iscariot and the Judas also known as THADDEUS. The popularity of the name throughout Christendom may owe something to the Apostle's character, as he is shown in the Bible as one of the more fallible and human of the Twelve. When Jesus appears after His Resurrection to the assembled Apostles, Thomas is not there, being too depressed to join them. When he is told what has happened, he declares that until he has touched Christ's wounds he will not believe; whence the expression 'doubting Thomas'. When this happened and his doubts were removed, he immediately declared Jesus to be God. Thomas became a particularly favoured name in medieval England, in honour of the immensely popular St Thomas à Becket (1118–70). The name is shortened to **Tom** or **Tommy** and, in the north, **Tam** and **Tammie**. 'Tommy' for a soldier comes from the use of the name Thomas Atkins on sample forms for recruitment by the War Office in the nineteenth century. **Tomas** is the Irish form of the name, currently popular there together with Thomas and Tom, and also the Welsh spelling.

There are a good number of feminine forms of the name. Formerly **Thomasina** or **Tomasina** was the most common, but this has now been easily outstripped in popularity by the Cornish **Tamsin**, with its variants **Tamzin** and **Tamzen**. This is the main source of the name TAMMY. Thomas and its variants is one of the core Western names, and is currently widely popular.

Thora

When the Viking raiders came to stay and settle in northern England, Scotland and Ireland, they brought with them a set of names based on their favourite god Thor, the god of thunder and fighting. Thora ('dedicated to Thor') is the only feminine name to have survived. There are many masculine names based on the god many of them rare. **Thurstan** or **Thurston** ('Thor's stone (?altar)'), **Torquil**, a contracted form of *Thorketill* ('Thor's cauldron') and **Turlough** (in Irish **Toirdhealbhach**), meaning 'like Thor' and often anglicised by TERENCE, are still found. More recently **Tor**, **Torrin** or **Torin** and **Tory** (**Torey**, **Torry**, also found for girls as shortenings of VICTORIA) have become quite fashionable. They are all forms of the name **Thor**. See also **Tormod** under NORMAN.

Thurayya see Soraya

Tia, Tiana

Tiana (sometimes **Tianna**) is an American name which can be a Cherokee variant of the name DIANA, or else a German form of Christiana. The more popular name **Tia** may be a short form of this, or of other names beginning or ending in the letters -tia; but it is also the Spanish word for 'auntie', often used as a term of affection. That it is regarded as an independent name is shown by spellings such as **Teah** and **Teia**. Tia has been popular in England since the early 2000s. (See also TIARA)

Tiago see James

Tiara, Tierra

This word for a jewelled headpiece was adopted unchanged from Latin into English, the Romans having borrowed the word from the Greek, where it meant 'turban'. The sound, however, may be more important than the meaning, for at the same time as girls began to be called Tiara, they were also being called **Tierra**, the Spanish for 'earth, land', and spellings such as **Tearra** and **Teaira** blur the distinction between the two. **Tia** is used as a pet form of these names.

Tiarnan see **Tiernan**

Tib, Tibbie, Tibby see **Isabel**

Ticia see **Laetitia**

Tiegue see **Tadhg**

Tiernan

Tiernan or **Tiarnan** is an Irish name from *tigern* 'lord, chief'. It was the name of an important twelfth-century Irish king. The name is currently popular in Northern Ireland. **Tierney** is a less common related name meaning 'lordly'.

Tierra see **Tiara**

Tiesha see **Laetitia**

Tiffany

Theophania is a Greek name meaning 'divine appearance', which was given to girls born around the time of the Epiphany, a word that comes from the same root. This became *Tiphaine* in French, and **Tiffania** or **Tiphany** in English. In medieval romance Tiphany appears as the name of the mother of the Three Kings whose gifts mark Epiphany. The name more or less disappeared in English-speaking countries, but was known as a French surname, which belonged to a jeweller who set up in New York. Tiffany's famous shop featured in the title of the very successful film *Breakfast at Tiffany's* (based on Truman Capote's novel, 1958), where, out of context, it could be understood as a proper name; and it is this that seems to have led to a revival of this name in recent decades.

Tilda, Tilly see **Matilda**

Timothy

This really belongs with the THEODORE group of names, for it comes from *Timotheos*, a Greek name meaning 'honouring God'. In the Acts of the Apostles, Timothy is a young man of Asia Minor, carefully brought up in religion by his mother EUNICE and grandmother LOIS, and who is chosen as an able companion and assistant by the Apostle PAUL. **Tim** and **Timmie** or **Timmy** are the usual short forms. In Ireland the name has been used to replace the native TADHG.

Tina see **Christine**

Tiphany see **Tiffany**

Tisha see **Laetitia, Patrick**

Titus

A Roman family name, Titus is probably of Etruscan origin and thus of unknown meaning. There was an Emperor Titus, chiefly remembered for his destruction of the Temple at Jerusalem, who was very popular with the people of Rome on account of his generosity to them, but luckily for them died young and thus avoided bankrupting the state as he looked set to do. Like so many other Roman names, its use is largely due to its appearance in the Bible. It was the name of a follower of St Paul who, with TIMOTHY, was the most trusted of his followers. The notoriety of Titus Oates, fabricator of the Popish Plot in the seventeenth century, probably helped a long-lasting decline in the name, but there are slight signs of a revival at the moment, possibly helped by the publicity given to the name by Titus Groan, hero of Mervyn Peake's *Gormenghast* books.

Toby

Toby is the English, **Tobias** the Greek form of a Hebrew name meaning 'Jehovah is good'. The name comes from the Apocryphal *Book of Tobit*, a highly romanticised account of how Tobias, with the help of the Archangel RAPHAEL, set out with his dog, won himself a wife and cured his father Tobit's blindness. It was a popular subject for painting, and since Tobias's dog is a notable feature of such works, Toby was transferred to the animal, and became the name of Mr Punch's dog. The American actor **Tobey** Maguire has introduced a different spelling. Toby is currently quite a popular choice in England.

Tod, Todd

A surname used as a first name, Tod is a dialect word for 'fox', and would originally have been given as a nickname to someone who either had red hair or else was known for his cunning. As a first name it has been in use from at least the latter part of the nineteenth century, for the expression 'on your tod', Cockney rhyming slang for 'on your own', refers to the American jockey Tod Sloan (1874–1933).

Toirdhealbhach see Thora

Tolomey see Bartholomew

Tom, Tomas, Tomasina, Tomina, Tommy see Thomas

Toni, Tonia, Tonie, Tonio, Tony see Antony

Tonya see Antony, Tania

Topaz see Jewel

Topher see Christopher

Tor, Torey see Thora

Tori, Toria, Torie see Victoria

Torin, Torrin see Thora

Tormod see Norman

Torquil see Thora

Torry see Thora

Tory see Victoria

Toya

Toya is a Mexican pet form of Victoria, which has been well used in recent years in the USA, particularly in combination in the forms **LaToya** and **Latoy**, for which see further under LAETITIA.

Trace, Tracey, Tracy see Theresa

Travis

This is a form of the surname **Travers**, which comes from the Old French word for 'a crossing', and would have been given to someone who lived at a ford or crossroads, or possibly someone who gathered tolls at such a place. It has been a popular boy's name in the USA since the later 1970s. **Travon** seems to be a development of this.

Trent, Trenton

Both these boys' names go back to the English river Trent, whose name dates back to prehistoric times and has tentatively been identified as meaning 'the flooder'. The river name became a surname, which was taken to America, where these names are most used. In the eighteenth century William Trent founded a settlement, now a city in New Jersey, which was known as Trenton ('Trent's town'), which in turn has become a first name.

Trevor

This is the English form of the Welsh name **Trefor**. It means 'large homestead' and is the name of a number of places in Wales. It has been in use in Wales since the tenth century, but only came to England in the middle of the nineteenth, and was particularly popular in the middle years of the twentieth century. **Trev** is the short form. Trevor is currently in decline in the UK having been popular two generations ago, but underwent a revival in the USA in the 1990s. **Trevon** seems to be an American variant.

Trey

Trey is used in the USA as a nickname given to a boy who was the third generation to bear the same name and had the Roman numeral III after his name, in the same way the JUNIOR is used for the second bearer of a name. These nicknames help distinguish between people with the same name. It has been derived from the Latin *tres* ('three'). It has subsequently become an independent name, perhaps influenced by TROY. Trey Parker, the creator of the cartoon series *South Park*, has recently made the name more widely known.

Tricia see Patrick

Trina see Katherine

Trinity

This is the vocabulary word used as a girl's name, mostly found in the USA. It fits in with the current trend for overtly religious names, such as HEAVEN and GENESIS, and is the most successful of them. However, some uses may be inspired by its being the name of a character in the very successful 1999 film *The Matrix*, particularly as its popularity showed a big jump between 1999 and 2000. The name is shortened to **Trini** or **Trinny**.

Triss see Beatrice

Tristan

Tristan, **Tristram** or **Tristam** is the hero of the tragic love-story of Tristan and ISOLDA. Sir Tristan of Lyonesse was famous for his skill as a huntsman, one of the best fighters in Arthurian legend, the bravest knight in Cornwall and a faithful follower of his uncle, King Mark, until he fell in love with Mark's wife. The meaning of the name is not known, but it has a complex history. In the romances his name is linked with the French word *triste* ('sorrowful'), and a story was told that after his father had been captured by an enchantress his mother went searching for her husband, even though her baby was due to be born. She fell into labour in the forest, and died from a combination of complications and exposure. Before she died, she held her son and said to her waiting woman (in Malory's words): 'Because I shall die of the birth … I charge thee, gentlewoman, that thou pray my lord, King Melodias, that when he is christened let call him Tristram, that is as much to say as a sorrowful birth'. However, this is an example of folk etymology, with the name being altered to fit a recognisable word, and a story made up to go with it. The early form of the name seems to have been Drustan, derived from the Pictish name Drust, and the form **Drystan** is occasionally used in the United States. The Scottish connection is not surprising, for some scholars interpret Tristan's homeland of Lyonesse as a form of the Scottish place name Lothian. There are, however, very early associations of the name with Cornwall. Near Castle Dore in Cornwall, in romance the capital of King Mark, a sixth-century tombstone was found inscribed in Latin 'Here lies Drustan son of Cynvawr', and it may be no coincidence that Cynvawr is recorded as the name, along with the later GERAINT, of one of the sixth-century Cornish kings. (See also BRONWEN.) The name is currently popular in the USA, where is is also spelt Tristen, Triston, Tristin and Tristain, and Tristan is popular in France. The feminine form Trista was boosted considerably by the character of Trista Evans on the soap opera *Days of Our Lives* (1996–2001). Later, it was the name of a personality on the 'reality' show *The Bachelorette* in 2003.

Trix, Trixie see Beatrice

Troilus see Cressida

Troy

As a surname Troy can be either from someone who originally lived in the French town of Troyes, or an Irish surname from the Gaelic for 'a foot soldier'. Modern use of the name as a first name also comes from the story of the great city of Troy in Asia Minor, whose siege and destruction by the Greeks is told in Homer's *Iliad* and by many later classical writers. Although the name has been used steadily since the nineteenth century in the USA, the modern use of the name most obviously comes from the success of the actor Troy Donahue (birth name Merle Johnson Jr) who became a teen heart throb in

1959. This explains why the period of greatest use for the name was in the 1960s. Troy has recently spread from being a boy's name to girls.

Trudi(e), Trudy see **Gertrude**

Tucker

Tucker is a surname now being used for boys in the USA. The name is an occupational one. In the past a tucker was a technical term for someone who fulls cloth.

Tudor, Tudyr see **Theodore**

Tuilelaith see **Tallulah**

Turlough see **Thora**

Ty see **Tyler, Tyrone**

Tybalt see **Theobald**

Tyler

This is a name that has been popular in the USA in recent years. It is simply a surname, a respelling of the occupation of tiler, used as a first name. Predominantly a boy's name, it is now also used for girls. It can be shortened to **Ty**. Tyler is very popular for boys in England, Scotland, the USA and Canada and Australia.

Tyrone

Tyrone is the name of an Irish county which, in its turn, gets its name from a person, for it means 'Owen's land'. Two American actors, father and son, called Tyrone Power who appeared in films in the first part of the twentieth century did much to spread the name there, while in the UK the director Tyrone Guthrie (1900–71) gave it fame. Guthrie was called Tony as a pet form of his name, but **Ty** is the more usual short form. The girl's name **Taryn** was invented by the younger Tyrone Power and his wife Linda Christian by combining letters from their names, and given to their daughter. Its use has spread, and it is now not uncommon both in the USA and UK. The form **Tarrin** comes from Lloyd Alexander's *Chronicles of Prydain* children's books. The same Gaelic element *ty*, meaning 'land, territory', is also found in **Tyree**, the name of an island off the coast of Scotland, now used for boys. The supermodel **Tyra** Banks has helped the spread of this feminine form. Occasional names such as **Tyrese** and **Tyshawn** are blends based on these names.

Tyrrel see **Terence**

Tyson

As a surname Tyson can either be a form of Dyson 'son of Denis' or from the Old French world *tison*, 'firebrand'. The name was already in use by the 1960s as a boy's first name, which may explain why the imprisonment of the most prominent holder of the surname, Mike Tyson, did not affect its popularity.

U

Uilliam see **Hugh, William**

Ulick see **Hugh, Ulysses, William**

Ulises see **Ulysses**

Ulric

This name appears in Old English as **Wulfric** ('wolf' combined with 'power'), which was the name of an English saint of the twelfth century who had been a self-indulgent parson in his younger days, devoted to hunting, but who reformed in later years, to end his days a recluse in the delightfully named Haselbury Plucknett in Somerset. It is also the name of a number of German saints, and modern use of Ulric is probably due to its introduction from Germany. This is certainly the case for **Ulrice**, the German feminine form, also found as **Ulrica** or **Ulrika**, all forms being pronounced the same way. Ulrica seems to have been a popular literary name in the nineteenth century, appearing, among others, as characters in two of Sir Walter Scott's books, *Ivanhoe* (1819) and *Count Robert of Paris* (1831).

Ulysses

This is the Latin form of **Odysseus**, Homer's great Greek hero, famous for his wisdom, cunning and eloquence and the faithfulness of his wife PENELOPE. It is little used in modern times, but when it occurs it is probably through an association with General Ulysses S. Grant (1822–85), commander of the Union armies in the American Civil War and 18th president of the United States. In Ireland **Ulick** (see HUGH, WILLIAM) is sometimes anglicised as Ulysses. The name is sometimes spelt **Ulises** in the USA.

Uma

Made famous by the actress Uma Thurman, whose father is a noted Buddhist scholar, Uma is one of the names of the Indian goddess Parvati and comes from the Sanskrit word for 'flax'. English speakers had been exposed to the name earlier, for it is used by R.L. Stevenson for a character in his spooky novella *The Beach of Falesa* (1893).

Umar see **Omar**

Umberto see **Humbert**

Umniya see **Aman**

Una, Unity see **Oonagh**

Unice see **Eunice**

Unique, Unity see **Oonagh**

Urban

This Latin name, meaning 'townsman', was chosen by eight medieval popes, probably because it was the opposite of PAGAN, which originally meant 'country dweller'. It is rarely found in modern times. There is a Welsh name **Urien**, which is thought to come from the same root, being a form of the Latin *urbigenus* ('town-born'). It was the name of a leader of the Northern Britons in the sixth century, who also appears as one of King Arthur's knights in the medieval romances.

Uriah see **Bathsheba**

Uriel

Uriel is a Hebrew name meaning 'God is my light'. It is the name of an angel who does not appear in the Bible, but who is counted by some as one of the Archangels. It is also the name of two minor characters in the Old Testament. **Uri** can either be a short form, or an independent name meaning 'light' and **Uriah** 'God is light' is basically the same name. For the Biblical Uriah see under BATHSHEBA.

Ursula

Ursula means 'little bear'. St Ursula was a very popular saint in the Middle Ages who had a church dedicated to her by the late fourth or early fifth century. According to legend, she and 11,000 virgin companions were martyred at Cologne by the Huns on their way back from a pilgrimage to Rome. She is said to have been a British princess fleeing from an unwanted marriage. Other than that she probably existed and that her companions were originally recorded as 10 in number, little can be confidently asserted about Ursula, for the stories about her are no less fictitious than those told about her masculine equivalent ORSON. Ursula Vernon is a popular artist and writer.

Usama

Usama or **Osama** means 'lion' in Arabic.

V

Vaclav see **Stephen**

Val see **Percy, Valery**

Valda, Valdemar see **Waldo**

Valery

Valery with its alternative spelling **Valerie** is the English form of the Roman family name **Valeria** (masculine **Valerian**), a name coming from the Latin verb *valere* ('to be strong, healthy, flourish'). From the same root comes **Valentine**, the name of a third-century martyr. Nothing is known about him for sure, for all the stories revolve around customs associated with St Valentine's Day, and these evolved from pagan Roman fertility customs associated with mid-February. Valentine's only connection is that his feast day falls on 14 February. In the Middle Ages the name is found in the romance of *Valentine and Orson*, in which Valentine is a brave and doughty prince. The name is especially given to children born on or about the saint's day and can be given to both sexes, although it is more commonly masculine, with **Valentina** being used as an alternative feminine. **Val** is used as a short form of these names for both sexes, and for women it has been elaborated into a new name, **Valene**. See also **Orson**

Van see **John**

Vance

Vance is an English surname, meaning 'fens' (try saying fens with a very strong west-country accent with the typical change of 'f' to 'v' and you will see how it got there). Vance Packard (1914–96) was an author and social commentator who wrote a very influential book called *The Hidden Persuaders* (1957) which showed how pubic opinion was manipulated by advertisers and politicians.

Vanda see **Wanda**

Vanessa

This is a name invented by Jonathan Swift (1667–1745) for a poem called *Cadenus and Vanessa* (1726), in which he declines the offer of marriage made to him by a young woman called Esther Vanhomrigh, Cadenus being an anagram of *decanus*, the Latin for his rank of Dean, and Vanessa a play on elements of her name. **Ness, Nessa** and **Nessie** are common short forms. The name Vanessa received a boost in the 1980s in the Americas with the successful telenovela *Vanessa* starring the very popular Lucia Mendes. The name is also popular in Austria, but not currently a common choice in the UK. Vanessa Paradis is a popular French singer and actress.

Vanora see **Jennifer**

Varun(a) see **Aditya**

Vashti

Vashti is the name of the Old Testament queen whose refusal to display herself at her husband's feast leads to her replacement by ESTHER. The name probably comes from the Persian for 'beautiful'. It is still in occasional use, but mainly in literary contexts, often with rather voluptuous connotations.

Vasilie see **Basil**

Vaughan
A Welsh first name and surname, Vaughan is the English form of the adjective *fychan*, a form of the Welsh word meaning 'little'. It would originally have been given to someone small as a nickname.

Velda see **Waldo**

Velma
This name is something of a mystery. It seems to have come into use in the United States in the 1880s, at a time when names such as THELMA were also popular. It may well be that the -elma sound was felt to be particularly attractive by parents, in the way that certain sounds seem to become strangely fashionable for a while, and that Velma was a name invented to fit this fashion. However, it has been linked with Wilhelmina (see WILLIAM), and there may be a progression of Wilhelmina moving to the pet form Wilma, then becoming **Vilma** (the German pronunciation), with Velma as a variant.

Venetia
This is the Latin name for the city of Venice, although in the past the name was associated with the name of **Venus**, the Roman goddess of fertility and love, and some uses may have been in this sense. A famous early bearer of the name was Venetia Stanley (1600–33). She was a lady of noble family and outstanding intellect, who set up house on her own in London, thereby earning the description by one contemporary of 'that celebrated beautie and courtezane'. In 1625 she secretly married her childhood playmate Sir KENELM Digby against his family's wishes. It was a love match and a happy marriage, and after Venetia's early death Digby erected an elaborate monument to her and was so overcome with grief that he went into complete seclusion for two years. Her death was lamented in verse by numerous poets, including Ben Jonson. The name **Venus** has gained some publicity from the sporting success of the tennis player Venus Williams which has led to an increase in use, although it is still rare. Venus's Greek counterpart, **Aphrodite**, is even rarer. These names probably never joined the main stream of European names because, as goddesses of fertility and love they had, in legend, many extra-marital affairs. One of the names of Aphrodite's most famous lovers, ADONIS, is occasionally used, but since it has entered general vocabulary as a term for a beautiful young man, it is a difficult name to live up to. (See also under JULIA.)

Vera
Vera looks as if it is from the Latin for 'truth', which would give it the same sense as the English name **Verity**; in fact, it comes from Russian and means 'FAITH'. It is sometimes used as a short form of VERONICA. The rare spelling **Viera** is closer to the Russian original. **Vere** is sometimes regarded as a masculine form of Vera, but is actually a French place name which became an aristocratic surname and then a first name. There is a rare pet form **Verita**.

Vergil see **Virgil**

Verity see **Vera**

Vernon
Vernon is a French place name which comes from a Gaulish word meaning 'where alders grow'. A Richard de Vernon was one of the Norman conquerors of England, and he founded a noble family. In the nineteenth century, when such practices were popular, the surname was adopted as a first name. **Verna** has been used as a feminine form of the name, but is usually traced back to the Latin word *vernus* ('spring').

Veronica
The story told of St Veronica says that she was a witness of Christ's suffering as he carried His cross through Jerusalem to the site of the crucifixion. Moved with pity, she used her veil to wipe the sweat from His face, and an image of His face, like that of the Turin shroud, was left on her veil and became a sacred relic. In fact, the name of the relic seems to have been transferred to the (possibly fictional) woman, for Veronica means 'true image or icon'. **Véronique**, the French form, is occasionally found. An alternative

interpretation of the name links it with the Macedonian Greek name **Berenice** ('bringer of victory'). Berenice was a popular name with the third-century BC rulers of Egypt, descendants of ALEXANDER's Macedonian conquerors, and a story is told of how one Berenice dedicated a lock of her hair at a temple as an offering for the safe return of her husband from war. The lock disappeared and a new constellation was seen in the sky, ever after known as the Lock of Berenice. The Greeks would have pronounced the name with the 'c' hard and the final 'e' pronounced; it was formerly given a soft 'c' and a final 'e' in England, but its modern pronunciation is reflected in the form **Bernice**. **Bunnie** or **Bunny** and **Bernie** are short forms of Bernice, with **Ron(n)i** or **Ronee** for Veronica.

Vesta

This is the name of the Roman goddess of the hearth and home. The name was the stage name of the music-hall stars Vesta Tilley (1864–1952) and Vesta Victoria, but was never widely used.

Vevina see Bevin

Victor, Victoria

The Latin for 'victory', both Victoria and Victor (the masculine form) are found at an early date on the Continent, but are very rare in Britain until the nineteenth century, when Queen Victoria was named after her German mother. **Vic** is used as a short form for both sexes and **Vicky**, **Tory** or **Tori(e)**, **Toria** and **Vita** for Victoria, with TOYA a Spanish-language pet form. **Queenie** was also used as a form for those named after Queen Victoria. Vita has been associated with the Latin word for 'life', but its most famous bearer, the writer Vita Sackville-West (1892–1962), was a Victoria. The pre-Roman British already had a name with the same meaning, used by the chieftainess and rebel leader the Romans called **Boadicea** or **Boudicca**. This name has come down to us as the Welsh name **Buddug** or **Buddic**. Earlier still we have a record of a pre-Roman chieftain called Bodvoc, which appears to be a masculine form. The masculine name **Gwythyr**, found in some of the earliest surviving Welsh literature, is said to be a form of Victor. Victoria is popular in the USA with Victor well used. In the UK the name was very popular in the 1960s and 70s and is once more well used.

Vida see David

Viera see Vera

Vilma see Velma, William

Vina see David, Lavinia

Vincent

Vincent is a name allied to VICTORIA, for it comes from the Latin verb for 'to conquer'. The name was popular in the Middle Ages, particularly among the French, who introduced it to England. At a later date, St Vincent de Paul (1580–1660), one of many saints called Vincent, brought the name fame. He organised societies of laymen to care for the poor and neglected, as well as founding the Vincentian Fathers and the Sisters of Charity. The Spanish form is **Vincente**. Vincent and Vincente are well used in the America. The actors **Vin** Diesel and **Vinnie** Jones show the short forms.

Violet

One of the best known of the flower names, Violet is also found in the French form **Violette**, in the Italian **Violetta** – famous as the name of the heroine of Verdi's opera *La Traviata* (1853) – and in the Latin form **Viola**, possibly influenced by Shakespeare's heroine of *Twelfth Night*. The flower and its colour seem to go back to a Greek word *ion*, which has the same meaning and which lies behind a group of less common girls' names. **Ione** means 'violet', and is the feminine of Ion, the name of the king of Athens who gave his name to the Ionian people. Edward Bulwer-Lytton seems to have invented it for the heroine of his highly successful novel *The Last Days of Pompeii* (1834). **Ianthe** ('violet flower') is an ancient name which has a long literary history. It was taken from ancient mythology by Ovid (43 BC–AD 18), picked up by a number of sixteenth- and seventeenth-century poets and playwrights, used by Byron for a pseudonym for the dedicatee of the poem which brought him fame, *Childe Harold's Pilgrimage*, and used by Shelley for his first daughter and for a character in *Queen Mab* (1813). **Iolanthe**, used by Gilbert and Sullivan for their opera, is a form of the name **Yoland** (**Yolande** or **Yolanda**), a name of disputed origin which may belong to this group.

Virgil

This is the usual form, as a first name, of the Latin poet, more correctly spelt **Vergil**. It is primarily an American name, as in the composer Virgil Thomson (1896–1989), although it can also be found in Ireland as an anglicisation of FERGUS. To the Romans, Virgil became almost the national poet, his epic *The Aeneid* becoming the accepted account of how Rome came to be. In the Middle Ages he was thought to have prophesied the coming of Christ in a poem which actually celebrated the birth of a grandchild of the Emperor AUGUSTUS; and from this he developed into a powerful magician in popular literature, with a magic looking-glass in which he could see whatever was happening in the world.

Virginia

Virginia is a Roman symbolic name. The Romans told a story of a corrupt ruler who lusted after a beautiful young girl called Virginia, who virtuously rejected his advances. He got a dependant of his to claim that the girl was actually his slave, and the ruler gave judgement in his favour, having agreed in advance that the girl would then be handed over into his power. Virginia's father realised what was happening and the fate which awaited his daughter and killed her on the spot, preferring her death to dishonour. Despite this ancient precedent, the real source of Virginia as a modern name is the American state named in honour of Elizabeth I, the Virgin Queen, by Sir Walter Raleigh when he founded a colony there. The first child born to the settlers was christened Virginia, and for a long time the name remained primarily an American one, although this is no longer the case. It is shortened to **Ginny** or **Jinny** and occasionally **Geena** (see GINA), and some **Gingers** are Virginias rather than redheads.

Vita see Victoria

Vivian

Derived from the Latin meaning 'lively', Vivian was originally a masculine name, with the elaborations **Vyvyan** and **Vyvian**. **Vivien** and **Vivienne** were the feminines. However, this distinction has now become blurred, and while you are unlikely to find the feminine forms used for men, women now use all the forms along with **Viviana** (an obscure early martyr) and **Vivianne**.

Vonda see Wanda

Vyvian, Vyvyan see Vivian

W

Wade

Wade was the name of an obscure character in Anglo-Saxon pagan legend, but modern use of this as a boy's name comes from the surname. Some bearers of the surname may in fact get it from the Anglo-Saxon name, but other Wades get their surname either from an ancestor who lived by a ford ('wade' in Middle English), or because they originally came from the Suffolk town called Wade. In Margaret Mitchell's *Gone With the Wind* Scarlett calls her son Wade Hampton Hamilton after Wade Hampton III (1818–1902) Civil War soldier and Governor of South Carolina.

Waldo

This comes from a Germanic word meaning 'power' and is also a pet form of **Waldemar** or **Valdemar**, meaning 'great ruler'. **Valda**, which has a variant **Velda**, is the feminine equivalent. The word 'Waldo', as used to mean a mechanical device for handling things by remote control, comes from a science-fiction novella by Robert Heinlein, where the hero is a physically handicapped man of that name who invents devices to compensate for his inabilities. When, soon afterwards, the nuclear industry developed means of extensive remote manipulation, the name of Heinlein's fictional devices was transferred to the real ones.

Walid

Walid comes from the Arabic for 'newborn' hence 'son'. In the eight century under the caliph Al-Walid-ibn-Abd-al-Malik the Arab world expanded greatly.

Walker

Walker is an English surname which comes, like TUCKER, from the actions of someone who fulls cloth. It has been used regularly in the USA as a boy's name since the nineteenth century, although it was rare in the 1950s–80s.

Wallace

The use of this as a surname probably arose from admiration of Sir William Wallace (c. 1274–1305) of *Braveheart* fame, the great Scottish patriot who fought against the English under Edward I and temporarily drove them out of his country, until he was captured and executed by them. In contemporary accounts his name is spelt *Walays*, or in Latin *Wallensis*, which means 'the Welshman'. It comes from the word *waleis*, which originally meant 'foreign' but came to be given to all the Celtic minorities in the British Isles, including those living in the Scottish border area from whom Wallace is thought to have been descended.

Walter

Walter is another of the Germanic names brought to England by the Norman Conquest. It is made up of elements *wald* and *hari* meaning 'rule' and 'army'. In the past, the pet forms were **Wat** and **Watty**, reflecting the old pronunciation which swallowed the 'l'; but now **Wally** and **Walt** are used.

Wanda

It has been said that Wanda is a form of 'Wend', an ancient tribe who inhabited Europe in the Dark Ages; but this is not well supported. It is a Slavic name, found in Polish folklore, but seems to have reached English speakers only when Ouida published a novel called *Wanda* in 1883. The variant **Vanda** reflects the German pronunciation of the name, and has the variant **Vonda.**

Warren

Warren is a surname used as a first name. Unlike the majority of such names, which only came into use in the nineteenth century, it has been a first name since the seventeenth century. The surname has a number of different sources. There was a Germanic name *Varin*, meaning 'to watch, guard', which the Normans brought over as *Guerin* and which became Warren in English; it can be from the French place name La Varenne (near Nantes), meaning 'warren'; or it can be a name given to someone who lived near a warren or was a warren-keeper. In the USA it probably came into general use in honour of General Joseph Warren killed in the battle of Bunker Hill in 1775.

Warwick

This is a surname and place name used as a first name. The town of Warwick, to judge by its meaning, was originally a suburb which grew up by a weir. Guy, Earl of Warwick, was a popular hero of medieval romance. There were also two real-life earls of Warwick in the fifteenth century whose lives could have come from the story-books – one a model of knightly courtesy and prowess, the other so influential in the Wars of the Roses that he has come down to us as Warwick the Kingmaker. The pub sign of the Bear and Ragged Staff is taken from the Warwick coat of arms. **Warrie** is used as a short form.

Wat, Watty see Walter

Waverly

Waverly is a surname, now used as a first name, often for girls. The surname was a place name made up of a first element with unclear meaning but which appears to have something to do with trees, while the final syllable means 'clearing'.

Wayne

This is most emphatically a twentieth-century name, since it owes its use to the popularity of the film star John Wayne. As a surname, it is the old word for 'a cart', and would have been given to a carter or cart-maker. **Waylon** is not an elaboration, but from another surname that refers to land fit for a road. Waylon Jennings (1937–2002) was a well-known country singer.

Wenceslas see Stephen

Wendy

Wendy has one of the best-recorded histories of any first name. It was introduced by J.M. Barrie in 1904 for the girl in *Peter Pan*. He said that he took it from the nickname that a child called Margaret Henley used for him: she regarded him as her friend, so called him 'Fwendy-Wendy'. *Peter Pan* was enormously successful and the name Wendy spread rapidly. Its spread must have been helped by its similarity to the Welsh names starting with GWEN which had been popular shortly before. With variants such as **Wenda** it is difficult to draw a line between Wendy and the Welsh Gwenda.

Wenonah see Winona

Wenzel see Stephen

Wesley

Another name with a clear history, Wesley was introduced as a first name in honour of John Wesley (1703–91), the founder of Methodism, and his brother Charles (1707–88), evangelist and hymn writer. **Wes** is the short form. The surname means 'west meadow'. **Weston**, another surname which has recently come into use as a first name, has a similar origin, meaning 'west farm'.

Whitney

This is an English place name meaning 'white island'. In the United States the Californian Mount Whitney is the highest peak in the country outside Alaska; it was named after Josiah Dwight Whitney (1819–96), the geologist who surveyed the Rockies and established the height of many of the mountains' highest peaks. He is probably the main American source of the name. Whitney has been used as a first name for both sexes, but is mostly feminine. **Whitley** ('white meadow' in Old English) is also used for girls, in part because of its similarity to Whitney, but mainly because it featured as a character name in the television series *A Different World* which was popular in the 1980s and 1990s. This show also introduced the name **Jaleesa**. The singer Whitney Houston, who has made the name so well known, was named after the actress Whitney Blake (1925–2002) whose birth name was Nancy Whitney.

Wilbert

An Old English name combining 'will' with 'bright', Wilbert is little used now, but it is known to generations of *Thomas the Tank Engine* fans as the first name of the Rev. Awdrey who created him.

Wilbur

This is a surname, probably from the Old English words meaning 'will' and 'fortress', used as a first name. It is mainly an American name, its use inspired by Wilbur Wright (1867–1912) who, together with his brother **Orville** (which appears to have been a surname invented by Fanny Burney for her novel *Evelina* (1778)), was a pioneer of aviation.

Wilfred

Wilfred, with its variant **Wilfrid**, is an Old English name made up of the elements 'will' and 'peace'. It was the name of an outstanding Northumbrian bishop in the seventh century, but it died out after the Norman Conquest until revived in the saint's honour by High Church Anglicans in the nineteenth century. **Wilf** and **Fred** are the short forms.

William

A Germanic name, William is compounded from elements meaning 'will' and 'helmet' (signifying 'protection'), and literally came over with the Conqueror, who was better known in his own time as William the Bastard. It rapidly became popular, and has remained among the favourite boys' names from the Norman Conquest to this day. It is shortened to **Will**, **Willie** or **Willy** and its variants **Bill**, **Billie** or **Billy**. In Welsh the name became **Gwilym** or **Gwillym**, with a short form **Gwil**. In Ireland **Ulick** (see also HUGH) may be a form of the name via **Uilliam**, while LIAM, the Irish short form of William, has become popular as a name in its own right and spread to other countries. **Guillaume** is the French form. **Wilhelmina** is the basic feminine form, taken from the German. This has evolved a large number of short forms such as **Elma**, **Willa**, **Wilma** or **Vilma**, **Mina**, **Minna**, **Minnie** and **Minella** which, along with the masculine pet forms, are used as independent female names (see also VELMA). William is widely popular in the English-speaking world, and Billy is also well used as an independent name.

Willow

Willow is one of the more recent plant names to have entered the stock of names. It had been used very quietly for some time, often in a literary context. Then in 1995 Disney brought out the film *Pocahontas* with the character of Grandmother Willow. However, what was really influential was the use of the name in the television series *Buffy the Vampire Slayer*. The hit series was first shown in 1997 and the name entered the America name charts in 1998. The name sometimes fills the role of a feminine form of Will(iam).

Wilma see William

Winifred

This is the English form of the Welsh name **Gwenffrewi** or **Gwenfrewy** ('blessed reconciliation': see further under GWEN). There is a half-way form **Gwinifrid** which was well used in the nineteenth century in Wales and shows how the change in the name came about. St Winifred was a seventh-century princess who, according to legend, rejected the advances of a prince who then decapitated her in fury. When her head was restored to her body she miraculously came back to life, and was allowed to end her days as a nun. Her relics were moved to Shrewsbury in 1138, which accounts for the name developing an English form. Short forms are **Win**, **Winnie** and **Freda**. The name was very popular at the end of the nineteenth century and beginning of the twentieth.

Winona
This is the name of a number of places in the United States, including a city and county in Minnesota, used as a first name. It is the Sioux word for 'first-born daughter', and was the name of the daughter of the Sioux Dakota chief Wapasha III. The name occurs as **Wenonah**, the mother of Hiawatha, in Henry Longfellow's poem (1855). It is also found in the form **Wyn(n)ona**. The name is known as that of the actress Winona Ryder who was named after the nearby city of Winona. The country singer Wynonna Judd shows an alternative spelling.

Winston
Winston owes its modern popularity as a boy's name to Sir Winston Churchill (1874–1965). It was a traditional name in his family. The first Sir Winston Churchill, father of the first Duke of Marlborough, was born in 1620. He was named Winston in honour of his mother, who was born Sarah Winston. The surname came from a place name made up of Old English elements meaning 'joy' and 'stone'.

Wulfric see Ulric
Wyatt
The modern use of Wyatt as a boy's name is probably linked to the fame of the Western lawman Wyatt Earp. As a surname, it is a contracted form of the Old English name *Wigheard*, formed from elements meaning 'battle' and 'brave'.

Wyn, Wynford, Wynn see Gwen
Wynona, Wynnona see Winona
Wyvonne see Yvonne

XYZ

Xan, Xandra, Xandrine see **Alexander**

Xanthe
The Greek for 'yellow', Xanthe is thus the equivalent of the Latin names FLAVIA and Fulvia. It is an uncommon name, but offers an option for parents looking to give their daughter an unusual initial.

Xavier
St Francis Xavier (1506–52), the patron saint of missionaries, got his name from the Spanish-Basque village where he was born. He was one of the founding members of the Jesuits and devoted his life to spreading Christianity in the Far East, particularly in India, China and Japan. He is buried in Goa (India), where his tomb is still a popular place of pilgrimage. Xavier is most often found as a second name, often following Francis. In Spain it is spelt **Javier**. It is occasionally spelt **Zavier**, and the X-men comics and films have introduced the spelling **Xzavier**. There are feminine forms **Xaviera** or **Javiera**, **Xavia** or **Zavia**, **Xaverine** and **Xavière**.

Xenia
This is the full form of the name also found as **Xena**, **Zena** or **Zina**. It comes from the Greek word for 'hospitable', which in turn comes from *xenos* ('stranger, foreigner'). The success of the television series *Xena, Warrior Princess* which first showed in 1995 increased use of the name for a few years.

Ximena
Also spelt **Jimena**, Ximena was the wife of Rodrigo Diaz, known as El Cid, hero of the great medieval Spanish epic named after him. The meaning of the name is unclear. Use is mainly restricted to Spanish speakers.

Xiomara
Like so many Spanish names, Xiomara is of obscure origin. It may go back to an Germanic name, which might mean 'famous in battle', but it might just as well go back to some early name, the origin and possibly even the language of which is now lost. The name is well used in Spanish-speaking America. The wife of the current President of Honduras is Xiomara de Zelaya; Xiomara Rivero is a Cuban athlete; Xiomara Reyes is a Cuban ballet dancer and a recent Miss Nicaragua is Xiomara Blandino.

Xzavier see **Xavier**

Yaakov see **Jacob**

Yadira
Yadira is a Spanish name, common throughout Latin America. There are many suggestions as to its meaning and origin, the most convincing is that it is a form of Jadira, 'Jade' said to have been a Moorish name. It is also said to be a Hebrew name meaning 'friend'. **Yadhira** Carrillo is a popular Mexican actress; Yadira Garcia Vera is Minister for Basic Industry in Cuba.

Yair
Yair is a Hebrew name meaning 'he shines' most often found in Spanish as JAIRO. However, Yair is also found among Spanish-speakers, and **Yahir**, the name of a popular Mexican singer and actor is probably a variant. **Yahaira** looks like a feminine form, but

is claimed by some to be a name from the Native American Taino language. It was popularised in the 1970s by the telenovella *Esmeralda*. Names beginning with Y are currently popular in Latin America and many of them are difficult to trace historically. Many have been linked to Arabic names, via the large-scale immigration to Latin America by Arabic speakers, particularly the Lebanese, but at the moment there has not been enough work done on the history of these names to say anything authoritatively about them. Names in this group include **Yareli**, **Yaritza**, and **Yuridia**. The latter has been given a high profile by the Mexican singer and actress Yuridia Gaxiola as well as by another Mexican singer and actress known simply as **Yuri**, whose full first name is Yuridia.

Yakov see Jacob

Yan(n), **Yannick** see John

Yaqub see Jacob

Yareli, **Yaritza** see Yair

Yasmin, **Yasmine** see Jasmine

Yehudi see Jude

Yesenia

This is a form of the plant name *Jessenia*, a type of tree found in South America. It became popular with Spanish speakers after it was used for the titular gypsy heroine of a 1970 melodramatic Mexican film set in the nineteenth century. This was later developed into a television series.

Ynyr see Honoria

Yoland, **Yolande**, **Yolanda** see Violet

Yonah see Jonah

Yosef see Joseph

Yoselin see Jocelyn

Ysabel see Isabel

Yseult, **Yseut**, **Ysold**, **Ysolda**, **Ysolde** see Isolda

Yuliana see Julia

Yuri, **Yuridia** see Yair

Yusuf see Joseph

Yvonne

This is the most common form of a group of names which come from a Germanic root meaning 'yew', the tree used for making longbows. **Yves**, the French form of Ivo (see IVOR), a popular name in France but rare elsewhere, developed two feminine diminutives, Yvonne and **Yvette**. There are a number of spelling variants, of which **Yvone** and **Evonne** are the most common. In the United States in the 1930s and 1940s it was considered a rather exotic name, and some users were not sure how to pronounce it, others how to spell it. This led to a number of extraordinary variations in both spelling and pronunciation, of which the most extreme were **Javonne** (see under JAVON), as if the name were Slavic, and **Wyvonne**.

Zabrina see Sabrina

Zac see Isaac, Zachary

Zachary

The English form of the Hebrew name **Zachariah** (**Zacharias** is the Greek), Zachary means 'God has remembered'. It is probably the most used of the masculine 'Z' names, particularly in its short form **Zac** (see also ISAAC). **Zach**, **Zack**, **Zacky** and **Zaz** have also been recorded as short forms. The name is attached to eight different people in the Bible, the most prominent of whom was the father of John the Baptist, who was punished with dumbness when he did not believe what the Angel GABRIEL told him of his future son, and on the restoration of his voice was inspired to compose the hymn of praise known as the 'Benedictus'. Zachary is currently popular in the USA, sometimes with an 'e' instead of the second a or with a 'ck' rather than 'ch', and it is used regularly in the UK

Zahra, Zahrah see Zara

Zaire

This appears to be the name of the African country, used as the name of the Democratic Republic of the Congo 1971–97, used as a first name, probably to mark African origin. The country name means 'the river that swallows all rivers' and refers to the Zaire or Congo river.

Zander, Zandra see Alexander

Zane

The use of this surname of unknown meaning for boys comes from the author Zane Grey (1872–1939), who was largely responsible for creating the western as a literary genre. He was christened Pearl Zane Grey, but not surprisingly chose to change this, and took his pen name from his middle name (his mother's maiden name) and his home town of Zanesville, Ohio. This in turn was named from its founder, Ebenezer Zane.

Zara

The English form of **Zahra(h)**, an Arabic name meaning 'to flower or achieve splendour', Zara was introduced by William Congreve as the name of an African queen in his play *The Mourning Bride* (1697). It was then used by Aaron Hill in 1735 as the title and name of the heroine of his translation of a melodramatic tragedy by Voltaire, in the original French called *Zaïre* (1733). However, it was rarely found in real life until the 1960s. Although the Princess Royal brought the name to the attention of the general public when she chose it for her daughter in 1981 it does not seem to have led to any marked increase in the name's use until more recently when Zara Philips has become well known in her own right. It is well used in the UK and Ireland, but in the USA the variant **Zaria(h)** is more likely to be used.

Zavia, Zavier see Xavier

Zayden

A new name for boys, coined by combining the striking letter Z with the fashionable -ayden/aiden ending.

Zaynab, Zeynep

These are forms of an Arabic girl's name, which comes from a scented plant which grows in the desert. It is strongly associated with the Prophet Mohammed, being the name of two of his wives and a daughter.

Zaz see Zachary

Zebedee

The father of the Apostles James the Great and John 'the disciple whom Jesus loved', Zebedee was a successful fisherman, working on the Sea of Galilee. His name means 'my gift'. However, the modern associations of this name are not biblical, for generations of children grew up linking the name with the spring-based puppet of television's *The Magic Roundabout* and the catch-phrase 'Time for bed, said Zebedee'.

Zeev see Zev

Zeke see Ezekiel

Zelda see Griselda

Zelma see Selma

Zena see Xenia

Zenaida see Zinaida

Zenobia

Zenobia was a queen of Palmyra in Syria, famous for her intellect and beauty. When her husband Odenathus died in AD 267 (some say by her hand), she took over the throne. At first the Roman emperors supported her, but she became over-ambitious, and when she invaded the Roman territories of Asia Minor and Egypt she was captured and deposed, and her city-state and its unique culture were obliterated. The name is interpreted as the Greek for 'force of Zeus', but it is probably an adaptation (which at that time could go a long way from the original) of her native name found in local inscriptions, which was Septimia Bathzabbai, meaning something like 'dowry of God'. The use of Zenobia as the name of a major character in Nathaniel Hawthore's 1852 novel *The Blithedale Romance* has led to the occasional use in the USA.

Zev

Zev or Zeev is a Hebrew name meaning 'wolf'.

Zillah

This is a Hebrew name meaning 'shade'. In Genesis she is the mother of Jabal and Jubal and co-wife of Lamech with ADAH. The name was used by the poet laureate Robert Southey (1774–1843) in a tale he took from a medieval source about the origin of the rose, in which a fair maiden of Bethlehem called Zillah rejects the advances of a sottish brute, is accused by him of having dealings with the devil, and is condemned to be burned at the stake. The flames destroy her false accuser, but she is unharmed and from the stake white roses blossom, 'the first ever seen on earth since paradise was lost'.

Zilpha

Zilpha, more correctly spelt **Zilpa**, is a biblical name from the Arabic meaning 'with the little nose'. She was a slave girl given to LEAH by her father Laban, and by her to her husband JACOB as a concubine to be a sort of surrogate mother for Leah. Zilpa became the mother of Gad and ASHER, from whom two of the 12 tribes of Israel descended.

Zina see Xenia

Zinaida

This is the Russian form of a Greek name meaning 'daughter of Zeus'. It is the name of two early martyrs, but its introduction to the English-speaking world is probably due to its use for the heroine of Turgenev's novella *First Love* (1860). **Zenaida** is an alternative form.

Zinnia

This is a modern flower name, the flower being named after J.G. Zinn, a German botanist.

Zion

Zion is the Hebrew name for the central citadel in Jerusalem, hence for Jerusalem as a whole. It is also used by Rastafarians as a general term for a land of freedom. In 1997 it was used by the singer Lauryn Hill as the name of her son. In this case the Rastafarian connection is probably important as the boy is the grandson of the Reggae singer Bob Marley. The name came into more general use thereafter, and has increased rapidly in popularity in the USA.

Zita

Zita seems to be from an Italian dialect word for 'child'. It was the name of a Tuscan saint of the thirteenth century, who at the age of 12 started work as a domestic servant. Her care over her work and her habit of giving food to the poor brought her into conflict with both her fellow servants and her employer, but her devotion and meek patience won her respect in the end, and she spent most of her later life in good works. She became the patron saint of domestic servants, with a bunch of keys as her emblem. Despite these lowly associations, Zita was the name of the last empress of Austria, who lost the throne after the dissolution of the Austro-Hungarian Empire at the end of World War I, but who lived on in retirement until 1989.

Zoe

Zoe or **Zoë** is the Greek word for 'life', and as such was used by Greek speakers for the Hebrew EVE. It was introduced to English speaker as the title of a novel by Geraldine Jewsbury in 1845 and has been popular in the UK since the 1970s, with a phonetic spelling, **Zowie**, an occasional variant. **Zoey** and **Zoie** are also occasionally used.

Zofia see Sophie

Zola

The name of the French writer Emile Zola (1840–1902), whose father was Italian, comes from an Italian dialect word meaning 'bank, mound of earth'. It has been used occasionally as a girl's name, most notably the lead singer of the Black American pop group The Platters, Zola Taylor (1938–2007), and the barefoot South African runner Zola Budd.

Zowie see Zoë (*see* Zoe)

Zubaida

This is a girl's name a pet form of Zubda the Arabic for butter or cream. It is used in the same way the 'the cream of ...' can be used in English, to indicate something that is the best.

Zuleika

This is a Persian name meaning 'brilliant beauty'. It is traditionally the name of both Joseph's and Potiphar's wives, but it first gained fame in the English-speaking world when Byron used it for the tragic heroine of his poem *The Bride of Abydos* (1813). Its greatest fame, however, comes from Max Beerbohm's comic novel *Zuleika Dobson* (1911). When this was broadcast on the radio and his heroine's name was, in his view, mispronounced, Beerbohm sent an angry telegram to the producer, which ran 'zuleika speaker not hiker beerbohm'. Although the pronunciation rhyming with speaker is the traditional one, that rhyming with hiker is now the more common. **Suleika** is a variant.